repository or
storage device

shared storage

repository with
state data

RAID-level

M000291407

...ge
...ent

LUNs

LUN masking

LUN migration

live storage migration

storage
replication

cloud storage
data management

hard disk

folder

firewall

virtual
firewall

hypervisor

virtualization
platform

virtual
infrastructure
manager

physical
network device

virtual
network device

resource
cluster

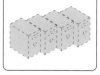

resource
pool

general machine
processable
document

policy

schema or
data model

human readable
document

human

user interface/
portal

workstation

virtual
desktops

mobile computer

mobile devices

firmware

conflict
symbol

malicious
component
or program

trusted
attacker

malicious
service
agent

attacker

security
element or
locked resource

public key

private key

attribute
token

digital
signature

certificate
revocation list

certificate

transition
arrow

business process/
workflow logic

actively
processing

zone or region

pattern or
process step

Praise for This Book

"Thomas Erl's text provides a unique and comprehensive perspective on cloud design patterns that is clearly and concisely explained for the technical professional and layman alike. It is an informative, knowledgeable, and powerful insight that may guide cloud experts in achieving extraordinary results based on extraordinary expertise identified in this text. I will use this text as a resource in future cloud designs and architectural considerations."

—*Dr. Nancy M. Landreville, CEO/CISO, NML Computer Consulting*

"This book continues the very high standard we have come to expect from ServiceTech Press. The book provides well-explained vendor-agnostic patterns to the challenges of providing or using cloud solutions from PaaS to SaaS. The book is not only a great patterns reference, but also worth reading from cover to cover as the patterns are thought-provoking, drawing out points that you should consider and ask of a potential vendor if you're adopting a cloud solution."

—*Phil Wilkins, Enterprise Integration Architect, Specsavers*

"This book provides an excellent read for anyone wanting to grasp the fundamentals and advanced concepts of cloud computing. The easy-to-understand format provides the reader with a clear direction on how to enable a more robust, dynamic, and efficient cloud environment while also providing vital information on how to effectively secure core components of the cloud. The reader, who might not have a full understanding of cybersecurity implications as they relate to cloud, will have the foundational knowledge to build out secure cloud environments. I would recommend this book to anyone serious about cloud security."

—*Sean Cope, CISSP CEH CNDA, FedRAMP Assessment Lead,*
Homeland Security Consultants

"A very well written book, providing details of how to achieve the characteristics of a cloud and hence enable businesses to achieve its benefits."

—*Kumail Morawala, CCP Certified Trainer*

"*Cloud Computing Design Patterns* is an excellent book to use when building or maintaining your cloud. The book is vendor neutral, which ensures that there are no conflicts of interest as far as the authors and publisher go. I think that the diagrams and illustrations are particularly helpful since some people seem challenged with trying to visualize virtual machines."

—*Laura Taylor, Relevant Technologies*

"*Cloud Computing Design Patterns* takes a disciplined approach to categorizing cloud design building blocks and simplifying inherent technology complexities. It explains, in a lucid manner, why a particular design pattern is needed and how to approach a pertinent solution. I found the security patterns sections more versatile in covering examples, such as hypervisor attack vectors, threat mitigation strategies, and mobile device management security. Written in a catalog style, this book takes you through a journey of development that is intuitive as well comprehensive enough."

—*Anant Mahajan*

"Readers will find it easy to read, comprehend, and apply the cloud pattern principles in practice that have already been adopted by the industry."

—*Matt Lorrain, Greg Ponto, and Michael E. Young,*
Security Standards & Architecture team, Esri

"The models seem to be consistent and thorough, which should make them approachable and of value in scoping the design of reliable implementations. Overall, this is a good basis for progressing a common understanding of the vision of cloud practice—well done."

—*Tom Cleary, Australian Computer Society (ACS)*

Cloud Computing
Design Patterns

Thomas Erl,
Robert Cope,
Amin Naserpour

PRENTICE HALL

NEW YORK • BOSTON • INDIANAPOLIS • SAN FRANCISCO

TORONTO • MONTREAL • LONDON • MUNICH • PARIS • MADRID

CAPE TOWN • SYDNEY • TOKYO • SINGAPORE • MEXICO CITY

ServiceTech PRESS

For information about buying this title in bulk quantities, or for special sales opportunities (which may include electronic versions; custom cover designs; and content particular to your business, training goals, marketing focus, or branding interests), please contact our corporate sales department at corpsales@pearsoned.com or (800) 382-3419.

For government sales inquiries, please contact governmentsales@pearsoned.com.

For questions about sales outside the U.S., please contact international@pearsoned.com.

Visit us on the Web: informit.com/ph

Library of Congress Control Number: 2015935087

ISBN-13: 978-0-13-385856-3
ISBN-10: 0-13-385856-1

Text printed in the United States on recycled paper at Courier in Westford, Massachusetts.

First printing: June 2015

Editor-in-Chief
Mark L. Taub

Senior Acquisitions Editor
Trina MacDonald

Development Editors
Natalie Gitt
Maria Lee

Managing Editor
Kristy Hart

Senior Project Editor
Betsy Gratner

Copy Editors
Natalie Gitt
Maria Lee

Senior Indexer
Cheryl Lenser

Proofreaders
Natalie Gitt
Maria Lee
Debbie Williams

Publishing Coordinator
Olivia Basegio

Cover Designer
Thomas Erl

Compositor
Bumpy Design

Graphics
Jasper Paladino

Educational Content Development
Arcitura Education Inc.

To our new addition.
—Thomas Erl

To my wife, Erin, for her patient support
and our sons, Sean and Troy.
—Robert Cope

Contents at a Glance

CHAPTER 1: Introduction 1

CHAPTER 2: Understanding Design Patterns. 9

CHAPTER 3: Sharing, Scaling and Elasticity Patterns 15

CHAPTER 4: Reliability, Resiliency and Recovery Patterns 97

CHAPTER 5: Data Management and Storage Device Patterns 167

CHAPTER 6: Virtual Server and Hypervisor Connectivity and
Management Patterns. 221

CHAPTER 7: Monitoring, Provisioning and Administration Patterns. 283

CHAPTER 8: Cloud Service and Storage Security Patterns. 335

CHAPTER 9: Network Security, Identity & Access Management and
Trust Assurance Patterns 395

CHAPTER 10: Common Compound Patterns. 471

APPENDIX A: Cloud Computing Mechanisms Glossary. .511

APPENDIX B: Alphabetical Design Patterns Reference 535

About the Authors 541

Index 543

Contents

CHAPTER 1: Introduction 1

Objective of This Book 2

What This Book Does Not Cover 2

Who This Book Is For 2

Origin of This Book 3

Recommended Reading 3

How This Book Is Organized 3

    Chapter 3: Sharing, Scaling and Elasticity Patterns 4

    Chapter 4: Reliability, Resiliency and Recovery Patterns 4

    Chapter 5: Data Management and Storage Device Patterns 4

    Chapter 6: Virtual Server and Hypervisor Connectivity and
    Management Patterns 4

    Chapter 7: Monitoring, Provisioning and Administration Patterns . . 4

    Chapter 8: Cloud Service and Storage Security Patterns 4

    Chapter 9: Network Security, Identity & Access Management
    and Trust Assurance Patterns 4

    Chapter 10: Common Compound Patterns 5

    Appendix A: Cloud Computing Mechanisms Glossary 5

    Appendix B: Alphabetical Design Patterns Reference 5

Additional Information 5

    Symbol Legend 5

    Pattern Documentation Conventions 5

    Updates, Errata, and Resources (www.servicetechbooks.com) . . . 6

    Cloud Computing Design Patterns (www.cloudpatterns.org) 6

    What Is Cloud? (www.whatiscloud.com) 6

    Referenced Specifications (www.servicetechspecs.com) 6

    The Service Technology Magazine (www.servicetechmag.com) . . 6

    CloudSchool.com™ Certified Cloud (CCP) Professional
    (www.cloudschool.com) 6

    Social Media and Notification 7

CHAPTER 2: **Understanding Design Patterns** 9

About Pattern Profiles 11
        Requirement 11
        Icon 11
        Problem 11
        Solution 12
        Application 12
        Mechanisms 12

About Compound Patterns 12

Design Pattern Notation 13
        Capitalization 13
        Page Number References 13

Measures of Design Pattern Application 13

Working with This Catalog 14

CHAPTER 3: **Sharing, Scaling and Elasticity Patterns** 15

Shared Resources 17
        Problem 17
        Solution 18
        Application 19
        Mechanisms 21

Workload Distribution 22
        Problem 22
        Solution 22
        Application 22
        Mechanisms 24

Dynamic Scalability 25
        Problem 25
        Solution 27
        Application 28
        Mechanisms 31

Service Load Balancing **32**
  Problem 32
  Solution 33
  Application 34
  Mechanisms. 36
Elastic Resource Capacity **37**
  Problem 37
  Solution 37
  Application 38
  Mechanisms. 40
Elastic Network Capacity **42**
  Problem 42
  Solution 43
  Application 43
  Mechanisms. 43
Elastic Disk Provisioning **45**
  Problem 45
  Solution 46
  Application 48
  Mechanisms. 49
Load Balanced Virtual Server Instances. **51**
  Problem 51
  Solution 52
  Application 53
  Mechanisms. 55
Load Balanced Virtual Switches **57**
  Problem 57
  Solution 58
  Application 58
  Mechanisms. 60
Service State Management **61**
  Problem 61
  Solution 61
  Application 62
  Mechanisms. 63

Storage Workload Management...........................64

   Problem 64

   Solution 64

   Application 66

   Mechanisms... 69

Dynamic Data Normalization 71

   Problem 71

   Solution 72

   Application 72

   Mechanisms... 73

Cross-Storage Device Vertical Tiering 74

   Problem 74

   Solution 76

   Application 76

   Mechanisms... 79

Intra-Storage Device Vertical Data Tiering 81

   Problem 81

   Solution 81

   Application 82

   Mechanisms... 85

Memory Over-Committing 86

   Problem 86

   Solution 87

   Application 88

   Mechanisms... 89

NIC Teaming 90

   Problem 90

   Solution 90

   Application 91

   Mechanisms... 92

Broad Access.....................................93

   Problem 93

   Solution 93

   Application 94

   Mechanisms... 94

CHAPTER 4: **Reliability, Resiliency and Recovery Patterns** **97**

Resource Pooling **99**
Problem 99
Solution 99
Application 100
Mechanisms 103

Resource Reservation **106**
Problem 106
Solution 107
Application 107
Mechanisms 110

Hypervisor Clustering **112**
Problem 112
Solution 112
Application 114
Mechanisms 117

Redundant Storage **119**
Problem 119
Solution 121
Application 121
Mechanisms 122

Dynamic Failure Detection and Recovery **123**
Problem 123
Solution 123
Application 123
Mechanisms 126

Multipath Resource Access **127**
Problem 127
Solution 128
Application 129
Mechanisms 131

Redundant Physical Connection for Virtual Servers.....132

Problem 132

Solution 133

Application 134

Mechanisms 136

Synchronized Operating State. 138

Problem 138

Solution 138

Application 139

Mechanisms 142

Zero Downtime. 143

Problem 143

Solution 143

Application 144

Mechanisms 144

Storage Maintenance Window 147

Problem 147

Solution 148

Application 148

Mechanisms 154

Virtual Server Auto Crash Recovery 155

Problem 155

Solution 156

Application 157

Mechanisms 158

Non-Disruptive Service Relocation 159

Problem 159

Solution 160

Application 160

Mechanisms 164

CHAPTER 5: Data Management and Storage
Device Patterns 167

Direct I/O Access...................................169
Problem 169
Solution 169
Application 169
Mechanisms..171

Direct LUN Access 173
Problem 173
Solution 174
Application 174
Mechanisms..176

Single Root I/O Virtualization 178
Problem 178
Solution 179
Application 179
Mechanisms..180

Cloud Storage Data at Rest Encryption 181
Problem 181
Solution 182
Application 182
Mechanisms..183

Cloud Storage Data Lifecycle Management 184
Problem 184
Solution 185
Application 185
Mechanisms..186

Cloud Storage Data Management 187
Problem 187
Solution 188
Application 188
Mechanisms..189

Cloud Storage Data Placement Compliance Check......190
Problem 190
Solution 191
Application 191
Mechanisms. 192

Cloud Storage Device Masking 194
Problem 194
Solution 194
Application 195
Mechanisms. 197

Cloud Storage Device Path Masking 198
Problem 198
Solution 198
Application 199
Mechanisms. 200

Cloud Storage Device Performance Enforcement.......201
Problem 201
Solution 202
Application 202
Mechanisms. 203

Virtual Disk Splitting 204
Problem 204
Solution 205
Application 206
Mechanisms. 209

Sub-LUN Tiering 210
Problem 210
Solution 210
Application 211
Mechanisms. 213

RAID-Based Data Placement 214
Problem 214
Solution 214
Application 215
Mechanisms. 217

IP Storage Isolation 218
  Problem 218
  Solution 218
  Application 218
  Mechanisms 220

**CHAPTER 6: Virtual Server and Hypervisor
Connectivity and Management Patterns** 221

Virtual Server Folder Migration 223
  Problem 223
  Solution 225
  Application 225
  Mechanisms 226
Persistent Virtual Network Configuration 227
  Problem 227
  Solution 227
  Application 228
  Mechanisms 229
Virtual Server Connectivity Isolation 231
  Problem 231
  Solution 232
  Application 233
  Mechanisms 234
Virtual Switch Isolation 235
  Problem 235
  Solution 236
  Application 236
  Mechanisms 238
Virtual Server NAT Connectivity 240
  Problem 240
  Solution 240
  Application 240
  Mechanisms 243

External Virtual Server Accessibility **244**

    Problem 244

    Solution 245

    Application 245

    Mechanisms 246

Cross-Hypervisor Workload Mobility **247**

    Problem 247

    Solution 248

    Application 250

    Mechanisms 250

Virtual Server-to-Host Affinity **252**

    Problem 252

    Solution 253

    Application 254

    Mechanisms 257

Virtual Server-to-Host Anti-Affinity **258**

    Problem 258

    Solution 261

    Application 261

    Mechanisms 264

Virtual Server-to-Host Connectivity **265**

    Problem 265

    Solution 266

    Application 266

    Mechanisms 266

Virtual Server-to-Virtual Server Affinity **267**

    Problem 267

    Solution 269

    Application 269

    Mechanisms 271

Virtual Server-to-Virtual Server Anti-Affinity **272**

    Problem 272

    Solution 275

    Application 275

    Mechanisms 277

Stateless Hypervisor **278**

Problem 278

Solution 278

Application 279

Mechanisms 282

**CHAPTER 7: Monitoring, Provisioning and
Administration Patterns. 283**

Usage Monitoring **285**

Problem 285

Solution 285

Application 286

Mechanisms 287

Pay-as-You-Go **288**

Problem 288

Solution 288

Application 289

Mechanisms 291

Realtime Resource Availability **292**

Problem 292

Solution 292

Application 293

Mechanisms 294

Rapid Provisioning **295**

Problem 295

Solution 296

Application 296

Mechanisms 299

Platform Provisioning **301**

Problem 301

Solution 301

Application 302

Mechanisms 304

Bare-Metal Provisioning 305
    Problem 305
    Solution 305
    Application 305
    Mechanisms 308

Automated Administration 310
    Problem 310
    Solution 310
    Application 311
    Mechanisms 314

Centralized Remote Administration .315
    Problem 315
    Solution 317
    Application 317
    Mechanisms 318

Resource Management 320
    Problem 320
    Solution 320
    Application 321
    Mechanisms 323

Self-Provisioning 324
    Problem 324
    Solution 325
    Application 325
    Mechanisms 329

Power Consumption Reduction 330
    Problem 330
    Solution 330
    Application 331
    Mechanisms 334

**CHAPTER 8: Cloud Service and Storage
Security Patterns** **335**

    Trusted Platform BIOS **337**
        Problem 337
        Solution 338
        Application 339
        Mechanisms 340

    Geotagging. **341**
        Problem 341
        Solution 341
        Application 342
        Mechanisms 343

    Hypervisor Protection. **344**
        Problem 344
        Solution 346
        Application 347
        Mechanisms. 349

    Cloud VM Platform Encryption. **350**
        Problem 350
        Solution 350
        Application 352
        Mechanisms. 353

    Trusted Cloud Resource Pools **354**
        Problem 354
        Solution 354
        Application 356
        Mechanisms 358

    Secure Cloud Interfaces and APIs. **360**
        Problem 360
        Solution 361
        Application 361
        Mechanisms. 363

Cloud Resource Access Control **364**

    Problem 364

    Solution 366

    Application 368

    Mechanisms 368

Detecting and Mitigating User-Installed VMs **369**

    Problem 369

    Solution 371

    Application 372

    Mechanisms 374

Mobile BYOD Security **376**

    Problem 376

    Solution 378

    Application 380

    Mechanisms 381

Cloud Data Breach Protection **382**

    Problem 382

    Solution 384

    Application 384

    Mechanisms 386

Permanent Data Loss Protection **387**

    Problem 387

    Solution 388

    Application 389

    Mechanisms 390

In-Transit Cloud Data Encryption **391**

    Problem 391

    Solution 391

    Application 392

    Mechanisms 394

CHAPTER 9: Network Security, Identity & Access Management and Trust Assurance Patterns 395

Secure On-Premise Internet Access 397
Problem 397
Solution 398
Application 400
Mechanisms. 403

Secure External Cloud Connection 404
Problem 404
Solution 404
Application 405
Mechanisms 408

Secure Connection for Scaled VMs. 409
Problem 409
Solution 412
Application 414
Mechanisms. 415

Cloud Denial-of-Service Protection. 416
Problem 416
Solution 418
Application 419
Mechanisms. 420

Cloud Traffic Hijacking Protection. 421
Problem 421
Solution 423
Application 423
Mechanisms. 424

Automatically Defined Perimeter 425
Problem 425
Solution 426
Application 427
Mechanisms. 429

Cloud Authentication Gateway. **430**

　Problem 430

　Solution 431

　Application 432

　Mechanisms 435

Federated Cloud Authentication **436**

　Problem 436

　Solution 438

　Application 439

　Mechanisms 443

Cloud Key Management **444**

　Problem 444

　Solution 445

　Application 446

　Mechanisms 447

Trust Attestation Service **448**

　Problem 448

　Solution 449

　Application 449

　Mechanisms 451

Collaborative Monitoring and Logging **452**

　Problem 452

　Solution 455

　Application 455

　Mechanisms 459

Independent Cloud Auditing **460**

　Problem 460

　Solution 461

　Application 463

　Mechanisms 464

Threat Intelligence Processing **465**

　Problem 465

　Solution 466

　Application 468

　Mechanisms 469

CHAPTER 10: Common Compound Patterns **471**

"Compound Pattern" vs. "Composite Pattern" 472

Compound Pattern Members 472

Joint Application vs. Coexistent Application 472

Private Cloud 474

Public Cloud 476

Software-as-a-Service (SaaS) 478

Platform-as-a-Service (PaaS) 480

Infrastructure-as-a-Service (IaaS) 482

Elastic Environment 484

Multitenant Environment 486

Resilient Environment 490

Cloud Bursting 492

Burst Out to Private Cloud 493

Burst Out to Public Cloud 496

Burst In 499

Secure Burst Out to Private Cloud/Public Cloud 501

Cloud Balancing 503

Cloud Authentication 505

Resource Workload Management 506

Isolated Trust Boundary 508

APPENDIX A: Cloud Computing Mechanisms Glossary . . . **511**

**APPENDIX B: Alphabetical Design Patterns
Reference** **535**

About the Authors **541**

Index **543**

Acknowledgments

- Khaja Ahmed, Amazon
- Wayne Armour, Armoured Networks
- Khalid Asad, IBM
- Alenka Brown, Mcclure Brown
- Antonio Bruno, Arcitura Certified Trainer
- Tom Cleary, Australian Computer Society
- Sean Cope, Homeland Security Consultants
- Damian Crosby, RMS
- Michael Dance Jr., BAH
- Michael Fulton, Proctor & Gamble
- Leszek Jaskierny, HP
- Clint Johnson, SJRB
- Ernest Kim, MITRE
- Michael J. Kristan, MITRE
- Vivek Kumar, Yahoo
- Dr. Nancy M. Landreville, NML Computer Consulting
- Matt Lorrain, Esri
- Kathleen Lynch
- Anant Mahajan
- Ahmad Manzoor, Advanced Global Communications Networks
- Kumail Morawala, CCP Certified Trainer
- Vasudevan Narayanan, IBM
- Bob Natale, MITRE
- Sharon Orser-Jackson, MITRE
- Greg Ponto, Esri
- Yves Roycie, keepmomentum
- Scott Rush, HP
- Vijay Srinivasan, Cognizant
- Umit Tacay, silverplatypus
- Laura Taylor, Relevant Technologies
- Katy Warren, MITRE
- Phil Wilkins, Specsavers
- Michael E. Young, Esri

Special thanks to the Arcitura Education CloudSchool.com research and development team that produced the Cloud Certified Professional (CCP) course modules upon which this book is based.

Chapter 1

Introduction

Objective of This Book

What This Book Does Not Cover

Who This Book Is For

Origin of This Book

Recommended Reading

How This Book Is Organized

Additional Information

Objective of This Book

A design pattern is a proven design solution for a common design problem that is formally documented in a consistent manner. Cloud computing design patterns provide proposed design practices and technology architectures, as well as established feature-sets offered by industry tools, technologies, products, and platforms. This book was written with one primary goal in mind: to provide a master design patterns catalog for cloud computing.

What This Book Does Not Cover

Due to the vendor-neutral basis of this book, it does not contain any significant coverage of commercial or vendor-specific cloud computing vendors, services, or technologies. Furthermore, it is important to note that this book documents design patterns only. It does not provide any introductory or tutorial-like coverage of general cloud computing topics. Such coverage is provided in *Cloud Computing: Concepts, Technology & Architecture*, a preceding title released as part of the *Prentice Hall Service Technology Series from Thomas Erl*. For more information about this and other titles in the series, visit www.servicetechbooks.com.

Who This Book Is For

This book is aimed at the IT professionals who:

- want to learn proven design solutions and practices for building, maintaining, and evolving cloud-based solutions and environments

- want to prepare themselves for common challenges associated with the design and architecture of cloud-based services and solutions

- want to gain vendor-neutral insight into the complexion of modern-day cloud computing technologies and innovations

Origin of This Book

As with the *Cloud Computing: Concepts, Technology & Architecture* title, this book is primarily comprised of content from Cloud Certified Professional (CCP) courses developed by Arcitura Education.

The manner in which this catalog componentizes cloud architecture into individually documented pattern profiles makes this book an ideal educational resource for learning and understanding both basic and advanced cloud computing technology concepts, as well as the deep mechanics and inner workings of modern-day cloud platforms.

While this book groups all patterns into a catalog that acts as a master technical reference, CCP courses organize patterns and mechanisms together with additional content into industry certification tracks that map to common cloud computing project roles, such as cloud architect, virtualization specialist, storage specialist, and security specialist.

Recommended Reading

Many of the design patterns in this book were inspired by or have roots in previously published pattern catalogs that may be of interest, especially if you are new to the world of design patterns:

- *Design Patterns: Elements of Reusable Object-Oriented Software* (E. Gamma, R. Helm, R. Johnson, J. Vlissides, Addison-Wesley 1994)

- *Patterns of Enterprise Application Architecture* (M. Fowler, Addison-Wesley 2003)

- *Pattern-Oriented Software Architecture* Volumes 1-5 (F. Buschmann, K. Henney, M. Kircher, R. Meunier, H. Rohnert, D. Schmidt, P. Sommerlad, M. Stal, Wiley 1996-2007)

Furthermore, the previously published title in the *Prentice Hall Service Technology Series from Thomas Erl* also dedicated to design patterns is *SOA Design Patterns* (T. Erl et al, Prentice Hall, 2008).

How This Book Is Organized

Unlike other titles in this series, this book does not group chapters into parts. The coverage of each chapter containing design patterns is relatively comprehensive, allowing the chapters themselves to provide sufficiently broad content separation.

The book begins with Chapters 1 and 2 providing introductory content, and then continues with the following primary chapters:

Chapter 3: Sharing, Scaling and Elasticity Patterns

Design patterns that provide basic and advanced design solutions focused on IT resource sharing, scaling, elasticity, and overall optimization.

Chapter 4: Reliability, Resiliency and Recovery Patterns

Design patterns that address a range of issues pertaining to failover, redundancy, and recovery of IT resources and cloud environments.

Chapter 5: Data Management and Storage Device Patterns

Design patterns focused on cloud storage architecture, cloud storage device configuration and management, as well as the management and optimization of cloud-hosted data.

Chapter 6: Virtual Server and Hypervisor Connectivity and Management Patterns

Design patterns that cover connectivity, accessibility, configuration, and related issues pertaining to virtual servers and hypervisors.

Chapter 7: Monitoring, Provisioning and Administration Patterns

This chapter groups administrative design patterns, such as those pertaining to runtime monitoring, IT resource provisioning, and general administrative features and controls.

Chapter 8: Cloud Service and Storage Security Patterns

Patterns focused on establishing security controls for cloud service architectures and cloud storage devices are covered in this chapter.

Chapter 9: Network Security, Identity & Access Management and Trust Assurance Patterns

This chapter provides a range of cloud security patterns that tackle common security requirements, as well as various forms of attack preventions.

Chapter 10: Common Compound Patterns

Many of the previously documented design patterns can be combined into super-patterns that represent common models or environments in the cloud computing industry, or provide larger, more complex design solutions. This chapter provides examples of some of the more relevant combinations through the definition of a series of compound design patterns.

Appendix A: Cloud Computing Mechanisms Glossary

Design patterns are applied with the involvement and implementation of different combinations of cloud computing mechanisms. This appendix provides concise definitions of all mechanisms associated with and referenced by the preceding design pattern profiles.

Appendix B: Alphabetical Design Patterns Reference

A quick reference list of cloud computing design patterns in alphabetical order, with page numbers.

Additional Information

These sections provide supplementary information and resources for the *Prentice Hall Service Technology Series from Thomas Erl*.

Symbol Legend

This book contains numerous diagrams that are labeled as *figures*. The primary symbols used throughout the figures are individually listed in the symbol legend located on the inside of the book cover. This legend is consistent with the symbol legend used in the *Cloud Computing: Concepts, Technology & Architecture* title.

Pattern Documentation Conventions

Each pattern in this book is documented in a consistent format according to a set of pre-defined notation conventions that are explained in the "Design Pattern Notation" section in Chapter 2.

Updates, Errata, and Resources (www.servicetechbooks.com)

Information about other series titles and various supporting resources can be found at the official book series Web site: www.servicetechbooks.com. You are encouraged to visit this site regularly to check for content changes and corrections.

Cloud Computing Design Patterns (www.cloudpatterns.org)

All of the pattern profile summary tables documented in this book are also published online at CloudPatterns.org. This site acts as an online reference tool and allows for the submission of new pattern candidates.

What Is Cloud? (www.whatiscloud.com)

A quick reference site comprised of excerpts from this book to provide coverage of fundamental cloud computing topics.

Referenced Specifications (www.servicetechspecs.com)

This site provides a central portal to the original specification documents created and maintained by primary standards organizations, with a section dedicated exclusively to cloud computing industry standards.

The Service Technology Magazine (www.servicetechmag.com)

The Service Technology Magazine is a monthly publication provided by Arcitura Education Inc. and Prentice Hall and is officially associated with the *Prentice Hall Service Technology Series from Thomas Erl.*

CloudSchool.com™ Certified Cloud (CCP) Professional (www.cloudschool.com)

The pattern profiles and mechanisms covered in this book originated from courses that are part of the Cloud Certified Professional (CCP) curriculum, an academic, vendor-neutral program dedicated to specialized areas of cloud computing.

Social Media and Notification

To be automatically notified of new book releases in this series, new supplementary content for this title, or key changes to the aforementioned resource sites, use the notification form at www.servicetechbooks.com or send a blank email to notify@arcitura.com.

Alternatively, connect via the official *Prentice Hall Service Technology Series from Thomas Erl* Facebook page, LinkedIn group, or Twitter account by visiting: www.servicetechbooks.com/community.

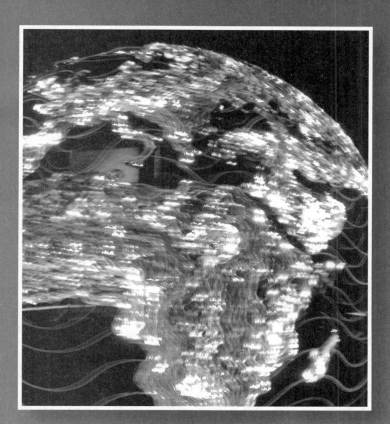

Chapter 2

Understanding Design Patterns

About Pattern Profiles

About Compound Patterns

Design Pattern Notation

Measures of Design Pattern Application

Working with This Catalog

The simplest way to describe a pattern is that it provides a proven solution to a common problem individually documented in a consistent format and usually as part of a larger collection. The notion of a pattern is already a fundamental part of everyday life. Without acknowledging it each time, we naturally use proven solutions to solve common problems each day. Patterns in the IT world that revolve around the design of automated systems are referred to as *design patterns*.

Design patterns are helpful because they:

- represent field-tested solutions to common design problems
- organize design intelligence into a standardized and easily referenced format
- are generally repeatable by most IT professionals involved with design
- can be used to ensure consistency in how systems are designed and built
- can become the basis for design standards
- are usually flexible and optional (and openly document the impacts of their application and even suggest alternative approaches)
- can be used as educational aids by documenting specific aspects of system design (regardless of whether they are applied)
- can sometimes be applied prior and subsequent to the implementation of a system
- can be supported via the application of other design patterns that are part of the same collection
- enrich the vocabulary of a given IT field because each pattern is given a meaningful name

Furthermore, because the solutions provided by design patterns are proven, their consistent application tends to naturally improve the quality of system designs.

Note that even though design patterns provide proven design solutions, their mere use cannot guarantee that design problems are always solved as required. Many factors weigh in to the ultimate success of using a design pattern, including constraints imposed by the implementation environment, competency of the practitioners, diverging business requirements, and so on. All of these represent aspects that affect the extent to which a pattern can be successfully applied.

A *pattern language* is a set of related patterns that act as building blocks in that they can be carried out in one or more pattern application sequences where each subsequent pattern builds upon the former. The notion of a pattern language originated in building architecture, as did the term "pattern sequence" used in association with the order in which patterns can be carried out.

The cloud computing design pattern catalog, in its entirety, provides an open-ended master pattern language for cloud computing. The extent to which different patterns are related can vary, but overall they share a common objective, and endless pattern sequences can be explored.

About Pattern Profiles

Each of the design patterns covered in this book is documented in a pattern profile comprised of the following parts:

Requirement

A requirement is a concise, single-sentence statement that presents the fundamental requirement addressed by the pattern in the form of a question. Every pattern description begins with this statement.

Icon

Each pattern description is accompanied by an icon image that acts as a visual identifier. The icons are displayed together with the requirement statements in each pattern profile as well as on the inside book cover. Note that compound patterns do not have icons.

Problem

The issue causing a problem and the effects of the problem are described in this section, which may be accompanied by a figure that further illustrates the "problem state." It is this problem for which the pattern is expected to provide a solution. Part of the problem description includes common circumstances that can lead to the problem (also known as "forces").

Solution

This represents the design solution proposed by the pattern to solve the problem and fulfill the requirement. Often the solution is a short statement that may be further followed by a diagram that concisely communicates the final solution state. "How-to" details are not provided in this section but are instead located in the Application section.

Application

This part is dedicated to describing how the pattern can be applied. In can include guidelines, implementation details, and sometimes even a suggested process.

Mechanisms

This section lists one or more common mechanisms that are implemented to apply the pattern. All mechanisms referenced are defined in Appendix A, *Cloud Computing Mechanisms Glossary*. Note that the application of a pattern is not limited to the use of its listed mechanisms.

Each pattern profile begins with the Requirement statement followed by a table containing concise Problem and Solution statements, an Application summary, and a Mechanisms list. This summary table is then followed by corresponding sections (with the same titles) that provide detailed descriptions.

About Compound Patterns

A *compound pattern* is a coarse-grained pattern comprised of a set of finer-grained patterns. Singled out in Chapter 10, *Common Compound Patterns*, are some of the more common and important cloud computing compound patterns.

When a pattern is classified as a "compound," it is important to note that just about any pattern can turn out to be a compound pattern. Every one of the other patterns described in this book can be decomposed into a set of more granular patterns. Their combination then results in the original pattern, thereby also making it a compound pattern.

The reason this perspective is important is because whether or not a pattern is labeled as being a compound pattern is always relative. It is just a matter of the granularity at which the pattern is documented in relation to other patterns in the same catalog. Note also that compound patterns can be nested.

The compound patterns covered in this book are classified as such because they relate to recognizable models, environments, and technology-sets in the contemporary cloud computing industry. In a different context, these patterns could be classified differently. The rectangle symbols used to represent design patterns are further distinguished with an asterisk in the bottom right corner when they represent compound patterns.

It is furthermore important to clarify how patterns can be combined into compounds. A compound pattern can represent a set of patterns that are applied together to a particular program or implementation in order to establish a specific set of design characteristics. This would be referred to as *joint application*. Alternatively, the member patterns that comprise a compound pattern can represent a set of related features provided by a particular program or environment. In this case, a *coexistent application* of patterns establishes a "solution environment" that may be realized by a combination of tools and technologies.

Design Pattern Notation

Capitalization

All design pattern names (including names of compound patterns) are capitalized throughout this book. The names for groups of related patterns are capitalized when displayed in figures but not when referenced in body text.

Page Number References

Each design pattern name is followed by a page number in parentheses. This number, which points to the first page of the corresponding pattern profile, is provided for quick reference purposes. The use of page number references has become a common convention among design pattern catalogs and publications. The only time the number is not displayed is when a pattern name is referenced within that pattern's profile section.

Measures of Design Pattern Application

It is important to acknowledge that most patterns do not propose a black or white design option. Design patterns can often be applied at different levels. Although the effectiveness of a given pattern will generally be equivalent to the extent to which it is realized, there may be practical considerations that simply limit the degree to which a pattern can be applied in the real world.

The point is to take into consideration and incorporate the design goals of a design pattern to whatever extent feasible, and to strive for an end-result that realizes the pattern to a meaningful extent as it pertains to fulfilling requirements and objectives.

Working with This Catalog

As previously established, this textbook is organized as a technical reference guide. Subsequent chapters group patterns based on parent categories. You do not need to read this book in any particular sequence. It is designed in a catalog format that allows readers to jump to any particular pattern profiles that are of immediate interest.

To maximize the functionality of this catalog, it is worth taking note of the following suggested usage guidelines:

- If you come across terms or references to models that you would like to learn more about, you will find them most formally defined in the *Cloud Computing: Concepts, Technology & Architecture* book or at www.whatiscloud.com.

- If you come across references to cloud computing mechanisms that you would like to learn more about, you will find concise definitions in Appendix A. Detailed descriptions of a subset of these mechanisms are available in the *Cloud Computing: Concepts, Technology & Architecture* book. You may also find more descriptive definitions online, at www.cloudpatterns.org.

- If you know the name of a pattern and would like to quickly locate it, use the alphabetical list provided in Appendix B. Each pattern listed is accompanied by the page number of its corresponding profile.

- If you would like to share information about patterns with others or if you would like to view pattern information online for quick reference purposes, use www.cloudpatterns.org to access and search through the pattern profile summary tables.

- If you are interested in how cloud computing design patterns map or relate to NIST architecture models, visit www.cloudpatterns.org. A subset of the patterns in this catalog has been mapped.

The cloud computing design patterns catalog is expected to grow over time as new developments and innovations emerge in the industry. Cloud computing professionals are welcome to submit candidate patterns via www.cloudpatterns.org for open review by the community and consideration for inclusion in the catalog.

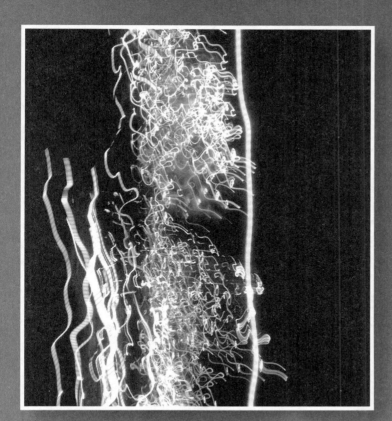

Chapter 3

Sharing, Scaling and Elasticity Patterns

Shared Resources
Workload Distribution
Dynamic Scalability
Service Load Balancing
Elastic Resource Capacity
Elastic Network Capacity
Elastic Disk Provisioning
Load Balanced Virtual Server Instances
Load Balanced Virtual Switches

Service State Management
Storage Workload Management
Dynamic Data Normalization
Cross-Storage Device Vertical Tiering
Intra-Storage Device Vertical Data
   Tiering
Memory Over-Committing
NIC Teaming
Broad Access

This collection of design patterns focuses on providing solutions for maximizing the potential usage of available IT resources in response to unpredictable usage requirements across multiple cloud consumers. Shared Resources (17), Dynamic Data Normalization (71), Memory Over-Committing (86), and NIC Teaming (90) directly enable and support the realization of multitenancy over large pooled resources, whereas ubiquitous cloud consumer access is enabled through the application of the Broad Access (93) pattern.

The majority of patterns in this chapter directly or indirectly enable the elasticity characteristic of cloud computing to support the automated ability of a cloud to transparently scale IT resources, as required in response to runtime conditions or as pre-determined by the cloud consumer or cloud provider.

Problem	Allocating dedicated IT resources to individual consumers can be wasteful and under-utilize their collective capacity.
Solution	Physical IT resources are shared by partitioning them into lower capacity virtual IT resources that are provisioned to multiple cloud consumers.
Application	Virtualization technology is used to create virtual instances of physical IT resources. Each virtualized IT resource can be assigned to a cloud consumer, while the underlying physical IT resource is shared.
Mechanisms	Audit Monitor, Cloud Storage Device, Cloud Usage Monitor, Hypervisor, Logical Network Perimeter, Resource Replication, Virtual CPU, Virtual Infrastructure Manager (VIM), Virtual RAM, Virtual Server

Problem

Organizations commonly purchase physical on-premise IT resources, such as physical servers and storage devices, and allocate each to specific applications, users, or other types of consumers (Figure 3.1). The narrow scope of some IT resource usage results in the IT resource's overall capacity rarely being fully used. Over time, the processing potential of each IT resource is not reached. Consequently, the return on the investment of each IT resource is also not fully realized. The longer these types of dedicated IT resources are used, the more wasteful they become, and more opportunities to further leverage their potential are lost.

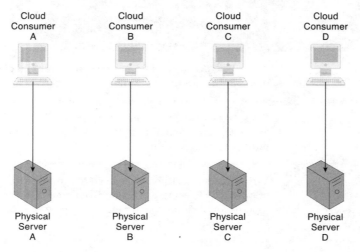

Figure 3.1

Each cloud consumer is allocated a dedicated physical server. It is likely that, over time, a significant amount of the physical servers' combined capacity will be under-utilized.

Solution

Virtual instances of physical IT resources are created and shared by multiple consumers, potentially to the extent to which the capacity of the physical IT resource can support (Figure 3.2). This maximizes the utilization of each physical IT resource, thereby also maximizing the return on its investment.

This pattern further forms the fundamental basis of a model by which virtual instances of the physical IT resource can be used (and leased) temporarily.

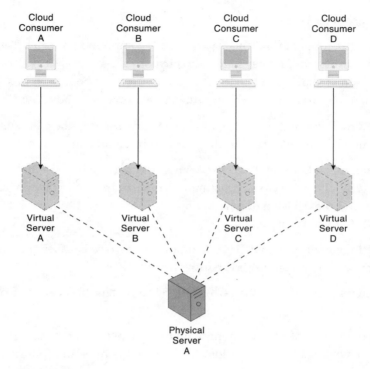

Figure 3.2

Each cloud consumer is allocated a virtual server instance of a single underlying physical server. In this case, the physical server is likely greater than if each cloud consumer were given its own physical server. However, the cost of one high-capacity physical server is lower than four medium-capacity physical servers and its processing potential will be utilized to a greater extent.

Application

The most common technology used to apply this pattern is virtualization. The specific components and mechanisms that are used depend on what type of IT resource needs to be shared. For example, the virtual server mechanism is used to share a physical server's processing capacity and the hypervisor mechanism is utilized to create instances of the virtual server. The VIM component can be further incorporated to manage hypervisors, virtual server instances, and their distribution.

It is important to note how the Shared Resources pattern is positioned among compound patterns, especially given its fundamental nature in relation to cloud platforms:

The Shared Resources pattern is:

- an optional member of the Private Cloud (474) compound pattern because, although common in private clouds, the virtualization of physical IT resources for cloud consumer sharing purposes is an option that can be chosen in support of the business requirements of the organization acting as cloud provider.

- a required member of the Public Cloud (476) compound pattern because of its inherent need to share IT resources to numerous cloud consumers.

- an optional member of the IaaS (482) compound pattern because the cloud provider may allow the cloud consumer access to administer raw physical IT resources and the decision of whether and how to use virtualization technology is left to the cloud consumer.

- a required member of the PaaS (480) compound pattern because the ready-made environment mechanism itself is naturally virtualized.

- a required member of the SaaS (478) compound pattern because SaaS offerings are naturally virtualized.

- a required member of the Multitenant Environment (486) compound pattern because this pattern provides a cloud technology architecture that specifically addresses the sharing of IT resources.

The sharing of IT resources introduces risks and challenges:

- One physical IT resource can become a single point of failure for multiple virtual IT resources and multiple corresponding cloud consumers.

- The virtualized physical IT resource may become over-utilized and therefore unable to fulfill all of the processing demands of its virtualized instances. This is referred to as a resource constraint and represents a condition that can lead to degradation of performance and various runtime exceptions.

- The virtualized instances of an underlying physical IT resource shared by multiple cloud consumers can introduce overlapping trust boundaries that can pose a security concern.

These and other problems raised by the application of this pattern are addressed by other patterns, such as Resource Pooling (99) and Resource Reservation (106).

Mechanisms

- *Audit Monitor* – When the Shared Resources pattern is applied, it can change how and where data is processed and stored. This may require the use of an audit monitor mechanism to ensure that the utilization of shared IT resources does not inadvertently violate legal requirements or regulations.

- *Cloud Storage Device* – This mechanism represents a common type of IT resource that is shared by the application of this pattern.

- *Cloud Usage Monitor* – Various cloud usage monitors may be involved with tracking the shared usage of IT resources.

- *Hypervisor* – A hypervisor can provide virtual servers with access to shared IT resources hosted by the hypervisor.

- *Logical Network Perimeter* – This mechanism provides network-level isolation that helps protect shared IT resources and their cloud consumers.

- *Resource Replication* – The resource replication mechanism may be used to generate new instances of IT resources made available for shared usage.

- *Virtual CPU* – This mechanism is used to share the hypervisor's physical CPU between virtual servers.

- *Virtual Infrastructure Manager (VIM)* – This mechanism is used to configure how physical resources are to be shared between virtual servers in order to send the configurations to the hypervisors.

- *Virtual RAM* – This mechanism is used to determine how a hypervisor's physical memory is to be shared between virtual servers.

- *Virtual Server* – Virtual servers may be shared or may host shared IT resources.

Workload Distribution

How can IT resource over-utilization be avoided?

Problem	IT resources subjected to high volumes of concurrent usage can suffer degraded performance, reduced availability and reliability, and can become susceptible to overall failure.
Solution	The IT resource is horizontally scaled and a load balancing system is used to distribute runtime workloads across multiple IT resources.
Application	Load balancing technology is incorporated into the cloud architecture and configured with appropriate load balancing algorithms to ensure effective workload distribution.
Mechanisms	Audit Monitor, Cloud Storage Device, Cloud Usage Monitor, Hypervisor, Load Balancer, Logical Network Perimeter, Resource Cluster, Resource Replication, Virtual Server

Problem

IT resources that are shared or are made available to consumers with unpredictable usage requirements can become over-utilized when usage demands near or exceed their capacities (Figure 3.3). This can result in runtime exceptions and failure conditions that cause the affected IT resources to reject consumer requests or shut down altogether.

Solution

The IT resource is horizontally scaled via the addition of one or more identical IT resources and a load balancing system further extends the cloud architecture to provide runtime logic capable of evenly distributing the workload across all available IT resources (Figure 3.4). This minimizes the chances that any one of the IT resources will be over-utilized (or under-utilized).

Application

This pattern is primarily applied via the use of the load balancer mechanism, of which variations with different types of load balancing algorithms exist. The automated scaling listener mechanism can also be used in a similar capacity to respond when an IT resource's thresholds are reached.

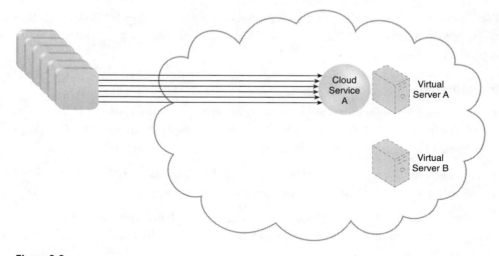

Figure 3.3

A group of cloud service consumers simultaneously access Cloud Service A, which is hosted by Virtual Server A. Another virtual server is available but is not being utilized. As a result, Virtual Server A is over-utilized.

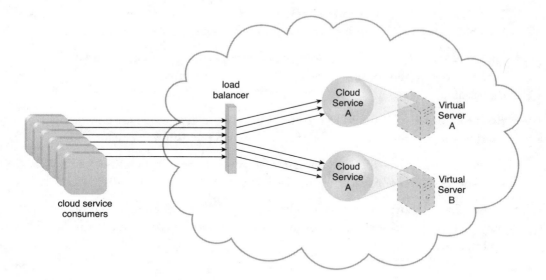

Figure 3.4

A redundant copy of Cloud Service A is implemented on Virtual Server B. The load balancer intercepts the cloud service consumer requests and directs them to both Virtual Server A and B to ensure even distribution of the workload.

In addition to the distribution of conventional cloud service access and data exchanges, this pattern can also be applied to the load balancing of cloud storage devices and connectivity devices.

Mechanisms

- *Audit Monitor* – When distributing runtime workloads, the types of IT resources processing data and the geographical location of the IT resources (and the data) may need to be monitored for legal and regulatory requirements.

- *Cloud Storage Device* – This is one type of mechanism that may be used to distribute workload as a result of the application of this pattern.

- *Cloud Usage Monitor* – Various monitors may be involved with the runtime tracking of workload and data processing as part of a cloud architecture resulting from the application of this pattern.

- *Hypervisor* – Workloads between hypervisors and virtual servers hosted by hypervisors may need to be distributed.

- *Load Balancer* – This is a fundamental mechanism used to establish the base workload balancing logic in order to carry out the distribution of the workload.

- *Logical Network Perimeter* – The logical network perimeter isolates cloud consumer network boundaries in relation to how and to where workloads may be distributed.

- *Resource Cluster* – Clustered IT resources in active/active mode are commonly used to support the workload balancing between the different cluster nodes.

- *Resource Replication* – This mechanism may generate new instances of virtualized IT resources in response to runtime workload distribution demands.

- *Virtual Server* – Virtual servers may be the target of workload distribution or may themselves be hosting IT resources that are part of workload distribution architectures.

Dynamic Scalability

How can IT resources be scaled automatically in response to fluctuating demand?

Problem	It is challenging to equip an IT resource to match its processing requirements. If the demand for the IT resource is below its capacity, then it is under-utilized and if the demand is above its capacity it is over-utilized or unable to meet the demand.
Solution	The IT resource can be integrated with a reactive cloud architecture capable of automatically scaling it horizontally or vertically in response to fluctuating demand.
Application	Dynamic horizontal scaling can be enabled via the use of pools of identical IT resources and components capable of dispersing and retracting workloads across each pool. Dynamic vertical scaling can be enabled via technology capable of swapping IT resource components at runtime.
Mechanisms	Automated Scaling Listener, Cloud Storage Device, Cloud Usage Monitor, Hypervisor, Pay-Per-Use Monitor, Resource Replication, Virtual Server

Problem

Manually preparing or extending IT resources in response to workload fluctuations is time-intensive and unacceptably inefficient. Determining when to add new IT resources to satisfy anticipated workload peaks is often speculative and generally risky. These additional IT resources can either remain under-utilized (and a failed financial investment), or fail to alleviate runtime performance and reliability problems when demand exceeds even the addition of their capacity.

The following steps are shown in Figures 3.5 and 3.6:

1. The cloud provider offers cloud services to cloud consumers.

2. Cloud consumers can scale the cloud services, as needed.

3. Over time, the number of cloud consumers increases.

4. The cloud provider's virtual server is overwhelmed with the increased workload capacity.

Figure 3.5

A non-dynamic cloud architecture in which vertical scaling is carried out in response to usage fluctuations (Part I).

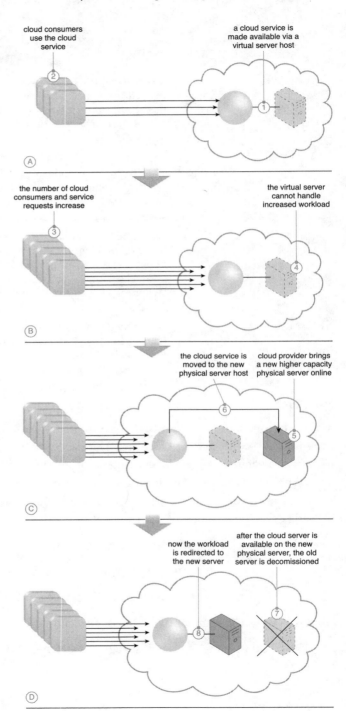

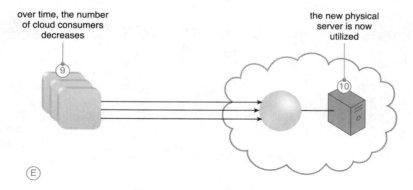

Figure 3.6

A non-dynamic cloud architecture in which vertical scaling is carried out in response to usage fluctuations (Part II).

5. The cloud provider brings a new, higher-capacity server online to handle an increased workload.

6. Because the required IT resources are not organized for sharing and are unprepared for allocation, the virtual server must have the operating system, required applications, and cloud services installed after being created.

7. Once the new server is ready, the old server is taken offline.

8. Now service requests are redirected to the new server.

9. After the peak usage period has ended, the number of cloud consumers and service requests naturally decrease.

10. Without properly implementing a process of under-utilized IT resource recovery, the new server's sizable workload capacity will not be fully utilized.

Solution

A system of predefined scaling conditions that trigger the dynamic allocation of IT resources can be introduced (Figure 3.7). The IT resources are allocated from resource pools to allow for variable utilization as dictated by demand fluctuations. Unneeded IT resources are efficiently reclaimed without requiring manual interaction.

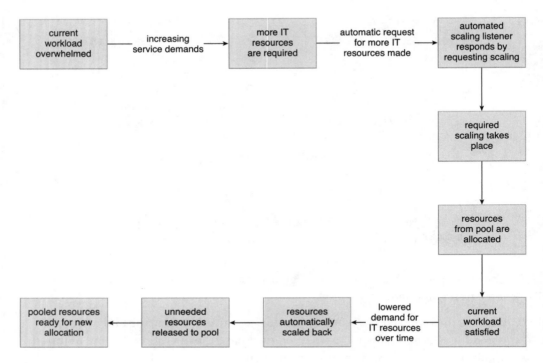

Figure 3.7

A sample dynamic scaling process.

Application

The fundamental Dynamic Scalability pattern primarily relies on the application of Resource Pooling (99) and the implementation of the automated scaling listener.

The automated scaling listener is configured with workload thresholds that determine when new IT resources need to be included in the workload processing. The automated scaling listener can further be provided with logic that allows it to verify the extent of additional IT resources a given cloud consumer is entitled to, based on its leasing arrangement with the cloud provider.

The following types of dynamic scaling are common:

- *Dynamic Horizontal Scaling* – In this type of dynamic scaling the number of IT resource instances is scaled to handle fluctuating workloads. The automatic scaling listener monitors requests and, if scaling is required, signals a resource replication mechanism to initiate the duplication of the IT resources, as per requirements and permissions. (Figures 3.8 to 3.10 demonstrate this type of scaling.)

- *Dynamic Vertical Scaling* – This type of scaling occurs when there is a need to increase the processing capacity of a single IT resource. For instance, if a virtual server is being overloaded, it can dynamically have its memory increased or it may have a processing core added.

- *Dynamic Relocation* – The IT resource is relocated to a higher capacity host. For example, there may be a need to move a cloud service database from a tape-based SAN storage device with 4 Gbps I/O capacity to another disk-based SAN storage device with 8 Gbps I/O capacity.

Figures 3.8 to 3.10 demonstrate dynamic horizontal scaling in the following steps:

1. Cloud service consumers are sending requests to a cloud service.

2. The automated scaling listener monitors the cloud service to determine if pre-defined capacity thresholds are being exceeded.

3. The number of service requests coming from cloud service consumers further increases.

4. The workload exceeds the performance thresholds of the automated scaling listener. It determines the next course of action based on a pre-defined scaling policy.

5. If the cloud service implementation is deemed eligible for additional scaling, the automated scaling listener initiates the scaling process.

6. The automated scaling listener sends a signal to the resource replication mechanism.

7. The resource replication mechanism then creates more instances of the cloud service.

8. Now that the increased workload is accommodated, the automated scaling listener resumes monitoring and the detracting or adding of necessary IT resources.

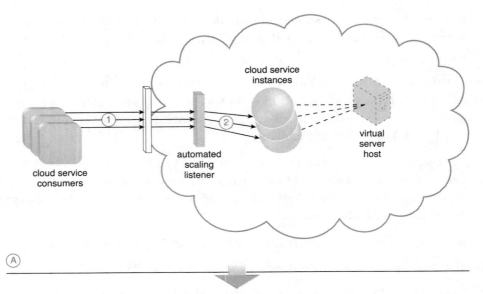

Figure 3.8
An example of a dynamic scaling architecture involving an automated scaling mechanism (Part I).

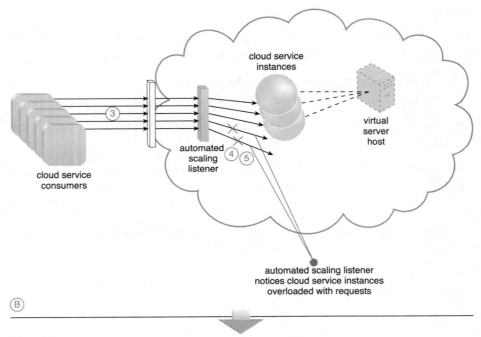

Figure 3.9
An example of a dynamic scaling architecture involving an automated scaling mechanism (Part II).

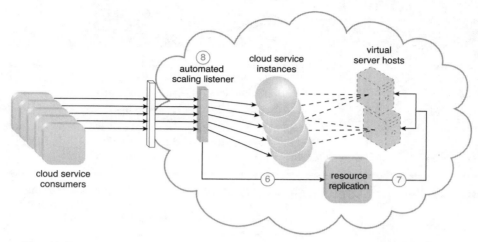

Figure 3.10

An example of a dynamic scaling architecture involving an automated scaling mechanism (Part III).

Mechanisms

- *Automated Scaling Listener* – The automated scaling listener is directly associated with the Dynamic Scalability pattern in that it monitors and compares workloads with predefined thresholds to initiate scaling in response to usage fluctuations.

- *Cloud Storage Device* – This mechanism and the data it stores may be scaled by the system established by this pattern.

- *Cloud Usage Monitor* – As per the automated scaling listener, cloud usage monitors are used to track runtime usage to initiate scaling in response to fluctuations.

- *Hypervisor* – The hypervisor may be invoked by a dynamic scalability system to create or remove virtual server instances. Alternatively, the hypervisor itself may be scaled.

- *Pay-Per-Use Monitor* – The pay-per-use monitor collects usage cost information in tandem with how IT resources are scaled.

- *Resource Replication* – This mechanism supports dynamic horizontal scaling by replicating IT resources, as required.

- *Virtual Server* – The virtual server may be scaled by the system established by this pattern.

Service Load Balancing

How can a cloud service accommodate increasing workloads?

Problem	A single cloud service implementation has a finite capacity, which leads to runtime exceptions, failure, and performance degradation when its processing thresholds are exceeded.
Solution	Redundant deployments of the cloud service are created and a load balancing system is added to dynamically distribute workloads across cloud service implementations.
Application	The duplicate cloud service implementations are organized into a resource pool. The load balancer is positioned as an external component or may be built-in, allowing hosting servers to balance workloads among themselves.
Mechanisms	Cloud Usage Monitor, Load Balancer, Resource Cluster, Resource Replication

Problem

Regardless of the processing capacity of its immediate hosting environment, a cloud service architecture may inherently be limited in its ability to accommodate high volumes of concurrent cloud service consumer requests. The cloud service's processing restrictions may be such that it is unable to leverage underlying cloud-based IT resources that normally support dynamic scalability. For example, the processing restrictions may originate from its architectural design, the complexity of its application logic, or inhibitive programming algorithms it is required to carry out at runtime. Such a cloud service may be forced to reject cloud service consumer requests when its processing capacity thresholds are reached (Figure 3.11).

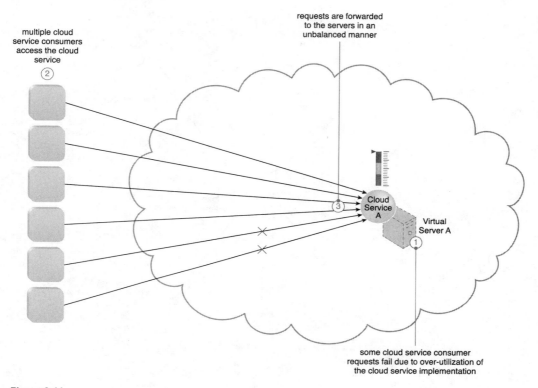

Figure 3.11

A single cloud service implementation reaches its runtime processing capacity and consequently rejects subsequent cloud service consumer requests.

Solution

Redundant implementations of the cloud service are created, each located on a different hosting server. A load balancer is utilized to intercept cloud service consumer requests in order to evenly distribute them across the multiple cloud service implementations (Figure 3.12).

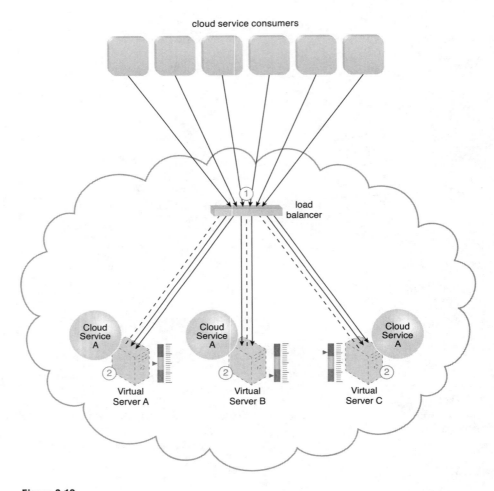

Figure 3.12

The load balancing agent intercepts messages sent by cloud service consumers (1) and forwards the messages at runtime to the virtual servers so that the workload processing is horizontally scaled (2).

Application

Depending on the anticipated workload and the processing capacity of hosting server environments, multiple instances of each cloud service implementation may be generated in order to establish pools of cloud services that can more efficiently respond to high volumes of concurrent requests.

The load balancer may be positioned independently from the cloud services and their hosting servers, as shown in Figure 3.12, or it may be built-in as part of the application or server's environment. In the latter case, a primary server with the load balancing logic can communicate with neighboring servers to balance the workload, as shown in Figure 3.13.

For this pattern to be applied, a server group needs to be created and configured, so that server group members can be associated with the load balancer. The paths of cloud service consumer requests to be sent through the load balancer need to be set and the load balancer needs to be configured to evaluate each cloud service implementation's capacity on a regular basis.

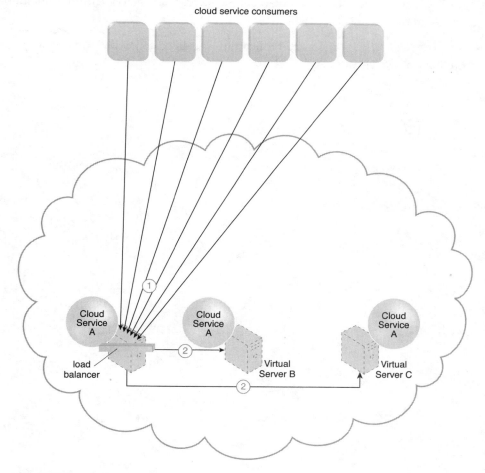

Figure 3.13

Cloud consumer requests are sent to Cloud Service A on Virtual Server A (1). The cloud service implementation includes built-in load balancing logic that is capable of distributing requests to the neighboring Cloud Service A implementations on Virtual Servers B and C (2).

Mechanisms

- *Cloud Usage Monitor* – In addition to performing various runtime monitoring and usage data collection tasks, cloud usage monitors may be involved with monitoring cloud service instances and their respective IT resource consumption levels.

- *Load Balancer* – This represents the fundamental mechanism used to apply this pattern in order to establish the necessary horizontal scaling functionality.

- *Resource Cluster* – Active-active cluster groups may be incorporated in a service load balancing architecture to help balance workloads across different members of the cluster.

- *Resource Replication* – Resource replication is utilized to keep cloud service implementations synchronized.

Elastic Resource Capacity

How can the processing capacity of virtual servers be dynamically scaled in response to fluctuating IT resource usage requirements?

Problem	When IT resources hosted by a virtual server impose processing requirements that exceed the virtual server's capacity, the performance and reliability of the hosted IT resources and the virtual server itself may be compromised.
Solution	An elastic provisioning system is established to dynamically allocate and reclaim CPUs and RAM for a virtual server in response to the fluctuating processing requirements of its hosted IT resources.
Application	Resource pools are utilized by scaling technology that interacts with the hypervisor and/or VIM to retrieve and return CPU and RAM resources at runtime, as per necessary processing capacity.
Mechanisms	Automated Scaling Listener, Cloud Usage Monitor, Hypervisor, Live VM Migration, Pay-Per-Use Monitor, Resource Replication, Virtual CPU, Virtual Infrastructure Manager (VIM), Virtual RAM, Virtual Server

Problem

When the processing capacity of a virtual server is reached at runtime, it becomes unavailable, resulting in scalability limitations and inhibiting the performance and reliability of its hosted IT resources (Figure 3.14).

Solution

Pools of CPUs and RAM are established for shared allocation. The runtime processing of a virtual server is monitored so that prior to capacity thresholds being met, additional processing power from the resource pool can be leveraged via dynamic allocation to the virtual server. This vertically scales the virtual server and, consequently, its hosted applications and IT resources as well.

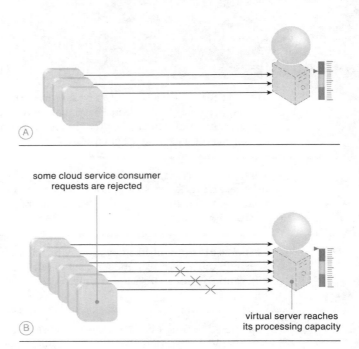

Figure 3.14
After the virtual server hosting the cloud service reaches its processing limit, subsequent cloud service consumer requests cannot be fulfilled.

Application

Resource Pooling (99) is applied to provision the necessary IT resource pools, and Dynamic Scalability (25) is applied to establish the automated scaling listener mechanism as an intermediary between cloud service consumers and any IT resources hosted by the virtual server that need to be accessed. Automated Administration (310) is further applied because intelligent automation engine scripts are needed to signal scaling requirements to the resource pool.

The following steps are shown in Figures 3.15 and 3.16:

1. Resource pools providing CPUs and RAM memory have been implemented and configured.

2. Cloud service consumers are actively sending requests.

3. The automated scaling listener is monitoring the requests.

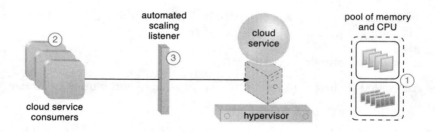

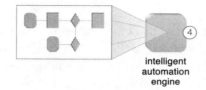

Figure 3.15

The application of the Elastic Resource Capacity pattern on a sample cloud architecture (Part I).

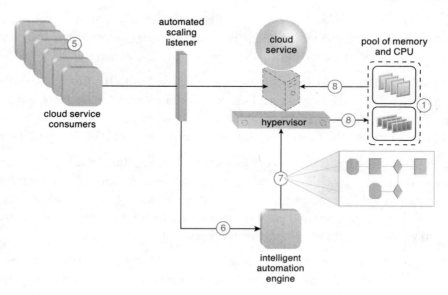

Figure 3.16

The application of the Elastic Resource Capacity pattern on a sample cloud architecture (Part II).

4. An intelligent automation engine script is deployed with workflow logic capable of notifying the resource pool using allocation requests.

5. Cloud service consumer requests increase.

6. The automated scaling listener signals the intelligent automation engine to execute the script.

7. The script runs the workflow logic that signals the hypervisor to allocate more IT resources from the resource pools.

8. The hypervisor allocates additional CPU and RAM to the virtual server, enabling it to handle the increased workload.

This type of cloud architecture may also be designed so that the intelligent automation engine script sends its scaling request via the VIM instead of directly to the hypervisor. Furthermore, in order to support dynamic resource allocation, virtual servers participating in elastic resource allocation systems may need to be rebooted for the allocation to take effect.

Mechanisms

- *Automated Scaling Listener* – The Elastic Resource Capacity pattern is reliant on the automated scaling listener mechanism for monitoring the workload and initiating the scaling process by indicating the type of scaling that is required.

- *Cloud Usage Monitor* – This mechanism is associated with the Elastic Resource Capacity pattern in how the cloud usage monitor collects the resource usage information of the allocated and released IT resources before, during, and after scaling, to help determine the future processing capacity thresholds of the virtual servers.

- *Hypervisor* – The hypervisor is responsible for hosting the virtual servers that house the resource pools that undergo dynamic reallocation. This mechanism allocates computing capacity to virtual servers according to demand, in alignment with the configurations and policies defined via the virtual infrastructure manager (VIM) by the cloud provider or resource administrator.

- *Live VM Migration* – If a virtual server requires additional capacity that cannot be accommodated by the current hypervisor, this mechanism is used to migrate the virtual server to another hypervisor that can offer the required capacity before adding more computing capacity at the destination.

- *Pay-Per-Use Monitor* – The pay-per-use monitor is related to this pattern in how the monitor is responsible for collecting all of the resource usage cost information, in parallel with the cloud usage monitor.

- *Resource Replication* – Resource replication is associated with this pattern in how this mechanism is used to instantiate new instances of the service or application, virtual server, or both.

- *Virtual CPU* – Processing power is added to virtual servers in units of gigahertz or megahertz, via the use of virtual CPU. This mechanism is used for allocating CPU according to the schedule and processing cycle of the virtual servers.

- *Virtual Infrastructure Manager (VIM)* – Virtual CPU and memory configurations are performed via this mechanism and forwarded to the hypervisors.

- *Virtual RAM* – Virtual servers are allocated the required memory via the use of this mechanism, which allows resource administrators to virtualize the physical memory installed on physical servers and share the virtualized memory between virtual servers. This mechanism also allows resource administrators to allocate memory in quantities greater than the amount of physical memory installed on the physical servers.

- *Virtual Server* – The Elastic Resource Capacity pattern relates to this mechanism in how virtual servers host the services and applications that are consumed by cloud consumers, and experience workload distribution when processing capacities have been reached.

Elastic Network Capacity

How can network bandwidth be allocated to align
with actual usage requirements?

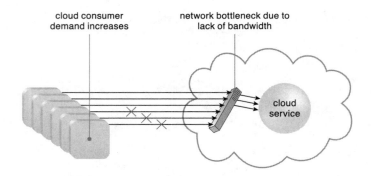

Problem	Network bandwidth is often fixed, resulting in performance bottlenecks, runtime exceptions, and failure when bandwidth capacity is reached.
Solution	A system is established to dynamically increase or decrease the amount of network ports or network bandwidth in response to actual bandwidth usage.
Application	Cloud consumer network traffic is isolated and each cloud consumer is allocated its own network ports, which are retrieved from and returned to a network pool, as per usage requirements.
Mechanisms	Automated Scaling Listener, Cloud Usage Monitor, Hypervisor, Logical Network Perimeter, Pay-Per-Use Monitor, Resource Replication, Virtual Server

Problem

Even if IT resources are scaled on-demand by a cloud platform, performance and scalability can still be inhibited when remote access to the IT resources is impacted by network bandwidth limitations (Figure 3.17).

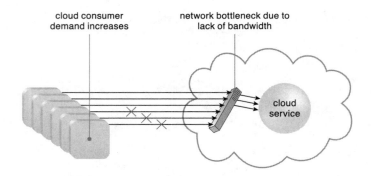

cloud consumer
demand increases

network bottleneck due to
lack of bandwidth

cloud
service

Figure 3.17

A scenario whereby a lack of available bandwidth causes performance issues for
cloud consumer requests.

Solution

A system is established in which additional bandwidth is allocated dynamically to the network to avoid runtime bottlenecks. This system ensures that individual cloud consumer traffic flows are isolated and that each cloud consumer is using a different set of network ports.

Application

The automated scaling listener mechanism and intelligent automation engine scripts are used to detect when traffic reaches a bandwidth threshold and to then respond with the dynamic allocation of additional bandwidth and/or network ports.

The cloud architecture may be equipped with a network resource pool containing network ports that are made available for shared usage. The automated scaling listener monitors workload and network traffic and signals the intelligent automation engine to increase or decrease the number of allocated network ports and/or bandwidth in response to usage fluctuations.

Note that when applying this pattern at the virtual switch level, the intelligent automation engine may need to run a separate script that adds physical uplinks specifically to the virtual switch. Alternatively, Direct I/O Access (169) can also be applied to increase network bandwidth that is allocated to the virtual server.

Mechanisms

- *Automated Scaling Listener* – The automated scaling listener is responsible for monitoring the workload and initiating the scaling of the network capacity.

- *Cloud Usage Monitor* – Cloud usage monitors may be involved with monitoring elastic network capacity before, during, and after scaling.

- *Hypervisor* – The hypervisor is used by this pattern to provide virtual servers with access to the physical network via virtual switches and physical uplinks.

- *Logical Network Perimeter* – The logical network perimeter establishes the boundaries necessary to allow for allocated network capacity to be made available to specific cloud consumers.

- *Pay-Per-Use Monitor* – This monitor keeps track of billing-related data pertaining to the dynamic network bandwidth consumption that occurs as a result of the application of this pattern.

- *Resource Replication* – Resource replication is utilized to add network ports to physical and virtual servers in response to workload demands.

- *Virtual Server* – Virtual servers host the IT resources and cloud services to which network resources are allocated and are themselves affected by the scaling of network capacity.

Elastic Disk Provisioning

How can the billing of cloud storage be based on actual, fluctuating storage consumption?

Problem	When cloud providers charge for fixed-disk storage allocation, the billing is based on the capacity of the disks, not their actual usage. As a result, cloud consumers are generally billed for more storage than they consume.
Solution	A dynamic storage provisioning system is established to dynamically allocate and remove (and collect billing data for) storage space at a granular level.
Application	Thin provisioning and dynamic allocation technology is used with cloud storage monitors to enable elastic storage space provisioning and the measuring of usage data for billing purposes.
Mechanisms	Cloud Storage Device, Cloud Usage Monitor, Hypervisor, Pay-Per-Use Monitor, Resource Replication, Virtual Server

Problem

Cloud consumers are commonly charged for cloud-based storage space based on fixed-disk storage allocation. This means that they are charged based on the capacity of the fixed disks, regardless of their actual data storage consumption.

For example, a cloud consumer may provision a virtual server with the Windows Server operating system and three 150 GB hard drives. When the cloud consumer installs the operating system, it is billed for using 450 GBs of storage space, even though the operating system may only use 15 GBs.

The following steps are shown in Figure 3.18:

1. The cloud consumer requests a virtual server with three hard disks, each with a capacity of 150 GB.

2. The virtual server is provisioned via the Rapid Provisioning and Automated Administration patterns, with a total of 450 GB disk space.

3. The 450 GB of storage space is allocated to the virtual server by the cloud provider.

4. The cloud consumer has not installed any software yet, meaning the actual used space is currently 0 GB.

5. Because 450 GB has been allocated and reserved for the cloud consumer by the cloud provider, the cloud consumer will be charged for 450 GB of disk usage as of the point of allocation.

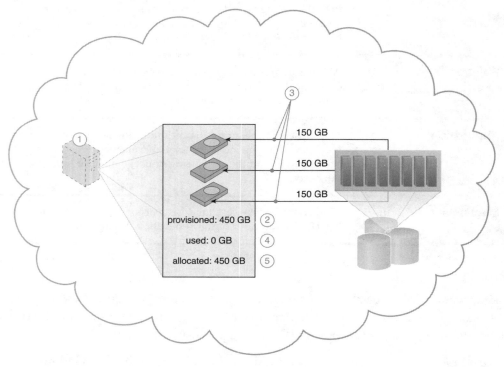

Figure 3.18
A scenario based on the use of a fixed-disk allocation based provisioning model.

Solution

A system of dynamic storage provisioning is established so that the cloud consumer is billed, on a granular level, for the exact amount of storage that was actually used at any given time. This system uses thin provisioning technology for the dynamic allocation of storage space and is further supported by runtime usage monitoring to collect accurate usage data for billing purposes.

The following steps are shown in Figure 3.19:

1. The cloud consumer requests a virtual server with three hard disks, each with a capacity of 150 GB.

2. The virtual server is provisioned via the Rapid Provisioning and Automated Administration patterns, with a total of 450 GB disk space.

3. 450 GB of disk space is set as the maximum allowed disk usage for this virtual server, but no physical disk space has actually been reserved or allocated yet.

4. The cloud consumer has not installed any software yet, meaning the actual used space is currently 0 GB.

5. Because the allocated disk space is equal to the actual used space (which is currently at zero), the cloud consumer is not charged for any disk space usage.

The cloud consumer will only be charged when the disk space has actually been used.

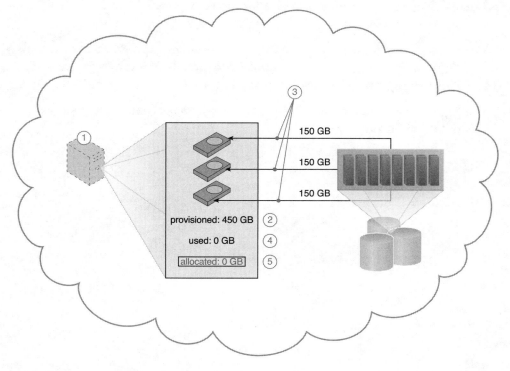

Figure 3.19

A scenario based on the use of a dynamic-disk allocation based provisioning model.

Application

Thin provisioning software is installed on servers that need to process dynamic storage allocation. A specialized cloud usage monitor is employed to track and report actual disk usage.

The following steps are shown in Figure 3.20:

1. A request is received from the cloud consumer and the provisioning for a new virtual server instance begins.

2. As part of the provisioning process, the hard disks are chosen as dynamic or thin provisioned disks.

3. The hypervisor calls a dynamic disk allocation component to create thin disks for the virtual server.

4. Virtual server disks are created via the thin provisioning program and saved in a folder of near-zero size. The size of this folder and its files grows as operating applications are installed and additional files are copied onto the virtual server.

5. The pay-per-use monitor mechanism tracks the actual dynamically allocated storage for billing purposes.

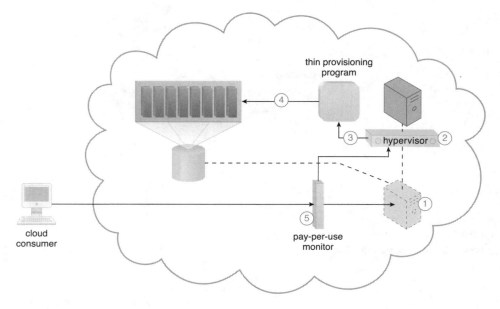

Figure 3.20
A sample cloud architecture resulting from the application of the Elastic Disk Provisioning pattern.

Because the allocated space is equal to the amount of used space after applying the pattern, the cloud consumer will only be charged for 15 GB of storage usage. Should the cloud consumer later install an application that takes up 6 GB of disk space, it will be billed for using 21 GB from thereon.

Figure 3.21 provides an example of before and after the application of the Elastic Disk Provisioning pattern.

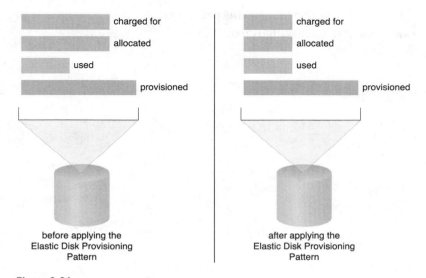

Figure 3.21

The fixed-disk allocation based provisioning model compared to the dynamic disk provisioning model.

Mechanisms

- *Cloud Storage Device* – This mechanism represents the cloud storage devices to which this pattern is primarily applied.

- *Cloud Usage Monitor* – Cloud usage monitors are used to track storage usage fluctuations in relation to the system established by this pattern.

- *Hypervisor* – The hypervisor is relied upon to perform built-in thin provisioning and to provision virtual servers with dynamic thin-disks in support of this pattern.

- *Pay-Per-Use Monitor* – The pay-per-use monitor is incorporated into the cloud architecture resulting from the application of this pattern in order to monitor and collect billing-related usage data as it corresponds to elastic provisioning.

- *Resource Replication* – Resource replication is part of an elastic disk provisioning system when conversion of dynamic thin-disk storage into static thick-disk storage is required.

- *Virtual Server* – The application of this pattern creates new instances of physical servers as virtual servers with dynamic disks.

Load Balanced Virtual Server Instances

How can a workload be balanced across virtual servers and their physical hosts?

Problem	If a runtime workload is improperly distributed across both virtual servers and their physical hosts, then some virtual servers become over-utilized, while others are under-utilized or running idle.
Solution	The workload is recalculated at runtime and virtual servers are correspondingly moved between hosting physical servers to ensure even distribution across virtual and physical layers.
Application	A capacity watchdog surveys physical and virtual servers and reports variance to the VIM, which interacts with a load balancer and live VM migration to dynamically adjust virtual server locations.
Mechanisms	Automated Scaling Listener, Cloud Storage Device, Cloud Usage Monitor, Hypervisor, Live VM Migration, Load Balancer, Logical Network Perimeter, Resource Cluster, Resource Replication, Virtual CPU, Virtual Infrastructure Manager (VIM), Virtual RAM, Virtual Server, Virtual Switch, Virtualization Monitor

Problem

When physical servers operate and are managed in isolation from one another, it is very challenging to keep cross-server workloads evenly balanced. One physical server can easily end up hosting more virtual servers or having to process greater workloads than neighboring physical servers (Figure 3.22).

Over time, the extent of over- and under-utilization of the physical servers can increase dramatically, leading to on-going performance challenges (for over-utilized servers) and constant waste (for the lost processing potential of under-utilized servers).

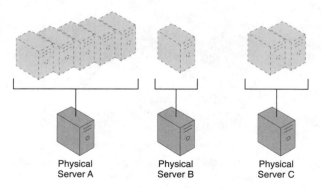

Figure 3.22
Three physical servers are encumbered with different quantities of virtual
server instances, leading to both over-utilized and under-utilized IT
resources.

Solution

A capacity watchdog system is established to dynamically calculate virtual server
instances and associated workloads and to correspondingly distribute the processing
across available physical server hosts (Figure 3.23).

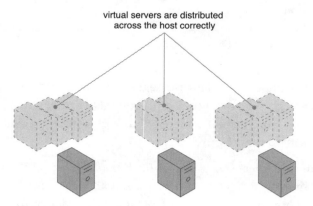

Figure 3.23
The virtual server instances are evenly distributed across the physical
server hosts.

Application

The capacity watchdog system is comprised of a capacity watchdog cloud usage monitor, the live VM migration program, and a capacity planner. The capacity watchdog monitor keeps track of physical and virtual server usage and reports any significant fluctuations to the capacity planner, which is responsible for dynamically calculating physical server computing capacities against virtual server capacity requirements. The capacity planner can decide to move a virtual server to another host to distribute the workload at which point it signals the live VM migration program to perform the move of the targeted virtual server from one physical host to another.

The following steps are shown in Figures 3.24 to 3.26:

1. The Hypervisor Clustering pattern is applied to create a cluster of physical servers.

2. Policies and thresholds are defined for the capacity watchdog monitor.

3. The capacity watchdog monitors physical server capacities and virtual server processing.

4. The capacity watchdog monitor reports an over-utilization to the VIM.

5. The VIM signals the load balancer to redistribute the workload based on pre-defined thresholds.

6. The load balancer initiates live VM migration to move the virtual servers.

7. Live VM migration transitions the selected virtual servers from one physical host to another.

8. The workload is balanced across the physical servers in the cluster.

9. The capacity watchdog continues to monitor the workload and resource consumption.

Figure 3.24

A cloud architecture scenario resulting from the application of the Load Balanced Virtual Server Instances pattern (Part I).

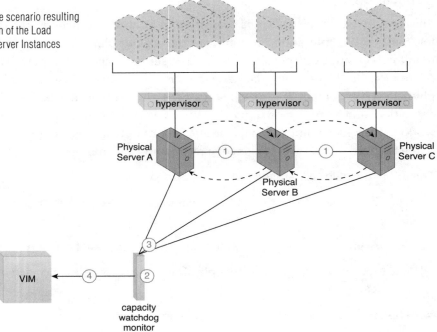

Figure 3.25

A cloud architecture scenario resulting from the application of the Load Balanced Virtual Server Instances pattern (Part II).

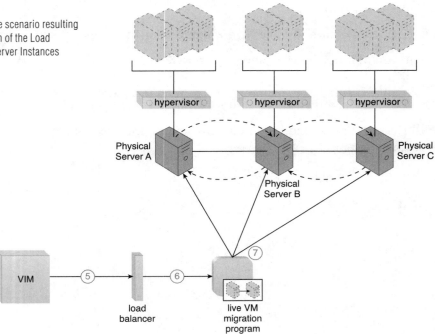

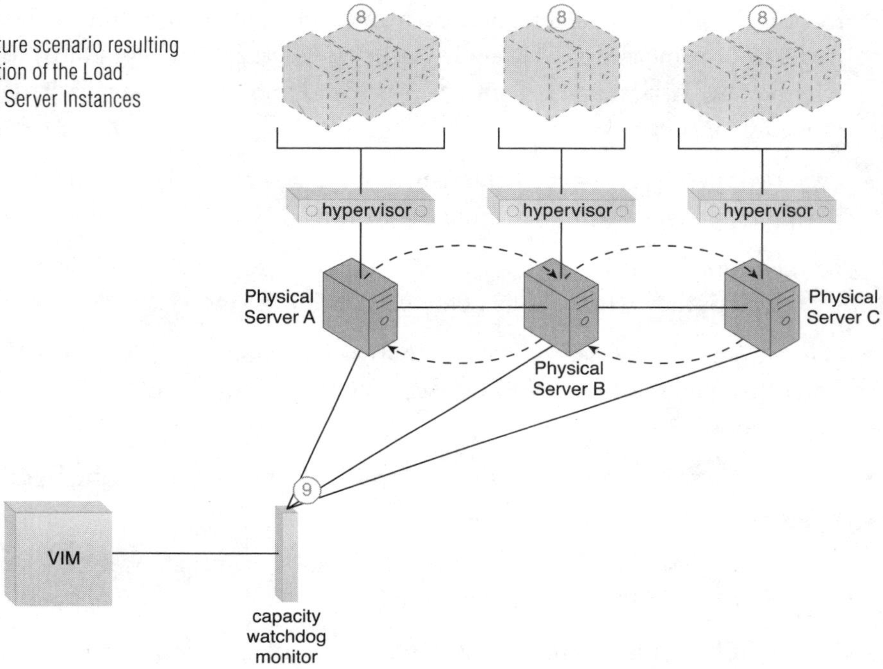

Figure 3.26

A cloud architecture scenario resulting
from the application of the Load
Balanced Virtual Server Instances
pattern (Part III).

Mechanisms

- *Automated Scaling Listener* – The automated scaling listener may be incorporated
  into the system established by the application of this pattern to initiate the process
  of load balancing and to dynamically monitor workload coming to the virtual
  servers via the hypervisors.

- *Cloud Storage Device* – If virtual servers are not stored on a shared cloud storage
  device, this mechanism is used to copy virtual server folders from a cloud storage
  device that is accessible to the source hypervisor to another cloud storage device
  that is accessible to the destination hypervisor.

- *Cloud Usage Monitor* – Various cloud usage monitors, including the aforementioned
  capacity watchdog monitor, may be involved with collecting and processing physical server and virtual server usage information.

- *Hypervisor* – Hypervisors host the virtual servers that are migrated, as required,
  and further form the cluster used as the backbone of the capacity watchdog
  system. They are used to host virtual servers and allocate computing capacity to

the virtual servers. The total available and consumed computing capacity of each hypervisor is measured by the virtual infrastructure manager (VIM) to determine whether any hypervisor is being over-utilized and needs to have virtual servers moved to another hypervisor.

- *Live VM Migration* – This mechanism is used to seamlessly migrate virtual servers between hypervisors to distribute the workload.

- *Load Balancer* – The load balancer mechanism is responsible for distributing the workload of the virtual servers between the hypervisors.

- *Logical Network Perimeter* – A logical network perimeter ensures that the destination of a given relocated virtual server is in compliance with SLA and privacy regulations.

- *Resource Cluster* – This mechanism is used to form the underlying hypervisor cluster in support of live VM migration.

- *Resource Replication* – The replication of virtual server instances may be required as part of the load balancing functionality.

- *Virtual CPU* – This mechanism is used to allocate CPU capacity to virtual servers. The amount of virtual CPU consumed by each virtual server running on a hypervisor is used to identify how the virtual servers are utilizing the hypervisor's CPU resources.

- *Virtual Infrastructure Manager (VIM)* – This mechanism is used to make all of the necessary configurations before broadcasting the configurations to the hypervisors.

- *Virtual RAM* – Virtual servers are allocated the required memory via the use of this mechanism, which helps to evaluate how virtual servers are utilizing the hypervisors' physical memory.

- *Virtual Server* – This is the mechanism to which this pattern is primarily applied.

- *Virtual Switch* – This mechanism is used to establish connectivity for the virtual servers after migrating between hypervisors to ensure that they will be accessible by cloud consumers and resource administrators.

- *Virtualization Monitor* – This mechanism is used to monitor the workload against the thresholds defined by the system administrator, in order to identify when the hypervisors are being over-utilized and require workload balancing.

Load Balanced Virtual Switches

How can workloads be dynamically balanced on physical network connections to prevent bandwidth bottlenecks?

Problem	When network traffic on the uplink port for a virtual switch increases, it can cause delays, performance issues, and packet loss because the affected virtual servers are sending and receiving traffic via only one uplink.
Solution	Network traffic is balanced across multiple uplinks between the virtual and physical networks.
Application	Extra network interface cards are added to the physical host to accommodate the virtual switch that is configured with multiple physical uplinks.
Mechanisms	Cloud Usage Monitor, Hypervisor, Load Balancer, Logical Network Perimeter, Physical Uplink, Resource Replication, Virtual Infrastructure Manager (VIM), Virtual Server, Virtual Switch

Problem

Virtual servers are connected to the outside world via virtual switches. When the network traffic on the uplink port increases, bandwidth bottlenecks can occur, resulting in transmission delays, performance issues, packet loss, and lag time because the virtual servers are sending and receiving traffic via the same uplink.

The following steps are shown in Figures 3.27 and 3.28:

1. A virtual switch has been created and is being used to interconnect virtual servers.

2. A physical network adapter has been attached to the virtual switch to be used as an uplink to the physical (external) network, connecting virtual servers to cloud consumers.

3. Cloud consumers can send their requests to virtual servers via the physical uplink. The virtual servers reply via the same uplink.

4. When the number of requests and responses increases, the amount of traffic passing through the physical uplink also grows. This further increases the number of packets that need to be processed and forwarded by the physical network adapter.

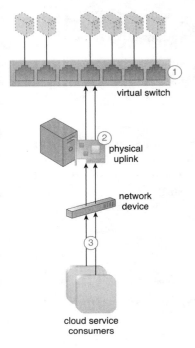

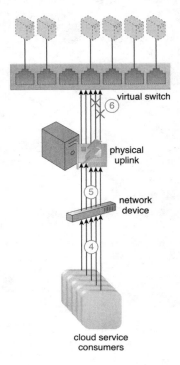

Figure 3.27
A sequence of events that can lead to network bandwidth bottlenecking is shown (Part I).

Figure 3.28
A sequence of events that can lead to network bandwidth bottlenecking is shown (Part II).

5. Because traffic increases beyond the physical adapter's capacity, it is unable to handle the workload.

6. The network forms a bottleneck that results in performance degradation and the loss of delay-sensitive data packets.

Solution

A load balancing system is established whereby multiple uplinks are provided to balance network traffic workloads.

Application

Balancing the network traffic load across multiple uplinks or redundant paths can help avoid slow transfers and data loss. Link aggregation can further be used to balance the traffic, thereby allowing the workload to be distributed across multiple uplinks at the same time. This way, none of the network cards are overloaded.

The following steps are shown in Figure 3.29:

1. Virtual servers are connected to the external network via a physical uplink, while actively responding to cloud consumer requests.

2. An increase in requests leads to increased network traffic, resulting in the physical uplink becoming a bottleneck.

3. Additional physical uplinks are added to enable network traffic to be distributed and balanced.

The virtual switch needs to be configured to support multiple physical uplinks. The number of required uplinks can vary on a server-by-server basis. The uplinks generally need to be configured as a team (also known as an NIC team) for which traffic shaping policies are defined.

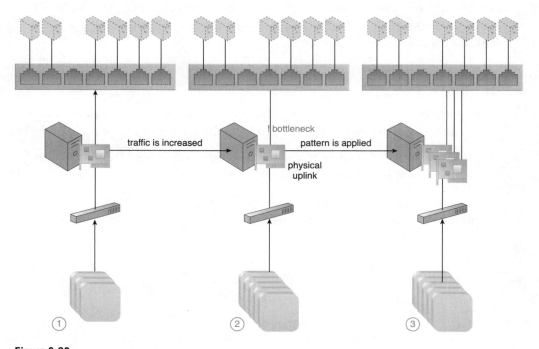

Figure 3.29
The addition of network interface cards and physical uplinks allows network workloads to be balanced.

Mechanisms

- *Cloud Usage Monitor* – Cloud usage monitors may be employed to monitor network traffic and bandwidth usage.

- *Hypervisor* – Hypervisors host and provide the virtual servers with access to both the virtual switches and external network. They are responsible for both hosting virtual servers and forwarding the virtual servers' network traffic across multiple physical uplinks to distribute the network load.

- *Load Balancer* – This mechanism supplies the runtime load balancing logic and performs the actual balancing of the network workload across the different uplinks.

- *Logical Network Perimeter* – The logical network perimeter can be used to create boundaries that protect and limit bandwidth usage for specific cloud consumers.

- *Physical Uplink* – The physical uplink mechanism is used to connect virtual switches to physical switches. The use of this mechanism enables each virtual switch to be connected to the physical network via two or more physical connections, for load-balancing purposes.

- *Resource Replication* – This mechanism is utilized to generate additional uplinks to the virtual switch.

- *Virtual Infrastructure Manager (VIM)* – This mechanism performs virtual switch configurations and attaches physical uplinks to the virtual switches.

- *Virtual Server* – Virtual servers host the IT resources that benefit from the additional uplinks and bandwidth via virtual switches.

- *Virtual Switch* – The virtual switch mechanism is used to connect virtual servers to the physical network and to cloud consumers.

Service State Management

How can stateful cloud services be optimized to minimize runtime IT resource consumption?

Problem	A cloud service designed to place significant data into memory for prolonged periods can consume excessive amounts of runtime processing, thereby unreasonably taxing the overall cloud infrastructure and imposing additional usage costs on cloud consumers.
Solution	The cloud service is designed to integrate with a state management system, allowing it to defer state data at runtime when necessary so as to minimize its IT resource consumption.
Application	A state management system requires a cloud storage device capable of temporarily holding and releasing state data exchanged by the cloud service. The cloud service itself needs to be equipped with logic to determine when and how to release and retrieve state data.
Mechanisms	Cloud Storage Device, Cloud Usage Monitor, Hypervisor, Pay-Per-Use Monitor, Resource Replication, State Management Database, Virtual Server

Problem

A cloud service may need to carry out functions that require prolonged processing across underlying IT resources or other cloud-based services that are invoked. While waiting for responses from IT resources or other cloud services, the primary cloud service may be unnecessarily consuming memory via the temporary storage of state data. The cloud service may also be storing RAM or CPU data, which represents memory consumed by the virtual server instance itself.

While retaining state data in-memory, the cloud service is considered to be in a stateful condition. When stateful, the cloud service is actively consuming infrastructure-level resources that could otherwise be shared within the cloud. Furthermore, the cloud consumer may be charged usage fees for the on-going consumption of these resources.

Solution

The cloud service architecture is designed to incorporate the use of the state management database mechanism, a specialized repository used for the temporary deferral of state data. This solution applies to custom cloud services that automate business tasks, as well as cloud service products (such as those based on cloud delivery models) offered by cloud providers.

Application

State information can be programmatically deferred by executing conditional logic within the cloud service, or it can be manually deferred by a cloud resource administrator using a usage and administration portal.

The following steps are shown in Figure 3.30:

1. The cloud consumer uses the usage and administration portal to request that the cloud service status be paused and deferred.

2. The request is forwarded to an API-enabled system that interacts with the state management database mechanism.

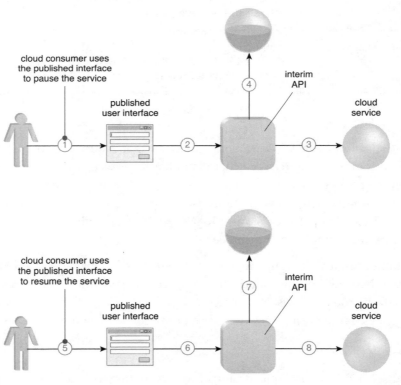

Figure 3.30

A sample scenario in which cloud service state data is manually deferred and restored.

3. The system reads the service status.

4. The system saves it to the state management database.

5. The cloud consumer requests that the service be reactivated via the usage and administration portal.

6. The cloud consumer request is forwarded to the system.

7. The system interacts with the state management database to retrieve the status of the cloud service.

8. The cloud service status is restored and cloud service activity resumes.

Note that resuming a paused cloud service may trigger a resource constraint, depending on how long the state data was deferred and how the IT resources required by the stateful cloud service are managed while the cloud service is stateless.

Mechanisms

- *Cloud Storage Device* – This mechanism is used in the same way as the state management database in relation to this pattern.

- *Cloud Usage Monitor* – Specialized cloud usage monitors may be employed for proactive monitoring of IT resource processing and server memory usage.

- *Hypervisor* – In some cases, state management database functionality is provided at the hypervisor level.

- *Pay-Per-Use Monitor* – This monitoring mechanism collects granular resource usage data for state data held in memory, as well as granular storage usage data for when state data is temporarily stored in a cloud storage device.

- *Resource Replication* – Resource replication is used to instantiate new instances of IT resources that may need to be deactivated and re-activated as part of state management deferral logic.

- *State Management Database* – This is the core mechanism used to implement a state management architecture.

- *Virtual Server* – This mechanism generally hosts the state management database and is responsible for providing the processing features used to transfer state data to and from the database.

Problem	When storage-related processing is limited to one cloud storage device, over-utilization can occur, while other storage devices are being under-utilized or not utilized at all, resulting in a non-optimized cloud storage architecture.
Solution	A storage capacity system is provided to distribute runtime workloads between different cloud storage devices, across the network, and to enable LUNs to be divided and managed.
Application	Cloud storage devices are combined into a resource pool from which they are scaled horizontally and in coordination with the use of a storage capacity monitor and LUN migration.
Mechanisms	Audit Monitor, Automated Scaling Listener, Cloud Storage Device, Cloud Usage Monitor, Load Balancer, Logical Network Perimeter

Problem

When cloud storage devices are utilized independently, the changes resulting from some devices being over-utilized while others remain under-utilized are significant. Over-utilized storage devices increase the workload on the storage controller and can cause a range of performance challenges (Figure 3.31). Under-utilized storage devices may be wasteful due to lost processing and storage capacity potential.

Solution

The LUNs are evenly distributed across available cloud storage devices and a storage capacity system is established to ensure that runtime workloads are evenly distributed across the LUNs (Figure 3.32).

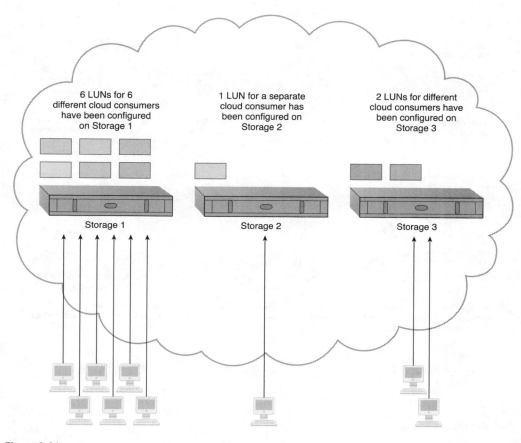

Figure 3.31

An imbalanced cloud storage architecture where six storage LUNs are located on Storage 1 for use by different cloud consumers, while Storage 2 and Storage 3 each host one and two additional LUNs respectively. Because it hosts the most LUNs, the majority of the workload ends up with Storage 1.

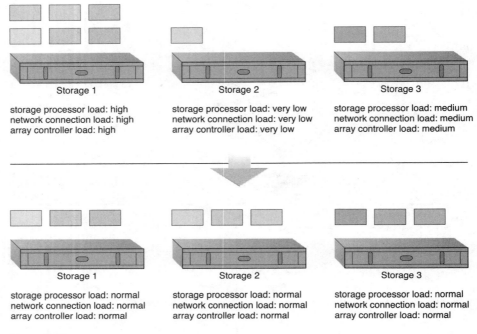

Figure 3.32
LUNs are dynamically distributed across cloud storage devices, resulting in more even distribution of associated types of workloads.

Application

Combining the different storage devices as a group allows LUN data to be spread out equally among available storage hosts. A storage management station is configured and an automated scaling listener is positioned to monitor and equalize runtime workloads among the storage devices in the group.

The following steps are shown in Figures 3.33 to 3.35:

1. The storage capacity system and the storage capacity monitor are configured to survey three storage devices in realtime. As part of this configuration, some workload and capacity thresholds are defined.

2. The storage capacity monitor determines that the workload on Storage 1 is reaching a predefined threshold.

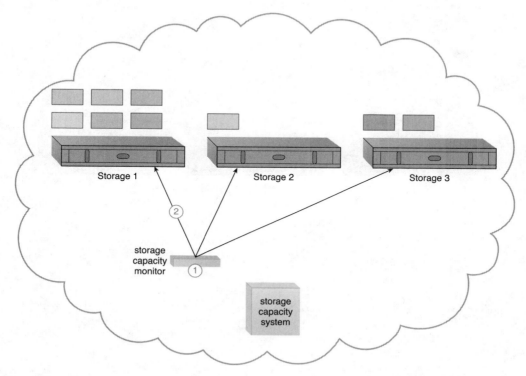

Figure 3.33

A cloud architecture resulting from the application of the Storage Workload Management pattern (Part I).

3. The storage capacity monitor informs the storage capacity system that Storage 1 is over-utilized.

4. The storage capacity system initiates workload balancing via the storage load/ capacity manager (not shown).

5. The storage load/capacity manager calls for LUN migration to move some of the storage LUNs from Storage 1 to the other two storage devices.

6. LUN migration transitions the LUNs.

Note that if some of the LUNs are being accessed less frequently or only at specific times, the storage capacity system can keep the hosting storage device in power-saving mode until it is needed.

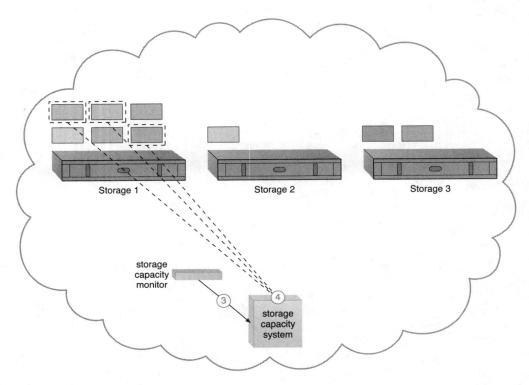

Figure 3.34

A cloud architecture resulting from the application of the Storage Workload Management pattern (Part II).

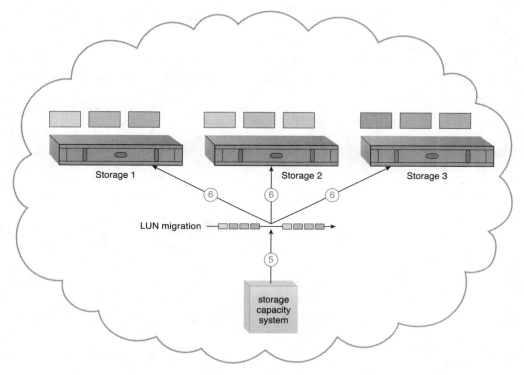

Figure 3.35

A cloud architecture resulting from the application of the Storage Workload Management pattern (Part III).

Mechanisms

- *Audit Monitor* – This monitoring mechanism may need to be involved because the system established by this pattern can physically relocate data, perhaps even to other geographical regions.

- *Automated Scaling Listener* – The automated scaling listener may be incorporated to observe and respond to workload fluctuations.

- *Cloud Storage Device* – This is the primary mechanism to which this pattern is applied.

- *Cloud Usage Monitor* – In addition to the capacity workload monitor, other types of cloud usage monitors may be deployed to track LUN movements and collect workload distribution statistics.

- *Load Balancer* – This mechanism can be added to horizontally balance workloads across available cloud storage devices.

- *Logical Network Perimeter* – This mechanism provides a level of isolation to ensure that cloud consumer data that is relocated to a new location remains inaccessible to unauthorized cloud consumers.

Dynamic Data Normalization

How can redundant data within cloud storage devices be automatically avoided?

Problem	Cloud consumers may store large volumes of redundant data within cloud storage devices, thereby bloating the storage architecture and compromising data access performance.
Solution	Data received by cloud consumers is automatically normalized so that redundant data is avoided and cloud storage device capacity and performance are optimized.
Application	Data de-duplication technology is used to detect and eliminate redundant data at block or file-based levels.
Mechanisms	Cloud Storage Device

Problem

Redundant data can cause a range of issues in cloud environments, such as:

- Increased time required to store and catalog files

- Increased required storage and backup space   .

- Increased costs due to increased data volume

- Increased time required for replication to secondary storage

- Increased time required to backup data

For example, a cloud consumer copies 100 MB of files onto a cloud storage device. If it copies the data redundantly, ten times, the consequences can be considerable:

- The cloud consumer will be charged for using 1,000 MBs (1 GB) of storage space even though it is only storing 100 MBs of unique data.

- The cloud provider needs to provide an unnecessary 900 megabytes of space on both the online cloud storage device and any backup storage systems (such as tape drives).

- It takes nine times the amount of time required to store and catalog data.

- If the cloud provider is performing a site recovery, the data replication duration and performance will suffer, since 1,000 MBs need to be replicated instead of 100 MBs.

In multitenant public clouds, these impacts can be significantly amplified.

Solution

A data de-duplication system is established to prevent cloud consumers from inadvertently saving redundant copies of data. This system detects and eliminates exact amounts of redundant data on cloud storage devices, and can be applied to both block and file-based storage devices (although it works most effectively on the former). The data de-duplication system checks each block it receives to determine whether it is redundant with a block that has already been received. Redundant blocks are replaced with pointers to the equivalent blocks that are already stored.

Application

A de-duplication system examines received data prior to passing it to storage controllers (Figure 3.36). As part of the examination process, it assigns a hash code to every piece of data that has been processed and stored. It also keeps an index of hashes and pieces. As a result, if a new block of data is received, its generated hash is compared with the current stored hashes to decide if it is a new or duplicate block of data.

Figure 3.36

In Part A, datasets containing redundant data unnecessarily bloat data storage. The Dynamic Data Normalization pattern results in the constant and automatic streamlining of data as shown in Part B, regardless of how denormalized the data received from the cloud consumer is.

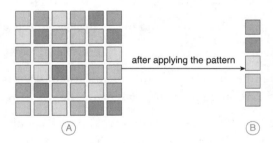

after applying the pattern

If it is a new block, it is saved. If the data is a duplicate, it is eliminated and a link (or pointer) to the original data block is created and saved in the cloud storage device. If a request for the data block is received at a later point, the pointer forwards the request to the original data block.

This pattern can be applied to both disk storage and backup tape drives. A cloud provider may decide to prevent redundant data only on backup cloud storage devices, while others may more aggressively implement the data de-duplication system on all cloud storage devices.

There are different methods and algorithms for comparing blocks of data and deciding whether they are duplications of other blocks.

Mechanisms

- *Cloud Storage Device* – This mechanism represents the cloud storage devices to which this pattern is primarily applied in relation to the normalization of both existing and newly added data.

Cross-Storage Device Vertical Tiering

How can the vertical scaling of data processing be carried out dynamically?

Problem	Increasing the processing capacity of data stored on cloud storage devices generally requires the manual vertical scaling of the device, which is inefficient and potentially wasteful.
Solution	A system is established whereby the vertical scaling of data processing can be carried out dynamically across multiple cloud storage devices.
Application	Using pre-defined capacity thresholds, LUN migration is used to dynamically move LUN disks between cloud storage devices with different capacities.
Mechanisms	Audit Monitor, Automated Scaling Listener, Cloud Storage Device, Cloud Usage Monitor, Pay-Per-Use Monitor

Problem

After working with a provisioned cloud storage device, a cloud consumer may determine that the device is unable to accommodate its necessary performance requirements. Conventional approaches to vertically scaling the cloud storage device include adding more bandwidth to increase IOPS (input/output per second) and adding more data processing power. This type of vertical scaling can be inefficient and time consuming to implement, and can result in waste when the increased capacity is no longer needed.

This approach is depicted in the following scenario in which a number of requests for access to a red LUN increased, requiring it to be manually moved to a high performance storage device.

The following steps are shown in Figure 3.37:

1. The cloud provider installs and configures a storage device.

2. The cloud provider creates the required LUNs for the cloud consumers.

3. Storage LUNs are presented to their respective cloud consumers, who begin using them.

4. The storage devices start forwarding requests to cloud consumer LUNs.

Figure 3.37

Conventional vertical scaling
of a cloud storage device.

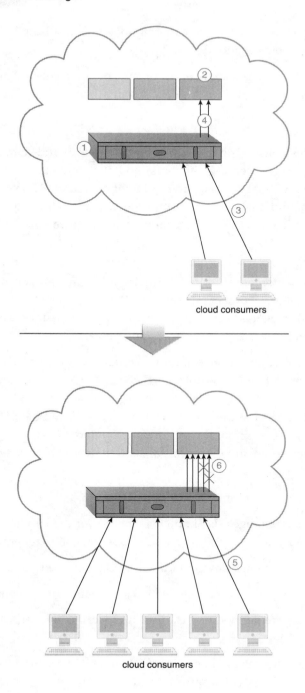

cloud consumers

cloud consumers

5. The number of requests increases significantly, resulting in high storage bandwidth and performance demands.

6. Some of the requests are rejected or time out due to performance capacity limitations.

Solution

A system is established that can survive bandwidth and data processing power constraints (thereby preventing timeouts) and that introduces vertical scaling between different storage devices possessing different capacities. As a result, LUNs can automatically scale up and down across multiple devices, allowing requests to use the appropriate level of storage devices to perform the tasks required by the cloud consumer.

Application

Although the automated tiering technology can move data to cloud storage devices with the same storage processing capacity, the new cloud storage devices with increased capacity need to be made available. For example, solid-state drives (SSDs) may be suitable devices for upgrading data processing power.

The automated scaling listener monitors requests sent to specific LUNs. When it identifies that a predefined threshold is reached, it signals the storage management program to move the LUN to a higher capacity device. Interruption is prevented because a disconnection during the transfer never occurs. While the LUN data is scaling up to another device, its original device remains up and running. As soon as the scaling is completed, cloud consumer requests are automatically redirected to the new cloud storage device.

The following steps are shown in Figures 3.38 to 3.40:

1. The primary storage (also known as the "lower capacity storage") is installed and configured, and responding to cloud consumer storage requests.

2. A secondary storage device with higher capacity and performance is installed.

3. The LUN migration is configured via a storage management program.

4. Thresholds are defined in the automated scaling listener, which monitors the requests.

5. The storage management program is installed and configured to categorize the storage based on device performance.

6. Cloud consumer requests are sent to the (lower capacity) primary storage device.

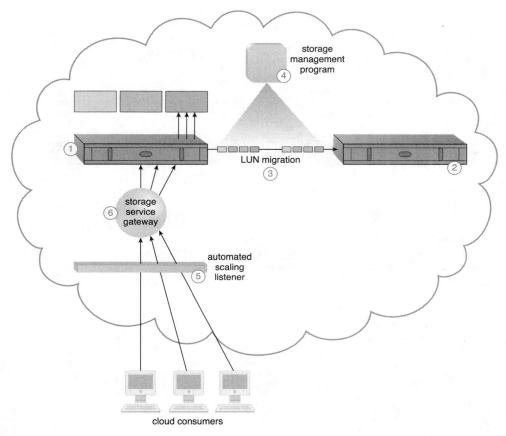

Figure 3.38

A cloud architecture resulting from the application of the Cross-Storage Device Vertical Tiering pattern (Part I).

7. The number of cloud consumer requests reaches the predefined request threshold.

8. The automated scaling listener signals the storage management program that scaling is required.

9. The storage management program calls the LUN migration program to move the cloud consumer's red LUN to a higher capacity storage device.

10. The LUN migration program initiates the move of the red LUN to a higher capacity storage device.

11. Even though the LUN was moved to a new storage device, cloud consumer requests are still being sent to the original storage device.

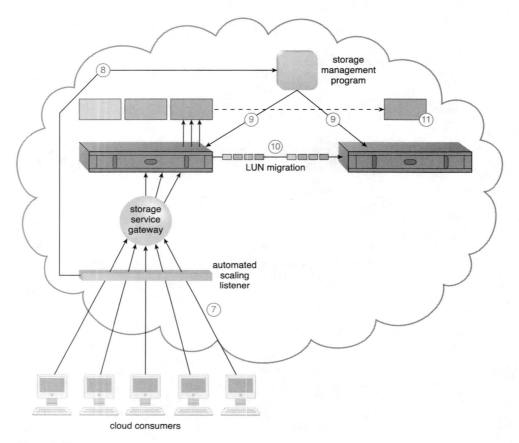

Figure 3.39

A cloud architecture resulting from the application of the Cross-Storage Device Vertical Tiering pattern (Part II).

12. The storage service gateway forwards the cloud consumer storage requests from the red LUN to the new storage device.

13. The red LUN is deleted from the lower capacity device (via the storage management and LUN migration programs).

14. The automated scaling listener monitors the cloud consumer requests for access to the higher capacity storage for the red LUN.

15. Usage and billing data is tracked and stored via the pay-per-use monitor mechanism.

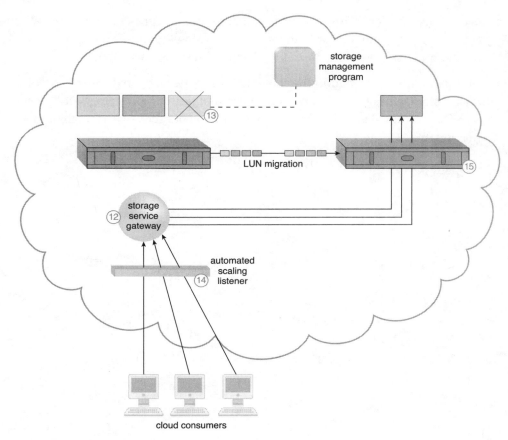

Figure 3.40

A cloud architecture resulting from the application of the Cross-Storage Device Vertical Tiering pattern (Part III).

Mechanisms

- *Audit Monitor* – This mechanism ensures that the relocation of cloud consumer data via the application of this pattern does not conflict with any legal or data privacy regulations or policies.

- *Automated Scaling Listener* – The automated scaling listener monitors the traffic from the cloud consumer to the storage device, and initiates the data transfer process across storage devices.

- *Cloud Storage Device* – This mechanism represents the cloud storage devices that are affected by the application of this pattern.

- *Cloud Usage Monitor* – This infrastructure mechanism represents various runtime monitoring requirements for tracking and recording the cloud consumer data transfer and usage at both source and destination storage locations.

- *Pay-Per-Use Monitor* – Within the context of this pattern, the pay-per-use monitor collects storage usage information on source and destination storage locations, as well as resource usage information for carrying out the cross-storage tiering functionality.

Intra-Storage Device Vertical Data Tiering

How can the dynamic vertical scaling of data be carried out within a storage device?

Problem	When required to maintain data within a single cloud storage device, the storage and processing capacity of the data will be limited to that of the device.
Solution	A cloud storage device capable of supporting multiple disk types is used to enable dynamic vertical scaling confined to the device.
Application	Complex cloud storage technology is utilized to establish storage tiers through which data can be scaled up or down via LUN migration.
Mechanisms	Automated Scaling Listener, Cloud Storage Device, Cloud Usage Monitor, Pay-Per-Use Monitor

Problem

When a cloud consumer has a firm requirement to limit the storage of data to a single cloud storage device, the capacity of that device to store and process data can become a source of performance-related challenges. For example, different servers, applications, and cloud services that are forced to use the same device may have data access and I/O requirements that are incompatible with the cloud storage device's capabilities.

Solution

A system is established to support vertical scaling within a single cloud storage device (Figure 3.41). This intra-device scaling system utilizes the availability of different disk types with different capacities.

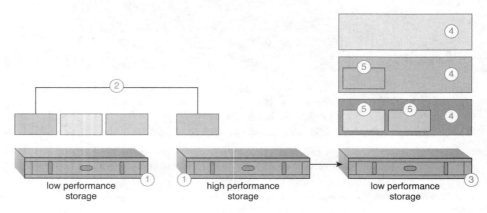

Figure 3.41

A conventional horizontal scaling system involving two cloud storage devices (1, 2) is transitioned to an intra-storage device system (3) capable of vertically scaling through disk types graded into different tiers (4). Each LUN is moved to a tier that corresponds to its processing and storage requirements (5).

Application

The cloud storage architecture requires the use of a complex storage device that supports different types of hard disks, in particular high-performance disks, such as SATAs, SASs, and SSDs. The disk types are organized into graded tiers, so that LUN migration can vertically scale the device based on the allocation of disk types that align to the processing and capacity requirements at hand.

After disk categorization, data load conditions and definitions are set so that the LUNs are able to either move to a higher or lower grade depending on when pre-defined conditions are met. These thresholds and conditions are used by the automated scaling listener when monitoring runtime data processing traffic.

The following steps are shown in Figures 3.42 to 3.44:

1. A storage device that supports different types of hard disks is installed.

2. Different types of hard disks are installed in the enclosures.

3. Similar disk types are grouped together to create different grades of disk groups based on their I/O performance.

4. Two LUNs have been created on Disk Group 1: LUN red and LUN yellow.

5. The automated scaling listener monitors the requests and compares them with the predefined thresholds.

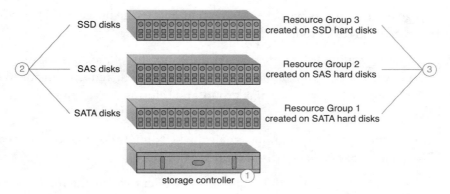

Figure 3.42

An intra-device cloud storage architecture resulting from the application of this pattern (Part I).

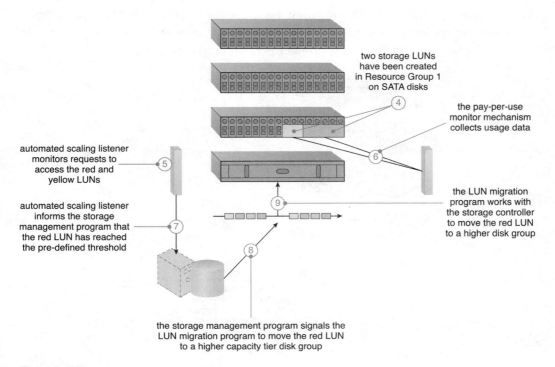

Figure 3.43

An intra-device cloud storage architecture resulting from the application of this pattern (Part II).

6. The usage monitor tracks the actual amount of disk usage on the red LUN based on free space and disk group performance.

7. The automated scaling listener realizes that the number of requests coming to the red LUN is reaching the predefined threshold, and the red LUN needs to be moved to a higher performance disk group, and informs the storage management program.

8. The storage management program signals the LUN migration to move the red LUN to a higher performance disk group.

9. The LUN migration works with the storage controller to move the red LUN to the higher capacity disk group.

10. The red LUN is moved to a higher performance disk group.

11. The usage monitor is still performing the same task of monitoring the disk usage. However, the difference is that the service price of the red LUN will be higher than before because it is using a higher performance disk group.

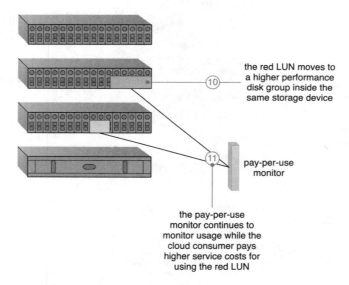

Figure 3.44

An intra-device cloud storage architecture resulting from the application of this pattern (Part III).

Mechanisms

- *Automated Scaling Listener* – The automated scaling listener monitors and compares the cloud storage device's workload with predefined thresholds, so that data can be distributed between disk type tiers, as per workload fluctuations.

- *Cloud Storage Device* – This is the mechanism to which this pattern is primarily applied.

- *Cloud Usage Monitor* – Various cloud usage monitors may be involved with the collection and logging of disk usage information pertaining to the storage device and its individual disk type tiers.

- *Pay-Per-Use Monitor* – This mechanism actively monitors and collects billing-related usage data in response to vertical scaling activity.

Memory Over-Committing

*How can multiple virtual servers be hosted on a single host
when the virtual servers' aggregate memory exceeds the
physical memory that is available on the host?*

Problem	A host needs to be able to host multiple virtual servers, even though their total memory configuration exceeds the host's own physical memory.
Solution	Memory virtualization is implemented to enable more virtual servers to be hosted on the same host, by allowing the host's physical memory to be exceeded by the total memory configuration of the virtual servers.
Application	One or more memory over-commitment components are implemented.
Mechanisms	Hypervisor, Virtual Infrastructure Manager (VIM), Virtual RAM, Virtualization Agent, Virtualization Monitor

Problem

Virtualization supports server consolidation, which is the hosting of multiple virtual servers on the same host or the physical server that is running the hypervisor. In the following example in Figure 3.45, six virtual servers are shown. Two virtual servers with 8 GBs each, two virtual servers with 4 GBs each, and two virtual servers with 2 GBs each have been defined. The virtual servers need a total of 44 GBs of memory.

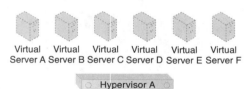

Virtual   Virtual   Virtual   Virtual   Virtual   Virtual
Server A Server B Server C Server D Server E Server F

Hypervisor A

Figure 3.45
The virtual servers require a total of 44 GBs of memory
to be hosted on the same hypervisor.

The virtual servers cannot be run if the host only has 32 GBs of physical memory available, which is less than the memory required by the virtual servers. Figure 3.46 illustrates a situation in which some of the virtual servers cannot be hosted or powered on by the same host as a result.

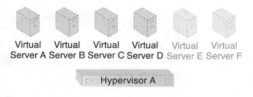

Figure 3.46
Two of the virtual servers cannot be powered on by
Hypervisor A.

The system cannot power on the remaining virtual servers when the amount of allocated memory reaches 32 GBs, because it has run out of memory.

Solution

Memory virtualization is implemented to enable more virtual servers to be hosted on
the same host by allowing its physical memory to be exceeded by the total memory
configuration of the virtual servers that require hosting (Figure 3.47).

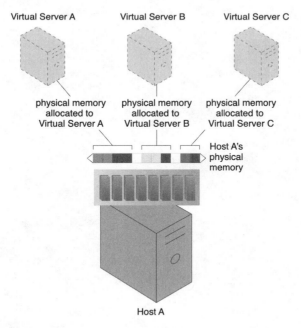

Figure 3.47
Virtual Servers A, B, and C are each allotted a portion of Host A's
physical memory.

Application

Figure 3.48 illustrates the steps that need to be applied. All of the virtual servers can be powered on after memory over-commitment is applied. The host is allowed to allocate an amount of memory that is greater than the amount of available physical memory.

Note that if Resource Reservation (106) needs to be applied to reserve a specific amount of memory for a virtual server, that amount will be deducted from the physical memory of the host and directly allocated to that virtual server. For example, if the host in Figure 3.49 has 32 GBs of memory and a virtual server has reserved 8 GBs, the amount of memory that remains available for the rest of the virtual servers is 24 GBs.

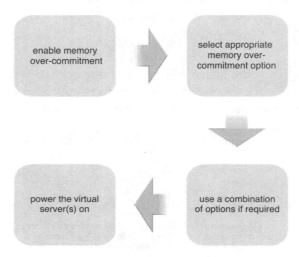

Figure 3.48

The four steps involved in applying the Memory Over-Committing pattern are shown.

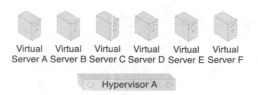

Figure 3.49

Virtual Servers A through F can all be powered on at Hypervisor A.

If an unsuitable memory over-committing technique is used and the over-committing limit is violated, then the host may end up not having sufficient memory. In this case, the host will have to swap to disk by using swap memory, which can have a significant performance impact on memory-intensive applications.

Mechanisms

- *Hypervisor* – The hypervisor mechanism is used to host virtual servers, and provides techniques and features for sharing and partitioning physical memory between multiple virtual servers for concurrent usage.

- *Virtual Infrastructure Manager (VIM)* – This mechanism establishes features for monitoring and analyzing the memory consumption and utilization status of hypervisors and virtual servers.

- *Virtual RAM* – Physical memory is partitioned and allocated to virtual servers in the form of virtual memory. This mechanism provides the virtual servers with access to the physical memory under the control of the hypervisor.

- *Virtualization Agent* – This mechanism provides techniques for improving memory utilization, and helps indicate to a given hypervisor which memory pages can be reclaimed from virtual servers if the hypervisor needs to free up physical memory.

- *Virtualization Monitor* – This mechanism establishes the tools and techniques required to actively monitor memory consumption, and send alerts and notifications whenever utilization thresholds are being met.

NIC Teaming

How can the capacity of multiple NICs be combined for virtual servers to use while improving availability?

Problem	The capacity of individual NICs may be insufficient to guarantee virtual server availability.
Solution	A single virtual switch is used to leverage multiple physical uplinks at the same time.
Application	Multiple NICs are bundled together, assigned to a virtual switch, and configured for concurrent usage.
Mechanisms	Hypervisor, Physical Uplink, Virtual Infrastructure Manager (VIM), Virtual Switch

Problem

The boot availability and capacity of a single physical uplink may sometimes be inadequate for the virtual switch.

In the following example, the virtual switch has two physical uplinks. Only one is active while the other is in standby mode. As illustrated in Figure 3.50, this arrangement does not provide sufficient availability or capacity, since only one physical uplink's capacity is in use at any one time.

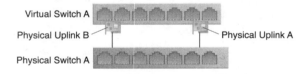

Figure 3.50
Virtual Switch A has two physical uplinks named Physical Uplinks A and B. Physical Uplink B is not active.

Solution

The capacity of multiple physical NICs needs to be combined so that their aggregated bandwidth can be available to keep the remaining NICs operational if one of the NICs goes down (Figure 3.51). NIC teaming is a feature that allows physical NICs to be bundled together to form a logical port. This can be used for:

- *Redundancy/High Availability* – When a virtual switch uses a teamed NIC network to connect to a physical network, traffic is sent via other available NICs should one of the physical NICs fail.

- *Load Balancing* – When a switch has uplinks consisting of multiple NICs, it can send traffic via all of the uplinks simultaneously to reduce congestion and to balance the workload and traffic.

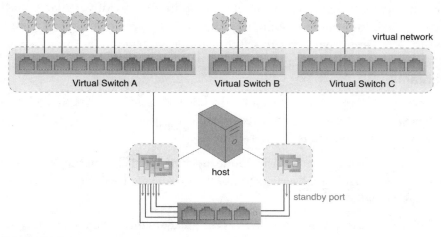

Figure 3.51

The physical NICs assigned to Virtual Switch A act as a team and simultaneously forward packets to balance the load. However, one of the two NICs that are teamed up for Virtual Switch C is not required to simultaneously forward traffic from both NICs. Instead, that NIC has been configured as a standby NIC. It will take over the forwarding of the packets to maintain redundancy and high availability, should anything happen to the original NIC.

Application

In Figure 3.52, multiple physical uplinks are added to the virtual switch. Figure 3.53 illustrates the connecting of the physical uplinks to the physical switch.

Figure 3.52

Six physical uplinks are added to Virtual Switch A.

Figure 3.53

Physical Switch A is now connected to the six physical uplinks.

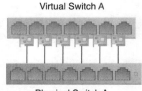

A NIC team is defined using a teaming policy, either via the VIM server or directly on the hypervisor. The physical switch needs to be configured in such a way that none of the physical uplinks are blocked. Implementing a teaming policy ensures that all of the physical uplinks remain active and that the aggregated bandwidth capacity is available for the virtual switch to use. If one of the physical uplinks fails or becomes disconnected, the other uplinks can remain operational to continue sending packets.

Applying this pattern increases the amount of uplink bandwidth available for the virtual switch while improving redundancy and availability. However, this pattern uses the physical NICs exclusively, meaning they cannot be used for anything else.

Mechanisms

- *Hypervisor* – This mechanism enables the creation of virtual servers and virtual switches, and also provides features that allow physical NICs installed on a physical server to be attached to virtual switches.

- *Physical Uplink* – This mechanism connects virtual switches to the physical network, and enables virtual servers to use the virtual switches to communicate with the physical network.

- *Virtual Infrastructure Manager (VIM)* – This mechanism is used to create and manage virtual switches and attach physical uplinks to virtual switches. The VIM also dictates configuration and utilization policies to hypervisors on how to utilize the physical uplinks.

- *Virtual Switch* – This mechanism is used to establish connectivity between virtual servers and the physical network, via the physical uplinks that are attached to the virtual switches.

Broad Access

How can cloud services be made accessible to a diverse range of cloud service consumers?

Problem	Cloud consumers may require access to a cloud service via cloud service consumer devices, protocols or data formats that the cloud service is not designed to support.
Solution	Runtime mapping logic is incorporated to transform data exchanges between the cloud service and different cloud service consumers.
Application	The mapping logic is added to the cloud service logic or positioned separately, within a multi-device broker mechanism that transforms data exchanged between the cloud service consumer and the cloud service.
Mechanisms	Multi-Device Broker

Problem

Cloud service implementations are commonly designed to support one type of cloud service consumer. However, different cloud consumers may need or prefer to access a given cloud service using different cloud service consumer devices, such as mobile devices, Web browsers, or proprietary user interfaces. Limiting the types of cloud service consumers and devices that a cloud service can support reduces its overall reuse and utilization potential.

Solution

Runtime mapping logic is incorporated into the cloud service architecture to support APIs for multiple types of cloud service consumer devices (Figure 3.54). Transport protocols, messaging protocols, data models, and other types of data sent to the cloud service are transformed at runtime into formats supported by the cloud service's native logic.

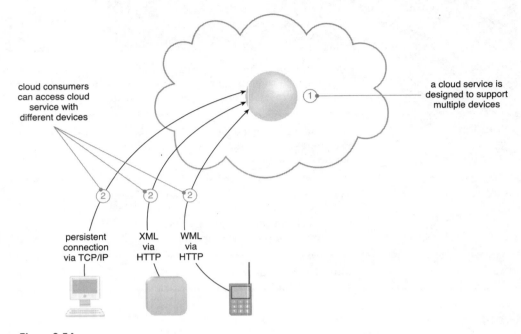

Figure 3.54

A cloud service containing runtime mapping logic is implemented (1) and made available to different kinds of cloud service consumer devices (2).

Application

The application of this pattern focuses on the creation and architectural placement of mapping logic. The multi-device broker is most commonly utilized as a component, separate from or within the cloud service architecture that houses the mapping logic (Figure 3.55). Some multi-device brokers can act as a gateway on behalf of multiple cloud services, thereby establishing themselves as the point of contact for cloud service consumers. Other multi-device brokers are positioned as service agents to transparently intercept messages upon which the mapping logic is carried out at runtime.

Alternatively, the mapping logic can be built right into the cloud service architecture by becoming an extension of the cloud service logic. A façade can be added to separate this logic as an independent component within the cloud service implementation.

Mechanisms

- *Multi-Device Broker* – The multi-device broker is a specialized mechanism that provides the runtime transformation logic used by cloud services to support different types of cloud service consumer devices.

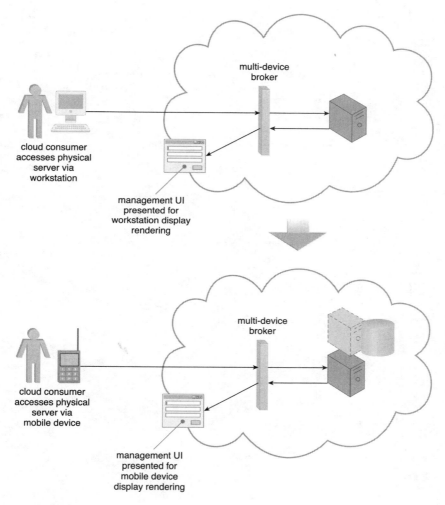

Figure 3.55

The cloud consumer (top) accesses and configures a physical server using a standard device and protocol that is now supported as a result of applying the Broad Access pattern. The cloud consumer (bottom) later accesses the cloud environment again to install a virtual server on the same physical server, and deploys an operating system and a database server. Both actions represent management tasks that can be accomplished via different devices brokered by the same centralized multi-device broker mechanism.

Chapter 4

Reliability, Resiliency and Recovery Patterns

Resource Pooling
Resource Reservation
Hypervisor Clustering
Redundant Storage
Dynamic Failure Detection and
  Recovery
Multipath Resource Access

Redundant Physical Connection for
  Virtual Servers
Synchronized Operating State
Zero Downtime
Storage Maintenance Window
Virtual Server Auto Crash Recovery
Non-Disruptive Service Relocation

Contingency planning efforts for continuity of operations and disaster recovery are concerned with designing and implementing cloud architectures that provide run-time reliability, operational resiliency, and automated recovery when interruptions are encountered, regardless of origin.

The patterns in this chapter address different aspects of these requirements. Starting with foundational patterns, such as Resource Pooling (99), Resource Reservation (106), Hypervisor Clustering (112), and Redundant Storage (119), which address basic failover and availability demands, the chapter continues with more specialized and complex patterns, such as Dynamic Failure Detection and Recovery (123) and Zero Downtime (143), which establish resilient cloud architectures that act as pillars for enterprise cloud solutions.

It is also worth noting that this set of patterns establishes and contributes to the availability leg of the security triad of confidentiality, integrity, and availability and is further complemented by several cloud security patterns in Chapters 8 and 9 in maximizing the reliability and resiliency potential by protecting against attacks that can compromise the availability of an organization's cloud-hosted IT resources.

Resource Pooling

How can IT resources be organized to support dynamic sharing?

Problem	When sharing identical IT resources for scalability purposes, it can be error-prone and burdensome to keep them fully synchronized on an on-going basis.
Solution	An automated synchronization system is provided to group identical IT resources into pools and to maintain their synchronicity.
Application	Resource pools can be created at different sizes and further organized into hierarchies to provide parent and child pools.
Mechanisms	Audit Monitor, Cloud Storage Device, Cloud Usage Monitor, Hypervisor, Logical Network Perimeter, Pay-Per-Use Monitor, Remote Administration System, Resource Management System, Resource Replication, Virtual CPU, Virtual Infrastructure Manager (VIM), Virtual RAM, Virtual Server

Problem

When assembling identical IT resources for sharing and scalability purposes (such as when applying Shared Resources (17) and Dynamic Scalability (25)), the IT resources need to carefully be kept synchronized so that no one IT resource differs from another.

Manually establishing and maintaining the level of required synchronicity across collections of shared IT resources is challenging, effort-intensive and, most importantly, error-prone. Variances or disparity between shared IT resources can lead to inconsistent runtime behavior and cause numerous types of runtime exceptions.

Solution

Identical IT resources are grouped into resource pools and maintained by a system that automatically ensures they remain synchronized (Figure 4.1). The following items are commonly pooled:

- physical servers
- virtual servers
- cloud storage devices

- internetwork and networking devices

- CPUs

- memory (RAM)

Dedicated pools can be created for each of these items, or respective pools can be further grouped into a larger pool (in which case each individual pool becomes a sub-pool).

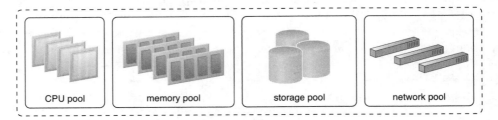

Figure 4.1
A sample resource pool comprised of four sub-pools of CPUs, memory, cloud storage devices, and virtual network devices.

Application

As stated previously, this pattern is primarily applied in support of Shared Resources (17) and Dynamic Scalability (25) in order to establish a reliable system of shared IT resource synchronization. The Resource Pooling pattern itself can be further supported by the application of Resource Reservation (106).

Provided here are common examples of resource pools:

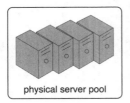

Physical server pools composed of ready-to-go, networked servers installed with operating systems and any other necessary programs or applications.

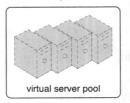

Virtual server pools are usually configured using templates that cloud consumers can choose from, such as a pool of mid-tier Windows servers with 4 GBs of RAM or a pool of low-tier Ubuntu servers with 2 GBs of RAM.

storage pool

Storage pools (or cloud storage device pools) that consist of file-based or block-based storage structures. Storage pools can contain empty or filled cloud storage devices. Often storage resource pools will take advantage of LUNs.

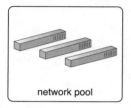

network pool

Network pools (or interconnect pools) are composed of different, preconfigured network connectivity devices. For example, a pool of virtual firewall devices or physical network switches can be created for redundant connectivity, load balancing, or link aggregation.

CPU pool

CPU pools are ready to be allocated to virtual servers. These are often broken down into individual processing cores (as opposed to pooling entire CPUs).

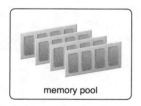

memory pool

Pools of physical RAM that can be used in newly provisioned physical servers or to vertically scale physical servers.

Resource pools can grow to become complex, with multiple pools created for specific cloud consumers or applications. To help with the organization of diverse resource pools, a hierarchical structure can be established to create parent, sibling, and nested pools.

Sibling resource pools are normally drawn from the same collection of physical IT resources (as opposed to IT resources spread out over different data centers) and are isolated from one another so that each cloud consumer is only provided access to its respective pool (Figure 4.2).

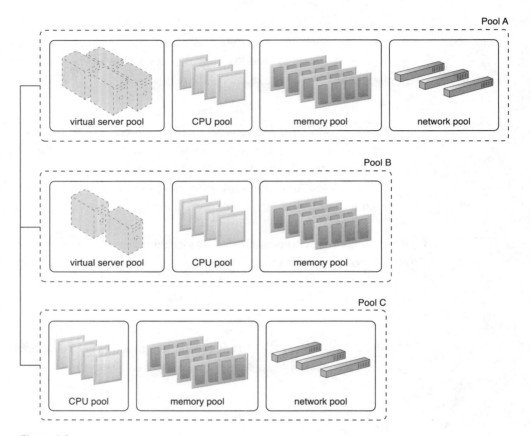

Figure 4.2

Pools B and C are sibling pools taken from the larger Pool A that has been allocated to a cloud consumer. This is an alternative to taking the IT resources for Pool B and Pool C from a general reserve of IT resources that is shared throughout the cloud.

In the nested pool model, larger pools are divided into smaller pools of the same kind (Figure 4.3). Nested pools can be used to assign resource pools to different departments or groups within the same cloud consumer organization.

After resources pools have been defined, multiple instances of IT resources from each pool can be created to provide an in-memory pool of "live" IT resources.

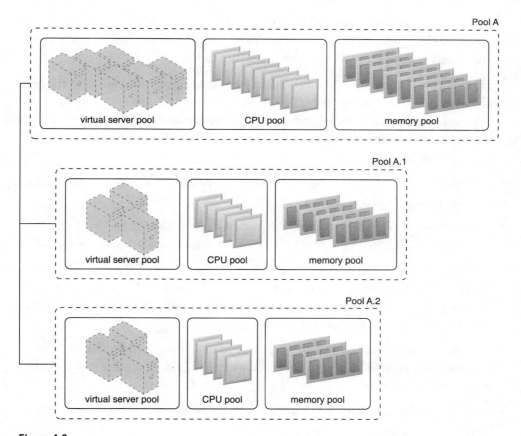

Figure 4.3

Nested Pools A.1 and A.2 are comprised of the same IT resources as Pool A, but in different quantities. Nested pools are generally used to provision cloud services that are rapidly instantiated using the same kind of IT resources with the same configuration settings.

Mechanisms

- *Audit Monitor* – This mechanism monitors resource pool usage to ensure compliance with privacy and regulation requirements, especially when pools include cloud storage devices or data loaded into memory.

- *Cloud Storage Device* – Cloud storage devices are commonly pooled as a result of the application of this pattern.

- *Cloud Usage Monitor* – Various cloud usage monitors can be involved with the run-time tracking and synchronization required by IT resources within pools and by the systems managing the resource pools themselves.

- *Hypervisor* – The hypervisor mechanism is responsible for providing virtual servers with access to resource pools, and hosting virtual servers and sometimes the resource pools themselves. Hypervisors further can distribute physical computing capacity between the virtual servers based on each virtual server's configuration and priority.

- *Logical Network Perimeter* – The logical network perimeter can be used to logically organize and isolate the resource pools.

- *Pay-Per-Use Monitor* – The pay-per-use monitor collects usage and billing information in relation to how individual cloud consumers use and are allocated IT resources from various pools.

- *Remote Administration System* – This mechanism is commonly used to interface with backend systems and programs in order to provide resource pool administration features via a front-end portal.

- *Resource Management System* – The resource management system mechanism supplies cloud consumers with the tools and permission management options to administer resource pools.

- *Resource Replication* – This mechanism can be used to generate new instances of IT resources for a given resource pool.

- *Virtual CPU* – This mechanism is used to allocate CPU to virtual servers, and also helps to determine whether a hypervisor's physical CPU is being over-utilized or a virtual server requires more CPU capacity. When a system has more than one CPU or when hypervisors belong to the same cluster, their total CPU capacity can be aggregated into a pool and leveraged by virtual servers.

- *Virtual Infrastructure Manager (VIM)* – This mechanism enables pools of resources to be created on individual hypervisors, and can also aggregate the capacity of multiple hypervisors into a pool from where virtual CPU and memory resources can be assigned to virtual servers.

- *Virtual RAM* – This mechanism is used to allocate memory to virtual servers, and to measure the memory utilization of hypervisors and virtual servers. When more than one hypervisor is present, a pool encompassing the combined memory capacity of the hypervisors can be created. This mechanism is also used to identify whether more memory should be added to a virtual server.

- *Virtual Server* – This mechanism is associated with the Resource Pooling pattern in how virtual server hosted IT resources are provisioned and consumed by resource pools that are assigned to cloud consumers. Virtual servers themselves may also be pooled.

Resource Reservation

How can shared IT resources be protected from conflicts that can arise from concurrent access?

Problem	When two or more cloud service consumers attempt to instantiate the same shared IT resource, runtime conflicts can occur, including resource constraints due to lack of capacity.
Solution	A system is established whereby a portion of an IT resource (or one or more IT resources) is set aside exclusively for a given cloud service consumer.
Application	The resource management system is used to define IT resource thresholds and to restrict access to reserved IT resources.
Mechanisms	Audit Monitor, Cloud Storage Device, Cloud Usage Monitor, Hypervisor, Logical Network Perimeter, Remote Administration System, Resource Management System, Resource Replication, Virtual CPU, Virtual Infrastructure Manager (VIM), Virtual RAM, Virtual Server

Problem

When applying Shared Resources (17) and Resource Pooling (99) we can give multiple cloud service consumers access to the same IT resources. Depending on how IT resources are designed for shared usage and depending on their available levels of capacity, concurrent access can lead to a runtime exception condition called *resource constraint*.

A resource constraint is a condition that occurs when two or more cloud consumers have been allocated to share an IT resource that does not have the capacity to accommodate the entire processing requirements of the cloud consumers. As a result, one or more of the consumers will encounter degraded performance or be rejected altogether. The cloud service itself may go down, resulting in all cloud consumers being rejected.

Other types of runtime conflicts can occur when an IT resource (especially one not specifically designed to accommodate sharing) is concurrently accessed by different cloud service consumers. For example, nested and sibling resource pools introduce the notion of *resource borrowing*, whereby one pool can temporarily borrow IT resources from other pools. A runtime conflict can be triggered when the borrowed IT resource is not returned due to prolonged usage by the cloud service consumer that is borrowing it. This can inevitably lead back to the occurrence of resource constraints.

Solution

An IT resource reservation system is established to protect cloud service consumers ("tenants") sharing the same underlying IT resources from each other. This system essentially guarantees a minimum amount of an IT resource for each cloud consumer by putting it aside and making it exclusively available only to the designated cloud service consumer. Potential conflicts, such as resource constraints and resource borrowing, are avoided because the reserved IT resources are never actually shared.

Application

Creating an IT resource reservation system requires the involvement of the resource management system mechanism that can be used to define IT resource usage thresholds for individual IT resources and resource pools. Reservations are created to lock the amount of IT resources that each pool must keep. The balance of IT resources within a pool can still be shared (and borrowed).

The following steps are shown in Figures 4.4 to 4.6:

1. A physical resource group is created.

2. A parent resource pool is created from the physical resource group by applying Resource Pooling (99).

3. Two smaller child pools are created from the parent resource pool, and resource limits are defined using the resource management system mechanism.

4. Cloud consumers are provided with access to their own exclusive resource pools.

5. There is an increase in requests from Cloud Consumer A, resulting in more IT resources being allocated.

6. Consequently, some IT resources are borrowed from Pool 2. The amount of borrowed resources, however, is pre-determined by the resource limit defined in Step 3, which ensures that Cloud Consumer B will not face resource constraints.

7. Cloud Consumer B now imposes more requests and usage demands and may soon need to utilize all available IT resources in the pool.

8. The resource management system forces Pool 1 to release the IT resources and move them back to Pool 2 to become available for Cloud Consumer B.

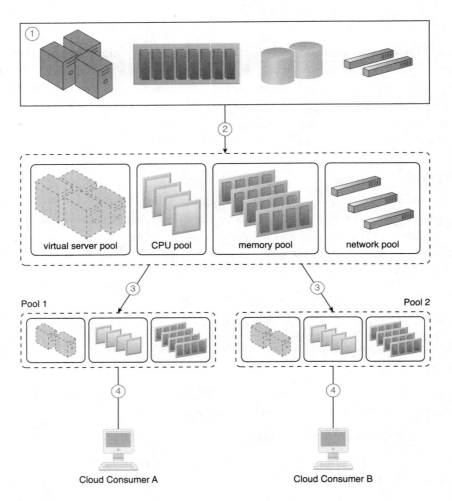

Figure 4.4

A resource pool hierarchy to which an IT resource reservation system is applied (Part I).

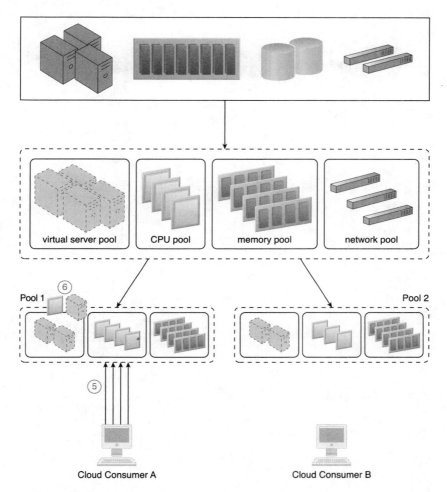

Figure 4.5

A resource pool hierarchy to which an IT resource reservation system is applied (Part II).

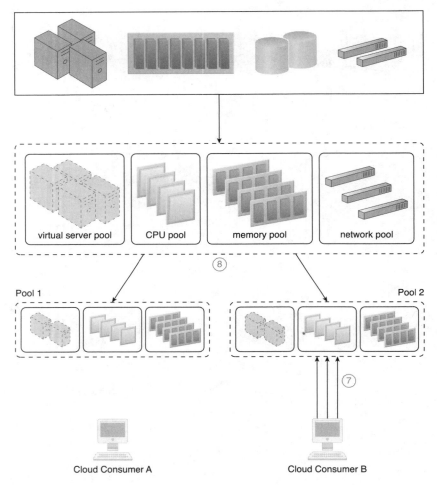

Figure 4.6

A resource pool hierarchy to which an IT resource reservation system is applied (Part III).

Mechanisms

- *Audit Monitor* – The audit monitor may be responsible for ensuring that the resource reservation system is acting in compliance with cloud consumer auditing, privacy, and other regulatory requirements. The audited information may also pertain to the geographical location of the reserved IT resources.

- *Cloud Storage Device* – This mechanism may be an IT resource reserved by this system.

- *Cloud Usage Monitor* – A cloud usage monitor may be involved with monitoring thresholds that trigger the allocation of reserved IT resources.

- *Hypervisor* – The hypervisor mechanism is associated with this pattern in its commitment to applying reservations for different cloud consumers in order to ensure that they are allocated the guaranteed amounts of IT resources. In support of this, it is responsible for locking, and pre-allocating the virtual servers' reserved computing capacity based on their configurations.

- *Logical Network Perimeter* – This mechanism ensures that reserved IT resources are made exclusively available to the appropriate cloud consumers.

- *Remote Administration System* – This system provides the tools necessary for custom front-ends to provide the administration controls necessary for cloud consumers to create and manage reserved IT resource allocations.

- *Resource Management System* – The resource management system provides essential features for managing IT resource reservations. These features may be encapsulated by a portal produced via the remote administration system mechanism.

- *Resource Replication* – The resource replication mechanism needs to stay updated on any cloud consumer IT resource consumption limitations to determine when new IT resource instances need to be replicated and provisioned.

- *Virtual CPU* – This mechanism is used to define the computing capacity a virtual server needs to have reserved. When this mechanism is used, a specific amount of CPU is explicitly allocated to each virtual server and not shared with other virtual servers.

- *Virtual Infrastructure Manager (VIM)* – This mechanism is used to configure the resources that are reserved for each virtual server.

- *Virtual RAM* – This mechanism is used to configure the memory that virtual servers need reserved and guaranteed. The memory that is reserved for each virtual server is not allocated to or shared with other virtual servers.

- *Virtual Server* – This mechanism hosts the reserved IT resources that are allocated.

Hypervisor Clustering

How can a virtual server survive the failure of its hosting hypervisor or physical server?

Problem	The failure of a hypervisor or its underlying physical server cascades to all hosted virtual servers further causing their hosted IT resources to fail.
Solution	Hypervisors are clustered across multiple physical servers, so that if one fails, active virtual servers are transferred to another.
Application	Heartbeat messages are passed between clustered hypervisors and a central VIM to maintain status monitoring. Shared storage is provided for the clustered hypervisors and further used to store virtual server disks.
Mechanisms	Cloud Storage Device, Hypervisor, Logical Network Perimeter, Resource Cluster, Resource Replication, Virtual Infrastructure Manager (VIM), Virtual Server, Virtual Switch, Virtualization Monitor

Problem

Virtual servers run on a hypervisor, and hardware resources are emulated for the virtual servers via the hypervisors. If the hypervisor fails or if the underlying physical server fails (thereby causing the hypervisor to fail), the failure condition cascades to all of its hosted virtual servers.

The following steps are shown in Figure 4.7:

1. Physical Server A hosts a hypervisor that hosts Virtual Servers A and B.

2. When Physical Server A fails, the hypervisor and the two virtual servers fail as well.

Solution

A high-availability hypervisor cluster is created to establish a group of hypervisors that span physical servers. As a result, if a given physical server or hypervisor becomes unavailable, hosted virtual servers can be moved to another physical server or hypervisor (Figure 4.8).

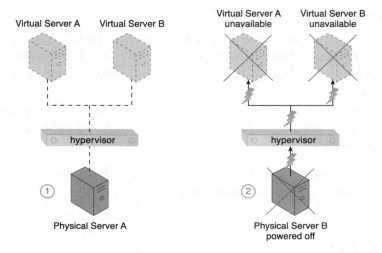

Figure 4.7
Two virtual servers experience failure after their host physical server goes down.

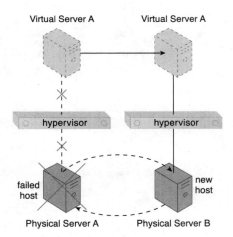

Figure 4.8
Physical Server A becomes unavailable, thereby bringing down its hypervisor. Because the hypervisor is part of a cluster, Virtual Server A is migrated to a different host (Physical Server B), which has another hypervisor that is part of the same cluster.

Application

A hypervisor cluster architecture is established and controlled via a central VIM, which sends regular heartbeat messages to the hypervisors to confirm that they are up and running. Any heartbeat messages that are not successfully acknowledged can lead the VIM to initiate the live VM migration program in order to dynamically move affected virtual servers to a new host. The hypervisor cluster utilizes a shared cloud storage device, which is used during the live migration of virtual servers by different hypervisors in the cluster.

Figures 4.9 to 4.12 provide examples of the results of applying the Hypervisor Clustering pattern, accompanied by numbered steps.

Figure 4.9

A cloud architecture resulting from the application of the Hypervisor Clustering pattern (Part I). These initial steps detail the assembly of required components.

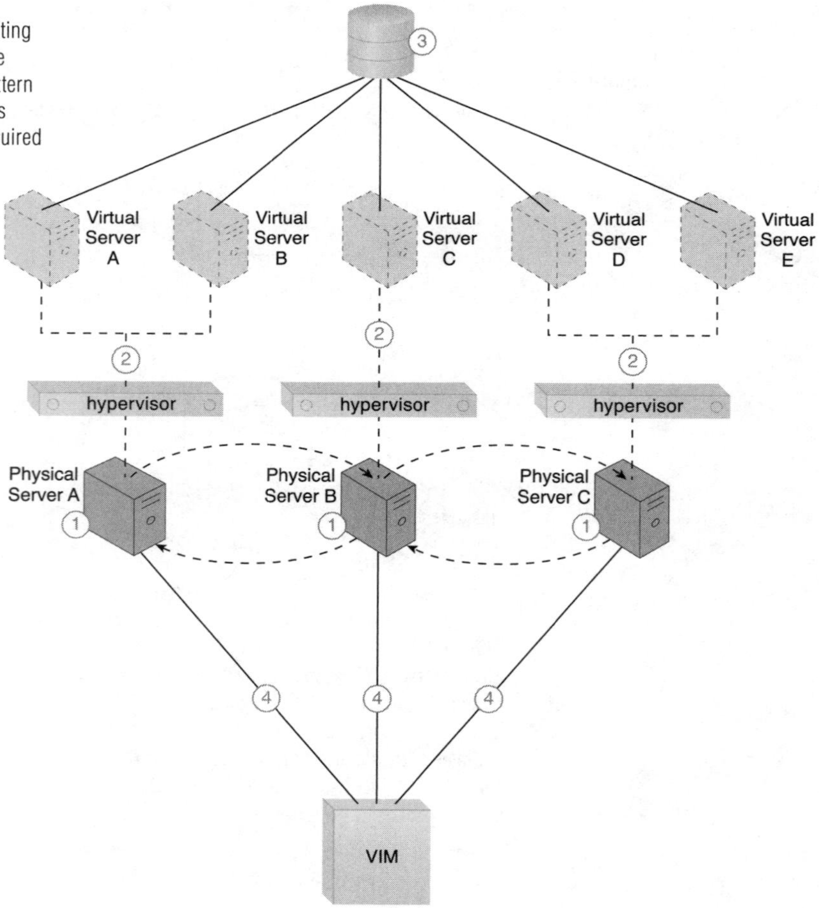

1. Hypervisors are installed on the three physical servers.

2. Virtual servers are created by the hypervisors.

3. A shared cloud storage device containing virtual server configuration files is positioned so that all hypervisors have access to it.

4. The hypervisor cluster is enabled on the three physical server hosts via a central VIM.

5. The physical servers exchange heartbeat messages with each other and the VIM, based on a predefined schedule.

Figure 4.10

A cloud architecture resulting from the application of the Hypervisor Clustering pattern (Part II).

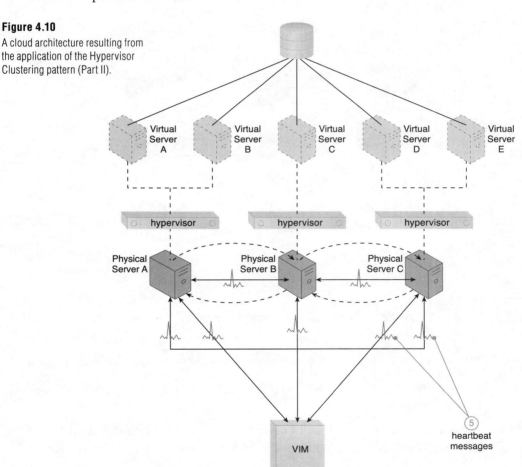

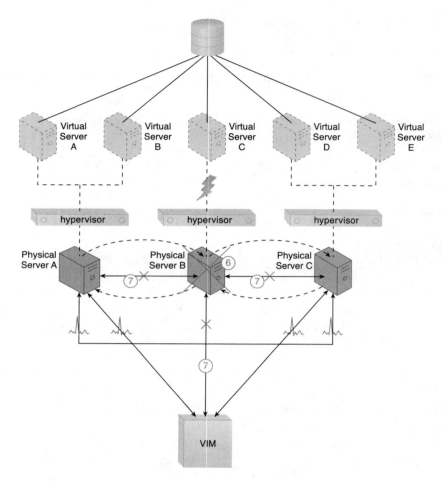

Figure 4.11

A cloud architecture resulting from the application of the Hypervisor Clustering pattern (Part III).

6. Physical Server B fails and becomes unavailable, jeopardizing Virtual Server C.

7. The VIM and the other physical servers stop receiving heartbeat messages from Physical Server B.

8. Based on the available capacity of other hypervisors in the cluster, the VIM chooses Physical Server C as the new host to take ownership of Virtual Server C.

9. Virtual Server C is live-migrated to the hypervisor running on Physical Server C, where it may need to be restarted before continuing to operate normally.

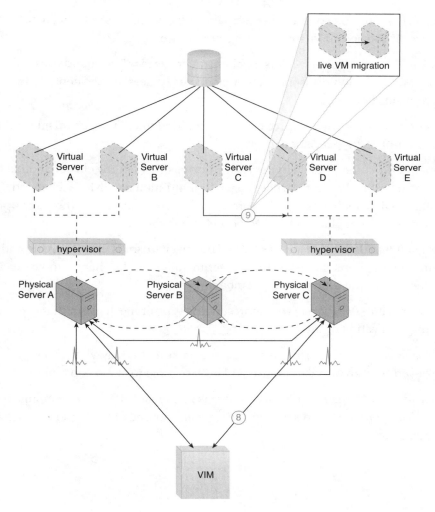

Figure 4.12
A cloud architecture resulting from the application of the Hypervisor Clustering pattern (Part IV).

Mechanisms

- *Cloud Storage Device* – The cloud storage device mechanism acts as a central repository that hosts the virtual server folders, so that the folders and virtual server configurations are accessible to all of the hypervisors participating in the cluster.

- *Hypervisor* – The hypervisor is the primary mechanism by which this pattern is applied. It acts as a member of the cluster and hosts the virtual servers. If a hypervisor fails, one of the other available hypervisors restarts its virtual machine to recover the hosted virtual servers from failure.

- *Logical Network Perimeter* – This mechanism creates logical boundaries that ensure that none of the hypervisors of other cloud consumers are accidentally included in a given cluster.

- *Resource Cluster* – The resource cluster is the fundamental mechanism used to create and initiate hypervisor clusters.

- *Resource Replication* – Each hypervisor informs others in the cluster about its status and availability. When a part of cluster configuration needs to be changed, for instance when a virtual switch is created, deleted, or modified, then this update may need to be replicated to all hypervisors via the VIM.

- *Virtual Infrastructure Manager (VIM)* – This mechanism is used to create and configure the hypervisor cluster, add cluster members to the cluster, and cascade the cluster configuration to cluster members.

- *Virtual Server* – Virtual servers represent the type of mechanism that is protected by the application of this pattern.

- *Virtual Switch* – This mechanism is used to ensure that any virtual servers retrieved from hypervisor failure will be accessible to cloud consumers.

- *Virtualization Monitor* – This mechanism is responsible for actively monitoring the hypervisors, and sending alerts whenever one of the hypervisors in the cluster fails.

Problem	When cloud storage devices fail or become inaccessible, cloud consumers are unable to access data and cloud services relying on access to the device may also fail.
Solution	A failsafe system comprised of redundant cloud storage devices is established so that when the primary device fails, the redundant secondary device takes its place.
Application	Data is replicated from the primary storage to the secondary storage device. A storage service gateway is used to redirect data access requests to the secondary storage device, when necessary.
Mechanisms	Cloud Storage Device, Failover System, Resource Replication

Problem

Cloud storage devices are subject to failure and disruption due to a variety of causes, including network connectivity issues, controller failures, general hardware failure, and security breaches. When the reliability of a cloud storage device is compromised, it can have a ripple effect, causing impact failure across any cloud services, cloud-based applications, and cloud infrastructure program and components that rely on its presence and availability.

The following steps are shown in Figure 4.13:

1. The cloud storage device is installed and configured.

2. Four LUNs are created, one for each cloud consumer.

3. Each cloud consumer sends a request to access its own LUN.

4. The cloud storage device receives the requests and forwards them to the respective LUN.

5. The cloud storage device fails and cloud consumers lose access to their LUNs. This may be due to the loss of the device controller (5.1) or loss of connectivity (5.2).

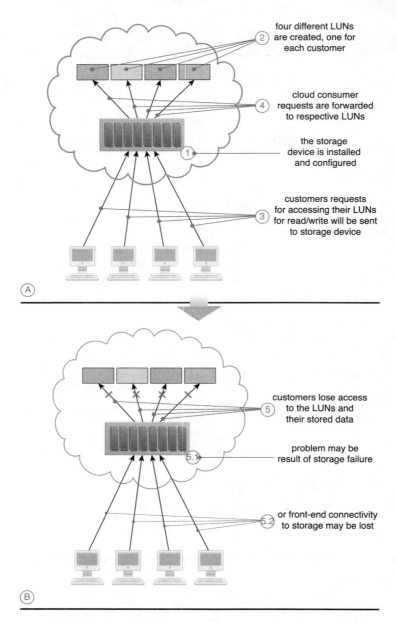

Figure 4.13

A sample scenario that demonstrates the effects of a failed cloud storage device.

Solution

A secondary redundant cloud storage device is incorporated into a system that synchronizes its data with the data in the primary cloud storage device. When the primary device fails, a storage service gateway diverts requests to the secondary device.

The following steps are shown in Figure 4.14:

1. The primary cloud storage device is replicated to the secondary cloud storage device on a regular basis.

2. The primary storage becomes unavailable and the storage service gateway forwards the cloud consumer requests to the secondary storage device.

3. The secondary storage forwards the requests to the LUNs, allowing cloud consumers to continue to access to their data.

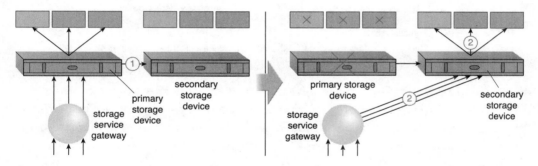

Figure 4.14
A simple scenario demonstrating the failover of redundant storage.

Application

This pattern fundamentally relies on the resource replication mechanism to keep the primary cloud storage device synchronized with any additional duplicate secondary cloud storage devices that comprise the failover system (Figure 4.15).

Cloud providers may locate secondary cloud storage devices in a different geographical region than the primary cloud storage device, usually for economic reasons. For some types of data, this may introduce legal concerns. The location of the secondary cloud storage device can dictate the protocol and method used for synchronization because some replication transport protocols have distance restrictions.

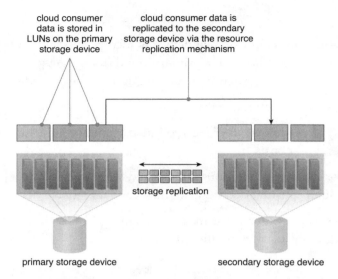

Figure 4.15
Storage replication is used to keep the redundant storage device synchronized.

Some cloud providers use storage devices with dual array and storage controllers to improve device redundancy. They may place the secondary storage device in a different physical location for cloud balancing and disaster recovery purposes. In this case, cloud providers may need to lease a network connection via a third-party cloud provider, to establish replication between two devices.

Mechanisms

- *Cloud Storage Device* – This is the mechanism to which the pattern is primarily applied.

- *Failover System* – The application of the Redundant Storage pattern results in a specialized failover system based on the use of duplicate storage devices and a storage service gateway.

- *Resource Replication* – The failover system created by the application of this pattern relies on this mechanism to keep cloud storage devices synchronized.

Dynamic Failure Detection and Recovery

How can the notification and recovery of IT resource failure be automated?

Problem	When cloud-based IT resources fail, manual intervention may be unacceptably inefficient.
Solution	A watchdog system is established to monitor IT resource status and perform notifications and/or recovery attempts during failure conditions.
Application	Different intelligent monitoring and recovery technologies can be used to establish the automation of failure detection and recovery tasks with a focus on watching, deciding upon, acting upon, reporting, and escalating IT resource failure conditions.
Mechanisms	Audit Monitor, Cloud Usage Monitor, Failover System, SLA Management System, SLA Monitor

Problem

Cloud environments can be comprised of vast quantities of IT resources being accessed by numerous cloud consumers. Any of those IT resources can experience predictable failure conditions that require intervention to resolve. Manually administering and solving standard IT resource failures in cloud environments is generally inefficient and impractical.

Solution

A resilient watchdog system is established to monitor and respond to a wide range of pre-defined failure scenarios. This system is further able to notify and escalate certain failure conditions that it cannot automatically solve itself.

Application

The resilient watchdog system relies on a specialized cloud usage monitor (that can be referred to as the intelligent watchdog monitor) to actively monitor IT resources and take pre-defined actions in response to pre-defined events (Figures 4.16 and 4.17).

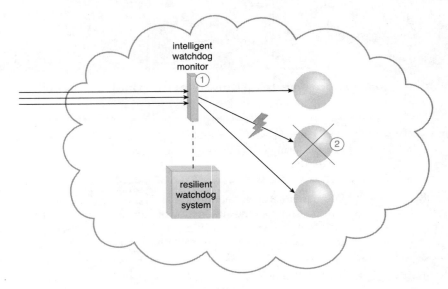

Figure 4.16

The intelligent watchdog monitor keeps track of cloud consumer requests (1) and detects that a cloud service has failed (2).

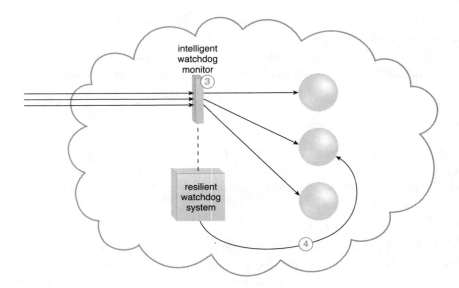

Figure 4.17

The intelligent watchdog monitor notifies the watchdog system (3), which restores the cloud service based on predefined policies (4).

The resilient watchdog system, together with the intelligent watchdog monitor, performs the following five core functions:

- watching
- deciding upon an event
- acting upon an event
- reporting
- escalating

Sequential recovery policies can be defined for each IT resource to determine how the intelligent watchdog monitor should behave when encountering a failure condition (Figure 4.18). For example, a recovery policy may state that before issuing a notification, one recovery attempt should be carried out automatically.

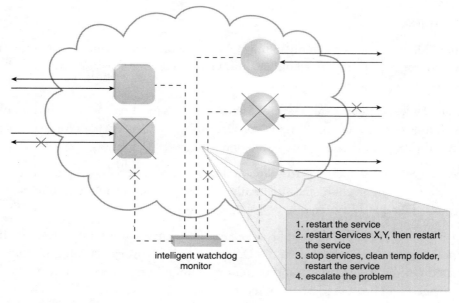

Figure 4.18

In the event of any failures, the active monitor refers to its predefined policies to recover the service step by step, escalating the processes as the problem proves to be deeper than expected.

When the intelligent watchdog monitor escalates an issue, there are common types of actions it may take, such as:

- running a batch file

- sending a console message

- sending a text message

- sending an email message

- sending an SNMP trap

- logging a ticket in a ticketing and event monitoring system

There are varieties of programs and products that can act as an intelligent watchdog monitor. Most can be integrated with standard ticketing and event management systems.

Mechanisms

- *Audit Monitor* – This mechanism may be required to ensure that the manner in which this pattern is carried out at runtime is in compliance with any related legal or policy requirements.

- *Cloud Usage Monitor* – Various specialized cloud usage monitors may be involved with monitoring and collecting IT resource usage data as part of failure conditions and recovery, notification, and escalation activity.

- *Failover System* – Failover is fundamental to the application of this pattern, as the failover system mechanism is generally utilized during the initial attempts to recover failed IT resources.

- *SLA Management System* and *SLA Monitor* – The functionality introduced by the application of the Dynamic Failure Detection and Recovery pattern is closely associated with SLA guarantees and therefore commonly relies on the information managed and processed by these mechanisms.

Multipath Resource Access

How can an IT resource be accessed when its pre-defined path is lost or becomes unavailable?

Problem	When the path to an IT resource is lost or becomes unavailable, the IT resource becomes inaccessible. This can jeopardize the stability of an entire cloud-based solution until the cloud provider is able to supply the cloud consumer with the lost or updated path.
Solution	Alternative paths to IT resources are provided to give cloud consumers a means of programmatically or manually overcoming path failures.
Application	A multipathing system that resides on the server or hypervisor is established to provide multiple alternative paths to the same, unique IT resource, while ensuring that the IT resource is viewed identically via each alternative path.
Mechanisms	Cloud Storage Device, Hypervisor, Logical Network Perimeter, Resource Replication, Virtual Server

Problem

Certain IT resources can only be accessed using an assigned path (hyperlink) that leads to the location of the IT resources. The path can be inadvertently lost or incorrectly defined by the cloud consumer or changed by the cloud provider. When a cloud consumer no longer possesses the correct and exclusive path to an IT resource, this IT resource becomes inaccessible and unavailable (Figure 4.19). When this unavailability occurs without warning at runtime, exception conditions can result that compromise the stability of larger cloud solutions that depend on the IT resource's availability.

Figure 4.19

Physical Server A is connected to LUN A via a single fiber channel, and uses the LUN to store different types of data. The fiber channel connection becomes unavailable due to an HBA card failure and invalidates the path used by Physical Server A, which has now lost access to LUN A and all of its stored data.

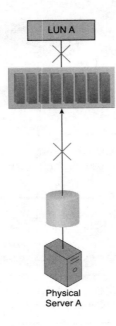

Solution

A multipathing system is established to provide alternative paths to IT resources providing cloud consumers with a means of programmatically or manually overcoming path failures (Figure 4.20).

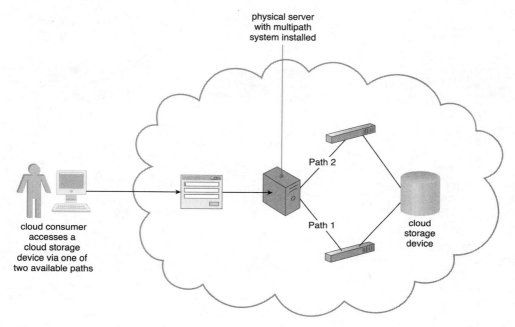

Figure 4.20

A multipathing system providing alternative paths to a cloud storage device.

Application

The application of this pattern requires the use of a multipathing system and the creation of alternative paths (or hyperlinks) that are assigned to specific IT resources. The alternative paths may be physical or virtual. The multipathing system resides on the server or hypervisor, and ensures that each IT resource can be seen via each alternative path identically.

The following steps are shown in Figure 4.21:

1. Physical Server A is connected to the LUN A storage device via two different paths.

2. LUN A is seen as different LUNs from each of the two paths.

3. The multipathing system is put in place and configured.

4. LUN A is seen as one identical LUN from both paths.

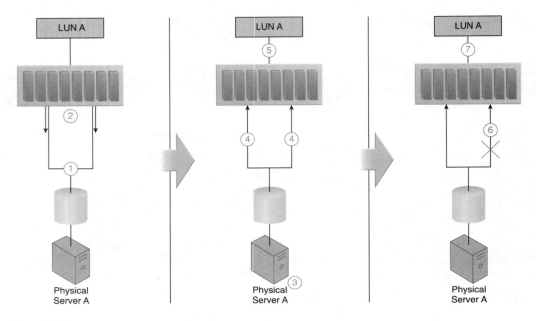

Figure 4.21

An example of a multipathing system.

5. Physical Server A has access to LUN A from two different paths.

6. A link failure occurs and one of the paths becomes unavailable.

7. Physical Server A can still use LUN A because the other link remains active.

In some cases, a specific driver is required by the operating system to ensure that it understands the redundant paths and does view two paths leading to the same IT resource as two separate IT resources, as shown in Figure 4.22.

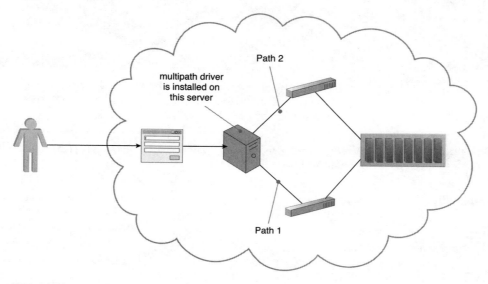

Figure 4.22

A multipath driver is installed on a server to ensure that the operating system understands the redundant paths and views two paths leading to the same IT resource as two separate IT resources.

Mechanisms

- *Cloud Storage Device* – The cloud storage device is a common IT resource that may require the creation of an alternative path in order to remain accessible by solutions that rely on data access.

- *Hypervisor* – An alternate path to a hypervisor is required to have a redundant link to the hosted virtual servers.

- *Logical Network Perimeter* – This mechanism guarantees that the privacy of cloud consumers is upheld even when multiple paths to the same IT resource are created.

- *Resource Replication* – The resource replication mechanism is required when it is necessary to create a new instance of an IT resource in order to generate the alternative path.

- *Virtual Server* – This mechanism is associated with Multipath Resource Access in how it hosts services that have multipath access via different links or virtual switches. In some cases, the hypervisor itself provides multipath access to the virtual server.

Problem	If the virtual switch uplink port used by a virtual server fails, the virtual server becomes isolated and unable to connect to the network or any of its hosted IT resources.
Solution	A redundant, physical backup network connection is established for virtual servers.
Application	A second physical network card is added to the physical host and is configured as a hot standby uplink port for the virtual switch.
Mechanisms	Failover System, Hypervisor, Logical Network Perimeter, Physical Uplink, Resource Replication, Virtual Infrastructure Manager (VIM), Virtual Server, Virtual Switch

Problem

A virtual server is connected to an external network via a virtual switch uplink port. If the uplink fails (due to, for example, cable disconnection or port failure), the virtual server becomes isolated and disconnects from the external network.

The following steps are shown in Figure 4.23:

1. A physical network adapter installed on the physical server host is connected to the physical switch on the network.

2. A virtual switch is created for use by two virtual servers. Because it requires access to the physical external network, the physical network adapter is attached to the virtual switch to be used as an uplink to the network.

3. The virtual servers communicate with the external network via the attached physical uplink network card.

4. A connection failure occurs, either because of a physical link connectivity issue between the physical adapter and the physical switch (4.1), or because of a physical network card failure (4.2).

5. The virtual servers lose access to the physical external network and are no longer accessible by their cloud consumers.

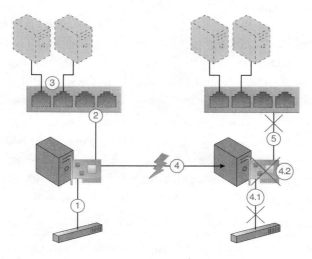

Figure 4.23

The steps that can lead to the separation of virtual servers from their external network connection.

Solution

One or more redundant uplink connections are established and positioned in standby mode. A redundant uplink connection is available to take over as the active uplink connection whenever the primary uplink connection becomes unavailable or experiences failure conditions (Figure 4.24).

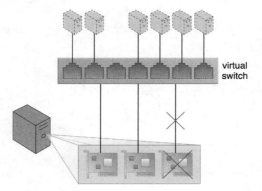

Figure 4.24

Redundant uplinks are installed on a physical server hosting several virtual servers. When one fails, another takes over to maintain the virtual servers' active network connections.

Application

While the main uplink is working, virtual servers connect to the outside via that port. As soon as it fails, the standby uplink will automatically become the active uplink, and the server will send the packets to the outside via the new uplink. This process is also transparent to virtual servers and users.

While the second NIC is connected and receives the virtual server's packets, it is not forwarding any traffic while the primary uplink is alive. If, and when, the primary uplink fails, the secondary uplink starts to forward the packets without any pause or interruption. If the failed uplink happens to come back into operation, it will take over the lead role and the second NIC goes into standby mode again.

The following steps are shown in Figures 4.25 and 4.26:

1. A new network adapter is added to support a redundant uplink.

2. Both network cards are connected to the physical external switch.

3. Both physical network adapters are configured to be used as uplink adapters for the virtual switch.

4. One physical network adapter is designated as the primary adapter, whereas the other is designated as the secondary adapter providing the standby uplink. The secondary adapter does not forward any packets.

5. The primary uplink forwards packets to the external network until it becomes unavailable.

6. When required, the secondary standby uplink automatically becomes the primary uplink and uses the virtual switch to forward the virtual servers' packets to the external network.

7. The virtual servers stay connected to the external physical network, without interruptions.

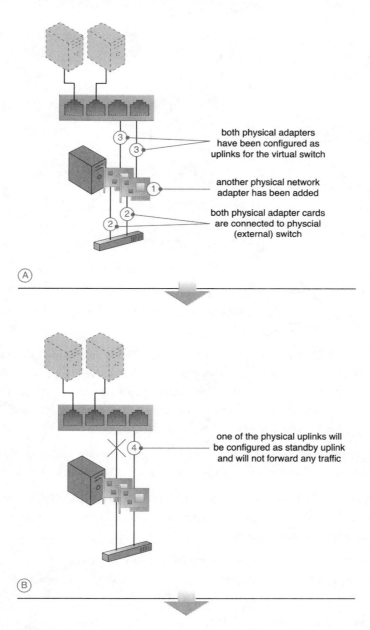

both physical adapters
have been configured as
uplinks for the virtual switch

another physical network
adapter has been added

both physical adapter cards
are connected to physcial
(external) switch

one of the physical uplinks will
be configured as standby uplink
and will not forward any traffic

Figure 4.25

An example scenario of the utilization of a redundant uplink (Part I).

Figure 4.26

An example scenario of the utilization of
a redundant uplink (Part II).

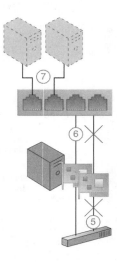

Mechanisms

- *Failover System* – The failover system is utilized to perform the failover of an unavailable uplink to a standby uplink.

- *Hypervisor* – The hypervisor hosts the virtual servers and some of the virtual switches, and provides virtual networks and virtual switches with access to the virtual servers. If a virtual switch's physical uplink becomes unavailable, this mechanism is responsible for forwarding the virtual servers' traffic using another available physical uplink on the virtual switch.

- *Logical Network Perimeter* – Logical network perimeters ensure that the virtual switches that are allocated or defined for each cloud consumer remain isolated.

- *Physical Uplink* – This mechanism is used to establish connectivity between virtual switches and physical switches. Additional physical uplinks can be attached to a virtual switch to improve redundancy.

- *Resource Replication* – Resource replication is used to replicate the current status of the active uplink to a standby uplink, so that the connection remains active without disruption.

- *Virtual Infrastructure Manager (VIM)* – This mechanism is used to configure virtual switches and their uplinks, and performs the configurations on the hypervisors so that they can use another available uplink should an active uplink fail.

- *Virtual Server* – This pattern is primarily applied in support of maintaining the network connections for virtual servers.

- *Virtual Switch* – This mechanism uses the attached physical uplinks to establish physical connection redundancy that allows virtual servers to be redundantly connected to cloud consumers and the physical network.

Synchronized Operating State

How can the availability and reliability of virtual servers be ensured when high availability and clustering technology is unavailable?

Problem	A cloud consumer may be prevented from utilizing high availability and clustering technology for its virtual servers or operating systems, thereby making them more vulnerable to failure.
Solution	A composite failover system is created to not rely on clustering or high availability features but instead use heartbeat messages to synchronize virtual servers.
Application	The heartbeat messages are processed by a specialized service agent and are exchanged between hypervisors, the hypervisor and virtual server, and the hypervisor and VIM.
Mechanisms	Cloud Storage Device, Failover System, Hypervisor, Resource Replication, State Management Database, Virtual Server

Problem

Technical restrictions, licensing restrictions, or other reasons may prevent a cloud consumer from taking advantage of clustering and high availability technology and products. This can seriously jeopardize the availability and scalability of its cloud services and applications.

Solution

A system comprised of a set of mechanisms and relying on the use of heartbeat messages is established to emulate select features of clustering and high availability IT resources (Figure 4.27).

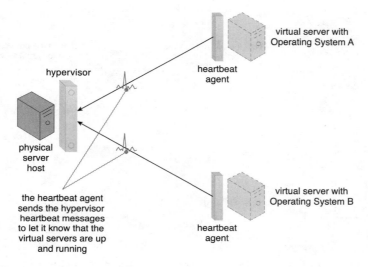

hypervisor

virtual server with
Operating System A

heartbeat
agent

physical
server
host

the heartbeat agent
sends the hypervisor
heartbeat messages
to let it know that the
virtual servers are up
and running

virtual server with
Operating System B

heartbeat
agent

Figure 4.27
Special heartbeat agents are employed to monitor heartbeat messages exchanged
between the servers.

Application

Heartbeat messages are processed by a heartbeat monitor agent and are exchanged
between:

- hypervisors

- each hypervisor and each virtual server

- each hypervisor and the central VIM

If an operating system is placed on a physical server, it needs to be converted into a
virtual server prior to the issuance of heartbeat messages.

The following steps are shown in Figure 4.28:

1. A virtual server is created from the physical server.

2. The hypervisor proceeds to host the virtual server.

3. The primary virtual server is equipped with fault tolerance and maintains a synchronized state via the use of heartbeat messages.

4. The secondary server that shares the synchronized state is available in case the primary virtual server fails.

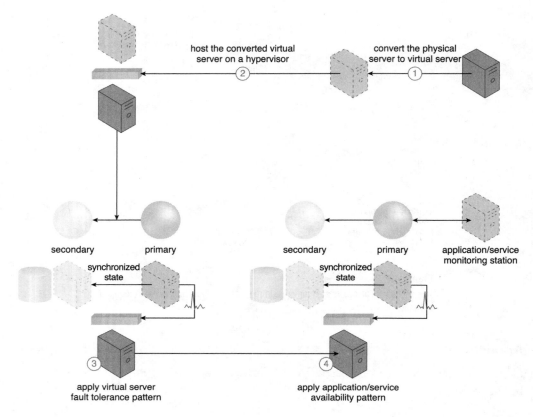

Figure 4.28

The cloud architecture resulting from the application of this pattern.

The application/service monitoring station monitors the servers and cloud services. In the event of failure, this station attempts recovery based on sequential pre-defined policies. If the primary server's operating system fails, procedures are in place to avoid downtime (Figure 4.29).

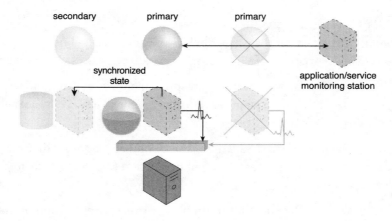

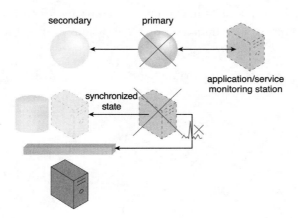

Figure 4.29

When the primary virtual server fails, along with its hosted cloud service, heartbeat messages are no longer transmitted. As a result, the hypervisor recognizes the failure and switches activity to the secondary virtual server that maintains the synchronized state. After the primary virtual server is back online, the hypervisor creates a new secondary for the new primary, and proceeds to save it as a synchronized non-active state.

Mechanisms

- *Cloud Storage Device* – Cloud storage devices may be used to host the primary and secondary (shadow) copies of virtual server data and cloud service instances.

- *Failover System* – The failover system is responsible for providing failsafe logic in support of switch cloud consumer requests from a primary virtual server to a secondary virtual server.

- *Hypervisor* – The hypervisor hosts the primary and secondary (shadow) state data, in addition to providing the features that resource replication needs to replicate the primary state.

- *Resource Replication* – Resource replication performs the replication of the primary virtual server state to a secondary (shadow) copy.

- *State Management Database* – The state management database actively stores and restores secondary operating state data in support of primary virtual server failure and recovery.

- *Virtual Server* – Virtual servers are the primary mechanism to which this pattern is applied.

Zero Downtime

How can downtime of virtual servers be avoided or eliminated?

Problem	It is challenging to provide zero downtime guarantees when a physical host acts as a single point of failure for virtual servers.
Solution	A fault tolerance system is established so that when a physical server fails, virtual servers are migrated to another physical server.
Application	A combination of virtual server fault tolerance, replication, clustering, and load balancing are applied and all virtual servers are stored in a shared volume allowing different physical hosts to access their files.
Mechanisms	Audit Monitor, Cloud Storage Device, Cloud Usage Monitor, Failover System, Hypervisor, Live VM Migration, Logical Network Perimeter, Physical Uplink, Resource Cluster, Resource Replication, Virtual CPU, Virtual Disk, Virtual Infrastructure Manager (VIM), Virtual Network, Virtual RAM, Virtual Server, Virtual Switch, Virtualization Agent, Virtualization Monitor

Problem

A physical server naturally acts as a single point of failure for the virtual servers it hosts. As a result, when the physical server fails or is compromised, the availability of any (or all) hosted virtual servers can be affected. This makes the issuance of zero downtime guarantees by a cloud provider to cloud consumers challenging.

Solution

A failover system is established so that virtual servers are dynamically moved to different physical server hosts in the event that their original physical server host fails. For example, in Figure 4.30, Virtual Server A is dynamically moved to another physical server host.

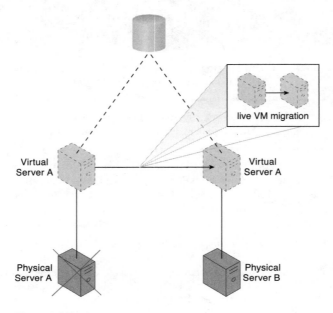

Figure 4.30

Physical Server A fails, triggering the live VM migration program to dynamically move Virtual Server A to Physical Server B.

Application

Multiple physical servers are assembled into a group that is controlled by a fault tolerance system capable of switching activity from one physical server to another, without interruption. Resource cluster and live VM migration components are commonly part of this form of high availability cloud architecture.

The resulting fault tolerance assures that, in case of physical server failure, hosted virtual servers will be migrated to a secondary physical server. All virtual servers are stored on a shared volume (as per Persistent Virtual Network Configuration (227)) so that other physical server hosts in the same group can access their files.

Live storage replication can further be utilized to guarantee that virtual server files and hard disks remain available via secondary storage devices.

Mechanisms

- *Audit Monitor* – This mechanism may be required to ensure that the relocation of virtual servers does not relocate hosted data to prohibited locations.

- *Cloud Storage Device* – A cloud storage device is used to store virtual server network configuration data shared by the physical servers. It stores virtual servers and virtual disks in a central repository so that other available hypervisors can access the files and power on the failed virtual servers in case one of the hypervisors fails.

- *Cloud Usage Monitor* – Incarnations of this mechanism are used to monitor the actual IT resource usage of cloud consumers to help ensure that virtual server capacities are not exceeded.

- *Failover System* – The failover system can be used to switch from a failed primary physical server to a secondary physical server.

- *Hypervisor* – The hypervisor of each affected physical server hosts the affected virtual servers.

- *Live VM Migration* – When multiple instances of the same service or virtual server are provisioned for the purpose of redundancy and availability, this mechanism is used to seamlessly distribute different instances of the same service between different hypervisors to make sure one hypervisor will not become a single point of failure.

- *Logical Network Perimeter* – Logical network perimeters provide and maintain the isolation that is required to ensure that each cloud consumer remains within its own logical boundary subsequent to virtual server relocation.

- *Physical Uplink* – Physical uplinks are used and deployed in a redundant model, so that the virtual servers and services will not lose their connectivity to the cloud service consumers if a physical uplink fails or becomes disconnected.

- *Resource Cluster* – The resource cluster mechanism is applied to create different types of active/active cluster groups that collaboratively improve the availability of virtual server-hosted IT resources.

- *Resource Replication* – This mechanism can create new virtual server and cloud service instances upon primary virtual server failure.

- *Virtual CPU* – The virtual CPU mechanism is used to provide CPU cycling, scheduling, and processing capabilities to the virtual servers.

- *Virtual Disk* – This mechanism is used to allocate local storage space to the hosted virtual servers.

- *Virtual Infrastructure Manager (VIM)* – This mechanism is used to control the availability and redundancy of the virtual servers and services, and initiates proper command when rebalancing the environment or recreating a new instance of a service or virtual server is required.

- *Virtual Network* – This mechanism is used to connect virtual servers and the services hosted on top of them.

- *Virtual RAM* – This mechanism is used to establish access for the virtual servers and applications to the physical memory installed on the physical server.

- *Virtual Server* – This is the mechanism to which this pattern primarily applied.

- *Virtual Switch* – This mechanism is used to connect hosted virtual servers to the physical network and external cloud service consumers using physical uplinks.

- *Virtualization Agent* – Virtual servers use this mechanism to send regular heartbeat messages to the hypervisor. A recovery process is initiated if the hypervisor does not receive heartbeats after an extended period of time.

- *Virtualization Monitor* – This mechanism is used to monitor the virtual servers' availability and operational status.

Storage Maintenance Window

How can access to data in a cloud storage device be preserved during a maintenance outage?

Problem	Hardware maintenance on cloud storage devices can require shutting down the device, resulting in loss of data access and disruption of service.
Solution	An outage prevention system is created to temporarily move the data without interruption during maintenance and other types of outages.
Application	LUN migration is applied to temporarily transfer data to a separate cloud storage device during the maintenance window.
Mechanisms	Cloud Storage Device, Failover System, Resource Replication

Problem

Cloud storage devices subject to maintenance and administrative tasks may need to be temporarily shut down, thereby causing an outage to cloud service consumers and IT resources that require access to the devices and the data they host (Figure 4.31).

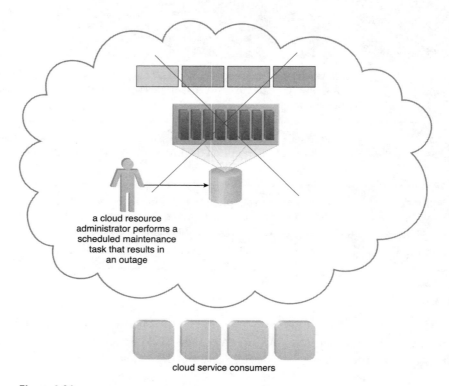

cloud service consumers

Figure 4.31

The maintenance task carried out by a cloud resource administrator causes an outage for the cloud storage device. Resultantly, the cloud storage device becomes unavailable to cloud service consumers.

Solution

Prior to a cloud storage device undergoing a maintenance outage, its data can be temporarily moved to a duplicate, secondary cloud storage device. Cloud service consumers are automatically and transparently redirected to the secondary cloud storage device and are unaware that the primary cloud storage device has been taken offline.

Application

Live storage migration is used to convert the data as a whole into an isolated mode and move it to the secondary cloud storage device, as shown in Figures 4.32 to 4.37.

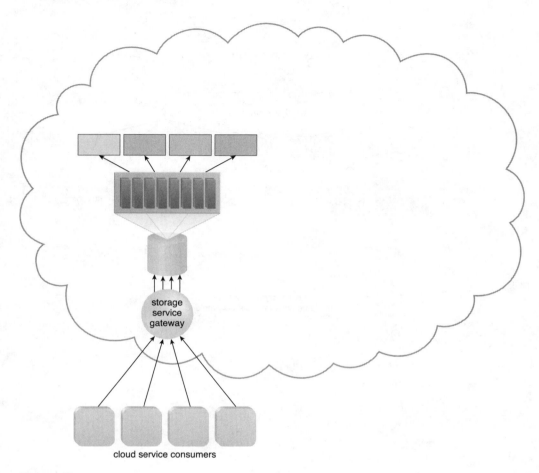

Figure 4.32

The cloud storage device is scheduled to undergo a maintenance outage.

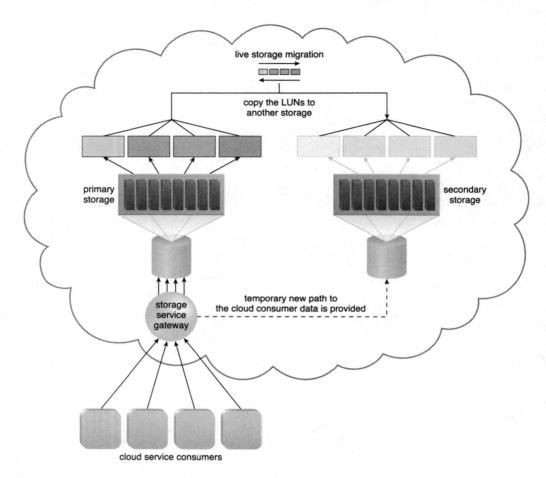

Figure 4.33

Live storage migration moves the LUNs from the primary storage device to a secondary storage device.

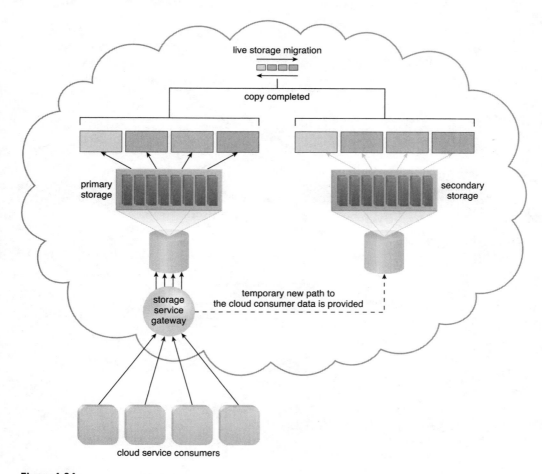

Figure 4.34

When the LUN's data has been migrated, requests for the data are forwarded to the duplicate LUNs on the secondary storage device.

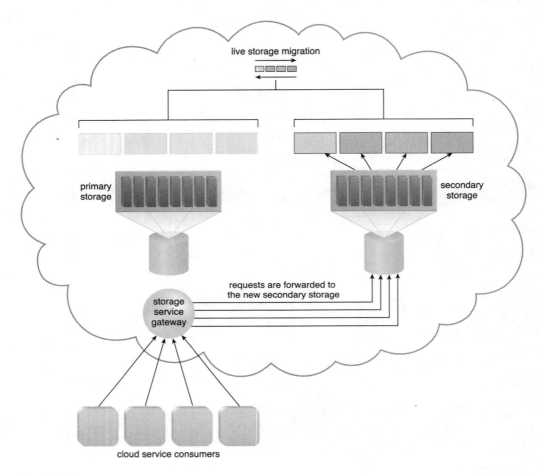

Figure 4.35

The primary storage is powered off for maintenance.

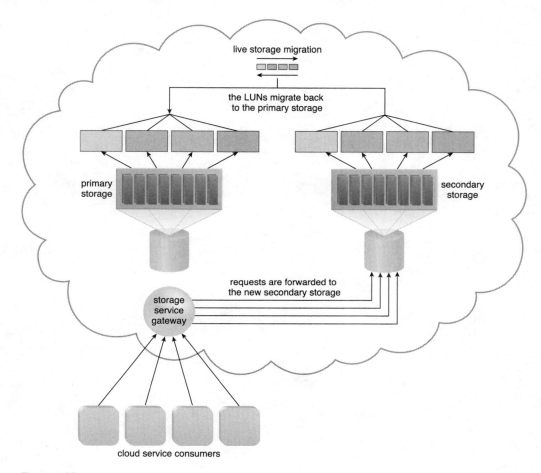

Figure 4.36

When it is confirmed that the maintenance task on the primary storage device has been completed, the primary storage is brought back online. Live storage migration subsequently restores the LUN data from the secondary storage device to the primary storage device.

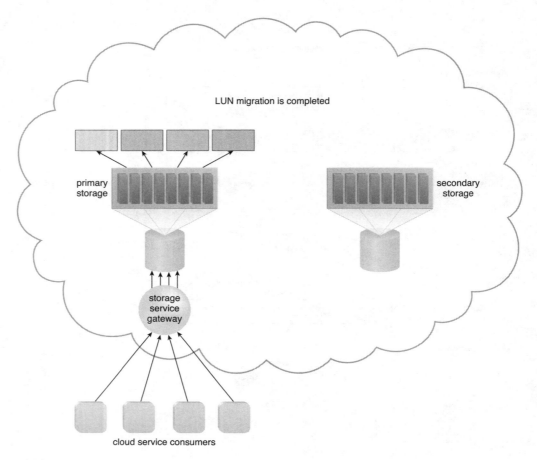

Figure 4.37

When the LUN migration is completed, all data access requests are forwarded back to the primary storage device.

Mechanisms

- *Cloud Storage Device* – This is the primary mechanism to which this pattern is applied.

- *Failover System* – Although the migration is often pre-scheduled when this pattern is applied, both manually and automatically initiated failover can be incorporated into this cloud architecture.

- *Resource Replication* – The resource replication mechanism is used to keep the primary and secondary storage devices synchronized.

Virtual Server Auto Crash Recovery

In the event that a virtual server's operating system crashes,
how can the hosted cloud services be automatically recovered?

Problem	A virtual server whose operating system suddenly fails needs to be able to have its hosted cloud services automatically recovered.
Solution	The virtual server's activity is constantly monitored and traced for recovery, in the event of an operating system failure.
Application	Applying this pattern involves specific techniques and mechanisms that are used by the hypervisor to check the operational status of the virtual server.
Mechanisms	Hypervisor, Virtualization Agent

Problem

When the operating system of a virtual server fails or crashes, the cloud services that are hosted on this virtual server also become unavailable. This can in turn cause an outage or even an SLA breach, since some organizations have little to no tolerance for outages.

The following steps are shown in Figure 4.38:

1. Cloud Service A is running on Virtual Server A.

2. Cloud consumers suddenly cannot access the service.

3. An investigation shows that Hypervisor A is working fine and has been allocating resources to Virtual Server A. However, Virtual Server A's resource usage is zero. Further investigation reveals that its operating system has crashed, which is why Cloud Service A is not working.

The system administrator has to manually reboot Virtual Server A in order to bring it back into operation.

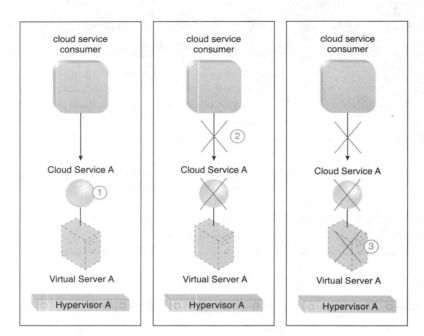

Figure 4.38
Cloud Service A becomes suddenly inaccessible to a cloud consumer.

Solution

Applying this pattern ensures that the operational status of a given virtual server is always being checked by the hypervisor on a routine basis. If the virtual server is not running or shows no signs of operation after a certain length of time, then the hypervisor takes action and restarts the virtual server automatically, to recover the virtual server from a crash.

The scenario that results is illustrated in Figure 4.39 in the following steps:

1. Hypervisor A is monitoring Virtual Server A's operational status.

2. Cloud Service A becomes unavailable due to an operating system failure on Virtual Server A.

3. Hypervisor A becomes aware of the nonoperational status of Virtual Server A immediately.

4. Hypervisor A restarts Virtual Server A.

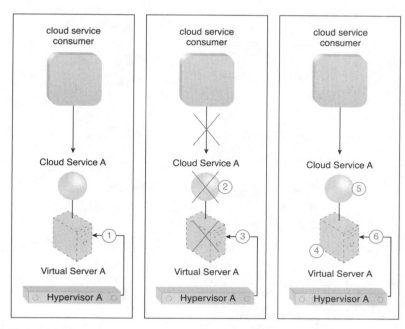

Figure 4.39

After the crash, Cloud Service A becomes available again.

5. Service resumes without requiring human interaction and cloud consumers can access the virtual server.

6. Hypervisor A continues to monitor the operational status of Virtual Server A.

Application

This pattern can be applied in different ways, depending on the brand and model of the hypervisor and the mechanism used to track the resource utilization of the virtual servers. The following chart in Figure 4.40 illustrates the steps involved in applying the pattern.

Different methods and mechanisms can be used to check the virtual server's operational status, such as a mechanism that can install an agent inside the virtual server that reports back to the hypervisor. Another mechanism is a hypervisor that checks the resource usage of the virtual server, including memory and CPU usage, at pre-defined intervals. A different method is to check the virtual server's network traffic and storage traffic for communication over the network and whether it is accessing or requesting any storage.

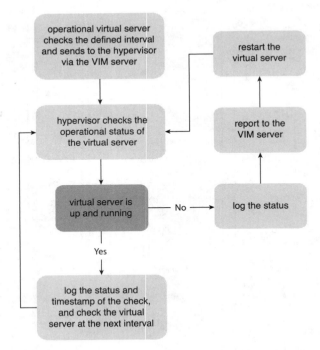

Figure 4.40
The steps involved in applying this pattern are shown.

While this pattern ensures that virtual servers, applications, and services are operational and can be automatically recovered in the case of an operating system failure, this pattern may also restart the virtual server as a result of a "false positive."

Mechanisms

- *Hypervisor* – The hypervisor mechanism hosts the virtual servers and is responsible for making sure the virtual servers are up and running. Any failed or crashed virtual servers are restarted by this mechanism.

- *Virtualization Agent* – This mechanism establishes one-way communication via specialized messages that are sent by the virtual servers to the host hypervisor at frequent and regular intervals to confirm virtual server operation.

Non-Disruptive Service Relocation

How can cloud service activity be temporarily or permanently relocated without causing service interruption?

Problem	There are circumstances under which redirecting cloud service activity or relocating an entire cloud service implementation is required or preferable. However, diverting service activity or relocating a cloud service implementation can cause outage, thereby disrupting the availability of the cloud service.
Solution	A system can be established whereby cloud service redirection or relocation is carried out at runtime by temporarily creating a duplicate implementation before the original implementation is deactivated or removed.
Application	Virtualization technology is used by the system to enable the duplication and migration of the cloud service implementation across different locations in realtime.
Mechanisms	Cloud Storage Device, Cloud Usage Monitor, Hypervisor, Live VM Migration, Pay-Per-Use Monitor, Resource Replication, SLA Management System, SLA Monitor, Virtual Infrastructure Manager (VIM), Virtual Server, Virtual Switch

Problem

A cloud service can become unavailable due to a number of reasons, such as:

- The cloud service encounters more runtime usage demand than it has processing capacity to handle.

- The cloud service implementation needs to undergo a maintenance update that mandates a temporary outage.

- The cloud service implementation needs to be permanently migrated to a new physical server host.

Cloud service consumer requests are rejected if a cloud service becomes unavailable, which can potentially result in exception conditions. Rendering the cloud service temporarily unavailable to cloud consumers is not preferred even if the outage is planned.

Solution

A system is established by which a pre-defined event triggers the duplication or migration of a cloud service implementation at runtime, thereby avoiding any disruption in service for cloud consumers.

An alternative to scaling cloud services in or out with redundant implementations, cloud service activity can be temporarily diverted to another hosting environment at runtime by adding a duplicate implementation onto a new host. Cloud service consumer requests can similarly be temporarily redirected to a duplicate implementation when the original implementation needs to undergo a maintenance outage. The relocation of the cloud service implementation and any cloud service activity can also be permanent to accommodate cloud service migrations to new physical server hosts.

Application

A key aspect to the underlying architecture is that the system ensures that the new cloud service implementation is successfully receiving and responding to cloud service consumer requests *before* the original cloud service implementation is deactivated or removed.

A common approach is to employ the live VM migration component to move the entire virtual server instance hosting the cloud service. The automated scaling listener and/or the load balancer mechanisms can be used to trigger a temporary redirection of cloud service consumer requests in response to scaling and workload distribution requirements. In this case either mechanism can contact the VIM to initiate the live VM migration process.

The steps involved in applying the Non-Disruptive Service Relocation pattern are illustrated in Figures 4.41 through 4.43.

1. The automated scaling listener monitors the workload for a cloud service.

2. As the workload increases, a pre-defined threshold within the cloud service is reached.

3. The automated scaling listener signals the VIM to initiate the relocation.

4. The VIM signals both the origin and destination hypervisors to carry out a runtime relocation via the use of a live VM migration program.

5. A second copy of the virtual server and its hosted cloud service are created via the destination hypervisor on Physical Server B.

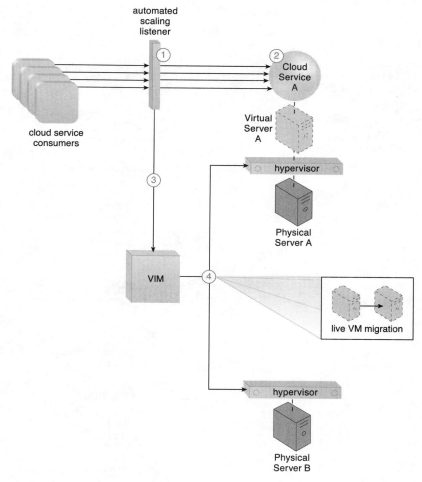

Figure 4.41

An example of a scaling-based application of the Non-Disruptive Service Relocation pattern (Part I).

6. The state of both virtual server instances is synchronized.

7. The first virtual server instance is removed from Physical Server A after it is confirmed that cloud service consumer requests are being successfully exchanged with the cloud service on Physical Server B.

8. Cloud service consumer requests are only sent to the cloud service on Physical Server B from hereon.

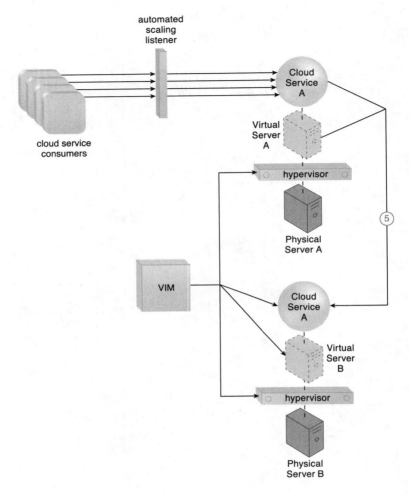

Figure 4.42
An example of a scaling-based application of the Non-Disruptive Service Relocation pattern
(Part II).

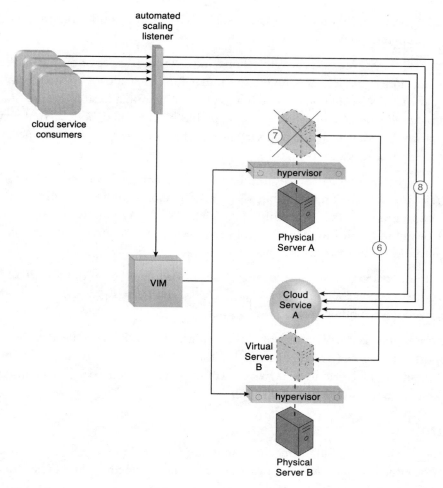

Figure 4.43

An example of a scaling-based application of the Non-Disruptive Service Relocation pattern (Part III).

Depending on the location of the virtual server's disks and configuration, this migration can happen in one of two ways:

- If the virtual server disks are stored on a local storage device or on non-shared remote storage devices attached to the source host, then a copy of the virtual server disks is created on the destination host (either on a local or remote shared/non-shared storage device). After the copy has been created, both virtual server instances are synchronized and virtual server files are subsequently removed from the origin host.

- If the virtual server's files are stored on a remote storage device shared between origin and destination hosts, there is no need to create the copy of virtual server disks. In this case, the ownership of the virtual server is simply transferred from the origin to the destination physical server host, and the virtual server's state is automatically synchronized.

Note that this pattern conflicts and cannot be applied together with Direct I/O Access (169). A virtual server with direct I/O access is locked into its physical server host and cannot be moved to other hosts in this fashion.

Furthermore, Persistent Virtual Network Configuration (227) may need to be applied in support of this pattern so that by moving the virtual server, its defined network configuration is not inadvertently lost, which would prevent cloud service consumers from being able to connect to the virtual server.

Mechanisms

- *Cloud Storage Device* – This mechanism is fundamental to the Non-Disruptive Service Relocation pattern in how it provides the storage required to host data pertaining to the virtual servers in a central location.

- *Cloud Usage Monitor* – Cloud usage monitors are used to continuously track IT resource usage and activity of the system established by the Non-Disruptive Service Relocation pattern.

- *Hypervisor* – The hypervisor is associated with this pattern in how it is used to host the virtual servers that are hosting the cloud services that need to be relocated. It is further used to transfer a virtual server's ownership and runtime, including CPU and memory state, from one hypervisor to another.

- *Live VM Migration* – This mechanism is responsible for transferring the ownership and runtime information of a virtual server from one hypervisor to another.

- *Pay-Per-Use Monitor* – The pay-per-use monitor is used to continuously collect the service usage costs of the IT resources at both their source and destination locations.

- *Resource Replication* – The resource replication mechanism is used to instantiate the shadow copy of the cloud service at its destination.

- *SLA Management System* – The SLA management system is responsible for acquiring SLA information from the SLA monitor, in order to obtain cloud service availability assurances both during and after the cloud service has been copied or relocated.

- *SLA Monitor* – This monitoring mechanism collects the aforementioned information required by the SLA management system.

- *Virtual Infrastructure Manager (VIM)* – This mechanism is used to initiate relocation, which can be automated in response to a threshold being reached or monitoring event.

- *Virtual Server* – Virtual servers generally host the cloud services at the source and destination locations.

- *Virtual Switch* – The virtual switch mechanism keeps virtual servers connected to and accessible over the network.

Chapter 5

Data Management and Storage Device Patterns

Direct I/O Access

Direct LUN Access

Single Root I/O Virtualization

Cloud Storage Data at Rest Encryption

Cloud Storage Data Lifecycle
Management

Cloud Storage Data Management

Cloud Storage Data Placement
Compliance Check

Cloud Storage Device Masking

Cloud Storage Device Path Masking

Cloud Storage Device Performance
Enforcement

Virtual Disk Splitting

Sub-LUN Tiering

RAID-Based Data Placement

IP Storage Isolation

The fundamental cloud computing model for enabling ubiquitous, on-demand, scalable network access to shared pools of configurable IT resources typically demands for the existence of and access to vast amounts of inexpensive storage that itself must be highly flexible, scalable, and configurable. As with other members of typical cloud architectures, cloud storage devices must have the ability to be rapidly provisioned and release storage resources and large amounts of data with minimal management effort or cloud provider interaction.

This set of patterns addresses key issues that pertain to common challenges and optimization requirements when configuring and managing cloud-based storage devices and the datasets they store.

Direct I/O Access

How can a virtual server overcome data transfer capacity thresholds imposed by its surrounding virtualization environment?

Problem	Virtualized networks and associated virtualized IT resources have capacity limitations that can unreasonably inhibit virtual server communication and data transfer performance.
Solution	The virtual server is allowed to circumvent the hypervisor and directly access the physical server's I/O card.
Application	The hypervisor transfers complete control of the physical server's I/O card directly to the virtual server, which is then able to recognize the I/O card as a hardware device.
Mechanisms	Cloud Storage Device, Cloud Usage Monitor, Hypervisor, Logical Network Perimeter, Pay-Per-Use Monitor, Resource Replication, Virtual Infrastructure Manager (VIM), Virtual Server

Problem

Access to the physical I/O cards that are installed on a physical server is usually provided to host virtual servers via I/O virtualization. However, virtual servers sometimes need to connect to and use an I/O card without any hypervisor interaction or emulation.

For example, there may be two application servers and one database connected to one another and installed as a virtual server. Direct access to the physical network must be made available in order to improve their connectivity (rather than sending traffic via the virtual network).

Solution

The cloud architecture permits connections to the physical I/O card directly by the virtual server, as an alternative to emulating such a connection via the hypervisor.

Application

To achieve this solution, the host CPU needs to support this type of access with the appropriate drivers installed on the virtual server for it to access the physical I/O card without hypervisor interaction, as shown in Figures 5.1 and 5.2. The virtual server will then be able recognize the I/O card as a hardware device.

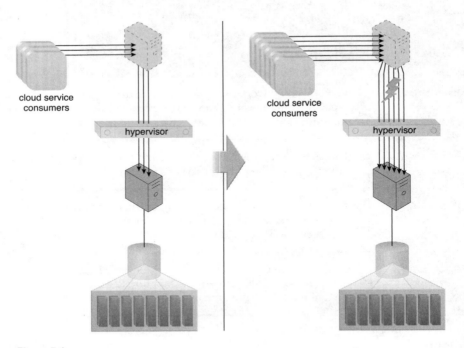

Figure 5.1

Part A (left) shows the virtual server accessing a database stored on a SAN storage LUN. Connectivity from the virtual server to the database occurs via a virtual switch. Part B (right) depicts an increase in the amount of requests. The resulting bandwidth and performance of the virtual NIC are inadequate.

Figure 5.2

In Part C, the virtual server
bypasses the hypervisor to
connect to the database server
via a direct physical link to the
physical server. The increased
workload can now be properly
handled.

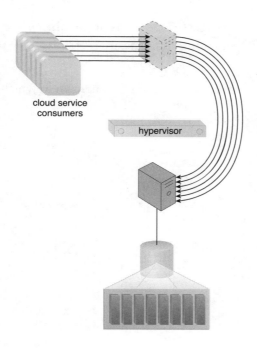

Mechanisms

- *Cloud Storage Device* – Whenever direct I/O access is used to dedicate a storage
  I/O card or host bus adapter (HBA) to a virtual server, this mechanism is used to
  establish the virtual server's access to data stored on the cloud storage device.

- *Cloud Usage Monitor* – The service usage data collected by runtime monitors can
  include and separately classify direct I/O access.

- *Hypervisor* – This mechanism hosts the virtual server that is carrying out the
  direct I/O access.

- *Logical Network Perimeter* – The logical network perimeter ensures that the allocated physical I/O card does not allow any cloud consumers to access other cloud
  consumers' IT resources.

- *Pay-Per-Use Monitor* – This mechanism collects information on the service usage
  costs of the allocated physical I/O card for billing purposes.

- *Resource Replication* – The Direct I/O Access pattern may rely on a resource replication mechanism to replace virtual I/O cards with physical I/O cards.

- *Virtual Infrastructure Manager (VIM)* – This mechanism is used to configure direct I/O access on the hypervisor, and configure I/O cards to be directly accessible to virtual servers.

- *Virtual Server* – The virtual server is the mechanism to which this pattern is primarily applied.

Direct LUN Access

How can a virtual server overcome performance limitations imposed by emulated file-based storage?

Problem	LUNs mapped via a host bus adapter on the hypervisor can restrict data access to emulated file-based storage, which can impose performance limitations.
Solution	The virtual server is granted direct access to block-based storage LUNs via the physical host bust adapter card.
Application	Raw device mapping technology is used to configure the hypervisor to enable access to raw, block-based LUNs to the virtual server.
Mechanisms	Cloud Storage Device, Cloud Usage Monitor, Hypervisor, Pay-Per-Use Monitor, Resource Replication, Virtual Infrastructure Manager (VIM), Virtual Server

Problem

Storage LUNs are typically mapped via a host bus adapter (HBA) on the hypervisor, with the storage space emulated as file-based storage to virtual servers. Sometimes, however, virtual servers need direct access to RAW block-based storage. For example, when implementing a cluster and using the LUN as the shared cluster storage device between two virtual servers, access via an emulated adapter may be insufficient.

The following steps are shown in Figure 5.3:

1. The cloud storage device is installed and configured.

2. The LUNs' mapping is defined so that each hypervisor has access to its own LUN and can also see the mapped LUNs.

3. The hypervisor shows the mapped LUNs to the virtual servers as normal file-based storage (and the virtual server uses it as such).

Figure 5.3

LUNs are required to use emulated, file-based storage.

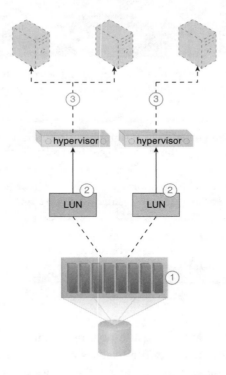

Solution

Virtual servers are granted direct access to block-based storage LUNs. Providing virtual servers with direct LUN access via a physical HBA card is effective because virtual servers that are part of the same cluster can use the LUN as a shared cluster volume for clustered databases. After implementing this solution, the required physical connectivity to the LUN and cloud storage device for the virtual servers is provided by the physical hosts.

Application

The LUNs are created and configured on the cloud storage device for LUN presentation to the hypervisors, which then needs to be configured using the raw device mapping to make the LUNs visible to the virtual servers as a block-based RAW SAN LUN, which is unformatted, un-partitioned storage. The LUN needs to be represented with a unique LUN ID for all of the virtual servers to use it as shared storage.

The application of the Direct LUN Access pattern by which virtual servers are given direct access to block-based storage LUNs is shown in Figures 5.4 and 5.5 in two parts.

1. The cloud storage device is installed and configured.

2. The required LUNs are created and presented to the hypervisors.

3. The hypervisors map the presented LUN directly to the virtual servers.

4. The virtual servers can see the LUNs as RAW block-based storage and can access them directly.

5. The virtual servers' storage commands are received by the hypervisors.

6. The hypervisors process and forward the requests to the storage processor.

Figure 5.4

A cloud architecture in which virtual servers are given direct access to block-based storage LUNs (Part I).

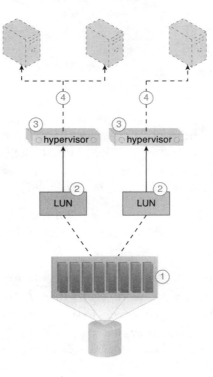

Figure 5.5

A cloud architecture in which virtual servers are given direct access to block-based storage LUNs (Part II).

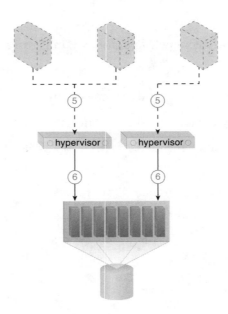

Mechanisms

- *Cloud Storage Device* – The cloud storage device mechanism provides virtual servers with direct access to the storage LUNs. Actual data is stored on the cloud storage device, which receives commands and requests from virtual servers and sends them to the physical disks for I/O read/write operations.

- *Cloud Usage Monitor* – This cloud usage monitor relates to the Direct LUN Access pattern in how it monitors and collects storage usage information that pertains to the direct usage of LUNs.

- *Hypervisor* – This pattern depends on the hypervisor to host and connect virtual servers to the cloud storage devices, and to forward virtual server requests. This mechanism enables virtual servers to send storage commands (typically SCSI commands) to the cloud storage device, after which the virtual servers can directly write on the cloud storage device instead of performing read/write operations on the virtual disk.

- *Pay-Per-Use Monitor* – The pay-per-use monitor may collect and separately classify service usage cost information via Direct LUN Access.

- *Resource Replication* – This mechanism may be involved with how virtual servers directly access block-based storage in replacement of file-based storage.

- *Virtual Infrastructure Manager (VIM)* – This mechanism enables virtual servers to be configured for direct access to specific LUNs that are visible to the hypervisor.

- *Virtual Server* – The virtual server is the mechanism to which this pattern is primarily applied.

Single Root I/O Virtualization

How can a single physical I/O device be virtualized and shared between multiple cloud service consumers?

Problem	A single I/O device needs to be provided to multiple cloud service consumers, but it has an inherent physical limitation of only being able to service one at a time.
Solution	The functionality of the physical I/O device is abstracted and its features are presented to multiple cloud service consumers, so that each only sees its own virtualized instance.
Application	PNIC hardware is used to virtualize the I/O device's functionality and the abstracted functions are presented via the use of virtualization techniques.
Mechanisms	Hypervisor

Problem

When direct access to the I/O card is permitted via the application of the Direct I/O Access (169) pattern, it can introduce a potentially severe limitation (Figure 5.6). Multiple cloud service consumers may need to have access to the I/O card's functionality, but it can only be accessed and used by one at any one time.

Figure 5.6

The Direct I/O Access (169) pattern is applied, which is sufficient for individual cloud service consumer access, but imposes a firm limitation should additional cloud service consumers require simultaneous access.

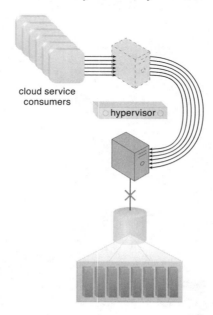

Solution

PNIC hardware that supports single root I/O virtualization (SRIOV) is used to abstract the I/O card's features and present them to cloud service consumers separately.

PNIC hardware devices have two types of functionality:

- *Physical Functionality (PF)* – replicates the actual hardware's capability and functionality

- *Virtual Functionality (VF)* – used to present multiple instances of the device to the hypervisor or virtual servers

Application

Application of this pattern requires the single root I/O virtualization feature to be enabled on the hardware I/O card. Note that the physical device will not be seen by the hypervisors or virtual servers when this feature is enabled. Instead, they will see the virtualized instances presented by the virtual functionality. The number of virtualized instances that can be created is dependent on a number of factors, such as hardware card type, vendor, model, and hypervisor.

The following steps are shown in Figure 5.7:

1. A physical NIC card that supports single root I/O virtualization is connected to a physical server that has the hypervisor installed and single root I/O virtualization feature enabled.

2. The device is abstracted into four instances, so the hypervisor sees four physical NICs.

3. Two instances of the NICs are attached to the virtual switch as physical uplinks.

4. Another uplink is assigned to a virtual machine to directly access the instance, similar to direct I/O access.

One single hardware I/O card can be abstracted and used by multiple cloud service consumers. Note that any cloud service consumers that use abstracted instances are locked onto the host and cannot be moved to another host without requiring downtime.

Applying this pattern eliminates the limitation set by the Direct I/O Access (169) pattern and allows two or more I/O devices to be accessible to each virtual server. Also, the virtual servers that use single root I/O virtualized instances cannot be moved to

Figure 5.7

A physical NIC card attached to a physical server supports the application of the Single Root I/O Virtualization pattern.

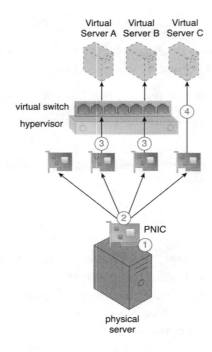

another host via the application of the Non-Disruptive Service Relocation (159) pattern and use of the live migration mechanism, unless they are disconnected from the abstracted device instance.

Mechanisms

- *Hypervisor* – This mechanism establishes features to replicate physical I/O cards that support single root I/O virtualization into multiple virtual instances via the use of physical and virtual functions. Each virtual instance can be directly connected to a virtual server or virtual switch, or used by the hypervisor.

Cloud Storage Data at Rest Encryption

How can cloud providers securely store cloud consumer data on cloud storage devices?

Problem	Data stored in a cloud environment requires security against access to the physical hard disks forming the cloud storage device.
Solution	Secure data on the physical hard disks in order to prevent unauthorized access.
Application	An encryption mechanism supported by the physical storage arrays can be used to automatically encrypt data stored on the disks and decrypt data leaving the disks.
Mechanisms	Cloud Storage Device, Cryptographic Key Management System (CKMS), Encryption

Problem

Cloud storage devices can be accessed via a single physical storage array (Figure 5.8).

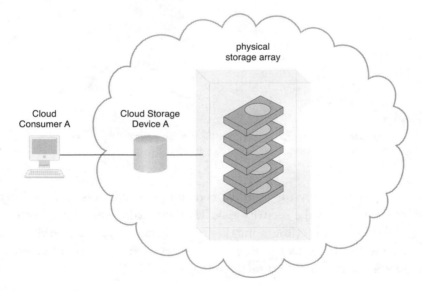

Figure 5.8

Cloud Consumer A stores data in a cloud environment that requires increased security.

Solution

Data is secured on the physical disks using an encryption mechanism, so that unauthorized access to the physical hard disks does not compromise data security.

Application

An encryption mechanism supported by the physical storage arrays can be used to automatically encrypt and protect data that will be automatically decrypted when the data leaves the physical hard disks (Figure 5.9).

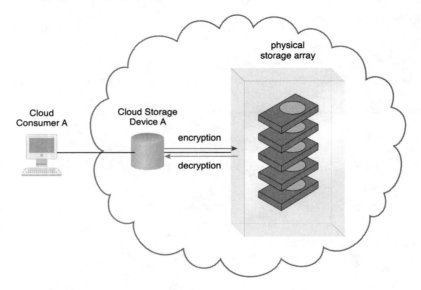

Figure 5.9

Data can be secured on physical disks by encrypting the data as it enters the physical storage array and decrypting data as it leaves the physical hard disks.

Using the same encryption key for multiple consumers or datasets in a multitenant cloud environment increases the security risk. Therefore, consider using shorter keys with simpler algorithms. A cryptographic key management system (CKMS) will be required to manage the keys. Depending on industry regulatory requirements, the cloud consumer may be required to directly manage the CKMS.

Mechanisms

- *Cloud Storage Device* – This mechanism represents the cloud storage devices that are affected by the application of this pattern.

- *Cryptographic Key Management System (CKMS)* – The CKMS is used to manage cryptographic keys.

- *Encryption* – This mechanism is used to encrypt and decrypt data traveling into or out of physical disks stored in a cloud environment.

Cloud Storage Data Lifecycle Management

How can data be stored and managed in a cloud environment based on a defined lifecycle?

Problem	Datasets no longer required by an organization can bloat databases causing performance challenges, and can further incur administration and maintenance burdens.
Solution	A solution can be introduced to automatically manage and migrate the data into a different type of cloud storage device, or delete the data based on its state in a defined lifecycle.
Application	A cloud storage data aging management mechanism monitors the state of data against a provided lifecycle in order to move data to a different cloud storage device or delete data after a defined lifecycle.
Mechanisms	Cloud Storage Data Aging Management, Cloud Storage Device, Data Transport

Problem

Over time, datasets can lose value to organizations, but must still be retained for security, regulatory, or compliance requirements (Figure 5.10).

For example, the size of Cloud Consumer A's data continues to increase, and they could be charged a cheaper price if it was moved to a less frequently accessed cloud storage device.

Figure 5.10

Cloud Consumer A stores data on Cloud Storage Device A.

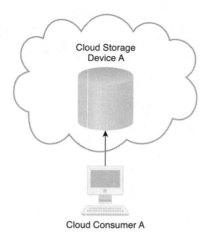

Cloud Storage
Device A

Cloud Consumer A

Solution

Implement a solution that automatically manages the data as well as moves data into different cloud storage devices based on a defined lifecycle. Outdated data can also be automatically deleted using this mechanism.

Application

Define the characteristics of the cloud storage devices in order to implement the data lifecycle management mechanism. A data transport mechanism should be implemented if the data requires migration to another cloud storage device. In combination, the mechanisms will manage the data at specific states in a defined lifecycle. The steps in applying this pattern are shown in Figure 5.11.

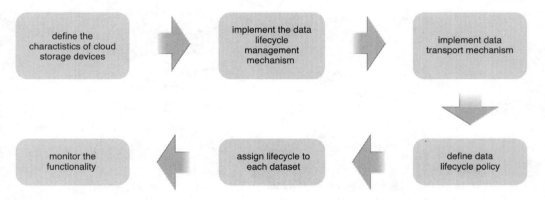

Figure 5.11
The steps in applying the Cloud Storage Data Lifecycle Management pattern are illustrated.

The cloud storage data aging management mechanism shown in Figure 5.12 can monitor and move data between Cloud Storage Devices A, B, and C based on a defined lifecycle from Consumer A of 6, 12, and 24 months, respectively.

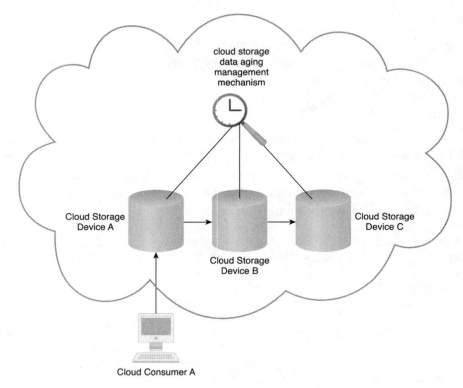

Figure 5.12

The cloud storage data aging management mechanism can be used in applying this pattern to manage datasets based on predefined policies.

Mechanisms

- *Cloud Storage Data Aging Management* – This mechanism is used to define and assign data lifecycle policies and monitor the data throughout its lifecycle in order to initiate movement using the data transport mechanism where defined.

- *Cloud Storage Device* – Data stored on the cloud storage device is managed by the cloud storage data aging management mechanism and moved by the data transport mechanism.

- *Data Transport* – When data is moved between different cloud storage devices, this mechanism can automatically perform the migration when requested by the cloud storage data aging management mechanism.

Cloud Storage Data Management

How can cloud consumers directly interact with data stored on a cloud storage device or provide access to other cloud consumers with appropriate permission levels?

Problem	Cloud consumers may not own or have permissions to the cloud-hosted storage devices that contain their data. This can limit their ability to access and manage datasets important to their business.
Solution	A solution is provided that enables cloud consumers to directly interact with data stored on a cloud storage device.
Application	A cloud storage management portal mechanism can be used to provide an interface or APIs for cloud consumers to interact with data stored on a cloud storage device.
Mechanisms	Cloud Storage Device, Cloud Storage Management Portal, Identity and Access Management (IAM)

Problem

Cloud consumers require a means of accessing and interacting with data stored in a cloud storage device. However, the fact that the cloud storage devices hosting their data may belong to third-party cloud providers can limit the extent to which cloud consumers can manage their own datasets (Figure 5.13).

Figure 5.13

Cloud consumers are unable to access data stored on a cloud storage device.

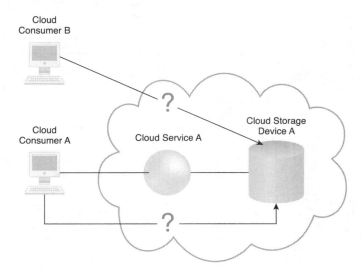

Solution

Implement a mechanism capable of providing access to data stored on a cloud storage device for cloud consumers.

Application

As depicted in Figure 5.14, a cloud storage management portal mechanism can be used to provide interfaces and APIs in order for cloud consumers to interact with datasets and cloud storage devices.

This mechanism can be linked to a self-service portal and usage and administration portal so that newly requested cloud storage devices can be automatically discovered and added to the list of accessible cloud storage devices. Cloud authentication control can be used and accessed so that data is only provided to authorized cloud consumers.

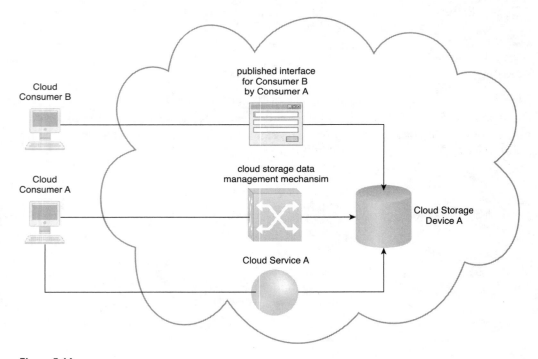

Figure 5.14

A cloud storage management portal mechanism provides the access for cloud consumers to manage data stored on a cloud storage device.

Mechanisms

- *Cloud Storage Device* – This mechanism represents the cloud storage devices to which this pattern is primarily applied.

- *Cloud Storage Management Portal* – This mechanism is used to establish communication between cloud consumers and cloud storage devices, and also to provide the required level of access and control over data stored in a cloud storage device.

- *Identity and Access Management (IAM)* – To enforce a centralized or federated model of authentication and authorization, this mechanism is used to integrate a cloud storage management portal mechanism with IAM.

How can cloud consumers ensure data that is stored on a cloud storage device is physically located in a region that meets required compliance policies?

Problem	Cloud consumer organizations may need to comply with regulatory data hosting policies that may place specific location requirements upon the storage devices used to host the data. However, when hosting data in a third-party cloud, there may be no way of knowing whether the cloud storage devices used meet these requirements.
Solution	A solution is implemented to monitor the location of a cloud storage device and send notifications should the storage conditions no longer satisfy compliance policies.
Application	The cloud storage data placement auditor mechanism is used to enforce policies defined by the cloud consumer (or cloud provider) on a specific dataset or cloud storage device.
Mechanisms	Attestation Service, Cloud Storage Data Placement Auditor, Cloud Storage Device, Geotag, Resource Replication, Trusted Platform Module (TPM)

Problem

There are a variety of corporate and governmental regulations that can require that certain types of data, especially private, confidential, or sensitive data, be physically located in the region native to the organization or in one of a list of approved regions. This was not a major concern with traditional data centers as their location was generally well known. However, when moving datasets into third-party cloud environments, organizations can lose the ability to govern storage devices to ensure compliance with such regulations. Furthermore, even if cloud storage devices initially are in compliance, cloud providers may opt to move them to other regions that may provide less expensive labor or infrastructure for their data centers, or perhaps for disaster recovery reasons (Figure 5.15).

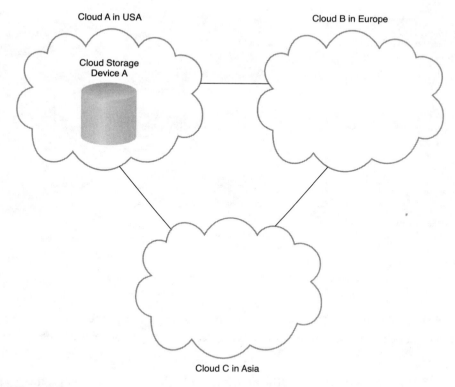

Figure 5.15

A cloud provider offers cloud storage in three regions. Initially the data may have been located in Cloud B, but has now been moved to Cloud A, unbeknownst to the cloud consumer.

Solution

A solution is implemented to ensure that a cloud storage device is only provisioned for use in a specific region, and that datasets stored on that cloud storage device will not be moved or copied into other regions.

Application

A cloud storage data placement auditor mechanism can be used to enforce policies defined by the cloud provider or cloud consumer on a specific dataset or cloud storage device. These policies are then attached to the dataset or cloud storage device and are automatically enforced.

The steps involved with the usage of this mechanism when applying this pattern are shown in Figure 5.16.

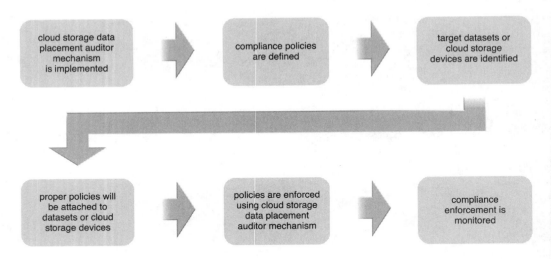

Figure 5.16

The steps in applying the Cloud Storage Data Placement Compliance Check pattern are illustrated.

A properly implemented cloud storage data placement auditor mechanism can prevent Cloud Storage Device A from being copied or replicated outside of the United States, as shown in Figure 5.17.

If this pattern is applied to prevent the replication of a dataset due to compliance requirements, integration between a resource replication mechanism and the cloud storage data placement auditor mechanism will be required.

Mechanisms

- *Attestation Service* – The attestation service receives the security status of the virtual servers from the TPM including location and is consulted when dispatching the workloads.

- *Cloud Storage Data Placement Auditor* – Monitors and enforces defined policies on a dataset or cloud storage device.

- *Cloud Storage Device* – This mechanism represents the cloud storage devices to which this pattern is primarily applied.

- *Geotag* – The geotag receptacle of the Trusted Platform Module (TPM) is provisioned with the compute platform geolocation.

- *Resource Replication* – To prevent dataset or cloud storage device replication as a result of compliance requirements, this mechanism can be integrated with the cloud storage data placement auditor mechanism.

- *Trusted Platform Module (TPM)* – The TPM is used as a trusted root for a secure boot of the physical and associated virtual servers and includes the geographic location of the servers and it reports the boot status to the trust attestation service.

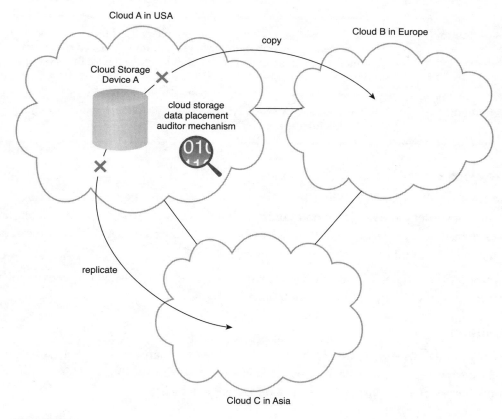

Figure 5.17

A cloud storage data placement auditor mechanism monitors and enforces policies on Cloud Storage Device A.

Cloud Storage Device Masking

How can data stored on a cloud storage device be isolated to specific consumers?

Problem	Data stored in a shared cloud environment can be vulnerable to unauthorized access by other cloud consumers.
Solution	A solution is implemented to isolate each cloud storage device from being presented to or accessed by unauthorized cloud consumers.
Application	A LUN masking mechanism can enforce defined policies at the physical storage array in order to prevent unauthorized cloud consumers from accessing a specific cloud storage device in a shared cloud environment.
Mechanisms	Cloud Storage Device, Cryptographic Key Management System (CKMS), Encryption, LUN Masking

Problem

Access to a cloud storage device may, by default, not be masked from unauthorized cloud consumers in a shared cloud environment. This can introduce inadvertent and malicious data access from unauthorized cloud consumers, cloud service consumers, or other neighboring IT resources.

Figure 5.18 illustrates Cloud Service Consumers A and B accessing respective cloud storage devices via a shared Physical Storage Array A.

Solution

A solution is implemented whereby a LUN masking mechanism is utilized to enforce policies at the physical storage array. This ensures that only authorized cloud service consumers can access the appropriate cloud storage device.

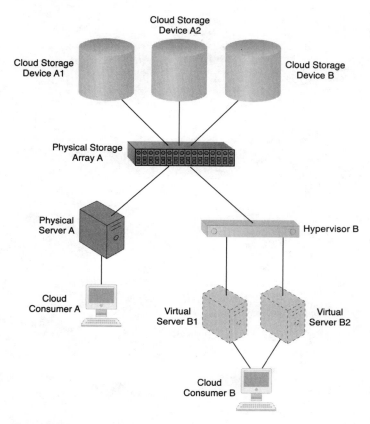

Figure 5.18
Cloud storage devices can be accessed via a single physical storage array.

Application

A LUN masking mechanism can be used to isolate and control which consumer has access to which cloud storage device. Physical Server A and Hypervisor B will not have access to the cloud storage devices without being reviewed against LUN masking policies by the LUN masking mechanism. As a result, Hypervisor B cannot view or access Cloud Storage Devices A1 and A2, and Hypervisor A cannot view or access Cloud Storage Device B (Figure 5.19).

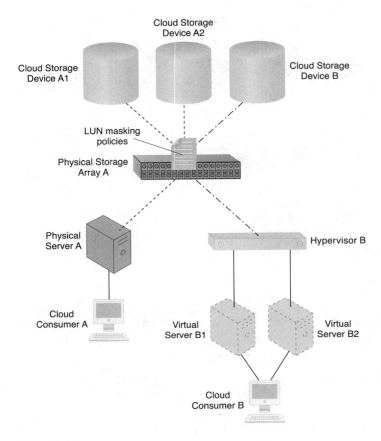

Figure 5.19

LUN masking policies can be enforced by a mechanism at Physical Storage Array A.

Many industry compliance regulations and best practices require an organization's sensitive data to be encrypted when at rest. The cloud consumer can encrypt data and employ a key manager to manage the encryption keys. The organization may also need to control its own cryptographic key management system (CKMS) to meet some industry regulations and best practices.

Mechanisms

- *Cloud Storage Device* – This mechanism represents the cloud storage devices to which this pattern is primarily applied.

- *Cryptographic Key Management System (CKMS)* - A CKMS, controlled by the organization to meet industry regulations and best practices, provides a system for managing encryption keys.

- *Encryption* – Encryption of data at rest is used to meet some industry compliance regulations and best practices to protect from data breaches.

- *LUN Masking* – This mechanism enforces a set of access control policies at the physical storage layer that manage which cloud storage device is accessible to which cloud consumer.

Cloud Storage Device Path Masking

How can data stored on a cloud storage device be isolated to specific consumers via certain pathways?

Problem	Cloud consumers can access cloud storage devices via alternative pathways that can compromise data security and integrity.
Solution	A solution is implemented at the hypervisor layer or physical server layer to limit access and utilization of certain available paths.
Application	The storage path masking mechanism is deployed inside the hypervisor or operating system installed on the physical server.
Mechanisms	Cloud Storage Device, Storage Path Masking

Problem

When multiple paths to a cloud storage device are available (such as when Multipath Resource Access (127) is applied), access to the cloud storage device by unauthorized cloud consumers becomes possible via the usage of alternative paths (Figure 5.20).

Solution

A solution is introduced to control and limit cloud consumer access to the utilization of certain available paths.

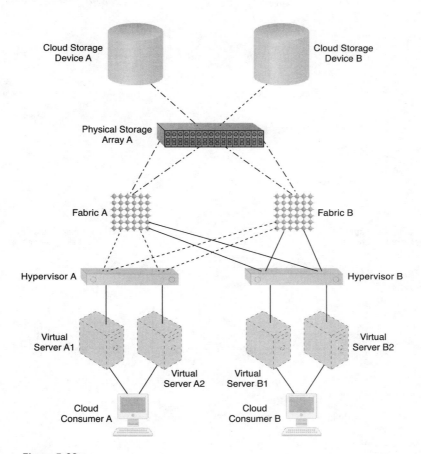

Figure 5.20

Redundancy of access to the cloud storage devices and physical storage device is implemented at Fabrics A and B, which connect each of the hypervisors to Physical Storage Array A. Cloud Consumer A and B can access both Fabric A and B via the two different dashed paths.

Application

The solution is implemented by using a storage path masking mechanism at the hypervisor layer or physical server layer. This limits access and utilization of available paths, as shown in Figure 5.21.

In case all unmasked paths from a physical server or hypervisor to a physical storage become unavailable, the physical server or hypervisor cannot communicate with the cloud storage device and a manual process is necessary to unmask the available masked paths and resume service.

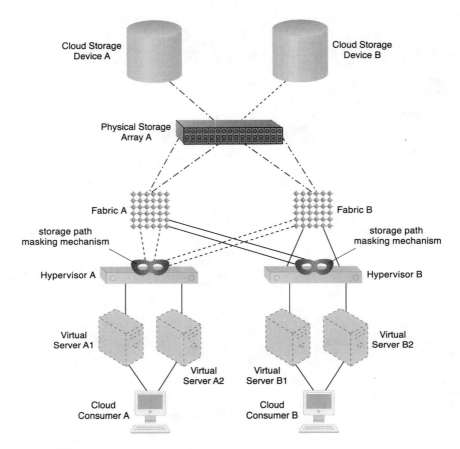

Figure 5.21

A storage path masking mechanism hides two of the previously visible paths to Hypervisor B.

Mechanisms

- *Cloud Storage Device* – This mechanism represents the cloud storage devices to which this pattern is primarily applied.

- *Storage Path Masking* – This mechanism is used to mask or hide the available paths from physical servers running operating systems or hypervisors to unauthorized cloud consumers.

Cloud Storage Device Performance Enforcement

How can data with different performance characteristics be stored on a cloud storage device compliant with the performance requirements of each dataset?

Problem	A cloud consumer can have different performance requirements for different datasets. If datasets with varying performance requirements reside on a cloud storage device with fixed performance capabilities, the performance requirements will not be met.
Solution	A solution is implemented with the ability to match and compare the performance characteristics of datasets against performance capabilities of a destination cloud storage device.
Application	A cloud storage device performance monitor mechanism manages data stored on a cloud storage device based on performance characteristics. This solution can also enforce policies that prevent data from being copied or moved elsewhere while sending an alert response.
Mechanisms	Cloud Storage Device, Cloud Storage Device Performance Monitor

Problem

A cloud consumer can contract three different cloud storage devices with varying storage performance characteristics, as follows:

- Cloud Storage Device A (Gold Tier)
- Cloud Storage Device B (Silver Tier)
- Cloud Storage Device C (Bronze Tier)

As depicted in Figure 5.22, a cloud consumer can copy different datasets onto a cloud, but needs to ensure that Datasets A, B, and C are stored on Cloud Storage Devices A, B, and C, respectively.

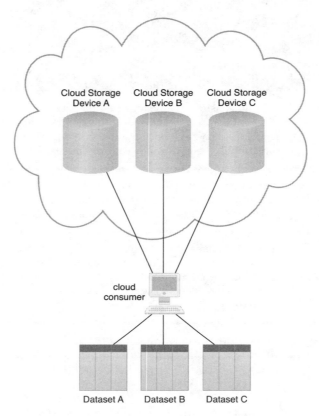

Figure 5.22
Different datasets with different performance requirements can be
stored on different cloud storage devices with varying price points.

Solution

A solution is introduced to automatically manage data based on its performance
requirements. This solution is further capable of moving data into different cloud storage devices when necessary. An alert can be raised to enforce policies that prevent datasets from being copied or moved to a different cloud storage device that does not meet
performance requirements.

Application

A cloud storage device performance monitor mechanism can be implemented as a specialized type of SLA monitor to identify and classify the performance characteristics of

cloud storage devices. A cloud provider would provide an API for cloud consumers to identify the performance characteristics of the different datasets.

By enforcing the performance requirements of each dataset, the cloud storage device performance monitor is able to generate an alert for a resource administrator to correct the performance mismatch or move the dataset to an appropriate cloud storage device.

Note that only some variations of this mechanism have the added ability to prevent data from being copied onto a cloud storage device that does not meet the defined performance requirements.

Mechanisms

- *Cloud Storage Device* – This mechanism represents the cloud storage devices to which this pattern is primarily applied.

- *Cloud Storage Device Performance Monitor* – This mechanism is used to check the performance characteristics defined for each dataset against the underlying cloud storage device or a destination cloud storage device for performance mismatch, which will then generate an alert or initiate the enforcement of a policy that prevents the dataset from being copied or moved.

Virtual Disk Splitting

How can a virtual disk be moved to another location that is either in the same cloud storage device or in a different cloud storage device?

Problem	Moving a virtual disk to a different location is sometimes required, but when the destination location is incompatible, the move may not be possible, losing functionality.
Solution	A solution is implemented that ensures that the destination location for a virtual disk is compatible prior to the attempted move.
Application	The virtual disk and its related files (log files, snapshots) are moved to a location that matches the virtual disk's requirements.
Mechanisms	Cloud Storage Device, Hypervisor, Virtual Disk, Virtual Infrastructure Manager (VIM), Virtualization Monitor

Problem

A virtual server may host an application that requires a different storage IOPS or throughput than other hosted applications. For instance, Figure 5.23 depicts Virtual Server A with three virtual disks, one of which is used to install a business-critical application that needs more storage I/O than the operating system. In this case, the virtual server needs to be moved to another storage tier or cloud storage device with greater I/O capacity.

Two cloud storage devices are shown in Figure 5.23. Cloud Storage Device B has a greater performance capacity and incurs higher usage fees than Cloud Storage Device A. Each cloud storage device has multiple internal LUNs with different I/O capacities and costs. For simplicity, the higher the number of LUNs means the greater the I/O capacity.

Virtual Server A has its operating system installed on Virtual Disk A, local backup and log files stored on Virtual Disk B, and an I/O-intensive business application (Application A) installed on Virtual Disk C. Application A recently began experiencing degraded performance. An investigation reveals that the current I/O capacity has not been sufficient ever since the number of Application A's cloud consumer requests began increasing.

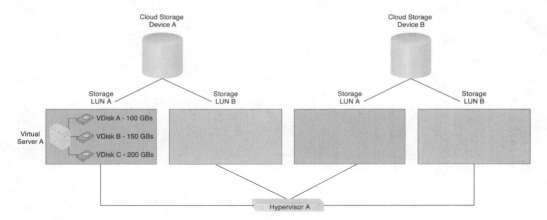

Figure 5.23
Virtual Server A has three VDisks named Virtual Disks A, B, and C. Virtual Disk C needs to be relocated to another storage location.

If Virtual Server A is moved to either LUN B on Cloud Storage Device A or another LUN on Cloud Storage Device B, cloud consumers will be charged for the amount of space used for all three virtual disks. However, Virtual Disks A and B do not require as much I/O capacity as Virtual Disk C. A solution that allows individual virtual disks to be moved to a different storage LUN without causing any outages or service impact on Virtual Server A is required.

Solution

The virtual disks are separated from each other by placing them into storage that can sustain their required performance levels. Typically, all virtual disks are stored inside the same folder in which the virtual server was first stored at its creation. This solution uses the live VM migration mechanism to move individual virtual disks to a different storage location (with a higher or lower I/O capacity) while the virtual server is kept in operation. This migration process needs to be supported by the host hypervisor, so that the I/O can be redirected to the new storage location after migration has been completed.

The scenario that results after this pattern is applied is depicted in Figure 5.24.

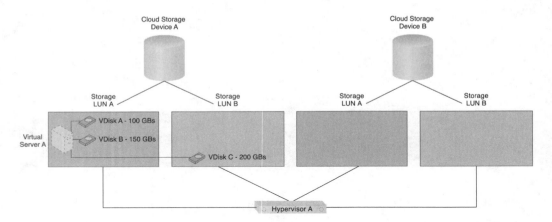

Figure 5.24
Virtual Disk C has been migrated to LUN B by a live VM migration mechanism to accommodate Application A's increasing requirements.

Application

In the example scenario shown in Figure 5.25, this pattern is applied to Virtual Server A. The virtual server is being forwarded requests from cloud consumers to use Application A on VDisk C. Figure 5.26 shows that the number of requests being sent for Application A has increased.

The increase in cloud consumer requests is creating a performance problem. Application A needs more I/O, a demand that cannot be accommodated by LUN A. This problem can occur even if the number of cloud consumer requests has not increased, as long as the other virtual servers being hosted on the same LUN are consuming most of the I/O.

The steps involved in applying this pattern are illustrated in Figures 5.27 and 5.28.

1. The automated scaling listener mechanism monitors the number of requests and measures the available I/O for VDisk C.

2. When the available I/O or number of requests reaches its pre-defined threshold, the VIM server receives a signal to move VDisk C.

3. The VIM server signals Hypervisor A to initiate moving VDisk C to LUN B on Cloud Storage Device A.

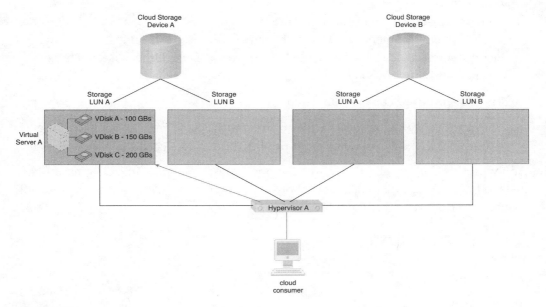

Figure 5.25

Cloud consumer requests for Application A on VDisk C are being sent to LUN A.

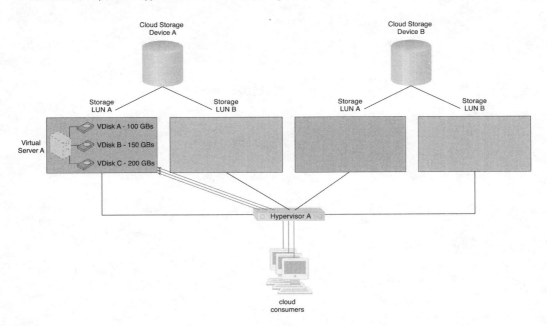

Figure 5.26

The number of cloud consumer requests being sent to LUN A increases.

4. Hypervisor A starts to create a synchronized copy of VDisk C on LUN B. Depending on the environment's structure, the hypervisor may offload this task to the cloud storage device to be performed at the storage layer. Otherwise, the hypervisor creates the copy via the network or storage network.

5. The synchronized copy is completed.

6. The cloud consumer requests are forwarded to VDisk C on LUN B and the original copy of VDisk C is deleted from LUN A.

Applying this pattern allows each of the applications or operating systems that are installed on a virtual disk to be hosted on a location that can accommodate their individual performance and bandwidth requirements.

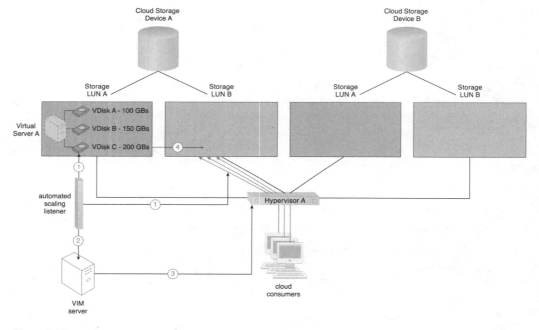

Figure 5.27

The steps for applying this pattern are shown.

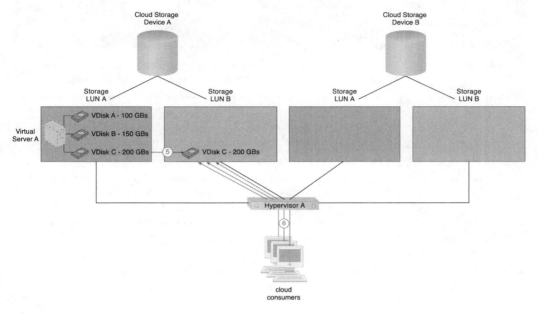

Figure 5.28
The steps for applying this pattern are shown.

Mechanisms

- *Cloud Storage Device* – This mechanism is used to host virtual server folders and their relevant files.

- *Hypervisor* – This mechanism is used to host virtual servers, and is also responsible for moving virtual disks between cloud storage devices based on pre-defined rules or thresholds.

- *Virtual Disk* – The virtual disk contains the virtual server's operating system, applications and data, and cloud consumer data, and can move between cloud storage devices to meet its own space or performance requirements.

- *Virtual Infrastructure Manager (VIM)* – This mechanism is used to configure thresholds and policies that dictate which actions the hypervisor should take. The VIM also moves virtual disks from one cloud storage device to another, and is used to manually initiate the disk splitting process.

- *Virtualization Monitor* – This mechanism is used to monitor disk IOPS and free disk space utilization, as well as to help make predictions that can improve disk-splitting policies and virtual disk placements.

Sub-LUN Tiering

How can a subset of data stored inside a LUN be moved without having to migrate the entire LUN?

Problem	A subset of data stored inside a LUN has increased performance requirements that cannot be fulfilled in its current location.
Solution	A solution is implemented capable of monitoring performance levels against required performance levels and coordinating the migration of datasets, as required.
Application	An automated scaling listener mechanism is used to monitor actual performance against required performance levels and can initiate necessary migration via a sub-LUN migration mechanism.
Mechanisms	Automated Scaling Listener, Cloud Storage Device, Sub-LUN Migration

Problem

Datasets can have specific performance requirements that separate them from other subsets of data stored within a LUN. When such requirements come about, it may be necessary for such datasets to be moved to a location that can fulfill the desired performance requirements.

For example, in Figure 5.29 LUN A is presented to Cloud Consumer A as Cloud Storage Device B with three different datasets. However, Dataset A2 needs to be placed on a higher performance storage tier without having to move LUN A. Moving the entire LUN will result in unnecessary charges for storage space utilization.

Solution

The solution has the intelligence necessary to check for locations that are compatible with dataset performance requirements and can further move datasets to those locations.

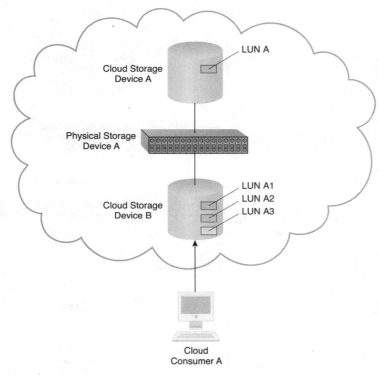

Figure 5.29
Cloud Consumer A stores data on LUN A.

Application

Data can be selectively moved to another tier via a sub-LUN migration mechanism that is activated by an automated scaling listener mechanism. The automated scaling listener mechanism can compare required performance levels against actual performance levels and initiate migration of data via a sub-LUN migration mechanism when necessary (Figure 5.30).

When migration is required, the sub-LUN migration mechanism can selectively migrate the dataset to another performance tier or cloud storage device (Figure 5.31).

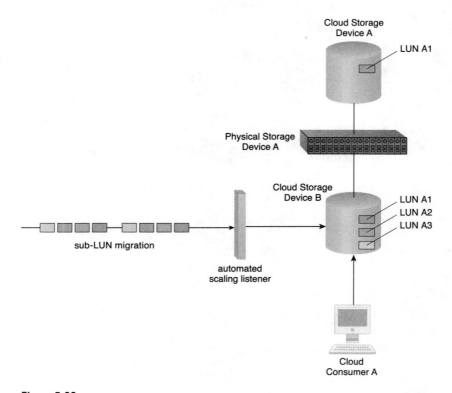

Figure 5.30

An automated scaling listener mechanism is connected to a sub-LUN migration mechanism after applying the Sub-LUN Tiering pattern.

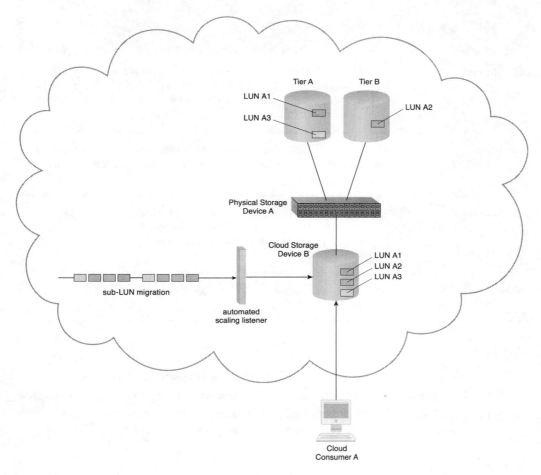

Figure 5.31

A sub-LUN migration mechanism moves Dataset A2 to a higher performance Tier B.

Mechanisms

- *Automated Scaling Listener* – This mechanism actively monitors the performance of a LUN and datasets in order to initiate migration where necessary.

- *Cloud Storage Device* – The cloud storage device is a common IT resource that may require the creation of an alternative path in order to remain accessible by solutions that rely on data access.

- *Sub-LUN Migration* – This mechanism is used to migrate required sub LUNs or datasets to different tiers or cloud storage devices.

Problem	Cloud storage devices can be provisioned with different underlying and back-end RAID levels. Data placed on a RAID level that is incompatible with its performance or protection requirements can be in jeopardy of underperforming or failing.
Solution	An interface is provided to cloud consumers that can communicate information about the available underlying RAID levels of cloud storage devices.
Application	A RAID identifier mechanism is used to inform the cloud consumer of RAID levels available for a selected cloud storage device by directly interacting with the cloud storage management portal mechanism.
Mechanisms	Cloud Storage Device, Cloud Storage Management Portal, RAID-level Identifier

Problem

Cloud storage devices are provisioned with different underlying and back-end RAID levels. A cloud provider will charge cloud consumers different prices based on the features, performance, and data protection levels required. Data copied to a cloud storage device needs to be stored with a required protection level (Figure 5.32).

Solution

An interface to the cloud consumer can provide information on the underlying RAID level of cloud storage devices via a RAID identifier mechanism that interacts directly with the cloud storage management portal mechanism.

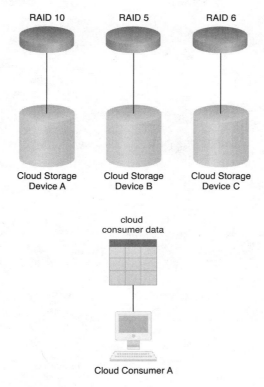

Figure 5.32
Consumer A will store data in a cloud storage device according to the RAID level that best satisfies its performance and data protection requirements.

Application

A RAID identifier mechanism is utilized to inform cloud consumers of the underlying RAID level for a requested cloud storage device via the cloud storage management portal mechanism, which allows the consumer to interact with a cloud storage device in order to copy or move data to and from the cloud without compromising the security of other cloud consumer's data (Figure 5.33).

Cloud consumers can select which cloud storage device best fulfills a set of requirements given the information provided by the RAID identifier mechanism.

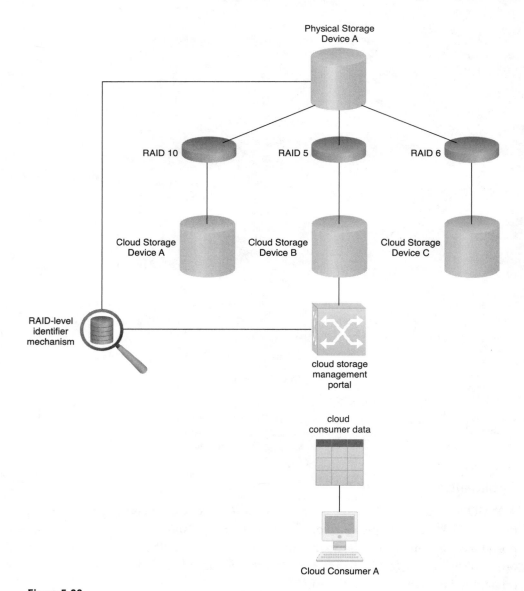

Figure 5.33

A RAID-level identifier mechanism will use the cloud storage management portal mechanism to return information on the specifics of the cloud storage devices to Cloud Consumer A.

Mechanisms

- *Cloud Storage Device* – This is the mechanism to which this pattern is primarily applied.

- *Cloud Storage Management Portal* – A cloud storage management portal mechanism allows the cloud consumer to view the RAID level of each cloud storage device and copy data into an appropriate cloud storage device.

- *RAID-level Identifier* – A RAID-level identifier identifies the underlying RAID level of each cloud storage device in order to forward the information to the cloud storage management portal mechanism.

IP Storage Isolation

How can IP storage be secured while using the same communication layer and channel as other networking traffic?

Problem	Storage traffic needs to share the same underlying network infrastructure as network traffic.
Solution	Implement a security mechanism that manages the appropriate levels of isolation for cloud storage devices.
Application	IP storage data can be protected from unauthorized users via a networking mechanism that is used to allocate a dedicated or virtually dedicated tunnel of traffic to IP storage.
Mechanisms	Cloud Storage Management Portal, LUN Masking, RAID-level Identifier, Storage Path Masking, Virtual Network

Problem

Storage traffic shares the same underlying network infrastructure as network traffic and must ensure security against unauthorized access to Cloud Storage Devices A and B.

Solution

A solution is introduced to ensure that isolation and security are enforced before data is returned to cloud consumers. In the scenario depicted in Figure 5.34, when the data leaves a cloud storage device and travels into the network for Hypervisors A or B, security is automatically enforced to ensure data travels to the appropriate cloud consumer.

Application

A LUN masking mechanism can be used between IP storage devices and the respective cloud consumers to implement the appropriate isolation. Isolation can be used at OSI Layer 2 to ensure cloud consumers communicate over a dedicated OSI Layer 2 network, while other cloud consumers can exist in a separate OSI Layer 2 domain. Quality of service mechanisms can ensure the required levels of network resources are available for IP storage.

Some storage vendors provide the APIs for storage resource administrators to interface with the cloud storage device and manually configure policies or automate the policy configuration. A standalone management interface can define the policies so that servers can only see and access the LUNs presented.

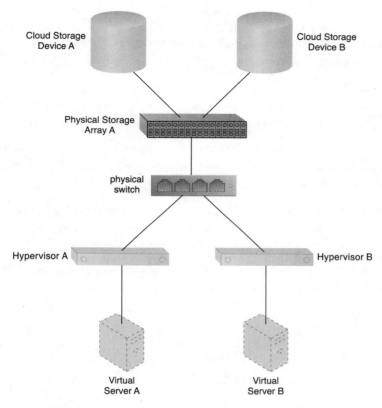

Figure 5.34

Virtual Server A and B require access to Cloud Storage Devices A and B without viewing or accessing each other's data.

A storage path masking mechanism can establish concurrent communication over the multiple available paths, while hiding some of the paths from the systems or applications (in Figure 5.34, this mechanism operates at Physical Switch A). A RAID-level identifier mechanism can be used to identify the RAID level of cloud storage devices and forward the information to a cloud storage management portal mechanism via provided APIs or SDKs. If no API or SDK is provided, then cloud storage resource administrators can manually populate the information by using available features and options, such as inventory tags or defined attributes, which attribute a value according to the RAID level of the cloud storage device.

Mechanisms

- *Cloud Storage Management Portal* – This mechanism is used to enable cloud consumers to interact with the data stored on cloud storage devices and restrict access based on defined policies.

- *LUN Masking* – This mechanism can manage which cloud consumers have access to view and interact with specific LUNs via available pathways.

- *RAID-level Identifier* – This mechanism can ensure data is stored in a cloud storage device with defined requirements that are managed by the cloud storage management portal mechanism.

- *Storage Path Masking* – This mechanism can isolate cloud storage devices by masking otherwise available pathways from cloud consumers to the cloud storage devices.

- *Virtual Network* – This mechanism is used as the network between a cloud storage device and a physical storage device or between cloud storage devices.

Chapter 6

Virtual Server and Hypervisor Connectivity and Management Patterns

Virtual Server Folder Migration

Persistent Virtual Network
  Configuration

Virtual Server Connectivity Isolation

Virtual Switch Isolation

Virtual Server NAT Connectivity

External Virtual Server Accessibility

Cross-Hypervisor Workload Mobility

Virtual Server-to-Host Affinity

Virtual Server-to-Host Anti-Affinity

Virtual Server-to-Host Connectivity

Virtual Server-to-Virtual Server
  Affinity

Virtual Server-to-Virtual Server
  Anti-Affinity

Stateless Hypervisor

Depending on which cloud delivery model a cloud resource administrator is working with, the extent to which hypervisor and virtual server configuration can be controlled can vary significantly. This set of patterns focuses on hypervisors and virtual servers.

Through the hypervisor, the cloud provider delivers interfaces to networking features, such as virtual network switches, that cloud consumers may use to configure custom virtual networks within the provider's infrastructure. This structure varies from SaaS and PaaS environments where much of the configuration and maintenance of IT resources is handled transparently for cloud consumers.

In an IaaS environment, on the other hand, cloud consumers will typically maintain complete control over the operation of the guest operating system in each virtual server, and all software layers above it. This allows for greater flexibility to apply the patterns covered in this chapter.

Virtual Server Folder Migration

How can a virtual server be kept on the same hypervisor when its configuration files and virtual disks are being moved to another location?

Problem	A virtual server needs to be kept on the same host while its configuration files and virtual disks are being transferred to another location.
Solution	The folder containing the virtual server's disks and configuration files is moved to another LUN or cloud storage device without modifying the virtual server host.
Application	The folder containing the virtual disks and configuration files is transparently relocated to another storage destination, without impacting the virtual server's operation or functionality.
Mechanisms	Cloud Storage Device, Hypervisor, Virtual Infrastructure Manager (VIM)

Problem

Certain situations will require a virtual server to be moved to another storage LUN or cloud storage device that offers higher performance or greater I/O throughput (Figure 6.1).

Figure 6.1

Three LUNs named Storage LUNs A, B, and C are configured on Cloud Storage Device A and made accessible for Hypervisors A and B to use. LUN A is shared between both hypervisors, meaning they share LUN B's available capacity and I/O throughput.

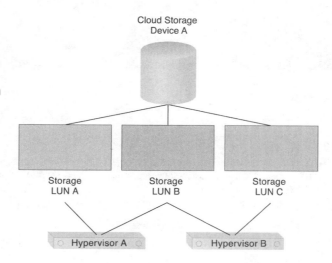

Cloud Storage Device A

Storage LUN A   Storage LUN B   Storage LUN C

Hypervisor A   Hypervisor B

Figure 6.2 shows each virtual server's placement in relation to their storage location and hypervisor. In Figure 6.3, the virtual servers have been replaced with virtual server folders.

Virtual Server C hosts a business-critical application belonging to a cloud consumer who cannot accommodate the downtime that is required to move the virtual server to another LUN or hypervisor.

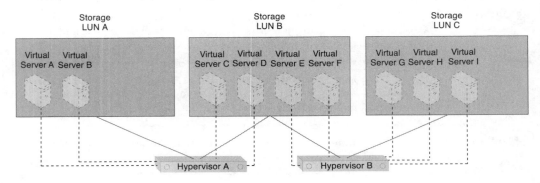

Figure 6.2
Virtual Servers A through I are distributed between Storage LUNs A, B, and C.

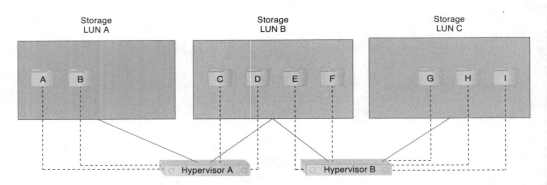

Figure 6.3
The virtual servers are represented by folder icons that contain the virtual servers' virtual disks (VDisks), configuration files, and log files. LUN B contains four virtual servers. Two are hosted on Hypervisor A and the other two are hosted on Hypervisor B. The number of cloud consumers using Virtual Server C increases over time, and LUN B's current I/O capacity is becoming inadequate. As a result, Virtual Server C is beginning to experience service-level degradation.

Solution

The target virtual server's folder can be moved to another storage LUN while Virtual Server C is still in operation without causing any negative impacts. A communication mechanism between the VIM server and hypervisor is used to initiate the process, as well as a replication mechanism to create a redundant copy of the virtual server folder on the destination storage LUN. Both folders are synchronized after the copying is finished, before the original copy is deleted.

Application

Figure 6.4 illustrates the architecture after the pattern is applied, in the following steps:

1. The migration process is initiated by the VIM server, which informs the hypervisor.

2. A copy of the virtual server folder is created at the new destination, LUN A.

3. The copying process continues until both copies are fully synchronized.

4. The hypervisor continues to send cloud consumer requests to the virtual server at the original location, LUN B.

5. Subsequent cloud consumer requests are forwarded to the new location, LUN A.

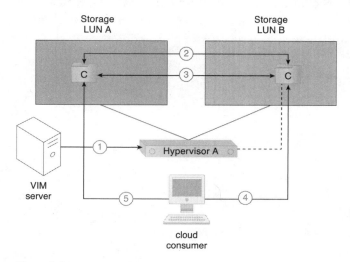

Figure 6.4
The steps comprising the application of this pattern are illustrated.

The mirror copying process can occur via the use of a variety of different specialized replication mechanisms, depending on the design of the environment and type of hypervisor and storage. For instance, a file-copying mechanism can be used as a hypervisor's subsystem, or the LUN migration and storage mechanisms can be applied at the storage layer.

Applying this pattern guarantees that the virtual server will not be moved to another hypervisor when its configuration files and log files are being moved to another storage location. The move can be performed at the storage layer and at the highest speed possible, if the cloud storage device allows the hypervisor to offload the copy operation to storage. Otherwise, the hypervisor performs the move via the network, which can affect other network traffic communication and may take longer if the virtual disk is larger in size.

Mechanisms

- *Cloud Storage Device* – This mechanism is used to store virtual server folders.

- *Hypervisor* – This mechanism is responsible for initiating virtual server folder migration from one cloud storage device to another.

- *Virtual Infrastructure Manager (VIM)* – This mechanism is used to configure policies and thresholds, and to define the conditions upon which a given hypervisor should automatically initiate virtual server folder migration. It can also be used to manually initiate virtual server folder migration.

Problem	When a virtual server is moved from one physical host to another, it loses its original network configurations, resulting in loss of network connectivity until the original configurations are recreated on the destination host.
Solution	The virtual server network configuration data is stored in a centralized location and replicated to the physical hosts, which makes it available to the destination host.
Application	The VIM is used to create and configure the virtual switch and to replicate the configuration data across the physical hosts.
Mechanisms	Hypervisor, Logical Network Perimeter, Physical Uplink, Resource Replication, Virtual Infrastructure Manager (VIM), Virtual Server, Virtual Switch

Problem

Network configurations and port assignments for virtual servers are generated when creating the virtual switch on the hosting physical server and the hypervisor responsible for hosting the virtual server. This configuration information resides within a virtual server's immediate hosting environment. If a virtual server is moved or migrated to another host (such as during an outage), it will lose network connectivity because the destination hosting environment will not have the required port assignments and network configuration information (Figure 6.5).

Solution

The network configuration information is stored in a centralized location and further replicated to physical server hosts. This way, when a virtual server is moved from one host to another, the destination host can gain access to the configuration, which can also be moved to the new host.

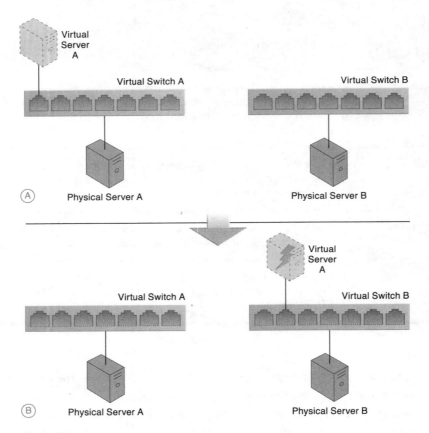

Figure 6.5

Part A shows a virtual server connected to the network through Virtual Switch A that was created on Physical Server A. Part B illustrates that after the virtual server is moved to Physical Server B, it is connected to Virtual Switch B that was created on Physical Server B. Because its configuration settings are missing, the virtual server cannot connect to the network.

Application

The system established by the application of this pattern includes a centralized virtual switch, a VIM, and configuration replication technology (Figure 6.6). The centralized virtual switch is shared by physical servers and configured via the VIM, which initiates replication of configuration settings to managed physical servers.

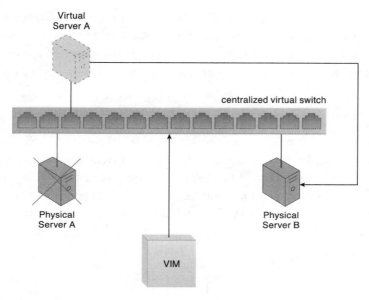

Figure 6.6

A virtual switch's configuration settings are maintained by the VIM, which ensures
that these settings are replicated to other physical servers. The centralized virtual
switch is published and each of the physical server hosts is assigned some of its
ports. When Physical Server A fails, the virtual server is moved to Physical Server
B. Because its network settings are stored on a centralized virtual switch shared
by both physical servers, it is retrieved and the virtual server maintains network
connectivity on its new host.

Mechanisms

- *Hypervisor* – The hypervisor hosts the virtual servers that require the replication
  of configuration settings across the physical hosts. It requests information about
  VIM-based virtual switches and loads the virtual switches into memory.

- *Logical Network Perimeter* – The logical network perimeter helps ensure that,
  before and after a virtual server is migrated, access to the virtual server and its IT
  resources is isolated to an authorized cloud consumer.

- *Physical Uplink* – This mechanism is used to connect the virtual switch to the
  physical switch and physical network.

- *Resource Replication* – The resource replication mechanism is used to replicate the
  virtual switch configurations and network capacity allocations across the hypervisors, via the centralized virtual switch.

- *Virtual Infrastructure Manager (VIM)* – Use of this mechanism enables a specialized VIM-based virtual switch to be created and broadcast to all of the hypervisors. Configurations and modifications to this type of virtual switch are maintained by the VIM and forwarded to the hypervisors as configuration updates.

- *Virtual Server* – This potential migration of this mechanism is what this pattern is dedicated to supporting.

- *Virtual Switch* – This mechanism connects virtual servers to the physical network via physical uplinks. A specialized type of virtual switch can be created via the VIM that is connected to all of the required hypervisors. If a virtual server is moved from one hypervisor to another, the virtual server can retain its network configurations because the virtual switch configurations are the same across the hypervisors.

Virtual Server Connectivity Isolation

How can a given virtual server be isolated and prevented from communicating with the external network while remaining in contact with other virtual servers and resources?

Problem	A virtual server's communication needs to be limited to only the virtual server and other resources it needs to remain in contact with, and isolated from all other parts of the external network.
Solution	The virtual server is not allowed to connect to any part of the solution that has a communication path to the external network or internal network, outside of what is required.
Application	The virtual server is isolated via the use of an additional virtual switch, thereby isolating it from the traffic of other virtual servers.
Mechanisms	Hypervisor, Physical Uplink, Virtual Firewall, Virtual Infrastructure Manager (VIM), Virtual Switch

Problem

In certain situations, a virtual server may not be allowed to communicate with a specific part of the network within the cloud environment, or with the cloud consumers outside of the cloud.

In Figure 6.7, Virtual Server A hosts an application that accesses a database hosted by Virtual Server B. Virtual Server A needs to remain accessible to respond to cloud consumer requests, while Virtual Server B is to only communicate with Virtual Server A. The virtual servers are both connected to Virtual Switch A, and the firewall has been configured to block all traffic to Virtual Server B's IP address so that it becomes isolated from the external network.

However, there are other virtual servers (Virtual Servers C and D) that are connected to the same switch that can still communicate with Virtual Server B, since their traffic will not pass the firewall. This does not meet the security requirements.

The cloud consumers cannot access Virtual Server B because the firewall blocks their requests. However, Virtual Servers C and D can still communicate with Virtual Server B because they are connected to the same switch. Also, traffic from another virtual or physical switch within the environment may still be able to send traffic to and access Virtual Server B, if permitted by the design of the environment.

Figure 6.7

Virtual Server B cannot be accessible to any other part of the external network or to the other virtual servers that are connected to Virtual Switch A.

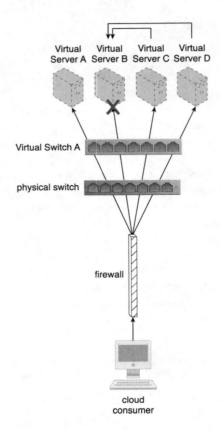

Solution

Virtual Server B is only allowed to communicate with Virtual Server A by restricting Virtual Server B's communication channel. After implementing the solution, the following scenario as illustrated in Figure 6.8 is produced.

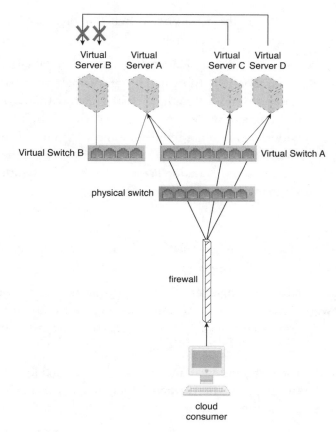

Figure 6.8

Virtual Server B is given its own virtual switch, so that it can be completely
isolated from all other virtual servers besides Virtual Server A.

Application

Two virtual switches need to be used for this solution. One virtual switch only has
virtual server-to-virtual connectivity, meaning it has no physical uplink to keep the
traffic inside the virtual switch. The other virtual switch has a physical uplink that
ensures that Virtual Server A can communicate with the other virtual servers and cloud
consumers.

Virtual Server B will have one or more virtual NICs attached to the internal virtual
switch that has no physical uplink. Virtual Server A has at least two virtual NICs. One
is attached to the internal virtual switch in order to communicate with Virtual Server B,

and the other one is attached to the other virtual switch in order to communicate with the other virtual servers and cloud consumers.

If the virtual servers that need to be in isolated communication with each other are distributed to different hypervisors, the functionality of this pattern becomes lost. All of the virtual servers that need to connect to the virtual switch without a physical uplink need to be hosted on the same hypervisor. Applying the Virtual Server-to-Virtual Server Affinity (267) pattern is therefore required to host the virtual servers together. Also note that if any pattern that may move the virtual servers to another hypervisor is being applied to the cloud environment, the Persistent Virtual Network Configuration (227) pattern is required to maintain their connectivity.

Mechanisms

- *Hypervisor* – The hypervisor mechanism is used to host virtual servers and create network partitioning via the use of virtual switches.

- *Physical Uplink* – This mechanism enables virtual switches to be connected to the physical network. Physical uplinks are also used to pass traffic from a virtual server attached to one virtual switch to other virtual servers attached to different virtual switches.

- *Virtual Firewall* – The virtual firewall mechanism can be used to control, limit, and isolate the traffic of one virtual switch from that of another switch, or of one virtual server from another.

- *Virtual Infrastructure Manager (VIM)* – This mechanism provides features and tools for creating multiple virtual switches and attaching their own dedicated uplinks if required.

- *Virtual Switch* – This mechanism is used to create different network connectivity points for virtual servers to isolate the connectivity of individual virtual servers from other virtual servers and the physical network.

Virtual Switch Isolation

How can network contention and bandwidth competition between virtual servers be decreased?

Problem	Network contention and bandwidth competition between virtual servers on the same virtual switch needs to be alleviated.
Solution	The virtual server traffic needs to be isolated.
Application	Virtual switches can be used as isolation mechanisms to reduce network contention and bandwidth competition.
Mechanisms	Hypervisor, Physical Uplink, Virtual Infrastructure Manager (VIM), Virtual Network, Virtual Switch

Problem

Placing virtual servers on the same virtual switch can increase their contention and competition for network bandwidth and I/O.

In Figure 6.9, Virtual Servers A and B both require a large amount of I/O to run a scalable application that is capable of consuming all of Physical Uplink A's available bandwidth. Virtual Servers A and B are becoming slower when responding to requests.

Figure 6.9

Only one physical uplink is available for the two virtual servers to use, resulting in longer response times for cloud consumer requests.

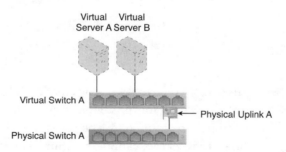

The cloud provider adds another physical uplink to Virtual Switch A in an attempt to prevent contention, but does not resolve the issue. As depicted in Figure 6.10, both virtual servers are using the new physical uplink's bandwidth and still competing for additional bandwidth.

Furthermore, the need for stronger security measures requires Virtual Servers A and B to be physically isolated from virtual server traffic so that they cannot communicate with each other.

Figure 6.10

Virtual Servers A and B require more bandwidth than the two physical uplinks can provide.

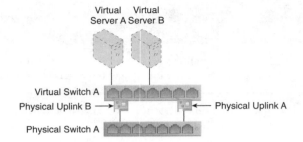

Solution

The virtual switch and physical uplink mechanisms are used to achieve the required level of isolation. As a result, Virtual Servers A and B are connected to different virtual switches that have individual physical uplinks, so that the two virtual servers cannot communicate with or impact one another, as shown in Figure 6.11.

Figure 6.11

Each virtual server is provided with access to a physical uplink and virtual switch that cannot be accessed by the other virtual server.

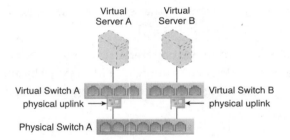

Application

As illustrated in Figure 6.12, two virtual switches that each have an individual physical uplink are defined and configured for the virtual servers. The physical uplinks are connected to the physical switch in Figure 6.13. The physical switch needs to be configured in such a way that the virtual servers cannot communicate with one another or impact each other's traffic. The virtual servers are then connected to the virtual switches, as shown in Figure 6.14.

Figure 6.12

Virtual Switches A and B are each provided with an individual physical uplink.

Figure 6.13

The two physical uplinks are connected to Physical Switch A.

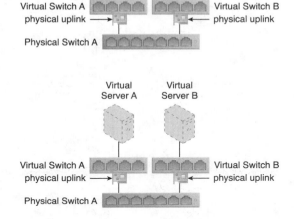

Figure 6.14

Virtual Servers A and B are connected to Virtual Switches A and B.

While the desired level of isolation can be achieved by applying this pattern to prevent network contention and create physical isolation between virtual servers, the number of available physical connections on the physical server becomes limited. Creating an individual virtual switch for every virtual server is not advised. Also, each virtual switch adds operation overhead to the hypervisor, which may be limited in the number of virtual switches it can support.

Preventing traffic and bandwidth competition requires a logical boundary to be created at the virtual networking layer by using the virtual switch mechanism and its physical uplink. Since virtual switches cannot share a physical uplink, a virtual switch with its own dedicated physical uplink can be allocated to different organizations inside a public cloud, or to different departments or services inside a private cloud.

For example, virtual servers communicate with external cloud service consumers via the NIC that is dedicated to their own virtual switch. This will ensure that the traffic of one virtual server does not impact the performance of other virtual servers. A protection layer is also created by isolating the network traffic of different cloud consumers or different departments from one another.

In Figure 6.15, Virtual Switches A and B are each connected to two different physical switches. If any of the physical switches or NICs encounter failure, the virtual servers remain connected to the virtual switch and external cloud service consumers. The application of the Load Balanced Virtual Switches (57) pattern makes the bandwidth capacity of the virtual switches equal to the aggregate capacity of both physical uplinks.

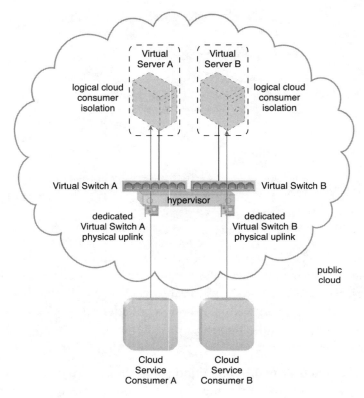

Figure 6.15

The virtual servers are still connected to the virtual switches and cloud service consumers even if a physical switch or NIC experiences failure.

Mechanisms

- *Hypervisor* – This mechanism is used to host and connect virtual servers to the network via virtual switches.

- *Physical Uplink* – This mechanism provides virtual switch-to-physical switch connectivity.

- *Virtual Infrastructure Manager (VIM)* – This mechanism is used to create and configure virtual switches and is also used to configure the virtual switches' physical uplinks.

- *Virtual Network* – This mechanism provides connectivity via multiple virtual switches that each have independent physical uplinks to isolate the network traffic of each virtual server.

- *Virtual Switch* – The virtual switch mechanism is used to connect virtual servers to the physical network, while virtual servers connect to other virtual switches via the use of physical uplinks.

How can a virtual server be published and communicate while keeping its actual IP address hidden?

Problem	A virtual server needs to be published and be able to send and receive packets without revealing its IP address to cloud consumers.
Solution	The virtual server communicates with the addition of a middle layer component that changes its IP address.
Application	The solution is applied via the use of a NAT protocol (or a comparable component).
Mechanisms	Hypervisor, Physical Uplink, Virtual Network, Virtual Switch

Problem

A cloud environment may need to fulfil security or privacy requirements that necessitate that the IP address of a virtual server be kept hidden from its cloud consumers. The traditional approach to addressing these requirements involves having the virtual server send out packets containing a false IP address. This approach is not recommended.

In Figure 6.16, Virtual Server A hosts a Web server that receives customer requests to access the company's Web page. The cloud provider wants to make sure the actual IP address of the virtual server is hidden from its cloud consumers by having Virtual Server A send packets using a false IP address.

Solution

There can be different layers of physical or virtual networking between the cloud consumer and the virtual server. The virtual server's IP address inside the packets is changed within so that it cannot be viewed by cloud consumers.

Application

Figure 6.17 shows that the packet is modified by the NAT server before it is sent off to the customers.

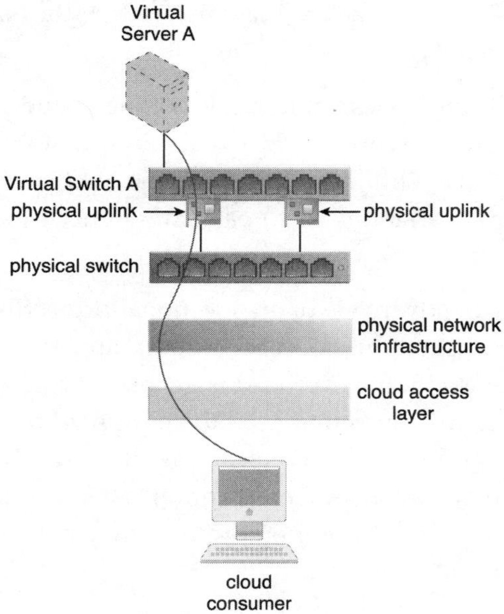

Figure 6.16

Virtual Server A's address needs to remain hidden from the cloud consumer.

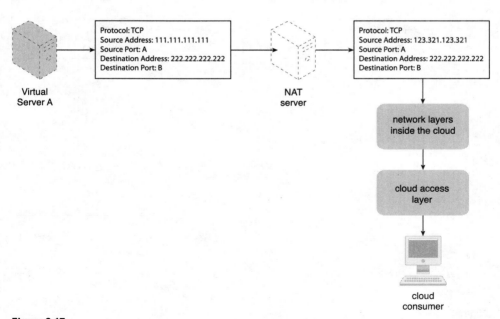

Figure 6.17

The sender IP address that the customers see in the packet is not Virtual Server A's real IP address.

When a customer sends a packet back to Virtual Server A, the NAT server modifies that packet as well, as shown in Figure 6.18.

To ensure that the NAT server does not lose track of the IP addresses and that the packets are sent or translated to the correct address, the information is stored in an internal database called a NAT table. Either static or dynamic NAT may be used. Note that the External Virtual Server Accessibility (244) pattern will need to be applied prior to the application of this pattern, as it is a prerequisite.

In addition to the security advantage of an additional protective layer over the virtual servers and services published for cloud consumers, applying this pattern also introduces performance overhead. This overhead is generated from the address translation and header exchange requirements that need to be fulfilled before the packets are sent to the cloud consumers and virtual servers, and is significantly higher when dynamic NAT or PAT is used. Moreover, service interruptions may result if encryption protocols are being used, as the security/encryption protocol may not validate the packets after they are modified by the NAT server.

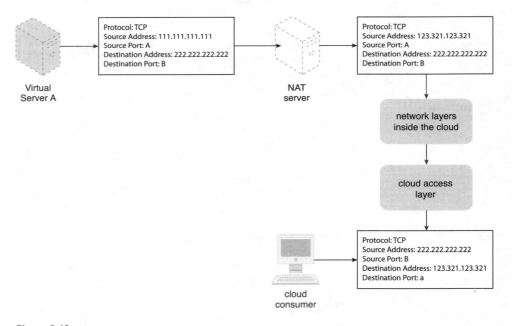

Figure 6.18
The packet is modified by the NAT server before it is sent back to Virtual Server A.

Mechanisms

- *Hypervisor* – This mechanism hosts virtual servers and enables the virtual servers to be connected to virtual switches.

- *Physical Uplink* – The physical uplink mechanism is attached to virtual switches and enables the virtual switches to communicate with physical components in the network.

- *Virtual Network* – This mechanism is comprised of multiple virtual switches that connect virtual servers to the NAT server. In some environments, the NAT server can also be part of the virtual network.

- *Virtual Switch* – The virtual switch mechanism is used to enable connectivity between virtual servers and systems outside of the virtual switch, via the physical uplink mechanism and NAT server.

External Virtual Server Accessibility

How can virtual servers and their hosted applications be made available to cloud consumers?

Problem	Cloud consumers need to be able to access virtual servers and their hosted applications and services.
Solution	The virtual servers are connected to a virtual switch that has at least one physical uplink that is accessible to cloud consumers.
Application	The virtual switch and its physical uplink are used in combination with various networking components to make the virtual servers and their cloud services available to cloud consumers.
Mechanisms	Hypervisor, Physical Uplink, Virtual Infrastructure Manager (VIM), Virtual Switch

Problem

After a virtual server is created, it needs to be made available to external cloud consumers. Figure 6.19 depicts Virtual Servers A and B as being currently inaccessible to cloud consumers. Virtual Server A has one virtual NIC attached to it that is connected to Virtual Switch A, which is an internal virtual switch only. This virtual server can communicate with Virtual Server C, which is connected to the same virtual switch but not connected with any cloud consumers. Virtual Server B, on the other hand, cannot communicate with Virtual Servers A or C or with any cloud consumers.

Figure 6.19

Virtual Servers A and B currently cannot communicate with any cloud consumers.

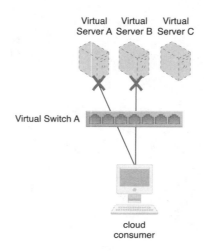

Solution

Each virtual server that needs to be accessible to cloud consumers has at least one attached or installed virtual NIC. Furthermore, the NIC needs to be connected to a virtual switch that can be accessed by the cloud consumers, as shown in Figure 6.20.

Figure 6.20

Cloud consumers can communicate with the virtual servers after the virtual switch's physical uplinks have been implemented.

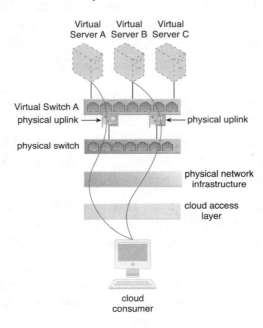

Application

Before applying this pattern, the virtual switch uses the physical uplink mechanism to connect to the physical network and become accessible. Adding the physical uplinks and configuring them properly enables the virtual switch to forward the traffic to the physical network. Also, each virtual server needs to have a minimum of one virtual NIC installed. The virtual NIC needs to be connected to the virtual switch before cloud consumers can send and receive traffic to and from the virtual servers.

Between the cloud consumer and virtual switch uplink, there exist a number of different layers of networking and security devices and mechanisms that control and forward traffic to the virtual switch. These components are out of the scope of this pattern. Note that the functionality of this pattern can be improved by applying it together with the Load Balanced Virtual Switches (57) and Redundant Physical Connection for Virtual Servers (132) patterns.

If the physical uplink of the virtual switch becomes unavailable, then the virtual servers themselves also become isolated and inaccessible. The Redundant Physical Connection for Virtual Servers (132) pattern can be applied to prevent this from occurring. Also, the virtual servers may become temporarily inaccessible or delayed in responding to requests if the physical uplink's bandwidth limit is reached. The Load Balanced Virtual Switches (57) pattern can be applied to prevent the virtual switch's physical uplinks from becoming a bottleneck.

Mechanisms

- *Hypervisor* – This mechanism is used to host virtual servers, and to establish virtual switches and the virtual switches' physical connectivity.

- *Physical Uplink* – This mechanism is used to connect virtual switches to physical switches and other physical components in the network, such as routers, firewalls, and physical servers.

- *Virtual Infrastructure Manager (VIM)* – This mechanism is used for creating and managing virtual switches, attaching and detaching their physical uplinks, and configuring the connectivity between virtual servers and physical uplinks via virtual switches.

- *Virtual Switch* – This mechanism enables virtual servers to communicate with cloud consumers via their attached physical uplinks, or via the uplinks connected to physical switches.

Problem	Virtual servers need to be moved between different models and/or different brands of hypervisors within or across different environments.
Solution	The virtual server is converted and/or exported into a common, supported format that is imported into the destination hypervisor.
Application	The OVF format is the most commonly used and supported format for virtual server exporting and importing.
Mechanisms	Cloud Storage Device, Hypervisor, Live VM Migration, Physical Uplink, Virtual Appliance, Virtual CPU, Virtual Disk, Virtual Infrastructure Manager (VIM), Virtual Network, Virtual Server Snapshot, Virtual Server State Manager, Virtual Switch

Problem

A virtual server and its hosted cloud services need to be moved to another hypervisor. However, the destination hypervisor is of a different brand or model that is incompatible with the virtual server.

Figure 6.21 depicts a scenario in which Cloud Service A is hosted on Virtual Server A. A component within the Cloud Service A architecture needs to be upgraded to a new version, but the new version requires Virtual Server A's operating system to be upgraded. The new operating system is not supported by Hypervisor A but is supported by Hypervisor B. However, Virtual Server A is not compatible with Hypervisor B because the two hypervisors are from different vendors.

Figure 6.21

Cloud Service A on Virtual Server A needs to be moved from Hypervisor A to Hypervisor B. The hypervisors are from different vendors.

Cloud Service A

Virtual Server A

Hypervisor A   Hypervisor B

Alternatively, a virtual server may need to be moved into an entirely new cloud that is operated and managed by a different cloud provider. In the following example shown in Figure 6.22, Virtual Server A and its hosted Cloud Service A need to be moved from Cloud A to Cloud B. However, the two clouds are operated by different cloud providers, leading to a range of incompatibilities.

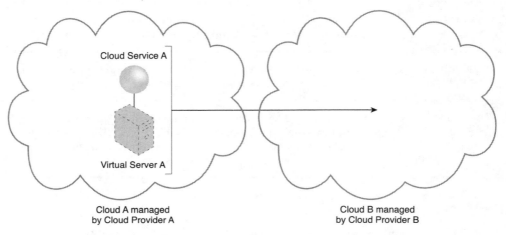

Figure 6.22

Virtual Server A needs to be moved from Cloud A to Cloud B, which is owned by a different cloud provider.

Solution

The virtual server is converted and exported from the original hypervisor into a format that can be recognized and imported at the destination hypervisor. Specifically, the standard open virtualization format is used to convert the virtual server to the Open Virtualization Format (OVF), as illustrated in Figures 6.23 and 6.24.

There may be no relationship between the two cloud environments that need to undergo a cross-cloud transition, in which case a method of moving the data from the origin cloud to the destination cloud will be required. This copying process can be performed via long-distance storage replication, file server, and data transfer or backup tapes.

Figure 6.23

Virtual Server A is exported to an OVF package at the origin hypervisor, and then imported from the OVF package to the destination hypervisor.

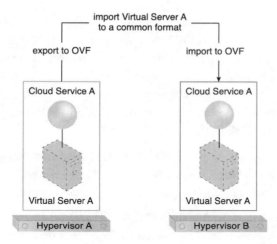

Figure 6.24

Virtual Server A is exported into an OVF package at Cloud A, and then imported from the OVF package into Cloud B.

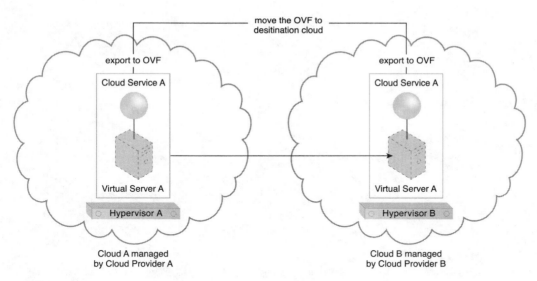

Application

Exporting the virtual server into OVF may require a system outage that needs to last until the OVF has been successfully transferred, imported, and powered on, to ensure that no changes have been made to the system. In some cases, manual human interaction may be required to configure the virtual server in the destination cloud. The virtual switch or virtual switch port configuration settings of the imported virtual server may also need to be modified.

Note that a cloud provider may publish required APIs on the usage and administration portal in order to provide cloud consumers with an opportunity to export/import their virtual servers in an IaaS delivery model. Also note that multiple virtual servers can be exported and imported together as a bundled workload.

Figure 6.25 lists the common steps required to apply this pattern.

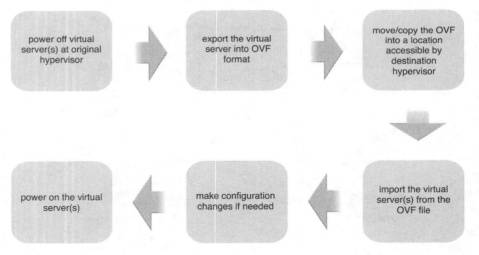

Figure 6.25
The six steps involved in the application of the Cross-Hypervisor Workload Mobility pattern.

Mechanisms

- *Cloud Storage Device* – This mechanism is used to host virtual server folders, which contain configuration files, log files, and virtual disks. During the migration process, this mechanism stores the virtual servers that have been converted into OVF format at the source location. At the destination location, the cloud storage device is used to copy the OVF file from the source, and hosts the virtual server folders after the virtual server is imported from the OVF file.

- *Hypervisor* – This mechanism is used to host virtual servers at both source and destination locations, and also provides features for exporting and importing virtual servers to and from OVF format.

- *Live VM Migration* – If both the source and destination locations are using a compatible hypervisor brand and version, this mechanism can be used to migrate virtual servers from one location to another without service interruption.

- *Physical Uplink* – This mechanism is used to establish connectivity between virtual switches and physical switches, in order to enable virtual servers to communicate with other virtual servers, cloud services, and cloud consumers.

- *Virtual Appliance* – The virtual appliance mechanism acts as a container that holds converted virtual servers and virtual server configurations. Use of this mechanism enables virtual servers to be imported pre-configured and pre-deployed.

- *Virtual CPU* – This mechanism is used to virtualize physical CPU for virtual servers, and provides the virtual servers with CPU frequency and CPU scheduling so that they can use the CPU resources for data processing.

- *Virtual Disk* – Virtual servers use this mechanism as persistent storage to store operating systems, applications, and data. Virtual disks are encapsulated into an OVF package during the migration process.

- *Virtual Infrastructure Manager (VIM)* – This mechanism is used to establish connectivity to the hypervisors at the source and destination locations in order to create OVF packages and import the packages at the destination location.

- *Virtual Network* – This mechanism is used to establish connectivity between virtual servers.

- *Virtual Server Snapshot* – If the current operating state of a virtual server needs to be retained before shutting down, this mechanism is used to create a point-in-time replica of the virtual server.

- *Virtual Server State Manager* – This mechanism is used to restore virtual servers to a snapshot point that had been taken previously.

- *Virtual Switch* – The virtual switch mechanism is used to establish connectivity for virtual servers to other virtual servers connected to different virtual switches, to cloud consumers, and to other physical servers and services via the use of the physical uplink mechanism.

Problem	A virtual server needs to be hosted on a particular host.
Solution	Affinity rules are used to ensure that the desired virtual server or workload is hosted on the target host.
Application	Affinity rules are applied and configured via the application of this pattern, and are dedicated and controlled by the VIM server.
Mechanisms	Hypervisor, Live VM Migration, Virtual Infrastructure Manager (VIM)

Problem

There are a number of reasons why a virtual server is only allowed to run on a specific operating system or application. Its desired computing capacity may only be available on a particular host, or it may need to be hosted by multiple hosts.

Figure 6.26 depicts a scenario in which the system administrator needs to make sure that Virtual Server A is only hosted on Hypervisors A and B. This may be because Hypervisors C and D are incompatible with Virtual Server A's operating system, or because Hypervisors C and D cannot accommodate the amount of physical resources required by Virtual Server A. This example is comprised of four hypervisors participating in a hypervisor cluster.

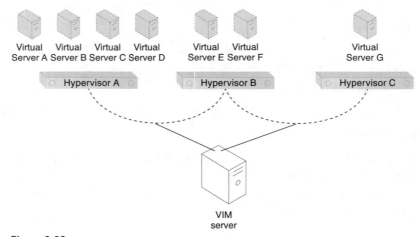

Figure 6.26

Virtual Server A can only be hosted on two of the four hypervisors belonging to a hypervisor cluster.

The Load Balanced Virtual Server Instances (51) pattern is applied to balance the virtual servers' workload across the hypervisors. The load balanced virtual server instances system attempts to balance the virtual servers' workload between Hypervisors A, B, and C, resulting in a distributed workload like the one shown in Figure 6.27.

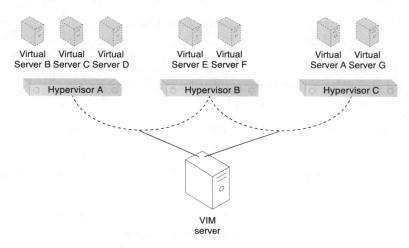

Figure 6.27

The virtual servers' workload is more evenly distributed between Hypervisors A, B, and C.

However, as a result of applying the pattern, Virtual Server A is moved to a hypervisor that is not Hypervisor A or B. This can conflict with its own hosting requirements or requirements set by the virtual server's applications or services, cloud consumer, or system administrator.

Solution

Affinity rules are used to ensure that the desired virtual server or workload is hosted on the target host. This guarantees that Virtual Server A can be moved between and hosted on only Hypervisors A and B. Virtual Server A will failover only to Hypervisor B, if Hypervisor A fails. Furthermore, when the load-balanced virtual server instances system is balancing the workload and Virtual Server A needs to be moved, it can only be moved to Hypervisor B.

Application

Virtual server-to-host affinity rules will be defined for and applied to Virtual Server A on the VIM server. These rules are broadcast to the hosts, and have the following impacts on failover and workload balancing:

- If workload balancing requires Virtual Server A to be moved from Hypervisor A, the VIM server dictates that it can only be moved to Hypervisor B.

- If Hypervisor A fails and the rest of the hypervisor cluster wants to power on the failed virtual servers, the other hypervisors will know that Virtual Server A can only be powered on at Hypervisor B.

Figures 6.28 and 6.29 illustrate the steps involved in applying the Virtual Server-to-Host Affinity pattern as follows:

1. The affinity rules are defined and cascaded by the VIM server so that Virtual Server A will only be hosted by Hypervisors A or B.

2. These affinity rules are attached to Virtual Server A and apply whenever Virtual Server A needs to be moved to or powered on at another hypervisor.

3. When the load-balanced virtual server instances system attempts to move the virtual servers to another hypervisor, it sees the affinity rule defined for the virtual servers and moves Virtual Server B to Hypervisor C.

4. The load-balanced virtual server instances system moves Virtual Server A to Hypervisor A.

In the following scenario in Figure 6.29, the Load Balanced Virtual Server Instances (51) pattern is applied to balance the workload between the hypervisors to prevent Virtual Servers A and B from over-utilizing Hypervisor A, while Hypervisors B and C are under-utilized.

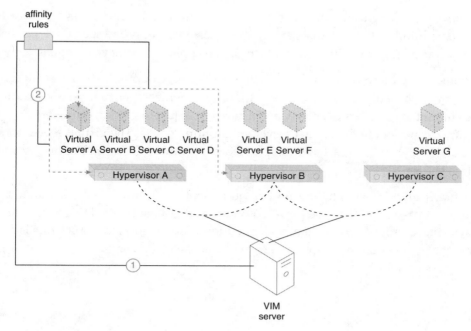

Figure 6.28

The steps involved in applying the Virtual Server-to-Host Affinity pattern are illustrated (Part I).

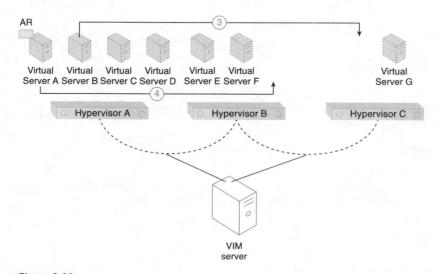

Figure 6.29

The steps involved in applying this pattern are illustrated (Part II).

In a multitenant environment, a customer may request a hypervisor as a service and want some or all of their virtual servers to be hosted on only the specific hypervisors they contracted (Figure 6.30). This pattern can be applied to achieve that goal.

Applying this pattern ensures that a virtual server or group of virtual servers can be hosted by a particular host. Imagine a scenario in which a virtual server requires a large amount of computing capacity and a hypervisor just received a hardware upgrade that can accommodate the virtual server's computing needs. The virtual server should always be hosted by this particular hypervisor, a requirement that can be met by applying this pattern.

Note that, in alignment with the affinity requirements, the virtual server will shut down if the host fails and will not be powered on at another host by the hypervisor clustering system. An affinity policy can be defined for multiple hosts to resolve this issue, to enable the hypervisor clustering system to power the virtual server on at another host in the event of failure.

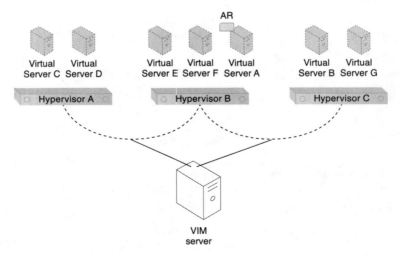

Figure 6.30

The workload is balanced between the hypervisors. Virtual Server A does not have any contact with any hypervisors other than Hypervisors A and B (Part III).

Mechanisms

- *Hypervisor* – This mechanism is used to host virtual servers individually or in groups.

- *Live VM Migration* – This mechanism checks the affinity rules defined for each virtual server before selecting the destination host hypervisor and initiating virtual server migration.

- *Virtual Infrastructure Manager (VIM)* – This mechanism is used to create, modify, remove, dictate, and control the affinity rules to ensure that virtual servers are placed on the correct host hypervisors.

Virtual Server-to-Host Anti-Affinity

How can a virtual server be guaranteed to not be hosted on a particular host or group of hosts?

Problem	A virtual server cannot be hosted on a specific host or group of hosts.
Solution	Anti-affinity rules are used to ensure that the virtual server or bundled workload will not be hosted on the target host or hosts.
Application	Virtual server-to-host anti-affinity rules are applied and configured, and controlled and dedicated by the VIM server to prevent the virtual server or workload from being hosted on the target host or group of hosts.
Mechanisms	Hypervisor, Live VM Migration, Virtual Infrastructure Manager (VIM)

Problem

A variety of reasons may prevent a virtual server or bundled workload from being allowed to be hosted on a particular host or group of hosts. These can include incompatibility between the virtual server's operating system and the target hypervisor, or the target hypervisor being unable to accommodate the amount of physical resources required by the virtual server. In such cases, a system needs to be set in place to prevent the virtual server or workload from being hosted on that particular host or group of hosts.

Figure 6.31 illustrates a scenario in which Hypervisors A and B are from two different vendors. However, Virtual Server A has not been operating normally on Hypervisor C after Hypervisor A failed.

The following steps are shown in Figures 6.32 and 6.33:

1. Hypervisor A fails.

2. The hypervisor clustering system powers on the virtual servers that were being hosted on Hypervisor A at other hypervisors, and Virtual Server B is powered on at Hypervisor B.

3. Virtual Server A is powered on at Hypervisor C.

4. Hypervisor A has failed, and the system administrator manually migrates Virtual Servers A and B between Hypervisors B and C to resolve the issue.

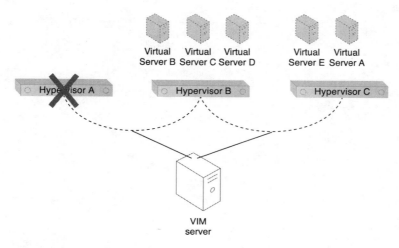

Figure 6.31

The hypervisor clustering system powers on Virtual Server A at Hypervisor C, causing instability. The system administrator had to manually move the virtual server to Hypervisor A in order to ensure it will operate normally.

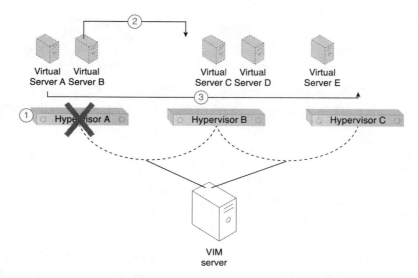

Figure 6.32

Virtual servers are powered on at different hypervisors upon Hypervisor A failure (Part I).

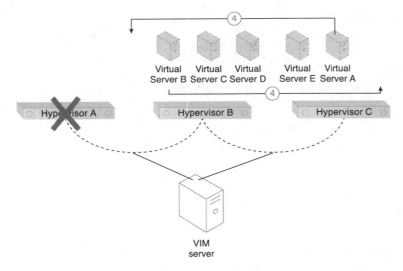

Figure 6.33

The virtual servers are migrated manually after Hypervisor A failure (Part II).

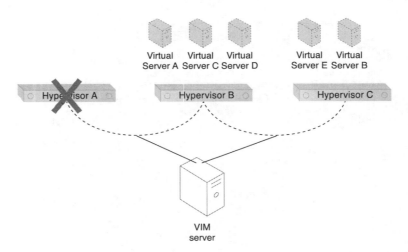

Figure 6.34

After being moved, Virtual Server A is operating normally on Hypervisor B (Part III).

After some time, the system administrator encounters performance issues with Virtual Server A and manually applies the Non-Disruptive Service Relocation (159) pattern to move Virtual Server A to Hypervisor B and Virtual Server B to Hypervisor C.

Solution

The virtual server/workload placement mechanism is used to prevent the virtual server or workload from being hosted on the target host or hosts by applying virtual server-to-host anti-affinity rules.

Application

In Figure 6.35, Virtual Server A is hosted on Hypervisor A. Hypervisors A, B, and C belong to the same hypervisor cluster. The Load Balanced Virtual Server Instances (51) pattern is applied to balance the workload across the hypervisor cluster. Virtual Server A cannot be hosted on Hypervisor C.

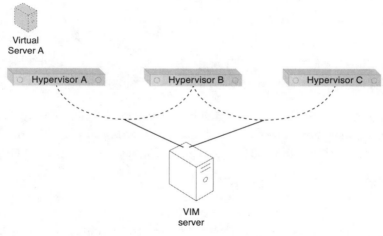

Figure 6.35

The Virtual Server-to-Host Anti-Affinity pattern is applied by configuring rules that create an anti-affinity relation between Virtual Server A and Hypervisor C. This configuration is performed via the VIM server and is replicated across the cluster.

The following steps are shown in Figure 6.36:

1. A virtual server-to-host anti-affinity rule is defined via the VIM server.

2. The rule is applied to Virtual Server C and Hypervisor C. This rule is part of Virtual Server A's profile, so that any mechanism, application, or service that needs to move Virtual Server A to another hypervisor will be made aware of the Hypervisor C limitation.

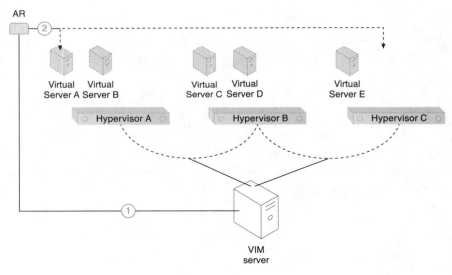

Figure 6.36

An anti-affinity rule is created and applied to the virtual server and hypervisor (Part I).

If Hypervisor A fails, the hypervisor clustering system will need to power on Virtual Server A at another hypervisor. After checking the anti-affinity rule, the hypervisor clustering system realizes that Virtual Server A cannot be powered on at Hypervisor C.

The following steps are shown in Figure 6.37:

1. Hypervisor A fails.

2. The hypervisor clustering system has to power on Virtual Servers A and B at another hypervisor. The hypervisor clustering system attempts to power on Virtual Server B at Hypervisor C.

3. Virtual Server A has an anti-affinity rule that prevents it from being hosted on Hypervisor C, so the hypervisor clustering system powers on Virtual Server A at Hypervisor B.

If the load-balanced virtual server instances system wants to move the workload between hypervisors for balancing, Virtual Server A can be moved between Hypervisors A and B only because the anti-affinity rule prevents Virtual Server A from being hosted on Hypervisor C (Figure 6.38).

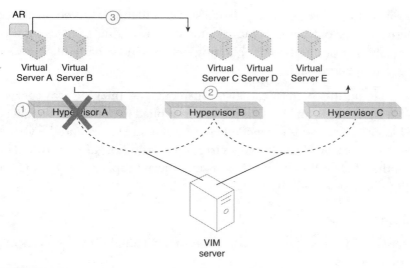

Figure 6.37

The steps involved in applying this pattern are shown (Part II).

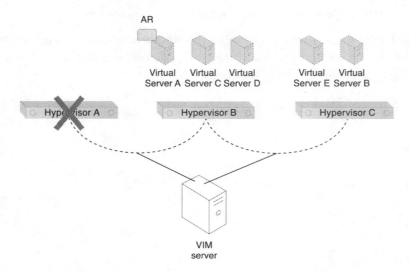

Figure 6.38

Virtual Server B is now powered on at Hypervisor C, while Virtual Server A has been powered on at Hypervisor B (Part III).

Applying this pattern ensures that a virtual server will not be hosted on a specific host. This pattern helps avoid performance degradation resulting from using a particular host, and resolves an application or operating system's incompatibility between the virtual server and hypervisor.

Note that applying this pattern can also cause outages. Imagine a hypervisor cluster comprised of Hosts A, B, and C. This pattern is applied to one of the virtual servers on Host A. This virtual server is currently being hosted on Host B, and the virtual servers that are being hosted by Host C have a virtual server-to-host affinity rule. This restriction means that if Host B fails and there is insufficient capacity on Host C, the virtual server will remain powered off.

Mechanisms

- *Hypervisor* – This mechanism is used to host individual virtual servers or groups of virtual servers.

- *Live VM Migration* – This mechanism is responsible for adhering to the defined anti-affinity rules as dictated by the virtual infrastructure manager, prior to selecting destination hosts and initiating virtual server migration.

- *Virtual Infrastructure Manager (VIM)* – This mechanism is used to create, modify, remove, dictate, and control the affinity rules that ensure that virtual servers are placed on the correct host hypervisors.

How can a virtual server and hypervisor communicate with one another securely without impacting other communication within the network?

Problem	A virtual server needs to have its communication restricted to only its host hypervisor, without affecting or having access to any other network communication.
Solution	A secure network-based channel of communication between the virtual server and hypervisor needs to be created.
Application	A new virtual switch is introduced, configured specifically to support this mode of communication.
Mechanisms	Hypervisor, Virtual Switch

Problem

A virtual server needs to communicate with only its host hypervisor, and cannot be connected to any other components within the network.

In Figure 6.39, Virtual Server A needs to be connected to only the hypervisor. The cloud consumer wants to ensure that the virtual server cannot communicate with any other virtual servers on the network.

Figure 6.39

All of the other virtual servers can communicate with Virtual Server A in the current configuration.

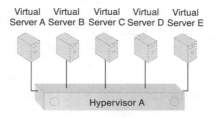

Solution

The application of this pattern primarily uses the virtual switch mechanism. Virtual Server A is isolated by implementing the virtual switches in such a way that restricts Virtual Server A's communication to only the hypervisor.

Application

This solution requires the creation of a new virtual switch that only provides connectivity to Virtual Server A and isolates this virtual server from other virtual servers. Applying the solution results in the scenario depicted in Figure 6.40.

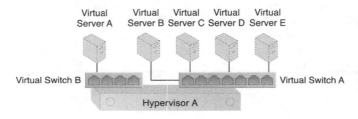

Figure 6.40

Virtual Switch B is configured to limit Virtual Server A's connectivity to the hypervisor only, which prevents Virtual Switch B from sending any of Virtual Server A's traffic to or from the network.

Applying this pattern helps achieve the level of isolation that is required by the cloud consumer by isolating Virtual Server A so that it can only communicate with the hypervisor. However, this pattern introduces an additional virtual switch, whose maintenance increases the hypervisor's overhead.

Mechanisms

- *Hypervisor* – This mechanism is used to host virtual servers and establish the virtual servers' network connectivity.

- *Virtual Switch* – The virtual switch mechanism is used for communication between virtual servers and their host hypervisors. In certain hypervisor models, a specialized virtual switch needs to be created for communication and a virtual NIC needs to be attached to the virtual servers. When a virtual switch is created in other hypervisor models, certain ports are reserved to provide this connectivity. These ports are hidden from the system administrators and can be seen and used by only the hypervisor and virtual servers.

Virtual Server-to-Virtual Server Affinity

How can a group of virtual servers and/or a bundled workload be guaranteed to be hosted by the same hypervisor?

Problem	A group of virtual servers or bundled workload needs to be hosted together on a particular host.
Solution	Affinity rules are used to ensure that the virtual server group or bundled workload is always hosted by and moved to the same destination host.
Application	Affinity rules are applied and configured via the application of the Virtual Server-to-Virtual Server Affinity pattern, and controlled and dedicated by the VIM server.
Mechanisms	Hypervisor, Live VM Migration, Virtual Infrastructure Manager (VIM)

Problem

Various situations may require multiple virtual servers or a bundled workload to be hosted together on the same hypervisor, such as the one illustrated in Figure 6.41.

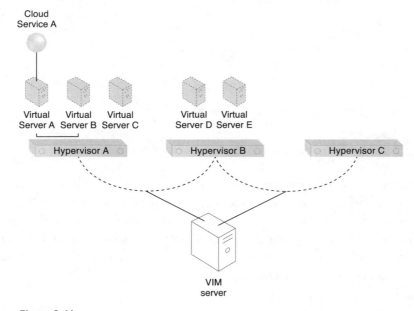

Figure 6.41

Cloud Service A is an application that uses Virtual Server B as its back-end database.

In the scenario depicted, a great deal of communication and traffic passes between Virtual Servers A and B. Cloud Service A is a delay-sensitive application whose functionality may be negatively impacted by latency. Both Virtual Servers A and B are to remain connected to the same virtual switch on the same host. This means that they will communicate only at the virtual switch layer and will not need to travel to and from the physical NICs, thereby decreasing latency. In this case, both virtual servers need to remain together even if they moved to another host.

The hypervisor clustering system will power on Virtual Servers A and B at another hypervisor if Hypervisor A fails, to result in the scenario shown in Figure 6.42.

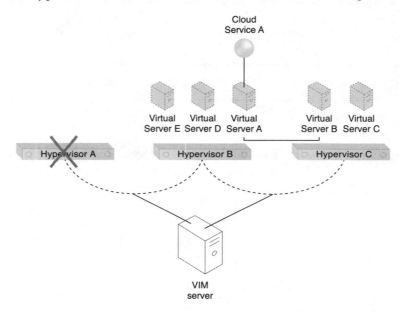

Figure 6.42
Virtual Servers A and B are powered on at Hypervisor B and Hypervisor C.

Virtual Servers A and B are placed on two different hypervisors, which means that the virtual servers' communication has to pass through the physical network and may have a performance impact on Cloud Service A's functionality. The system administrator wants to ensure that the two virtual servers will always be hosted together on the same hypervisor, and that their traffic and communication will move across only one virtual switch to prevent latency and performance issues.

Solution

The virtual server/workload placement mechanism is used to apply the virtual server-to-virtual server affinity rule to dictate a configuration that keeps the two virtual servers together. This configuration will then be replicated to the hosts and other relevant mechanisms. For instance, if Virtual Server A needs to be moved to Hypervisor B at a later date, Virtual Server B will be moved to Hypervisor B at that time automatically.

Application

To apply this pattern, the Virtual Server-to-Virtual Server Affinity rule needs to be configured on the VIM server. The VIM server then replicates this configuration to the hosts and related mechanisms. In the next scenario shown in Figure 6.43, the Hypervisor Clustering (112) and Load Balanced Virtual Server Instances (51) patterns have been applied together, and Hypervisor A fails.

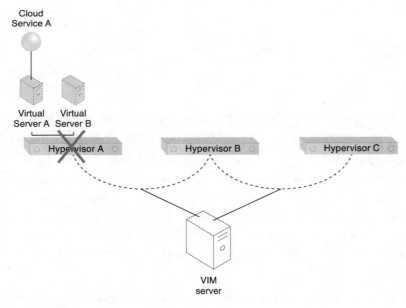

Figure 6.43
Virtual Servers A and B are powered on at Hypervisor A, which abruptly fails.

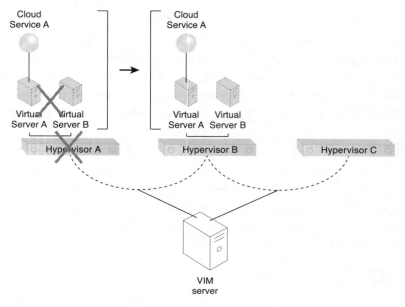

Figure 6.44

After Hypervisor A experiences failure, both virtual servers are powered on at Hypervisor B.

Since the Hypervisor Clustering pattern has been applied, Virtual Servers A and B will be powered on at another hypervisor, such as Hypervisor B (Figure 6.44).

The load-balanced virtual server instances system then balances the workload between Hypervisors B and C by moving either Virtual Server A or B to Hypervisor C. However, the defined affinity rule prevents this move to ensure that the required affinity is met and that the virtual servers are kept together. Moving both virtual servers to Hypervisor C balances the resource consumption of Hypervisors B and C, so they are moved to Hypervisor C. If there were no consumption benefits, they would have remained on Hypervisor B.

Applying this pattern helps improve service performance and decrease latency and the network traffic that travels via the physical network layer. The target virtual servers need to be connected to the same virtual switch during the application of this pattern, so that all virtual server communication will remain at the hypervisor layer and not traverse the physical NIC or physical switch. If one of the virtual servers needs to be moved, then all of the virtual servers that are part of the affinity policy will need to be moved together. This can result in an enormous workload, as well as a great deal of service relocation. If the underlying host fails, it will need to be confirmed that the host's computing capacity can accommodate all of the virtual servers' capacity requirements.

Mechanisms

- *Hypervisor* – This mechanism is used to host virtual servers and can host multiple virtual servers together.

- *Live VM Migration* – This mechanism is responsible for ensuring correct virtual server hosting, by checking and adhering to any relevant affinity rules prior to selecting the destination host for migration.

- *Virtual Infrastructure Manager (VIM)* – This mechanism is used to create, modify, and remove any affinity rules dictating which virtual servers need to be kept together. These policies are forwarded to the hypervisor and live VM migration mechanisms prior to virtual server migration.

Problem	Certain virtual servers or bundled workloads need to be hosted on different hosts.
Solution	Anti-affinity rules are used to ensure that the virtual servers or bundled workload are never simultaneously hosted together by the same destination host.
Application	Affinity rules are applied and configured by the application of the Virtual Server-to-Virtual Server Anti-Affinity pattern, and are controlled and dedicated by the VIM server.
Mechanisms	Hypervisor, Live VM Migration, Virtual Infrastructure Manager (VIM)

Problem

Certain situations require two or more virtual servers or workloads to be hosted on different hypervisors. In Figure 6.45, there is a strict security requirement that Virtual Servers A and B cannot share the same hosting hypervisor. Virtual Server A is accessible to both internal and external users, while Virtual Server B is only accessible to internal users and runs a highly critical application.

Virtual Server B needs to be hosted in a different location in case Hypervisor A becomes compromised, so that its failure does not impact Virtual Server B. Consider a scenario in which the solution that was originally implemented resembles the environment in Figure 6.46.

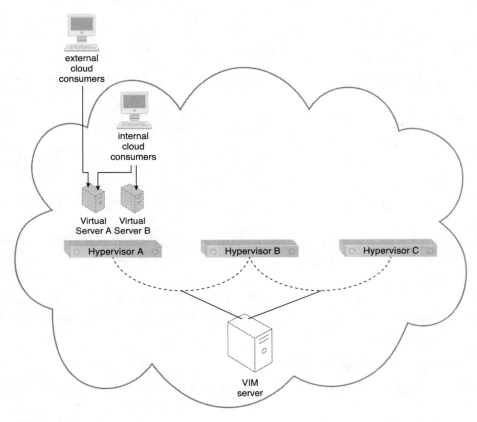

Figure 6.45
Virtual Servers A and B are being hosted by Hypervisor A, and need to be hosted on different hypervisors.

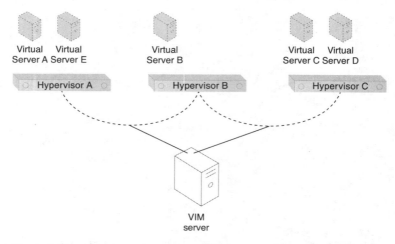

Figure 6.46
Virtual Server B is being hosted by Hypervisor B.

If Hypervisor B fails, the hypervisor clustering system will power on Virtual Server B at either Hypervisor A or C. Virtual Server B is powered on at Hypervisor A, resulting in the scenario depicted in Figure 6.47.

1. Hypervisor B experiences failure.

2. Virtual Server B is powered on at Hypervisor A to join Virtual Servers A and E.

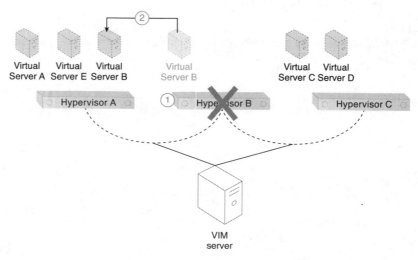

Figure 6.47
Virtual Server B is moved to Hypervisor A.

The hypervisor clustering system ends up powering on Virtual Server B at Hypervisor A, which violates the pre-defined requirements because both Virtual Servers A and B are now being hosted on the same hypervisor.

Solution

A system that guarantees that Virtual Servers A and B will always be hosted on separate hypervisors is used to address this problem. The solution is implemented via the VIM server, and applies virtual server-to-virtual server anti-affinity rules to prevent the two virtual servers from being hosted on the same host at the same time.

Application

The virtual server-to-virtual server anti-affinity rules are configured for Virtual Servers A and B. This configuration will then be replicated to the hosts and any relevant applications and mechanisms. For instance, Virtual Server A will be placed on Hypervisor A and Virtual Server B placed on Hypervisor B, as shown in Figure 6.48.

1. The virtual server-to-virtual server anti-affinity rule (AR) is defined via the VIM server.

2. The rule is applied to Virtual Servers A and B.

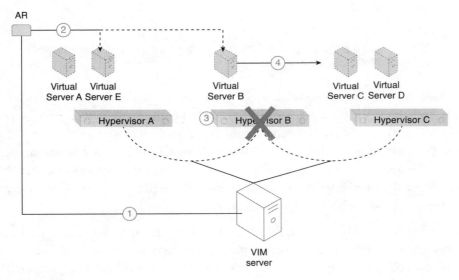

Figure 6.48
The steps comprising the application of the pattern are illustrated (Part I).

3. Hypervisor B crashes. The hypervisor clustering system needs to power on Virtual Server B elsewhere. However, the system will not allow Virtual Server B to be powered on at Hypervisor A because of the anti-affinity rule defined for Virtual Servers A and B.

4. Virtual Server B is powered on at Hypervisor C.

Figure 6.49 depicts the scenario that results after Hypervisor B fails.

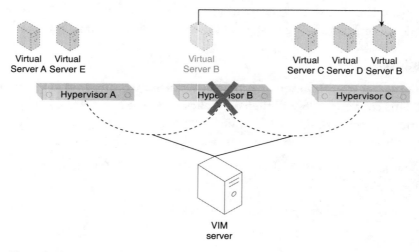

Figure 6.49

Virtual Server B is moved to Hypervisor C, after the system learns of the anti-affinity rule defined for Virtual Servers A and B (Part II).

The same holds true if the Load Balanced Virtual Server Instances (51) pattern has been applied and either Virtual Server A or B needs to be manually moved. If multiple virtual servers are running similar capacity-intensive applications, the virtual servers may need to be separated to be hosted on different hypervisors in order to sustain service-level performance. Applying this pattern provides a feature that ensures that the virtual servers will not be hosted on the same host, although outages are more likely since the number of possible hosting locations is reduced.

For instance, imagine a scenario in which two hosts have failed. The only host that can host the virtual servers is currently hosting a virtual server that is part of this anti-affinity rule, meaning the virtual servers will face downtime. This problem can be eliminated by using a scaled-out hypervisor cluster instead of a scaled-up architecture. Conversely, the number of hosts in the scaled-up architecture can be increased, or more physical computing capacity can be added to the hosts.

Mechanisms

- *Hypervisor* – This mechanism is used to host virtual servers, and can be further used as an isolation point whenever a virtual server has an anti-affinity rule defined against another virtual server. The second virtual server will always be hosted on a different hypervisor than the original virtual server.

- *Live VM Migration* – Virtual servers need to be migrated in accordance with any applicable virtual server-to-virtual server anti-affinity rules, so that virtual servers that have anti-affinity rules defined against another virtual server will be hosted on different hypervisors.

- *Virtual Infrastructure Manager (VIM)* – This mechanism is used for defining, modifying, and advertising the virtual server-to-virtual server anti-affinity rules. The hypervisor and live VM migration mechanisms adhere to these rules prior to migrating, powering on, or restarting any virtual server.

Stateless Hypervisor

How can a hypervisor be deployed with a minimal amount of downtime, while allowing for quick updating and upgrading?

Problem	A method of deploying hypervisors that allows them to be easily updated and upgraded without causing too much downtime is required.
Solution	A hypervisor is booted from a boot image and its configurations are loaded every time the hypervisor restarts.
Application	A boot server that can load a given hypervisor and its configurations into memory every time the hypervisor restarts is implemented.
Mechanisms	Cloud Storage Device, Virtual Infrastructure Manager (VIM)

Problem

Updating all the hypervisors across a larger cloud environment is a time-consuming procedure that introduces room for human error. Maintaining version consistency across the hypervisors further becomes an issue if the environment has a larger number of hypervisors. For instance, a cloud environment that contains 600 hypervisors would require a lengthy amount of time to update all of the hypervisors and deploy their security patches, a process which would need to be repeated on a regular basis.

Solution

In Figure 6.50, the hypervisor image is booted up into the host's memory and the configuration parameters are applied to the hypervisor to make it ready for operation.

Figure 6.50

The components involved in applying this pattern and their interactions are shown.

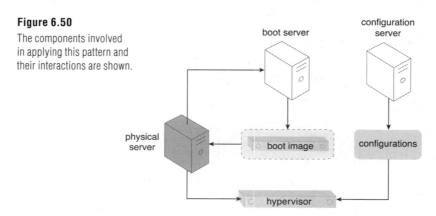

Application

A boot server that contains and maintains the last tested boot image is required in order to apply the solution (Figure 6.51). A configuration server that stores and maintains the configuration settings for the hypervisor is also required (Figure 6.52).

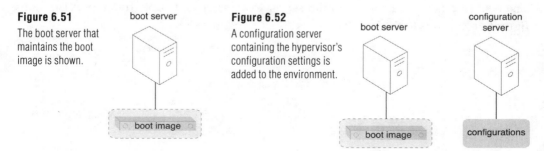

Figure 6.51
The boot server that maintains the boot image is shown.

Figure 6.52
A configuration server containing the hypervisor's configuration settings is added to the environment.

Every raw physical server that powers on has to locate the boot server via a certain method of communication, which is, in this case, the dynamic host configuration protocol (DHCP) server. As shown in Figure 6.53, the DHCP server is used to allocate the IP address to the hypervisor every time it powers on and point the hypervisor to the boot server.

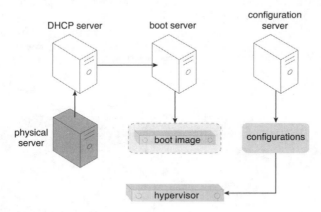

Figure 6.53
The DHCP server points the hypervisor to the boot server when it powers on.

After every restart, DHCP provides the physical server with the IP address and points the physical server to the boot server. The boot server transfers the boot image to the physical server, which loads the boot image into memory. The hypervisor is now up and running, as shown in Figure 6.54.

The next step is for the configuration server to transfer and apply the hypervisor configuration settings to the hypervisor, as shown in Figure 6.55.

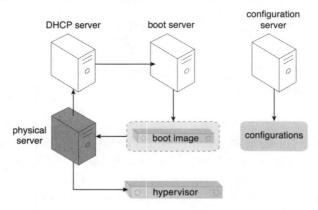

Figure 6.54
After the physical server loads the boot into its memory, the hypervisor is powered on and becomes operational.

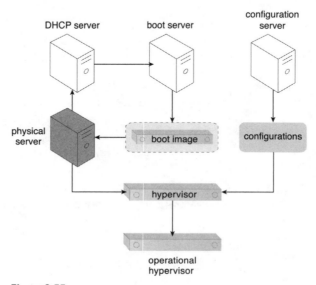

Figure 6.55
The configuration settings are applied to the hypervisor, which becomes operational.

Application of this pattern reduces the amount of time required to deploy hypervisors and eliminates the need to maintain and update each hypervisor individually, since updating the boot image upgrades each hypervisor to the latest version after its next reboot. However, if a corrupted boot image is used, then each hypervisor that reboots after loading the corrupted image will become impacted.

Also, in the event that the DHCP server, boot server, and/or configuration server are unavailable, none of the impacted hypervisors will be able to recover from the reboot. This risk can be mitigated by implementing a solution that allows hypervisors to save the latest boot image on the local hard disk so that they can boot from the local boot image. However, it is recommended for the solution components to be highly available to prevent this situation from occurring entirely.

Stateless hypervisors are hypervisors that are installed on a physical server. These hypervisors store their configurations and settings in allocated local cloud storage devices, which limits the hypervisor in a number of ways. They are also not installed or configured on the local or remote storage. As a result, no configurations and settings are stored locally in the hypervisor's local or remote storage. In this type of hypervisor, a hypervisor boot image is loaded to the server's RAM. The hypervisor configurations and settings are loaded after the boot image is loaded into the RAM. Improving consistency, security, confidentiality, and data integrity requires stateless hypervisor communications with deployment servers and VIM servers to be physically isolated. Note that mechanisms like a vLAN can be used instead of a physical channel. Stateless hypervisor communications are to be conducted over a secure and encrypted channel. Figure 6.56 depicts how stateless hypervisors boot up and become operational.

1. The physical server powers on and sends a request over the network to locate the deployment server.

2. The deployment server sends the hypervisor boot image to the physical server. The physical server loads the hypervisor boot image into the RAM.

3. The hypervisor is loaded after the boot image has been loaded into the RAM. The hypervisor locates the VIM server and sends a configuration request to the server.

4. The VIM server sends the configurations and settings to the hypervisor.

5. The hypervisor loads the configurations and settings into the RAM and applies them as instructed by the VIM server.

6. The hypervisor is ready to operate and can power on the virtual servers.

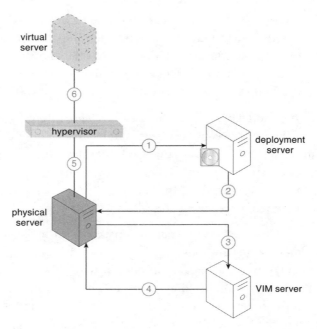

Figure 6.56

A stateless hypervisor becomes operational after this pattern is applied.

Mechanisms

- *Cloud Storage Device* – This mechanism is used to store temporary boot images, as well as the boot image that physical servers need to use to load the hypervisor image into memory for operation.

- *Virtual Infrastructure Manager (VIM)* – This mechanism is used to create and set the required configurations prior to booting the image to the physical servers. The VIM can also be used to create certain configuration policies to boot a specific image on a specific server, or to load certain configurations on each physical server after booting the hypervisor.

Chapter 7

Monitoring, Provisioning and Administration Patterns

Usage Monitoring

Pay-as-You-Go

Realtime Resource Availability

Rapid Provisioning

Platform Provisioning

Bare-Metal Provisioning

Automated Administration

Centralized Remote Administration

Resource Management

Self-Provisioning

Power Consumption Reduction

A primary goal for cloud providers is to deliver not only affordable but easy-to-use resources for organizational computing requirements. The patterns in this chapter are primarily provided in support of that goal.

Monitoring and situational awareness are enabled by patterns such as Usage Monitoring (285), Pay-as-You-Go (288), and Realtime Resource Availability (292) supporting cloud consumers with critical SLA assessment and verification capabilities.

Automated Administration (310) is an example of a solution to how the cloud provider can automate provisioning requirements met on-demand. This pattern can be combined with Centralized Remote Administration (315) and Rapid Provisioning (295) in support of Platform Provisioning (301) to relieve cloud consumers of the burden of implementing the underlying infrastructure of their cloud environments.

Problem	IT resources that are shared can generate a variety of runtime scenarios that, if not tracked and responded to, can cause numerous failure, performance, and security concerns and can further make usage-based reporting and billing impossible.
Solution	Cloud usage monitors are utilized to track and measure the quantity and nature of runtime IT resource usage activity.
Application	Various specialized cloud usage monitors can be incorporated into a cloud architecture, most of which will interact with other IT resources to transfer or process collected usage data.
Mechanisms	Audit Monitor, Automated Scaling Listener, Cloud Usage Monitor, Load Balancer, Pay-Per-Use Monitor, SLA Monitor

Problem

When making IT resources available for access and shared usage by multiple cloud consumers, the manner in which actual usage occurs can be highly unpredictable. IT resources may be subject to high usage volumes by individual cloud consumers performing a large amount of runtime processing or high volumes of cloud service consumers concurrently accessing the virtualized instances of the IT resources. Either way, infinite runtime scenarios can develop, leading to possible runtime exception conditions, security breaches, and other types of runtime failure.

Furthermore, for IT resources and cloud services to be commercialized in support of the Pay-as-You-Go (288) pattern, the cloud architecture needs to support the ability for runtime usage to be accurately measured.

Solution

IT artifacts and systems capable of monitoring, collecting and processing usage data and metrics are incorporated into the cloud architecture to enable the inherent measured usage characteristic of cloud environments, and to further offer a range of specialized usage monitoring and data collection functions (Figure 7.1).

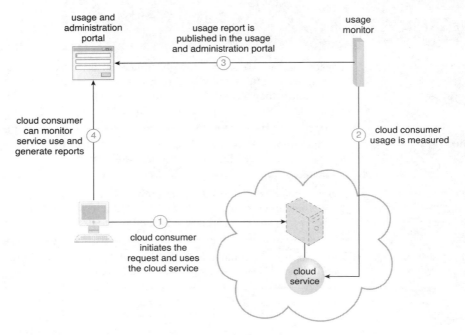

Figure 7.1

A usage monitor measures IT resource use and collects corresponding usage data that is stored and made available for reporting purposes.

Application

This pattern is fundamentally applied via the use of the cloud usage monitor mechanism. This broad, infrastructure-level mechanism encompasses a variety of specialized monitoring-based mechanisms that fulfill different forms of usage monitoring requirements and can be implemented as a monitoring agent, resource agent, or polling agent.

Regardless of which type of cloud usage monitor is used, there are common components that can accompany the implementation of a monitoring IT resource:

- *Usage Monitoring Station* – A system that the cloud usage monitor directly communicates with and to which it may transmit collected usage data.

- *Usage Database* – A repository used to store usage data received by usage monitoring stations or directly by cloud usage monitors.

- *Data Saver* – A middleware component used to save and update collected usage data.

- *Usage Reporter* – A middleware component used to retrieve usage data from the usage database and present it in human-readable reports. The usage reporter is generally integrated with a usage and administration portal.

- *Custom Reporter* – A tool used to design custom usage reports.

Mechanisms

- *Audit Monitor* – This mechanism is a used when auditing-related usage monitoring is required.

- *Automated Scaling Listener* – The mechanism is used when monitoring pertaining to dynamic scaling is required.

- *Cloud Usage Monitor* – This mechanism represents a range of specialized monitoring programs and agents that can fulfill specialized applications of this pattern.

- *Load Balancer* – This monitor appraises runtime workload usage prior to carrying out load balancing algorithms.

- *Pay-Per-Use Monitor* – This mechanism is used when billing-related usage monitoring is required.

- *SLA Monitor* – This mechanism is used when quality-of-service and other SLA-related usage monitoring is required.

Pay-as-You-Go

How can a cloud consumer be billed accurately for the actual amount of its IT resource usage?

Problem	Purchasing or leasing an entire IT resource can lead to fees significantly disproportionate to the actual amount that the IT resource is utilized.
Solution	A system is introduced to measure actual IT resource consumption at a granular level and to correspondingly bill only for the measured usage.
Application	Runtime usage monitoring is enabled to track actual IT resource usage and a billing system is established to process collected usage data into billing information.
Mechanisms	Billing Management System, Cloud Usage Monitor, Pay-Per-Use Monitor

Problem

When purchasing an IT resource, such as a physical server, the total cost of purchase and subsequent ownership may not correspond with the return on investment (ROI) of the server's actual runtime usage. Similarly, when leasing an IT resource for a fixed fee (or when leasing coarse portions of an IT resource at fixed fees), the amount of actual usage of the IT resource may not correspond to the capacity for which fees were charged (Figure 7.2).

Solution

A cloud architecture is established that is capable of collecting actual cloud consumer usage data and providing it to a management system used to process and report actual cloud consumer usage data for billing and chargeback purposes.

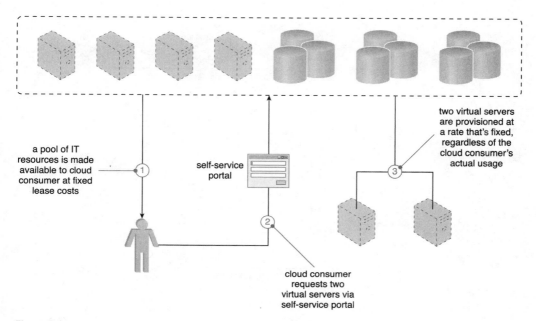

Figure 7.2

A cloud consumer that leases and pays fixed fees for two entire virtual servers may not actually use their entire processing capacity.

Application

This pattern is applied together with the Usage Monitoring (285) pattern to establish the use of the pay-per-use monitor mechanism as the primary component responsible for collecting and storing billing-related usage data at runtime. Also implemented by this pattern is the billing management system mechanism that processes, reports on, and generates billing information and documents based on the collected usage data.

The following steps are shown in Figure 7.3:

1. The cloud consumer accesses the cloud service via the usage and administration portal.

2. The pay-per-use monitor logs the usage data.

3. The pay-per-use monitor sends usage data to a usage monitor station.

4. The data from the pay-per-use monitor is normalized and saved to a usage database.

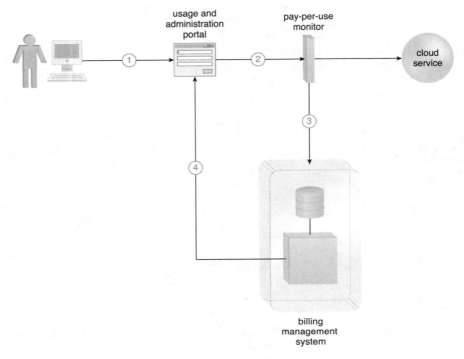

Figure 7.3
A basic cloud architecture resulting from the application of the Pay-as-You-Go pattern.

A human-readable report of realtime usage is published on the usage and administration portal for the cloud consumer to view.

Related components that can also comprise this cloud architecture include:

- *Data Source Loader* – A program that collects data from a usage database and delivers it to the chargeback calculation engine for processing.

- *Chargeback Calculation Engine* – After retrieving the required data, this engine generates chargeback or billing documents based on the cloud provider's pricing metrics.

- *Chargeback Database* – After determining the charges for usage, this information is stored in a database for future use and reporting.

Note that a given billing management system may include some or all of these components. Figure 7.4 shows a cloud architecture comprised of pay-per-usage and billing components.

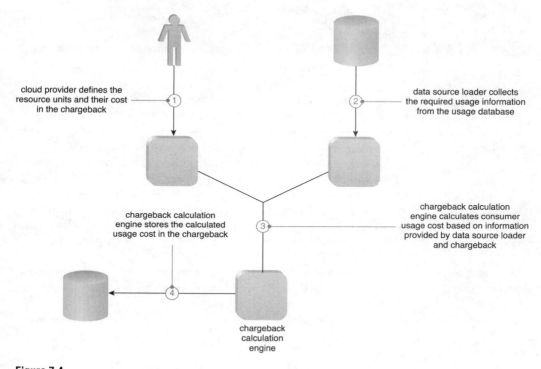

cloud provider defines the
resource units and their cost
in the chargeback

data source loader collects
the required usage information
from the usage database

chargeback calculation
engine stores the calculated
usage cost in the chargeback

chargeback calculation
engine calculates consumer
usage cost based on information
provided by data source loader
and chargeback

chargeback
calculation
engine

Figure 7.4

An example of a cloud architecture comprised of pay-per-usage and billing components.

Mechanisms

- *Billing Management System* – This fundamental mechanism is responsible for calculating recurring service costs in accordance with the goals of this pattern.

- *Cloud Usage Monitor* – Specialized cloud usage monitors may collect IT resource usage information that is stored in a usage database that may be used by the billing management system for some of its calculations.

- *Pay-Per-Use Monitor* – This monitor is core to the application of the Pay-as-You-Go pattern in that it is responsible for collecting runtime IT resource usage data used by the billing management system.

Realtime Resource Availability

How can cloud consumers access current availability status information for IT resources?

Problem	Conventional IT resource usage and status reporting occurs at some point subsequent to the corresponding collection of usage and status data. This delay makes it impossible for cloud consumers to determine the current availability and status of a given IT resource.
Solution	A monitoring and reporting system is established to provide realtime (or near realtime) reporting of IT resource availability and status information.
Application	The status of an IT resource is constantly monitored and transmitted to a monitoring station from which an availability reporter extracts and streams the usage data to a portal where it can be viewed and monitored by the cloud consumer.
Mechanisms	Audit Monitor, Cloud Usage Monitor, SLA Management System, SLA Monitor

Problem

An SLA includes various metrics to define service quality guarantees, a primary one of which is service availability. For a cloud consumer to be able to check on and assess the availability of a cloud service or IT resource, it needs to be able to receive up-to-date availability information on-demand. Most management systems used in clouds provide tools for generating usage and status reports after data is collected and stored and then subsequently requested by cloud consumers or cloud providers. The final step is for the data to be presented and rendered in a report. Because of the time it takes to complete these steps, the cloud consumer is given only historical availability data.

Solution

The system established by this pattern is similar to conventional usage data collecting and reporting architectures in that it consists of a usage monitor that collects the availability data and sends it to a monitoring station for storage. What distinguishes this system is the use of an availability reporter component that is capable of instantly retrieving and streaming the availability data so that it can be sent, on an on-going basis, to a front-end for viewing.

Application

This pattern is commonly applied together with the Centralized Remote Administration (315) pattern, as the usage and administration portal is generally the most convenient location for the streamed availability data to be displayed.

The following steps are shown in Figure 7.5:

1. A specialized monitor (not shown) collects and stores availability data in a dedicated database as part of a monitoring station.

2. The availability reporter instantly extrapolates the availability data from the monitoring station and streams it to the usage and administration portal.

3. The cloud consumer can view the realtime stream of availability report data via the usage and administration portal.

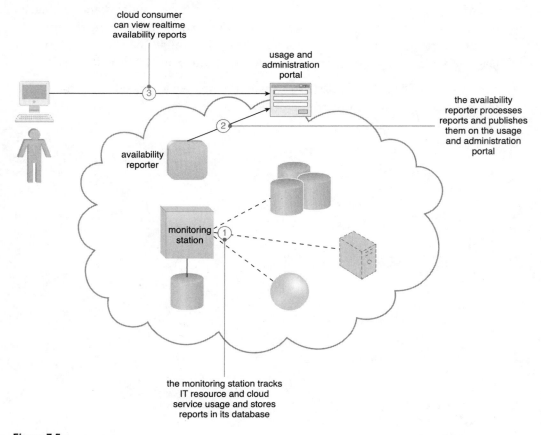

Figure 7.5

A cloud architecture resulting from the application of the Realtime Resource Availability pattern.

In the absence of a usage and administration portal, a separate service availability portal can be created, dedicated to the display of IT resource availability and status data. This type of system can also involve the use of a report access manager to manage the list of authorized IT resources for which a given cloud consumer can view availability and status data.

Mechanisms

- *Audit Monitor* – The audit monitor mechanism is related to this pattern in how it audits realtime IT resource availability data and the publication of the availability reports themselves.

- *Cloud Usage Monitor* – Specialized cloud usage monitors may track runtime usage data relevant to the reporting of IT resource availability information.

- *SLA Management System* – The SLA availability guarantees inputted and managed by this system directly relate to the availability reporting produced by the application of this pattern. The SLA availability metrics and values may be displayed on a usage and administration portal alongside the realtime availability data.

- *SLA Monitor* – The SLA monitor mechanism is responsible for collecting the uptime and availability information of IT resources.

Rapid Provisioning

How can the provisioning of IT resources be automated and made available to cloud consumers on-demand?

Problem	When a cloud consumer chooses what IT resources it would like to lease, having the actual provisioning of these IT resources performed manually can require too much time and human interaction to be sufficiently effective and responsive.
Solution	A system can be established to execute and coordinate the automation of a range of provisioning tasks and processes.
Application	Complex auto-provisioning systems can be assembled, each generally comprised of a rapid provisioning engine and an automated provisioning program.
Mechanisms	Cloud Storage Device, Hypervisor, Resource Replication, Virtual Server

Problem

A conventional provisioning process can involve a number of tasks that are traditionally completed manually by administrators and technology experts that prepare the requested IT resources as per pre-packaged specifications or as per custom client requests. In cloud environments, where higher volumes of customers are serviced and where the average customer requests higher volumes of IT resources, manual provisioning processes are inadequate and can even lead to unreasonable risk due to uncompetitive response times and human error.

For example, consider a cloud consumer that requests 25 Windows servers be installed, configured and updated, along with some applications. Half of the applications are to be identical installations while the other half need to be customized. In this scenario, each deployment of the operating system can take 30 minutes, followed by additional time and effort to apply necessary security patches and operating system updates (several of which may require server reboots). Finally, the applications need to be deployed and configured. A manual or semi-automated approach to this project will require an extended amount of time and will introduce a reasonable chance of human error contributing to mistakes in one or more of the new server installations.

Solution

A sophisticated system is introduced to enable the automation of the provisioning of a wide range of IT resources, individually or together. The system relies on an automated provisioning program, a rapid provisioning engine, along with scripts and templates to allow for IT resources to be provisioned on-demand, at the time when the cloud consumer requests the IT resources via a self-service portal.

Application

The application of this pattern can vary, depending on the types of IT resources that need to be rapidly provisioned. A multitude of individual components are available to coordinate and automate various aspects of IT resource provisioning. The assembly of these components comprises a large part of the resulting cloud architecture.

Components that can comprise the system include:

- *Server Templates* – Templates of virtual image files used for automating the instantiation of new virtual servers.

- *Server Images* – Similar to server templates, but used for provisioning physical servers instead.

- *Application Packages* – Collections of applications and other software that is packaged for automated deployment.

- *Application Packager* – The software used to create application packages.

- *Custom Scripts* – Scripts that automate administrative tasks, as part of an intelligent automation engine.

- *Sequence Manager* – A program used to organize sequences of automated provisioning tasks.

- *Sequence Logger* – A component that logs the execution of automated provisioning task sequences.

- *Operating System Baseline* – A configuration template applied after the operating system is installed to quickly prepare it for usage.

- *Application Configuration Baseline* – A configuration template with settings and environment parameters needed to prepare new applications for usage.

- *Deployment Data Store* – The repository that stores virtual images, templates, scripts, baseline configurations, and other related data.

The system produced by the application of this pattern is typically further integrated with the self-service portal resulting from the Self-Provisioning (324) pattern as well as various scripts and the use of the intelligent automation engine, as part of the application of the Automated Administration (310) pattern.

The various artifacts used to establish the provisioning systems are typically stored within a deployment repository supplied by the cloud provider, as shown in Figure 7.6. Figure 7.7 provides a sample cloud architecture resulting from the application of Rapid Provisioning.

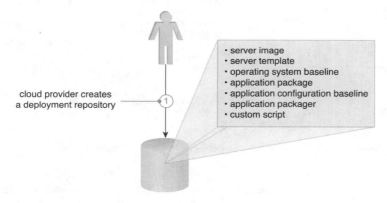

Figure 7.6
The cloud provider creates a deployment repository that stores system components.

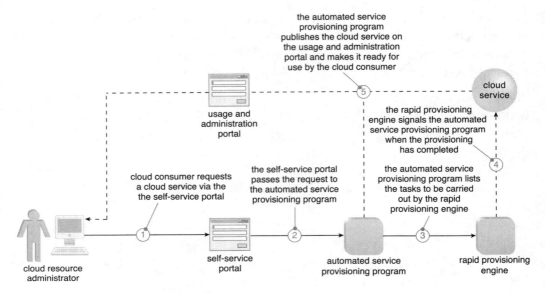

Figure 7.7

A sample cloud architecture resulting from the application of the Rapid Provisioning pattern.

The preceding example is significantly simplified. The following step-by-step descriptions provide better insight into the mechanics behind a typical rapid provisioning engine. This scenario involves a number of the previously listed system components.

1. A cloud consumer requests a new server through the self-service portal.

2. The sequence manager forwards the request to the deployment engine for an operating system to be prepared.

3. If the request is for building a virtual server, then the deployment engine uses the virtual server templates for provisioning. Otherwise, the deployment engine sends the request to provision a physical server.

4. If there was an already pre-defined image for the type of operating system requested, then it will be used for the provisioning of the operating system. Alternatively, the regular deployment process will be followed to install the operating system.

5. When the operating system is ready, the deployment engine informs the sequence manager.

6. The sequence manager updates the logs and sends them to the sequence logger for storage.

7. The sequence manager requests that the deployment engine apply the operating system baseline to the provisioned operating system.

8. The deployment engine applies the requested operating system baseline.

9. The deployment engine informs the sequence manager that the operating system baseline is applied.

10. The sequence manager updates and sends the logs of past steps to the sequence logger for storage.

11. The sequence manager requests that the deployment engine install the applications. (There may be more than one application that the sequence manger provides in its list.)

12. The deployment engine deploys the applications on the provisioned server.

13. The deployment engine informs the sequence manager that the applications have been installed.

14. The sequence manager updates and sends the logs of past steps to the sequence logger for storage.

15. The sequence manager requests that the deployment engine apply the application's configuration baseline.

16. The deployment engine applies the application's configuration baseline.

17. The deployment engine informs the sequence manager that the application configuration has been applied.

18. The sequence manager updates and sends the logs of past steps to the sequence logger for storage.

Mechanisms

- *Cloud Storage Device* – The cloud storage device provides the storage space that is needed to host and provision IT resources, in addition to application baseline information, templates, and scripts.

- *Hypervisor* – This mechanism is used to rapidly create, deploy, and host the virtual servers.

- *Resource Replication* – The resource replication mechanism is related to this pattern in how it is used to generate replicated instances of IT resources in response to rapid provisioning requirements.

- *Virtual Server* – The virtual server may be provisioned or may host provisioned IT resources.

Platform Provisioning

How can cloud consumers build and deploy cloud solutions without the burden of having to create and manage the underlying infrastructure?

Problem	Cloud consumers are often motivated to utilize cloud platforms to build and deploy solutions so that necessary IT resources can be leased instead of purchased. However, when presented with raw cloud-based IT resources, the burden of having to set up and maintain them may not be desirable.
Solution	A system can be established whereby ready-made platforms with packaged, pre-configured IT resources can be provided as turn-key environments for cloud consumers that do not wish to assume significant administrative responsibilities.
Application	Auto-deployment packages are created, comprised of various bundles of pre-configured IT resources deployed on pre-configured operating systems. These packages can be provisioned on-demand.
Mechanisms	Hypervisor, Ready-Made Environment, Resource Management System, Resource Replication, Virtual Server

Problem

Even though leasing IT resources offers economical benefits over purchasing and owning the same IT resources on-premise, organizations often do not see the benefit in having the on-staff administrative expertise and the overall responsibilities that come with setting up, configuring, and the on-going maintenance of raw, leased IT resources, such as those provided by IaaS platforms.

Solution

A provisioning system is established to deliver ready-made environment instances (stored as virtual machines) on-demand. Different packages of IT resources can be bundled into individual ready-made environments, enabling cloud providers to offer pre-defined and customized PaaS products.

Application

This pattern focuses specifically on the automated provisioning of the ready-made environment mechanism, and typically relies on the application of the Automated Administration (310) and Rapid Provisioning (295) patterns to establish a system capable of dynamically provisioning auto-deployment packages on-demand.

Each package is prepared with a ready-made environment that includes a base operating system and can be further equipped with pre-configured applications, databases, development tools, and other IT resources. The intelligent automation engine is utilized to carry out the auto-deployment via customized scripts. Each variation of offered PaaS services can be published in a service catalog accessible via the self-service portal implemented as a result of applying the Self-Provisioning (324) pattern.

The following steps are shown in Figure 7.8:

1. A cloud consumer logs into a self-service portal and requests the creation of a new ready-made environment.

2. The self-service portal forwards the request to the automated service provision.

3. The request platform is located.

3.1. The cloud consumer requests customization to the platform.

3.2. The platform is customized.

4. After several minutes, the platform is provisioned and is made available for the cloud consumer on the usage and administration portal.

4.1. The customized platform is provisioned and made available on the usage and administration portal for the cloud consumer.

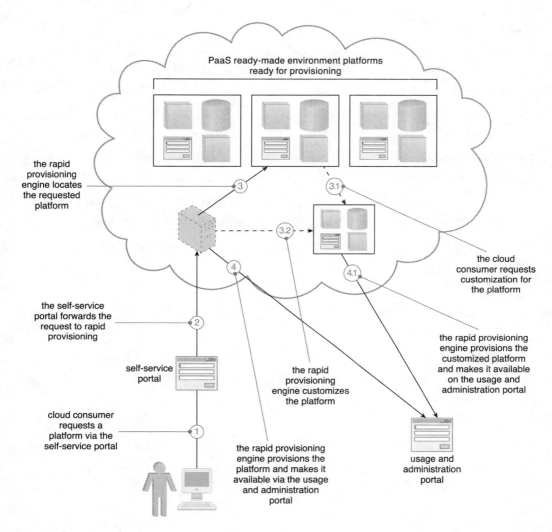

Figure 7.8
An example of the cloud architecture resulting from the application of the Platform Provisioning pattern.

Mechanisms

- *Hypervisor* – The hypervisor is responsible for hosting the virtual server, which hosts the development environments or platforms that are provided to cloud consumers.

- *Ready-Made Environment* – Ready-made environments are the primary platforms provisioned by the system established by this pattern.

- *Resource Management System* – This mechanism supplies cloud consumers with the tools and options they need to manage provisioned platforms.

- *Resource Replication* – The resource replication mechanism is used to replicate the requested platforms (usually from the pre-defined platform templates).

- *Virtual Server* – This mechanism is used to host the provisioned platforms.

Bare-Metal Provisioning

How can operating systems be remotely deployed on bare-metal servers?

Problem	Both cloud providers and cloud consumers require the ability to remotely provision bare-metal servers. This process begins with the remote deployment of operating systems. However, establishing a remote connection for provisioning purposes is not possible without software being already installed on bare-metal servers.
Solution	Contemporary server features are utilized to install remote management support into the server ROM to establish the required remote bare-metal provisioning system.
Application	Specialized discovery and deployment agents can be utilized within the remote bare-metal provisioning system to locate and provision available bare-metal servers with operating systems dynamically.
Mechanisms	Cloud Storage Device, Hypervisor, Logical Network Perimeter, Resource Management System, Resource Replication, SLA Management System

Problem

The remote provisioning of servers is common because remote management software is generally a native component of a server's operating system. However, bare-metal servers do not have pre-installed operating systems (or any other software) meaning access to conventional remote management programs is unavailable.

Solution

Most contemporary servers provide the option for remote management support to be pre-installed in the server's ROM. Some vendors offer this feature only through an expansion card, while others have the required components already integrated into the chipset. A bare-metal provisioning system can be designed to utilize this feature with specialized service agents that can be used to discover and effectively provision entire operating systems remotely.

Application

The remote management software that is integrated with the server's ROM becomes available upon server start-up. A Web-based or proprietary user interface, like the portal provided by the remote administration system mechanism, is usually used to connect to the server's native remote management interface. The IP address of the remote management interface can be configured manually, through the default IP, or alternatively set through the configuration of a DHCP service. IP addresses in IaaS platforms can be forwarded directly to cloud consumers so that they can perform bare-metal operating system installations independently.

Although remote management software is used to enable connections to server consoles and for the deployment of operating systems, it raises two concerns:

- Manual deployment on multiple servers can be vulnerable to inadvertent human and configuration errors.

- Remote management software can be time-intensive and require significant runtime IT resource processing.

The bare-metal provisioning system addresses these issues via the use of the following components:

- *Discovery Agent* – A type of monitoring agent that searches and finds available servers that are then assigned to cloud consumers.

- *Deployment Agent* – A management agent that is installed into a physical server's memory to be positioned as a client for the bare-metal provisioning deployment engine.

- *Discovery Section* – A software component that scans the network and locates available servers with which to connect.

- *Management Loader* – The component responsible for connecting to the server and loading the management options for the cloud consumer.

- *Deployment Component* – The feature responsible for installing the operating system on the selected servers.

The bare-metal provisioning system further provides an auto-deployment feature that allows cloud consumers to connect to the deployment software and provision more than one server or operating system at the same time.

The deployment software connects to the servers via their management interfaces, and uses the same protocol to upload and operate as an agent in the physical server's RAM, after which the bare-metal server becomes a raw client with a management agent installed. The deployment software then uploads the required setup files to deploy the operating system.

Deployment images, operating system deployment automation, or unattended deployment and post installation configuration scripts can be used via the intelligent automation engine mechanism and the self-service portal to further extend this functionality.

The following steps are shown in Figures 7.9 and 7.10:

1. The cloud consumer connects to the deployment solution.

2. The cloud consumer uses the deployment solution to perform a search by using the discovery agent.

3. The available physical servers are shown to the cloud consumer, who selects the target server for usage.

4. The deployment agent is loaded to the physical server's RAM via the remote management system mechanism.

5. The cloud consumer selects an operating system and method of configuration via the deployment solution.

6. The operating system is installed and the server is operational.

7. The status of the new server is reported to the VIM.

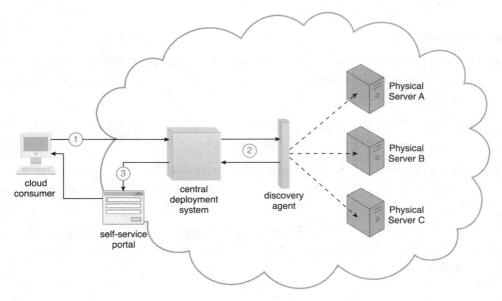

Figure 7.9

A sample cloud architecture resulting from the application of the Bare-Metal Provisioning pattern (Part I).

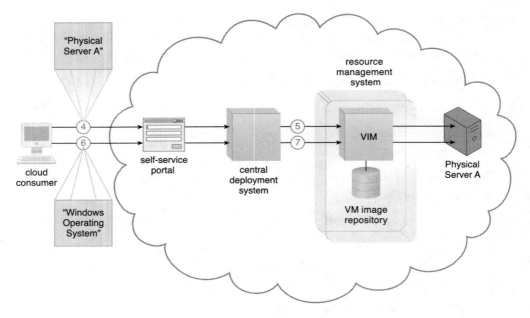

Figure 7.10

A sample cloud architecture resulting from the application of the Bare-Metal Provisioning pattern (Part II).

Mechanisms

• *Cloud Storage Device* – This mechanism is used to store operating system templates and installation files, as well as deployment agents and deployment packages for the provisioning system.

• *Hypervisor* – This pattern can be used to deploy a hypervisor on a physical server as part of operating system deployments.

• *Logical Network Perimeter* – This mechanism is used by the provisioning system to ensure that raw physical servers can only be accessed by the appropriate cloud consumers.

• *Resource Management System* – This mechanism is pivotal to the application of this pattern in that it interacts with the deployment agent to load the physical server's RAM.

- *Resource Replication* – This mechanism is implemented to replicate IT resources by deploying a new hypervisor on a physical box in order to balance the hypervisor workload during or subsequent to provisioning.

- *SLA Management System* – The SLA management system mechanism ensures that the availability of physical bare-metal servers is in accordance with pre-defined SLA stipulations.

Automated Administration

How can common administrative tasks be carried out consistently and automatically in response to pre-defined events?

Problem	IT resources undergo numerous administrative tasks that need to be repeatedly and efficiently carried out and become subject to human error and slow response times when performed manually.
Solution	The workflow logic of administration tasks suitable for automation is programmed using scripts and deployed in a platform capable of executing these scripts in response to pre-defined runtime events.
Application	An intelligent automation engine is implemented to establish a system capable of storing, managing, and executing the automation scripts.
Mechanisms	Automated Scaling Listener, Cloud Storage Device, Cloud Usage Monitor, Hypervisor, Resource Replication, Virtual Server

Problem

There are numerous administrative and maintenance tasks that need to be performed on physical servers, virtual servers, and other IT resources. By default, many of these tasks are performed manually by humans.

Various frequently recurring circumstances at times necessitate the execution of these tasks to be immediate and on-demand. However, performing certain types of administrative tasks manually is impractical and inefficient due to the potential for human error, and the synchronization that is required to simultaneously carry out the same task across different platforms.

Solution

An automation system that supports multiple connectivity options is created to run commands and scripts on diverse platforms (Figure 7.11). Different scripts need to be integrated together to run in a common workflow that uses extra extensions. This engine may also generate reports on each separate step of the workflow.

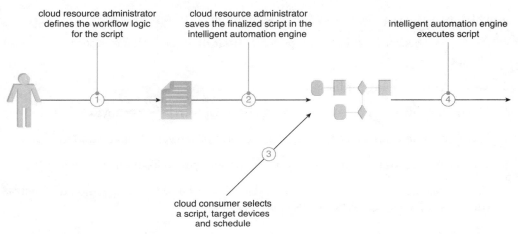

Figure 7.11

The cloud resource administrator defines the workflow logic (1) and expresses it in a series of scripts that is incorporated into an intelligent automation engine repository (2). The cloud resource administrator then selects the workflow, the systems it will run on, and its execution schedule (3). The intelligent automation engine runs the workflow and reports the results (4).

Application

An automation system, referred to as an intelligent automation engine, is implemented as a workflow management application that is capable of executing various scripts. The workflow logic is expressed in scripts via sequenced steps that are in a pre-determined order with conditional logic. Conditions pertaining to environmental factors can be defined so that additional scripts and logic can be automatically triggered when environmental parameters change.

The intelligent automation engine includes a repository that is used to store artifacts, such as workflow scripts, log files, and connectivity configurations, as well as a user interface that allows for the creation and editing of scripting templates. The engine may further support connections to other system monitors to integrate monitoring data with script execution.

Intelligent automation engines support a range of common connection methods, such as SSH, RDP, and RCMD, in addition to various authentication methods. Other templates are supplied so that different connection methods can be more easily used.

The following steps are shown in Figure 7.12:

1. The cloud resource administrator defines the workflow logic.

2. Script execution schedule times can be added while the workflow logic is being created or at a later point.

3. Existing scripts can be reused and added to the current workflow.

4. Access to the scripts is protected to ensure that they can only be run by authorized clients.

5. The scripts are ready for use.

6. The intelligent automation engine saves the scripts in its repository.

7. Security credentials for accessing and executing each script can be added.

8. The scripts can be used by the automated service provisioning programs.

9. The scripts are published via the self-service portal and the usage and administration portal for access and usage by cloud consumers.

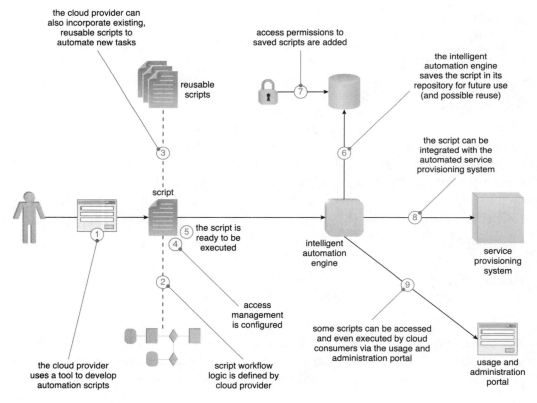

Figure 7.12

An overview of how the components can be assembled as a result of the application of this pattern.

Figure 7.13 depicts sample workflow logic that can be programmed in a script.

There are circumstances in the patching workflow shown in Figure 7.13 that will test the ability of the intelligent automation engine to make logical decisions. For example, the script will need to be programmed with responses to the following scenarios:

- the patch is installed successfully or unsuccessfully

- a reboot is required (if the reboot is successful, the engine must have a way to detect this, and if the reboot is unsuccessful, the engine must log the error)

Figure 7.13

This scenario depicts a physical server that needs patching, which is a routine task and a prime candidate for automation. The physical server is part of a cluster, so the script needs to ensure that the physical server is properly taken offline and monitoring is disabled before initiating the patching process.

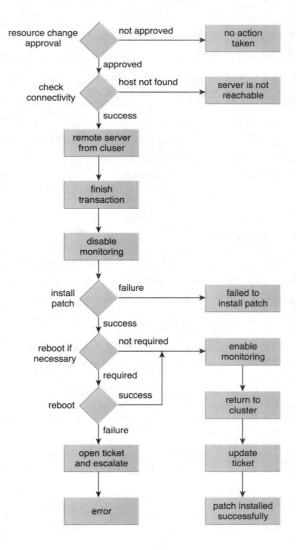

- after the patch is completed, the physical server's status needs to be changed to "online" and brought back into the cluster

Scripted workflows can at times require an extended period of time to complete, which makes handling error conditions more difficult. Additional challenges that arise when applying this pattern pertain to integrating scripts across different platforms and systems.

Mechanisms

- *Automated Scaling Listener* – The automated scaling listener notifies the intelligent automation engine when scaling of an IT resource is required.

- *Cloud Storage Device* – This mechanism can be used to store data related to the intelligent automation engine, such as workflow logic and custom scripts.

- *Cloud Usage Monitor* – This mechanism is associated with the Automated Administration pattern for two reasons, the first being that the automated scaling listener is a variant of the broader infrastructure-level cloud usage monitor mechanism. A second reason is that the intelligent automation engine runs workflows that can scale and release current IT resources according to cloud consumer usage demand.

- *Hypervisor* – The intelligent automation engine can pass commands and workflow logic to the hypervisor to be executed.

- *Resource Replication* – Whenever a virtualized instance of an IT resource is required, the resource replication mechanism may be initiated by the intelligent automation engine to generate the instance.

- *Virtual Server* – The intelligent automation engine either runs a workflow that sends commands directly to the virtual server for processing, or sends the commands or workflows to be run by the hypervisor to manage or modify the virtual server.

Centralized Remote Administration

How can diverse administrative tasks and controls be consolidated for central remote access by cloud consumers?

Problem	Cloud consumers can end up having to manage a range of diverse cloud-based IT resources, each with distinct administrative functions. The disparity in user-interfaces and reporting features can make remote administration burdensome and prone to human error.
Solution	The cloud provider can consolidate diverse management features for different IT resources into a single, custom portal that standardizes administrative controls as well as provides cross-IT resource reporting features.
Application	A usage and administration portal is developed by the cloud provider to interface with systems and APIs offered by back-end products, IT resources and mechanisms, and to further support different levels of access based on pre-assigned permissions.
Mechanisms	Audit Monitor, Billing Management System, Cloud Usage Monitor, Logical Network Perimeter, Multi-Device Broker, Pay-Per-Use Monitor, Remote Administration System, Resource Management System, SLA Monitor

Problem

Cloud platforms commonly provide cloud consumers with access to proprietary administration front-ends and portals for individual IT resources, meaning cloud providers essentially make out-of-the-box features externally available. Pre-built administration user interfaces can be sufficient for simpler cloud platforms and any cloud consumers that only require access to a modest number of IT resources. However, these user interfaces become inadequate once a greater number of IT resources need administering, especially by larger cloud consumer organizations that employ a number of cloud resource administrators.

Inconsistencies in the presentation of administrative controls and features and the processes they require can lead to human error and recurring inefficiencies as cloud resource administrators are required to learn how to perform the same tasks using different tools.

In the example illustrated in Figure 7.14, the cloud consumer wants to monitor the usage of IT resources that are allocated to each branch of its organization. The cloud consumer also requires the option of providing each branch manager with control over the IT resources at its own branch. Security and administrative risks are introduced if branch managers were provided with the same level of access as the cloud consumer that established the IT environment.

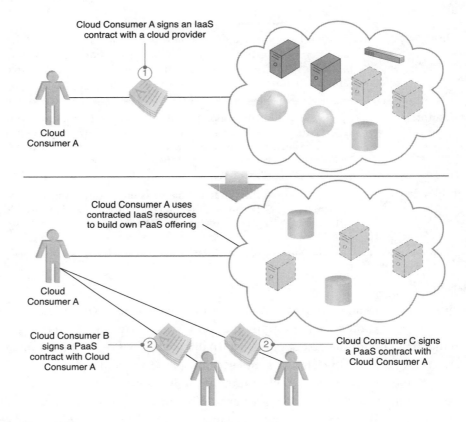

Figure 7.14

Cloud Consumer A leases an IaaS platform from a cloud provider (1) with the intention of offering its own PaaS platform to other cloud consumers (thereby assuming the role of a cloud provider). After the new PaaS platform is made available by Cloud Consumer A, Cloud Consumers B and C lease instances of the platform (2). Cloud Consumer A (acting as a cloud provider) needs a means of offering management features and usage tracking and reporting of the various IT resources that are available via the PaaS platform, while ensuring that each cloud consumer is granted an appropriate level of control.

Solution

A custom usage and administration portal can be created to support different levels of security access, while consolidating the administrative functions of a range of IT resources for consistent and standardized presentation (Figure 7.15).

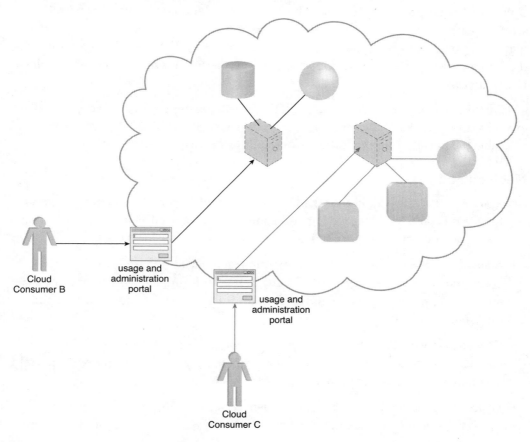

Figure 7.15
Cloud Consumers B and C can access and manage their provisioned IT resources using the usage and administration portal.

Application

The usage and administration portal generally provides two broad sets of features: management controls and reporting. Management controls consolidate similar IT resource management functions into standardized front-end controls presented to the cloud resource administrator. Reporting features can also consolidate usage data from multiple IT resources into summarized analysis reports and realtime dashboard statistics. Single sign-on technology is commonly used to enable cloud resource administrator credentials to propagate the authorization and authentication of all affected, underlying IT resources.

Unless the cloud provider chooses to build the usage and administration portal from scratch, the remote administration system mechanism is most commonly used as the main component around which the portal's architecture is built. The mechanism is then further integrated with various back-end management systems and API-enabled IT resources.

This pattern is commonly combined with the Self-Provisioning (324) pattern to further extend the feature-set of the centralized portal, as well as the Broad Access (93) pattern to enable the portal to support access from multiple devices and protocols.

Mechanisms

- *Audit Monitor* – The audit monitor is associated with this pattern in how it monitors cloud consumer usage to log IT resource access, as well as information about the cloud consumers themselves (such as their geographic locations).

- *Billing Management System* – The billing management system produces and generates the IT resource usage cost and chargeback information, which may be streamed or published on the usage and administration portal for cloud consumer viewing.

- *Cloud Usage Monitor* – The cloud usage monitor collects usage information about cloud services and IT resources managed via the usage and administration portal and may also monitor the usage of the administration portal itself.

- *Logical Network Perimeter* – This mechanism creates a logical isolation that separates each cloud consumer's management and usage tools and reports, to prevent viewing and access by other unauthorized cloud consumers.

- *Multi-Device Broker* – The application of the multi-device broker provides the features and tools that allow cloud consumers to use different devices running different operating systems to connect to the usage and administration portal.

- *Pay-Per-Use Monitor* – The pay-per-use monitor gathers IT resource usage information to be used by the billing management system. This billing information may be provided in a realtime report on the usage and administration portal.

- *Remote Administration System* – This mechanism provides fundamental technologies, APIs, and templates used for the creation and configuration of usage and administration portals.

- *Resource Management System* – The resource management system provides tools and management options necessary for cloud consumers to manage IT resources and is generally integrated with and abstracted by the usage and administration portal.

- *SLA Monitor* – The SLA monitor relates to this pattern by supplying the runtime usage data relevant to SLA-based reports that may be published on the usage and administration portal for cloud consumer viewing, as per the Realtime Resource Availability (292) pattern.

Resource Management

How can a cloud consumer safely manage an IT resource without impacting neighboring IT resources?

Problem	When cloud consumers access and manage deployed IT resources that coexist with other IT resources as part of a live production environment, management changes to an IT resource may inadvertently negatively impact others.
Solution	A set of tools and back-end controls are provided by the cloud provider to protect the management activity of one cloud consumer from others.
Application	Cloud consumers are given limited access levels and management options and their management activity is further confined to their respective logical network perimeters.
Mechanisms	Audit Monitor, Cloud Usage Monitor, Logical Network Perimeter, Remote Administration System, Resource Management System

Problem

When a cloud consumer carries out management tasks on an IT resource, neighboring IT resources (belonging to the same or different cloud consumer) can be inadvertently impacted.

For example, the logical network perimeter established for one cloud consumer may encompass IT resources that are shared by other cloud consumers. This means the same physical server may be hosting virtual servers that belong in different logical network perimeters. In Figure 7.16, all IT resources belong to the same cloud consumer.

Solution

A set of tools and back-end controls are provided by the cloud provider to specifically limit the access levels and management options of each cloud consumer to the IT resources for which it is granted access.

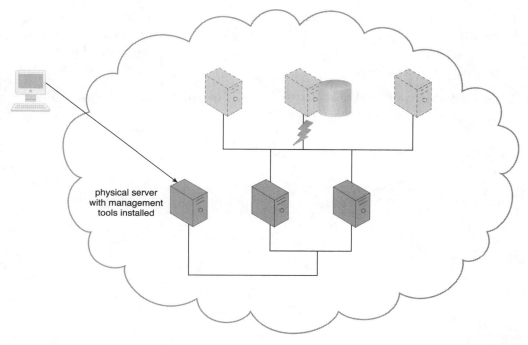

Figure 7.16

In this example, the cloud consumer makes a remote management change to a physical server, which accidentally affects a virtual server hosting a database in another part of the cloud environment. In this scenario, all IT resources belong to the same cloud consumer.

Application

This pattern is applied via front-end portal controls and corresponding back-end scripts and logic, and is therefore typically combined with the Centralized Remote Administration (315) pattern. The controls established by this pattern essentially confine each cloud consumer's access to within its designated logical network perimeter and further enforce the levels of access the cloud consumer has to IT resources within the perimeter.

The tools established by this pattern can further include a sandbox environment that allows cloud consumers to safely test and execute management changes before committing the changes to the production environment. The sandbox environment limits the amount of access cloud consumers have to physical resources, and also allows for the monitoring of commands and configuration requests (Figure 7.17). It provides two key features:

1. An auditing system is put in place to audit commands and requests *prior* to passing them to actual IT resources. This way, any conflicts or misconfigurations can be detected and notified to the cloud consumer before they are applied to the production environment.

2. Log files are maintained to keep a record of all commands and requests made. This can aid troubleshooting.

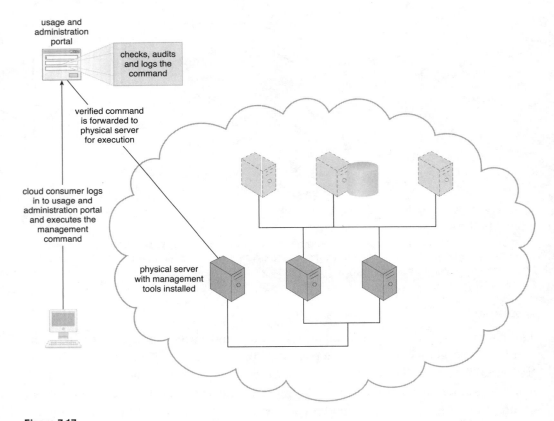

Figure 7.17

Cross-IT resource management tools and logic are used to check (and optionally audit and log) commands before allowing them to be executed.

Mechanisms

- *Audit Monitor* – This mechanism is responsible for auditing resource management activity for security and legal reasons.

- *Cloud Usage Monitor* – Cloud usage monitors may be used to track usage information relevant to the system created by the application of this pattern.

- *Logical Network Perimeter* – This mechanism isolates the IT resource access and management paths for cloud consumers, in order to provide a level of isolation that prevents cloud consumers from accessing the IT resources of others.

- *Remote Administration System* – To enable remote access to resource management features, the remote administration system enables the creation of custom portals and front-ends.

- *Resource Management System* – This mechanism provides cloud consumers with the options, tools, and access permissions that they require to manage the provision IT resources.

Problem	Manual or semi-automated IT resource provisioning processes required by cloud providers can be time-consuming and inefficient and can impose unnecessary delays and effort upon cloud consumers.
Solution	A self-service portal is established with the ability to interface with back-end systems required for the automated provisioning of IT resources.
Application	In addition to offering front-end controls for cloud consumers to choose IT resources for automated provisioning, the self-service portal is also equipped with the ability to receive a feed of current IT resources that are available for provisioning.
Mechanisms	Audit Monitor, Cloud Usage Monitor, Logical Network Perimeter, Multi-Device Broker, Remote Administration System

Problem

A cloud provider may require that a cloud consumer interact with sales staff to have new IT resources provisioned or, subsequent to receiving the provisioning request, an approval process may be required and cloud resource administrators may further have to manually perform the provisioning. These types of processes can unreasonably prolong the time it takes for a cloud consumer to gain access to the required IT resources and can further demand extra effort and communication from the cloud consumer organization.

A burdensome provisioning experience can make cloud consumers wary of further transactions with the cloud provider and can inhibit the cloud consumer organization's overall ability to be responsive to fulfilling their own business automation requirements.

Solution

The cloud provider makes a self-service portal available that provides cloud consumers with a live, up-to-date list of available cloud services and IT resources that can be automatically provisioned after the cloud consumer submits the request online.

Some cloud providers will still require a human-driven approval process that is carried out upon receiving a provisioning request via a self-service portal. However, this process is often expedited so that approved requests are fulfilled within hours instead of days.

Application

The Self-Provisioning pattern can be applied together with the Centralized Remote Administration (315) pattern to establish a sophisticated consumer-facing front-end comprised of a combination of the features of the usage and administration portal and the self-service portal. The respective portals can still be displayed independently but by standardizing both, they can be integrated as part of the same overall Web application to ensure a consistent experience for consumer-side cloud resource administrators.

The following steps are shown in Figure 7.18:

1. The cloud consumer connects to the self-service portal, established by the Self-Provisioning pattern, via a multi-device broker that provides accessible connectivity to this cloud consumer and others that may need to connect with different devices.

2. The cloud consumer selects the desired cloud service from an inventory of services listed and described in a service catalog published on the self-service portal.

3. The selected cloud service is provisioned.

4. The provisioned cloud service is published to the usage and administration portal, established by the Centralized Remote Administration (315) pattern, making it available for management by the cloud consumer.

5. The cloud consumer can use tools published on the usage and administration portal to manage the cloud service implementation.

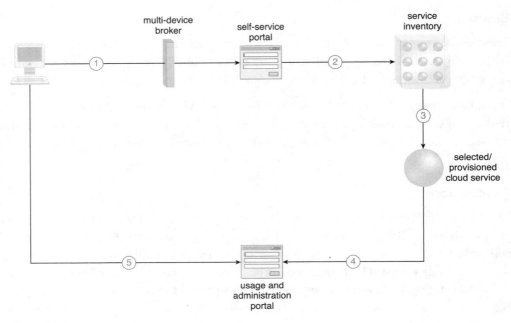

Figure 7.18

A simple cloud architecture in which both the self-service portal and usage and administration portal play roles in relation to how cloud services are provisioned online.

The self-service portal needs to be integrated with whatever separate approval process a cloud provider requires, along with the security system used to grant different levels of access and control. Cloud consumers are typically organized into access groups and granted service provisioning permissions based on the outcome of the approval process or prior profile information. Users who then log into the self-service portal on behalf of a cloud consumer organization will only be able to view and request from a list of IT resources that corresponds to their permission level.

Figures 7.19 and 7.20 illustrate the common steps that are required in order to navigate the permission approval process of a self-service portal.

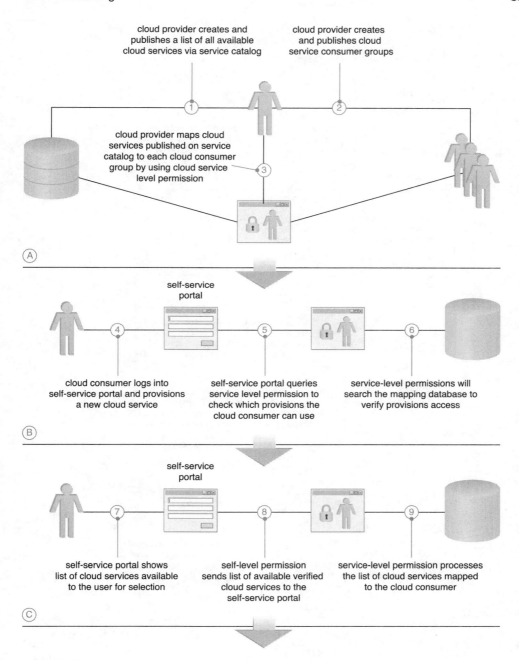

cloud provider creates and publishes a list of all available cloud services via service catalog

cloud provider creates and publishes cloud service consumer groups

cloud provider maps cloud services published on service catalog to each cloud consumer group by using cloud service level permission

cloud consumer logs into self-service portal and provisions a new cloud service

self-service portal queries service level permission to check which provisions the cloud consumer can use

service-level permissions will search the mapping database to verify provisions access

self-service portal shows list of cloud services available to the user for selection

self-level permission sends list of available verified cloud services to the self-service portal

service-level permission processes the list of cloud services mapped to the cloud consumer

self-service portal

self-service portal

Figure 7.19

Common steps required to navigate the permission approval process of a self-service portal (Part I).

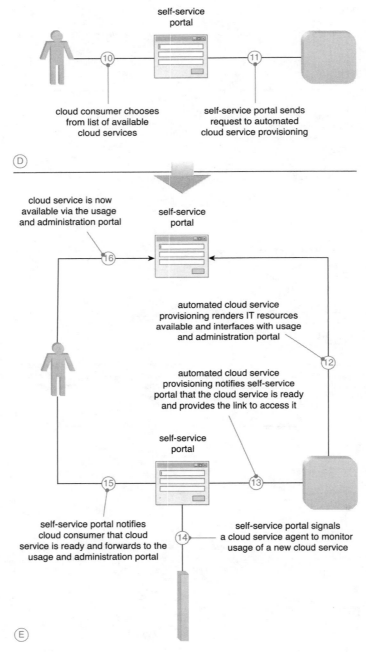

Figure 7.20

Common steps required to navigate the permission approval process of a self-service portal (Part II).

Mechanisms

- *Audit Monitor* – Auditing of self-service portal usage is required when information about the cloud consumers and their geographical locations or access points needs to be collected.

- *Cloud Usage Monitor* – Specialized cloud usage monitors may be employed to collect data of how self-service portal features are used.

- *Logical Network Perimeter* – The logical network perimeter isolates the options made available via a given instance of a self-service portal as they are offered to each cloud consumer.

- *Multi-Device Broker* – This mechanism is primarily utilized to broaden the access to the self-service portal via different types of cloud service consumer devices.

- *Remote Administration System* – The self-service portal that results from the application of this pattern may rely heavily on the tools and back-end interfaces provided by this mechanism.

Power Consumption Reduction

*How can a hypervisor's resources be guaranteed to be used
efficiently to minimize data center power and cooling costs?*

Problem	A hypervisor's resources need to be used in the most efficient way possible in order to minimize data center power and cooling expenses.
Solution	The host's capacity is utilized in the most efficient manner possible, so that the host hypervisors that are not being used are powered off.
Application	The capacities of the hosts are evaluated, virtual servers are distributed between the hosts, and the hosts that do not end up running any virtual servers enter into standby mode.
Mechanisms	Hypervisor, Live VM Migration, Virtual Infrastructure Manager (VIM), Virtualization Monitor

Problem

Figure 7.21 shows a cloud environment with four hypervisors participating in a hypervisor cluster. For simplicity, all of the virtual servers have the same virtual memory and virtual CPU configuration specifications. Each hypervisor can run eight virtual servers using 70% of its capacity, while the remaining 30% capacity is kept available for administration tasks like backups. Only two hypervisors are required to fully run the environment. The remaining two hypervisors are powered on unnecessarily and are consuming extra power, creating excess heat, and require UPS and cooling. A solution that can place the unnecessary hypervisors into a shutdown or standby mode and bring them back into operation on demand is required.

Solution

The capacity of the hypervisors is first evaluated before selecting the hypervisors that are to remain powered on to host the virtual servers. The virtual servers are moved to the selected hosts and the remaining hypervisors enter into standby mode. When the operational hosts' capacity is close to being exceeded, more hosts are called to leave standby mode and become operational as well. Applying this solution can bring substantial cost savings, depending on the size and design of the cloud environment.

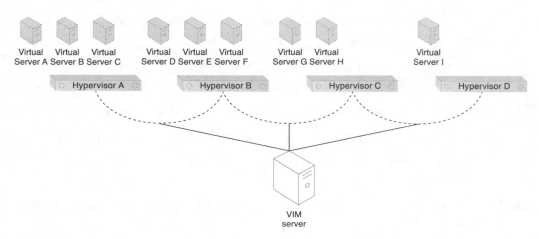

Figure 7.21

The hypervisors in this hypervisor cluster can each host eight virtual servers.

Application

The maximum utilization of each host is 70%, and the two hosts are capable of running all of the virtual servers without reaching their capacity limit of 70%. In some situations, an extra host may be kept powered on to meet the level of availability that is required by cloud consumers or applications. Bringing the host back into operation from standby mode may take several minutes, which certain SLAs may not be able to accommodate. Figure 7.21 illustrates the scenario prior to applying the pattern, while Figures 7.22 to 7.24 illustrate the steps involved in the application of this pattern.

If the Load Balanced Virtual Server Instances (51) pattern has been applied, the workload will be balanced between the hosts that are currently operational. An outage may result if there is no "hot" standby host to remain powered on, especially if demand is increasing or a host has abruptly failed. Any given virtual server may become shut down or remain powered off after a hypervisor failure, before the standby host becomes operational.

The following steps are shown in Figures 7.22 to 7.24:

1. A specialized capacity monitoring service agent monitors the capacity and workload of the hosts.

2. The monitoring results are sent to the VIM server, or sent to a capacity advisor application that forwards the results to the VIM server.

3. The VIM server initiates the workload movement via the application of the Non-Disruptive Service Relocation pattern.

4. The virtual servers are moved to the hosts that have been selected to stay operational.

5. The other hosts go into standby mode upon being signaled by the VIM server.

6. The capacity monitoring agent continues to monitor the workload on the hosts.

7. The capacity monitor signals the VIM server whenever the hosts' utilization nears 70%.

8. The VIM server signals one of the hosts to come out of standby mode via the use of the wake-on LAN (WOL).

9. After the host becomes operational, the system established by the application of the Non-Disruptive Service Relocation pattern moves some of the virtual servers to the host that has been powered back on.

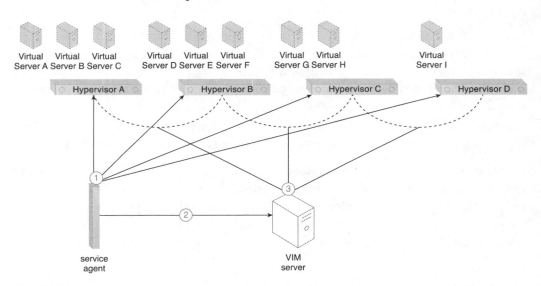

Figure 7.22
The Power Consumption Reduction pattern is applied (Part I).

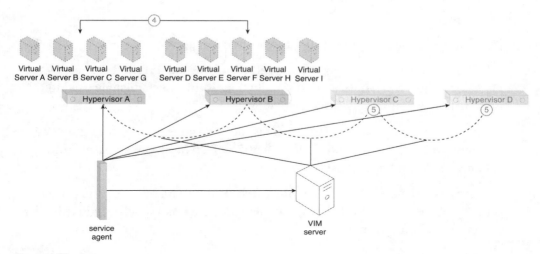

Figure 7.23

The Power Consumption Reduction pattern is applied (Part II).

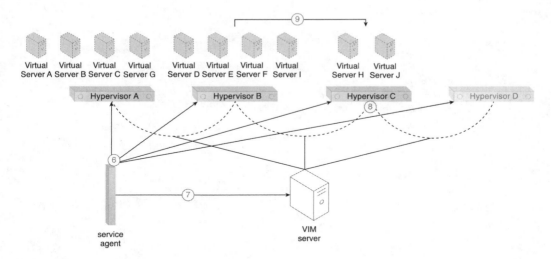

Figure 7.24

The Power Consumption Reduction pattern is applied (Part III).

Mechanisms

- *Hypervisor* – This mechanism is used to host virtual servers.

- *Live VM Migration* – If virtual servers need to be evacuated from their host hypervisor so the host can be placed into standby mode, this mechanism is used to migrate the virtual servers to a different host.

- *Virtual Infrastructure Manager (VIM)* – This mechanism is used to configure power consumption policies and thresholds, identify which hosts can be placed into standby mode, and bring hosts out of standby mode when required.

- *Virtualization Monitor* – This mechanism actively monitors resource and power utilization, and can be used to notify system administrators if certain resource or power utilization thresholds are met.

Chapter 8

Cloud Service and Storage Security Patterns

Trusted Platform BIOS

Geotagging

Hypervisor Protection

Cloud VM Platform Encryption

Trusted Cloud Resource Pools

Secure Cloud Interfaces and APIs

Cloud Resource Access Control

Detecting and Mitigating
  User-Installed VMs

Mobile BYOD Security

Cloud Data Breach Protection

Permanent Data Loss Protection

In-Transit Cloud Data Encryption

The foundations of security consist of supplying confidentiality, integrity, and availability of services. The patterns contained in this chapter provide important solutions for these key security requirements and aggressively approach threat mitigation by enabling security features suitable for cloud service and cloud storage architectures that are part of potentially volatile cloud environments.

Trusted Platform BIOS

How can the BIOS on a cloud-based environment be protected from malicious code?

Problem	Malware and rootkits can start before the operating system is launched, completely bypassing operating system security and remaining completely hidden.
Solution	Using security validation from the silicon up and remote monitoring of the platform security status, cloud consumers can verify that they are using compute platforms that meet their security assurance requirements.
Application	Trusted compute platforms are made available by the cloud provider with trusted platform modules (TPMs), which are hardware security modules (HSMs) that enable security assurance by validating digital signatures of code, starting at the basic input/output system (BIOS) using a measured boot.
Mechanisms	Digital Signature, Hardware Security Module (HSM), Trusted Platform Module (TPM)

Problem

The basic input/output system (BIOS) is firmware stored on non-volatile memory that persists between power cycles. The BIOS initializes and tests the system hardware components and loads a boot loader or an operating system from a mass memory device. The BIOS is implicitly trusted, enabling malicious code running at the BIOS level to take control of a computer system. It can compromise any components that are loaded during the boot process, including the hypervisor, operating system and VMs. Malware written into the BIOS can be used to re-infect machines, even after new operating systems have been installed or hard drives have been replaced. Since the BIOS loads first, there is no opportunity for anti-malware products to authoritatively scan the BIOS.

Rootkits are malware that run in kernel mode and have the same privileges as the operating system. As shown in Figure 8.1, different types of rootkits can load during different phases of the startup process, including:

1. *BIOS/firmware rootkits* – A rootkit consists of tools or programs that access administrator-level privileges to a computer or computer network.

Figure 8.1

A typical sequence of machine startup files.

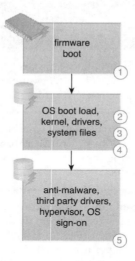

2. *OS boot load bootkits* – A bootkit extends the functionality of a rootkit and contains malware that infects a system's volume boot record, which allows it to burrow further into a system than the standard malware that infects the master boot record and load each time the system is booted.

3. *Kernel rootkits* – A kernel rootkit subverts system binaries of the kernel, providing as much privilege as any other kernel code. It can replace system call handlers with its own to-hide files, processes, and connections. The file access system calls can be overwritten to cause false data to be read from or written to files or devices on the system.

4. *Driver rootkits* – A driver rootkit resides as part of a device driver that is infected with malware.

5. Other boot files can be infected, including third party drivers, anti-malware, the hypervisor, and the operating system.

Solution

A tamperproof root of trust is established starting from the physical resources extending to the virtual resources and components in the computing stack, including the hypervisor. The concept of trust and the trust assurance level relies on a verifiable chain of integrity that is established from the silicon up, through the firmware BIOS, OS boot load, hypervisor, operating system, and other elements of the computing stack.

Application

The chain of trust is anchored in a tamper-resistant root in the hardware of the trusted platform module (TPM), where launch measurements or hashes are stored. The TPM is a type of hardware security module (HSM) that protects keys in hardware. The TPM has an endorsement private key that can sign messages that are validated by the TPM's public key. The environment controller compares those signed measurements against known good values and detects variations that can indicate a compromise of one or more launch components.

During the initial part of the boot process, the firmware checks for an embedded signature inside of the TPM. If that signature matches against a database of signatures in firmware, that module is allowed to execute. Shortly after the system is powered on, and before handoff to the OS loader occurs, the firmware checks the signature of firmware code that exists on hardware peripherals such as network cards, storage devices, or video cards.

Phases of a trusted compute platform boot include the following, as illustrated in Figure 8.2:

1. *Secure firmware boot* – Resources with firmware that use a TPM can be configured to load only trusted operating system boot loaders.

2. *Trusted boot* – The OS boot load checks the integrity of every component of the startup process before loading it.

3. *Early launch anti-malware* – Early launch anti-malware tests the integrity of all drivers before they load, and prevents unapproved drivers from loading.

4. *Measured boot* – The platform's firmware logs the boot process, and sends it to a trusted server that registers the platform's security assurance status.

The implications are that resources need to be procured from trusted sources that have TPMs installed. Procedures must be developed according to industry compliance guidelines for maintaining and updating firmware in order to maintain the security assurance level of the resource.

Figure 8.2

A platform startup sequence with a trusted BIOS.

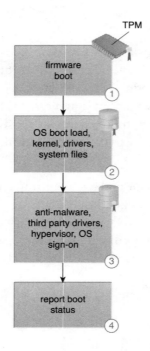

Mechanisms

- *Digital Signature* – A digital signature is used to provide integrity of code.

- *Hardware Security Module (HSM)* – The HSM protects the TPM keys and critical data.

- *Trusted Platform Module (TPM)* – The TPM provides a tamper-resistant HSM to hold keys and provide cryptographic processes.

Geotagging

How can the geographic location of cloud-based data and workloads be automatically communicated?

Problem	Control of data, workload locality, and data sovereignty are requirements for federal and industrial compliance and regulatory issues. Without knowledge of where a cloud consumer's workload is executed, it may not be possible to meet industrial compliance and regulatory requirements for data sovereignty.
Solution	When trusted resource pools are generated, the geolocation is supplied as part of the compliance and regulatory assurance attributes.
Application	Assets are geotagged using TPMs and are added to trusted resource pools that contain the same security assurance levels and geolocation regions.
Mechanisms	Geotag, Platform Trust Policy, Trusted Platform Module (TPM)

Problem

Cloud computing technologies are designed to be agile, providing geographically dispersed resources to process workloads. Unrestricted workload migration can conflict with cloud consumers' respective laws and industry compliance requirements for data and privacy. Cloud consumers often need to reliably identify the location of physical servers on which the data and workloads reside.

Some governments require that workloads stay within the country or within specific geographic boundaries. With interstate commerce, some retailers need to operate out of specific states for tax purposes. For intellectual property management, some companies need to accomplish research and development in certain geographic locations. Some companies need to stay out of countries with laws that allow their governments to legally access the company's information.

Solution

Geotagging enables monitoring and control of processing and workload movement within a geolocation. Geotagging supports the need for organizations to ensure their workloads are executed only in trusted servers located in authorized geographical areas. Adding to the Trusted Platform BIOS (337) pattern, geo-fencing policies and technologies are established to inform consumers of the location of compute resources.

Figure 8.3 illustrates a trusted platform module (TPM) that is loaded with the geolocation of the server being secured. Policies and processes are set up so that workloads are marked with assurance level and geolocation requirements, and those workloads are initiated and migrated only to servers that meet those prerequisites.

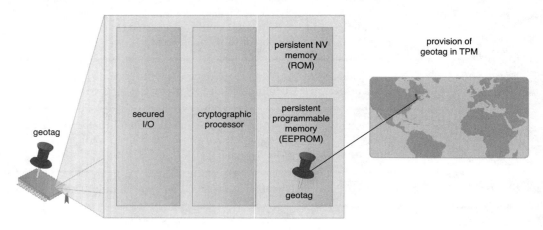

Figure 8.3
The geolocation is configured in the TPM.

Application

The process of using geotags to determine geolocation enables the establishment of a cloud server's location by provisioning that metadata to the server's TPM root of trust. The hardware root of trust is created by the administrator, generating the server's unique identifier and platform metadata stored in the tamperproof TPM. This information is referenced using secure protocols to assert the integrity and security assurance level of the platform, including location, based on the platform trust policy, and reported to an attestation service.

Geo-fencing policies are established with associated monitoring and control of the resources in order to meet the cloud consumer's requirements. Monitoring applications are implemented so that the cloud consumer can monitor and conduct compliance audits concerning the cloud resources' security status, including geolocation.

An implication of the application of the Geotagging pattern is that procedures need to be developed, and the implementation of initial configuration, monitoring, maintenance, and auditing of those procedures is required.

Mechanisms

- *Geotag* – The geotag is used to establish the geolocation of the compute platform.

- *Platform Trust Policy* – The platform trust policy is consulted to determine the trust level of the compute platform.

- *Trusted Platform Module (TPM)* – The TPM is used to hold integrity data and compute integrity checks on the initial boot, including geolocation.

Hypervisor Protection

How can a hypervisor be secured and monitored?

Problem	The hypervisor is vulnerable to threats from multiple vectors and, if compromised, could attack any other component that is shared by the same hypervisor.
Solution	A system is established whereby mitigations are implemented from the silicon up the stack to protect against hypervisor attack vectors.
Application	A hardened hypervisor is installed and verified using a trusted platform, and mitigations are added to protect against vulnerabilities.
Mechanisms	Digital Signature, Hardened Virtual Server Image, Host-Based Security System (HBSS), Trusted Platform Module (TPM)

Problem

Cloud computing infrastructure can depend on an architecture where physical resources are shared by multiple virtual machines allocated to multiple consumers. A compromise of the hypervisor puts all the guest operating systems at high risk. Because attacks against the hypervisor can be rooted in the processor, traditional defenses such as firewalls and intrusion detection and prevention systems (IDPSs) are not capable of stopping them. Combining multiple systems onto a single piece of physical hardware can cause a larger impact if a security compromise occurs.

Hypervisor vulnerabilities may allow an attacker to manipulate the assets inside the cloud facility, creating denial of service by a shutdown of running virtual machines, data leakage from the copy and transfer outside the cloud of virtual machines, data compromise from replacement of virtual machines with modified copies, or direct financial damage from replication and launch of many copies of the virtual machines running up the cloud consumer's cost.

Virtualization comes in two types:

- Type 1, or *bare-metal virtualization*, also known as *native virtualization*, involves the hypervisor running directly on the underlying hardware without a host operating system, or a hypervisor that is built into the computer's firmware.

- Type 2, or *hosted virtualization,* involves the hypervisor running on top of the host operating system, which can be most any common operating system. Hosted virtualization architectures have a layer of software, the hypervisor, running in the guest operating system that provides the utilities to control virtualization while in the guest operating system. Hosted virtualization architectures also allow applications to run alongside the hosted virtualization application, unlike bare-metal architectures that can only run applications within virtualized systems.

Figure 8.4 shows multiple vectors that can be used to mount attacks to vulnerable hypervisors:

A. A hardware rootkit uses device or platform firmware, such as the operating system BIOS or a router, network card, or hard drive, to create a persistent malware image in the hardware. The rootkit hides in firmware and can take over a VM. The attacker can gain root-level access to a system, for example by stealing credentials or launching an exploit. Once the attacker has root-level access, the rootkit can be injected into the system.

B. With a compromised host, a hacker can create new rogue VMs or a hyperstack or hyperjack attack. In a hyperstack attack, the original hypervisor is replaced with a rogue hypervisor that becomes aware of all communication between the hypervisor and VMs. A hyperjack attack is a compromise of the hypervisor, similar to a rootkit infection on a physical computer.

C. VMs can communicate over a hardware or emulated hardware backplane rather than a network. Networks rely on tools that watch traffic as it flows across routers and switches, but these tools cannot view traffic as it moves in a hypervisor's network.

D. VMs can have direct memory and device access intended to minimize overhead. As an example, an attack scenario can involve the migration of a malicious VM into a trusted zone. The rogue VM can be moved from one host to another, and possibly be replicated to a remote site using SAN replication. A rogue VM can have a VM root kit.

E. Attackers may attempt to break out of a guest operating system in order to access the hypervisor, another guest operating system, or the underlying host operating system. When a VM is detected by a compromised host operating system, the attacker can craft specific exploits against the VM and hypervisor. Threats to attack the hypervisor from the VM include virtualized memory attacks, virtualized I/O attacks, and virtualized CPU attacks.

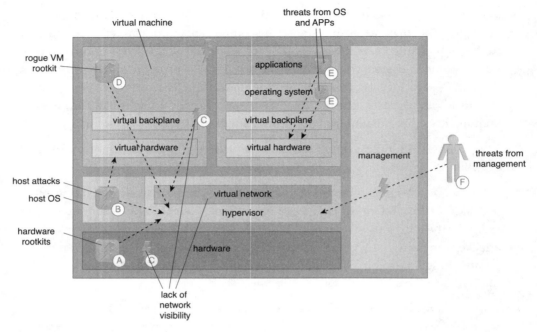

Figure 8.4
Examples of hypervisor attack vectors.

F. Other than managing virtualized resources, the hypervisor normally supports APIs for administration, launching, migrating, and terminating virtual machine instances. There are channels, data items, and APIs that can be compromised by an attacker.

Solution

A system is established that either directly or indirectly mitigates the hypervisor threats from the various attack vectors. Securing a hypervisor involves actions that are standard for any type of software, such as installing updates as they become available. Depending on the required assurance level, multi-role administration can provide for physical access control of the hardware on which the hypervisor runs.

Recommendations specific to hardening hypervisors include disabling unused virtual hardware and other hypervisor services, such as the clipboard and file sharing. If available, the hypervisor's capabilities can be used to monitor the security of a guest operating system running within it, as well as the security of activity occurring between guest operating systems. The hypervisor itself must also be monitored for signs of compromise.

Application

The hypervisor normally has the ability to monitor a guest operating system while it is running, which is known as introspection. Introspection can provide full auditing capabilities that may otherwise be unavailable. A Type 2 hypervisor running on an operating system adds complexity and more vulnerability to the host. Choosing Type 1 virtualization by replacing a host operating system with a hypervisor may improve security by reducing the operating system attack surface.

During hypervisor execution, the trustworthiness of the cloud server platform should be audited periodically. Ideally, this contributes to continuous monitoring. Hypervisors require physical security and should be configured using multi-role administrators.

The hypervisor itself should be carefully monitored for signs of compromise. This includes using self-integrity monitoring capabilities that hypervisors may provide, as well as the monitoring and analysis of hypervisor logs on an ongoing basis.

The following security measures are shown in Figure 8.5:

A. The BIOS must be booted with a measured boot from a trusted platform module (TPM) to create a trusted basic I/O system (BIOS) boot.

B. Before each hypervisor launch, the trustworthiness of the cloud server platform is verified or measured. The BIOS must be booted with a measured boot and the Type 1 hypervisor must in turn have its configurations verified through integrity checking before launching to ensure that the assumed level of trust is still in place. As a follow up to the measured boot, the Type 2 hypervisor securely boots the operating system by checking the integrity of its images to create a trusted compute platform.

C. To mitigate loss of network visibility, network traffic can be exposed between virtualized hosts to the physical network already in place, which requires the system on which the hypervisor is running to have multiple network interfaces. The virtual backplane can be disabled, and physical network interface cards can be used instead for networking or, as an alternative, to institute specialized virtual network monitoring. Physical networking will slow network communications compared to a virtual-only network, but will provide for reliable security monitoring. If reliable virtual network monitoring tools are available, this can be avoided.

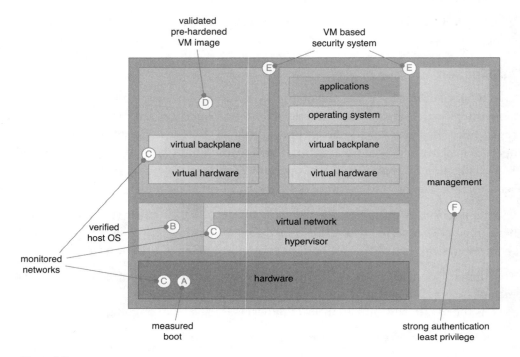

Figure 8.5

Examples of hypervisor threat mitigations.

D. From the trusted platform, a signed hardened virtual server image can be booted by checking its integrity. This requires creation of a signed VM image to check integrity and securely manage configuration control. Direct access to portions of I/O space or memory is trapped, and shared disk space eliminated or monitored.

E. Because hosted virtualization systems are run under a host operating system or a Type 1 hypervisor, the security of every guest operating system relies on the security of the host operating system or Type 1 hypervisor. An operating system and applications can be installed, configured, hardened, and tested in a single image, signed for integrity checking, in turn creating a hardened virtual server image, and then distributed to many hosts. Each virtual image should contain a VM host-based security system (HBSS) to mitigate against vulnerabilities of the OS and applications.

F. Strong authentication and the least privilege principle are implemented for management of VMs. The virtualization management system can be restricted to authorized administrators, possibly with separation of duties, who must use strong credentials to authenticate. A dedicated management network that is separate from all other networks and that can only be accessed by authorized administrators is an important best practice for any management function. Management communication carried over untrusted networks must be encrypted using FIPS-approved methods that encapsulate the management traffic. Logs must be configured to monitor both successful and unsuccessful attempts, and audits should confirm proper access.

Mechanisms

- *Digital Signature* – A trusted digital signature is used to protect the integrity of the boot code and system components.

- *Hardened Virtual Server Image* – Hardened virtual server images are used to prove security by verifying digital signatures.

- *Host-Based Security System (HBSS)* – HBSSs are installed on VM hosts to counter host-based vulnerabilities.

- *Trusted Platform Module (TPM)* – Trusted platform modules are used as an initial root of trust, starting at the silicon.

Cloud VM Platform Encryption

How can VM backups, snapshots, and live migration be secured?

Problem	VM backups, snapshots, and live migration create files that encapsulate the entire VM. These files can then be copied or moved outside the application that the cloud consumer controls, making them vulnerable to attacks.
Solution	Encrypted containers are provided for use and storage of the various types of VM backups and replications.
Application	A key manager is used to manage keys for encryption of the various types of VM storage that are pre-provisioned to receive backups and snapshots of consumer VMs or to receive replications and live migrations.
Mechanisms	Cryptographic Key Management System (CKMS), Virtual Server

Problem

VM backups, snapshots, and live migrations contain data for storage, RAM memory, CPU register status, and other metadata. The details of how this data is secured are hidden from the cloud consumer, which can cause data to be leaked. Figure 8.6 shows an example of data leakage.

Solution

The solution requires encryption that needs a key management system to accomplish the required security foundation architecture. The key manager encrypts the encryption keys and, depending on the requisite assurance level, provides for separation of duties (SOD) which requires multiple administrators to complete a specific administration task. Multiple administrators each have administration keys that must be used in conjunction with other administrator keys, which are split keys that require the use of multiple keys in order to unencrypt or accomplish administrative tasks.

Cloud VM Platform Encryption

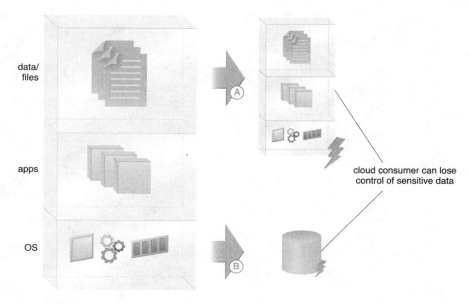

data/
files

apps

OS

cloud consumer can lose
control of sensitive data

Figure 8.6

Live migration or replication of the VM can potentially cause the consumer to lose control of the VM security (A). Storage of backups and snapshots with machine status can put the file security out of the consumer's control (B).

Figure 8.7 shows pre-configured VMs encrypted with consumer controlled encryption as follows:

1. In preparation for live migration or replication, an encrypted virtual server is pre-configured with consumer controlled encryption that will receive the migration or replication.

2. Live migration or replication is pre-configured and targeted to the encrypted server.

3. An encrypted virtual server is created for storage requirements.

4. The VM is configured to save all suspend, backup, and snapshot files to the encrypted server so that even memory snapshot files are encrypted when written to the disk.

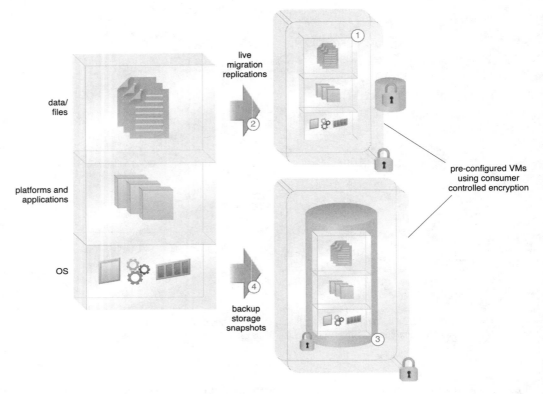

Figure 8.7
Pre-configured VMs encrypted with consumer controlled encryption.

Application

Application of this pattern renders data unreadable whenever it is stored, cloned, or replicated. It protects VMs even in a multitenant environment. A trusted execution environment is used to secure an operating VM.

In Figure 8.8, encrypted VMs are provisioned to receive backup, snapshots, migration data, and any other type of data that needs to be protected from leakage.

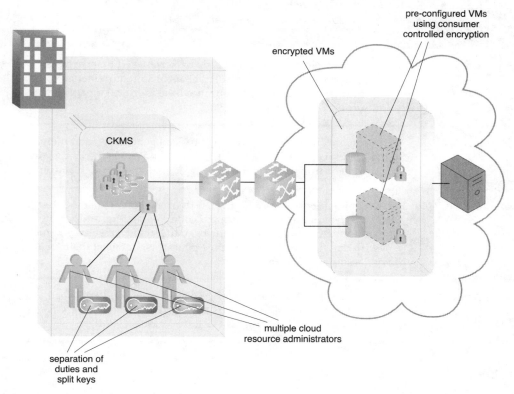

Figure 8.8
Key management and the Cloud VM Platform Encryption pattern.

Mechanisms

- *Cryptographic Key Management System (CKMS)* – The CKMS is used to manage encryption of VM resources.

- *Virtual Server* – Virtual servers are pre-configured with encryption to receive replications and backups of consumer VMs.

Problem	Cloud platform pool security needs to be achieved to meet cloud consumer compliance and regulatory security requirements. Verification of the platform assurance level is critical for regulated industries.
Solution	Trusted resource pools made up of trusted geotagged computers are made available by the cloud provider, and can be verified by the consumer through direct monitoring or evidence through auditing.
Application	Achieving security through the use of trusted platform modules (TPMs), validating digitally signed code, geotagging, and remote monitoring of the platform security status, cloud consumers can verify that they are using compute platforms that meet their security assurance requirements.
Mechanisms	Audit Monitor, Attestation Service, Certificate, Cloud Workload Scheduler, Cloud-based Security Groups, Digital Signature, Geotag, Platform Trust Policy, Trusted Platform Module (TPM)

Problem

Consumers have security requirements for the compute platforms they are using, usually governed by industry compliance regulations. The massive pooled resources of a cloud provider must be secured and grouped for a cloud consumer in order to meet their computing requirements and specifications, including security assurance levels. Cloud service providers must create boundaries, sometimes encompassing multiple platforms, to create a trusted pool for consumer workloads. Figure 8.9 illustrates multiple hardware resources forming a resource pool of virtual servers.

As a result of cloud consumer security requirements, cloud resources need to be secured in a way that meets verifiable security levels of assurance.

Solution

The concept of trust and trust assurance levels relies on a verifiable chain of integrity that is forged from the silicon up, starting with a trusted compute platform established through a secure boot. This creates the security assurance level of the platform, which

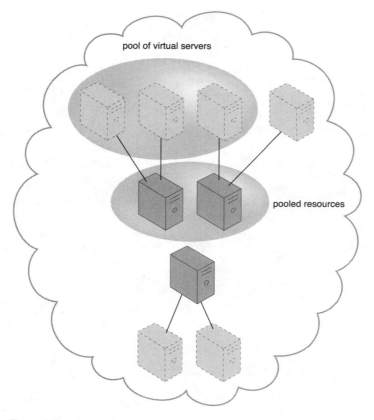

Figure 8.9
Fundamental resource pooling.

can include the geolocation. The compute platform registers its security status with an attestation service, which provides a secure service for reporting the security assurance level of a resource. The resource scheduler, referring to the attestation service, configures pools of resources to meet the requirements specified by the consumer and makes them available. This includes provisioning for the security of any excess capacity specified for capacity on demand.

Figure 8.10 provides an example of the end state of pooled virtual machines associated with pooled hardware servers in accordance with the security assurance level of the hardware servers. These virtual servers are then allocated to cloud consumers according to their security requirements.

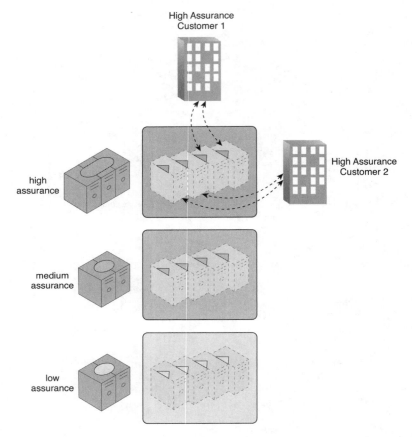

Figure 8.10
Resources pooled by security assurance level.

Application

When creating a trusted resource pool environment, security administrators install agents on target hosts, normally through an orchestrated and automated workflow, and configure certificates and keys so that the agent can use secure communication to authenticate with an attestation service. Administration processes then provision the attestation service database with the platform trust policy containing the security assurance level requirements of the cloud resources.

Secure resource pools are created so that workload placement can be:

- monitored and enforced based on consumer security requirements and boundary controls.

- verified and provided in audit and compliance reports to cloud consumers in order to meet their security and regulatory compliance requirements. Those compliance requirements often include proof of geographic location of the compute platforms.

The following actions are required to create and use a trusted resource pool, as illustrated in Figure 8.11:

1. The hardware server boots using the trusted platform module (TPM) to verify the BIOS, OS, and drivers.

2. The hypervisor launches, checking the integrity of the hypervisor image.

3. VMs boot, checking the integrity of the VM image.

4. System resources are registered with the attestation service including hardware boot status, hypervisor, and VM security status, which provides attestation of the authenticity of a platform. This assures that an authentic VM operating system starts in a trusted environment, which can then be considered trusted to a specified level of assurance. Attestations are signed with the TPM's private key and verified with the TPM's public key contained in the TPM certificate.

5. The cloud consumer specifies workload cloud resource requirements, including security assurance and location.

6. The cloud workload scheduler refers to the attestation service and schedules workloads on demand, meeting the cloud consumer security requirements by designating the compute resources with the required security level. The workload is placed on the resource pool with the proper security assurance level.

The cloud provider continuously monitors the platform hypervisor to ensure the required security assurance level is available and maintained. The auditing service maintains a record of the security status for reference by the cloud consumer.

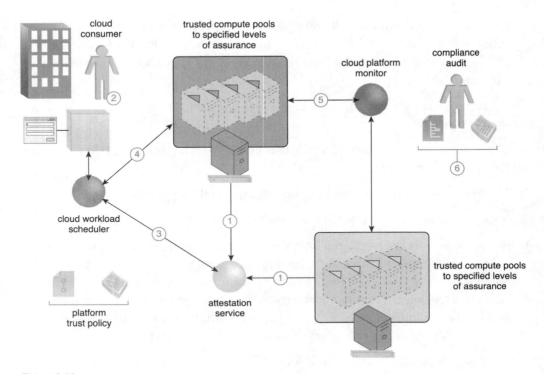

Figure 8.11
A sequence for creating and using trusted resource pools.

Mechanisms

- *Audit Monitor* – The audit monitor provides security event information for security logging and auditing purposes.

- *Attestation Service* – The attestation service registers the security assurance level of a platform and pools for reference by workflow scheduling functions.

- *Certificate* – The public keys in certificates are used to verify attestations signed with a TPM's private key.

- *Cloud Workload Scheduler* – The cloud workload scheduler schedules workloads according to their security assurance requirements by referring to the attestation service for cloud resources with the appropriate security levels.

- *Cloud-based Security Groups* – Cloud-based security groups support resource segmentation and access control referencing platform trust policy by delineating where different security measures can be applied.

- *Digital Signature* – Code is digitally signed so that it can be validated as being authentic.

- *Geotag* – The geotag is used to provide the server's geographic location for compliance auditing.

- *Platform Trust Policy* – The platform trust policy provides the security policy required by the platform in order to meet a specified level of assurance.

- *Trusted Platform Module (TPM)* – The TPM is used to securely verify the boot process.

Secure Cloud Interfaces and APIs

How can APIs be secured against unauthorized access?

Problem	On-premise and cloud-based resource interfaces and APIs are, by default, vulnerable to attacks through a number of vectors and methods.
Solution	A cloud identity and access management (IAM) system is instituted to differentiate intruders from legitimate consumers.
Application	An authentication gateway service (AGS) and an IAM system are implemented to identify and authenticate legitimate consumers and grant them access, while denying access to intruders.
Mechanisms	Authentication Gateway Service (AGS), Identity and Access Management (IAM)

Problem

Cloud computing providers create software interfaces and APIs that consumers use to manage and interface to cloud services. Service consumption, provisioning, management, orchestration, and monitoring are all performed using these interfaces. The security and availability of cloud services relies on the security of these interfaces and APIs.

In Figure 8.12, the API needs to distinguish authorized on-premise and cloud consumers from intruders:

A. Both authorized consumers and attackers can originate attacks on-premise, in the cloud, or via the Internet.

B. Legitimate users are granted access to resources after they are authorized.

C. Intruders are separated from legitimate users.

D. Legitimate components or services are separated from compromised components and services.

E. Intruding malware can be installed and form attacks.

F. Legitimate components and services can be compromised and used to form attacks.

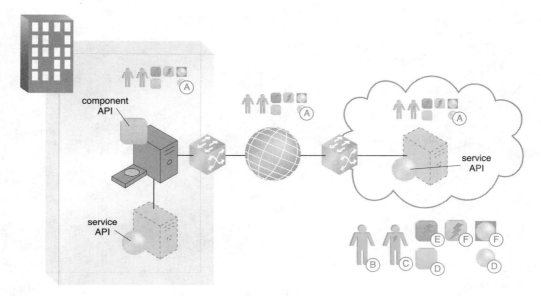

Figure 8.12
Common cloud API authentication requirements.

Solution

A cloud identity and access management (IAM) system is instituted to provide identities, authentication services, and support for access control to differentiate intruders
from legitimate consumers. If an API does not support authentication or authentication
to the security level of assurance required, an authentication proxy is placed in front of
the API.

Application

As part of an IAM, an authentication gateway service (AGS) is installed on-premise for
authentication to on-premise and cloud provider services on behalf of cloud consumers.
Consumers can be users or non-person entities (NPEs), which are services or components that require authentication for access.

Figure 8.13 illustrates a solution in the following steps:

1. Both authorized consumers and attackers request resources from on-premise,
   from the Internet, and from the cloud.

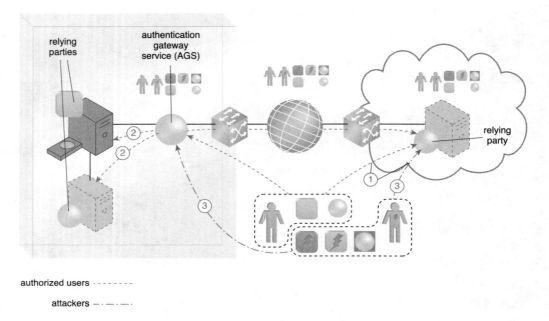

authorized users - - - - - - - -

attackers — · — · — ·

Figure 8.13
The AGS authenticates cloud consumers for access to APIs.

2. Authorized users and authorized components or services are authenticated and, if they have the proper privileges, are granted access to resources.

3. Intruding malware, compromised components or services, and intruders are rejected by the AGS.

Identification, authentication and access control, encryption, and activity monitoring of these interfaces must be designed to protect against both accidental and malicious attempts to circumvent security. An IAM system that supports access control mechanisms must be implemented to establish identities for cloud consumers and their attributes. The AGS uses the identities for authentication, and relying party resources verify authentication from the AGS and make an access decision that is usually based on attributes of the requesting authenticated consumer. If relying party resources can provide authentication to the required level of security assurance, it may not be desirable to use the authentication proxy. Establishment of identities and identity claims on tokens that meet the desired level of assurance may be all that is required.

An impact of applying this pattern is the need to establish the required IAM security assurance level, and establish the functions of the IAM to the corresponding level. Participating on-premise and cloud resources or relying parties must be configured or developed to authenticate consumers.

Mechanisms

- *Authentication Gateway Service (AGS)* – The AGS is used to provide positive authentication of consumers to providers.

- *Identity and Access Management (IAM)* – IAM is a system used to establish identities for consumption by the AGS and provide attributes to support access control for relying parties.

Cloud Resource Access Control

How can cloud consumer attributes be made available to determine cloud resource access control in multiple proprietary clouds?

Problem	Proprietary cloud providers each have their own methods and protocols for authentication and access control, which contributes to vendor lock-in.
Solution	A cloud single sign-on (SSO) architecture is established, incorporating an authentication gateway service (AGS) and attribute authority for implementation of cloud resource access control.
Application	An AGS and attribute authority connected to a secure token service (STS) are implemented and provisioned with the organization's cloud consumers' accounts and attributes. An attributed based access control (ABAC) mode of access control is instituted as the cloud service provider using the organization's SSO infrastructure.
Mechanisms	Attribute Authority, Attribute-Based Access Control (ABAC) System, Cloud-based Security Groups, Secure Token Service (STS), Single Sign-On (SSO)

Problem

Current public cloud providers lack compatibility and interoperability of their identity and access management (IAM) solutions. For example, some of the leading cloud providers only support identity-based authorization for their cloud consumers, and those solutions are not interoperable. Completely delegating access control to a cloud provider, including policy management, storage, and security enforcement, requires a strong trust relationship which may not be possible to meet security assurance level requirements, can create implementation dependency between a cloud consumer and the cloud provider, and can cause vendor lock-in.

In Figure 8.14, Organization A has developed SaaS but is relying on the cloud provider's IAM. Organization A's services are distributed between two proprietary cloud providers, Cloud Provider A and Cloud Provider B. This can be done strictly for continuity of operations (COOP) and failover purposes by creating a second instance of the service in a second cloud. Alternately, there may be a reason to put part of the functionality in Cloud Provider A and part of it in Cloud Provider B.

The following steps are shown in Figure 8.14:

1. Cloud Consumer A accesses Service A located in Cloud Provider A using Cloud Provider A's IAM.

2. For Cloud Consumer A to obtain access to Service B located in Cloud Provider B requires IAM incompatible with Cloud Provider A's IAM. For example, Cloud B may require separate identity tokens and a separate database for the cloud consumer's attributes.

As a result, if a proprietary cloud provider's IAM is incompatible with other cloud providers, the cloud consumer can become locked into a single cloud or encounter IAM complexities to incorporate more than one proprietary cloud.

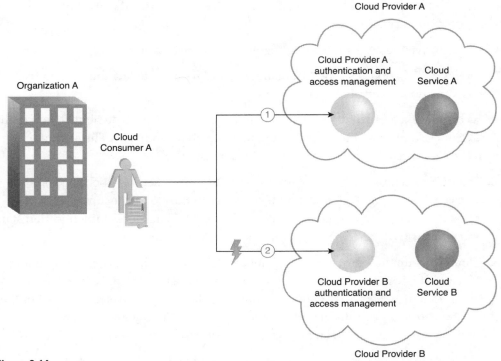

Figure 8.14

Cloud services distributed between Cloud Provider A and Cloud Provider B.

Solution

An IAM architecture is established by the cloud consumer, providing the separation of cloud computing resource provider and IAM provider. The cloud consumer specifies and manages security policies and consumes services from an attribute service. The attribute service provider can be a third party cloud IAM service provider, a cloud consumer established private cloud-based IAM, or a cloud consumer on-premise established IAM infrastructure. An attribute service and AGS managed by the organization enable them to choose different cloud providers without vendor lock-in when considering IAM.

In Figure 8.15, the diagram assumes that the attribute service has been provisioned with Organization A's cloud consumer attributes. Organization A has developed Service A and Service B to use the tokens issued by the AGS, which uses the attributes supplied by the attribute service.

1. Cloud Consumer A is directed to the AGS for authentication.

2. The AGS authenticates Cloud Consumer A and requests an attribute token from Organization A's attribute service.

3. Incorporating an STS function, the attribute service issues an attribute token to the AGS for Cloud Consumer A, referring to an attribute authority. The attribute token has a short lifespan, typically around 2 to 3 minutes.

4. The AGS provides the attribute token to Cloud Consumer A, which supports access control as an SSO model with attributes of the cloud consumer. The attributes will be used by the cloud service providers to determine authentication state and access privileges.

5. Cloud Consumer A provides the attribute token to Service A to prove authentication and support an access decision for its resources. Cloud Consumer A is also required to use their certificate and a holder-of-key (HOK) assertion as part of the attribute exchange protocol with the cloud service. Without an HOK check, the attribute token can be stolen and used by an attacker.

6. Using an SSO architecture, the cloud consumer provides the attribute token to Service B to prove authentication and support an access decision for its resources. Again, Cloud Consumer A is required to do an HOK check as part of the attribute exchange protocol.

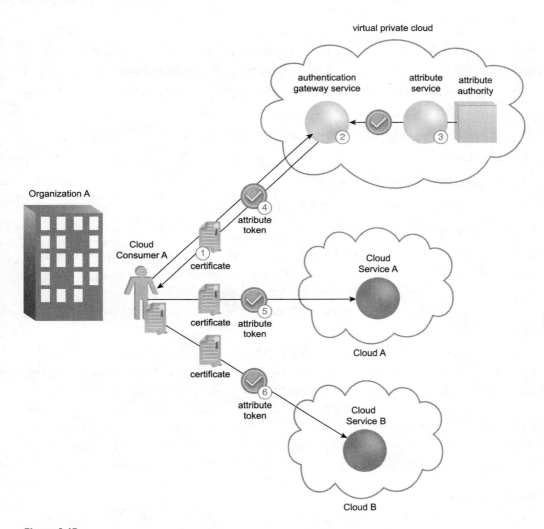

Figure 8.15
An example of an attribute service and access control in multiple proprietary clouds.

Application

The AGS and attribute service must be provisioned with the organization's cloud consumers' accounts and attributes. The pattern uses an attribute-based access control (ABAC) IAM model. Most IAM models can be supported by the pattern, including the following:

- Identity-based access control (IBAC) with access control lists (ACLs)

- Role-based access control (RBAC)

- Attribute-based access control (ABAC)

- Role- and attribute-based access control (RABAC)

- Policy-based access control (PBAC)

Each model has advantages and disadvantages, and requires various configurations of directories and databases. The level of complexity increases in the same sequence as the models are listed. The HOK profile for SSO together with mitigations against cross-site scripting (XSS) and cross-site request forgery (CSRF) attacks provide a strong cloud vendor neutral solution.

The implications are that the separation of IAM and customized access control enforcement in different cloud providers reduces trust management issues and provides flexibility for cloud consumers to develop their own security policies based on organizational requirements, without relying on cloud providers' enforcement mechanisms in a rigid cloud provider environment. The cloud consumer must use their own service or a third party attribute service for support in controlling access to their services, as well as their own or a third party IAM for identities and authentication.

Mechanisms

- *Attribute Authority* – Attribute services use the attributes of the attribute authority when issuing attributes in the form of tokens to the cloud consumer.

- *Attribute-Based Access Control (ABAC) System* – ABAC is one of several access control mechanisms that can be used with this pattern.

- *Cloud-based Security Groups* – Cloud-based security groups limit unauthorized access to IT resources.

- *Secure Token Service (STS)* – The STS is an attribute service that mints tokens for the AGS to provide to the cloud consumer for SSO purposes, after authentication.

- *Single Sign-On (SSO)* – The SSO is used for consumers to sign on or prove authentication to two separate services after authenticating to the AGS.

Problem	Virtual machines that are installed from cloud consumer templates need to be discovered and secured from any known vulnerabilities. An IaaS consumer has the ability to install VMs that have not been vetted for security by the cloud provider.
Solution	A system that includes an internal usage policy is established, providing network and endpoint security that is VM-aware in order to locate and identify virtual machines and report and secure them.
Application	Using host-based security, including host-based VM discovery software, emergent VMs can be discovered and reported for further processing.
Mechanisms	Hardened Virtual Server Image, Hardware-Based VM Discovery System, Host-Based Security System (HBSS), Hypervisor, Virtual Infrastructure Manager (VIM)

Problem

A virtual server, also called a virtual machine (VM), uses virtualization software known as a hypervisor that emulates a physical server. Virtual servers are used by cloud providers to share the same physical server with multiple cloud consumers by providing cloud consumers with individual virtual server instances. Figure 8.16 shows three virtual servers being hosted by two physical servers. The number of instances a given physical server can share is limited by its capacity. The first physical server hosts two virtual servers and the second physical server hosts one virtual server.

Figure 8.16

Virtual servers share the same physical server.

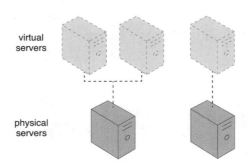

virtual servers

physical servers

In an IaaS environment, VMs are easily created, resulting in a risk of misconfiguration or operator error opening a security hole. A consumer can install a virtualization application and then be free to download pre-configured virtual machines from the Internet or to copy VMs locally to the system using removable media such as a USB thumb drive.

Consumer installed VMs can result in VM machines that are not being patched and monitored that contain vulnerabilities. Rogue VMs can appear on user desktop systems in particular. Rogue VMs can impose new vulnerabilities and consume resources and bandwidth. If these machines are not visible to the organization they cannot be remedied. VM sprawl is the propagation of virtual systems across the enterprise in an uncontrolled manner and this contributes to the issue.

A VM vulnerability, among other things, can allow a guest-to-host breakout exploit where the malware from one VM infects the host operating system. Once infected a host server is able to compromise any virtual environment running on it where it can create and launch its own rogue malicious virtual machine. Discovering virtual systems and the services running on them is as important as discovering physical machines.

Figure 8.17 shows a VM that has been installed in an unknown state of security provisioning:

A. The physical server.

B. A VM installed from an approved, hardened VM template from a VIM server.

C. A VM installed from an unknown, unapproved VM template.

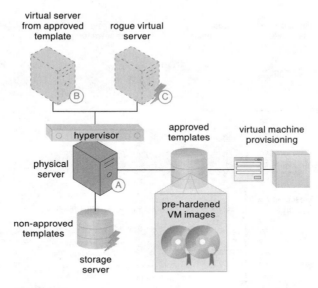

Figure 8.17

An installed rogue virtual server threatening approved server and other resources.

Solution

A system is established that can discover and monitor emergent VMs using a combination of tools and concepts. A hardware-based VM discovery system is installed to monitor and audit the security configurations of VMs periodically.

As an illustration, Figure 8.18 shows software installed on the host OS to discover and monitor VMs created on the subject host.

1. A non-approved VM is installed on a hardware server.

2. The VM discovery system discovers a rogue VM.

3. The VM discovery system quarantines the VM.

4. The discovery system alerts an administrator.

5. The administrator takes steps to configure and patch the VM to meet security requirements for use. Alternately, they could make the determination that an approved template can meet the requirements of the consumer and replace the vulnerable template.

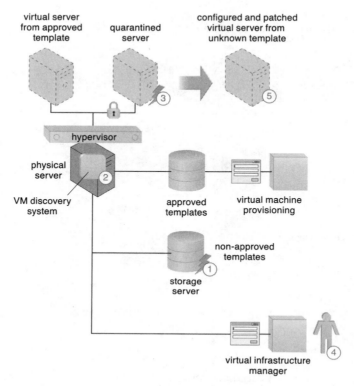

Figure 8.18
An enterprise VM discovery system.

Application

First, policy-based management and use of a virtualization management framework is necessary. VM lifecycle security policy can be created, which requires VMs to be pre-hardened, approved, and published to official templates for use in the infrastructure. As a first step to prevent VMs from accessing the physical LAN, the virtual machine network services should be disabled as a default, depending on the installed virtualization software. The application of the pattern is demonstrated in Figure 8.19.

Hardware-based VM discovery systems need to be installed and coordinated across network boundaries to monitor and audit the security configurations of VMs periodically. An enterprise VM discovery system is introduced that discovers virtualization in use throughout the organization's endpoints. Both the cloud service provider and cloud consumer on-premise resources need network mapping and scanning systems

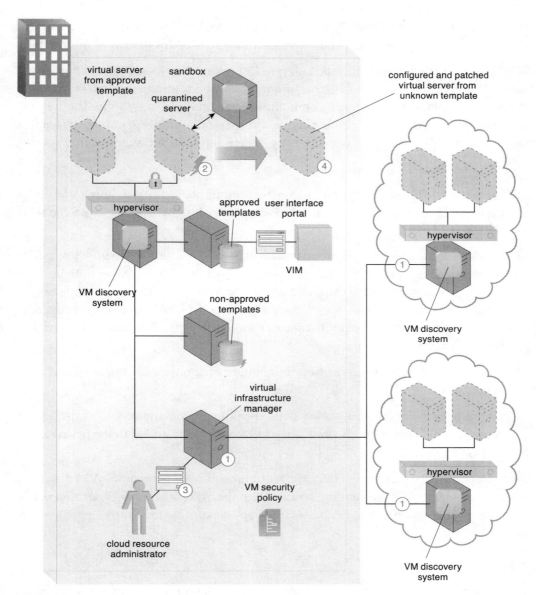

Figure 8.19
An enterprise VM discovery system.

to provide VM asset discovery. These tools must be deployed in a way that accounts for network security segmentation and provides for aggregation of discovery information.

The VM discovery system is installed on physical resource hosts as part of a host-based security system (HBSS). It must create and monitor policy and have visibility into the status of virtual machines running on both servers and desktop systems. The solution has to discover VMs from multiple vendors running on multiple operating systems. It must associate VMs with hosts and identify system software and vulnerability status.

Figure 8.19 depicts the following steps:

1. A master VM discovery system monitor communicates with each host's VM discovery system, and it sets the security policy describing what security profile the VMs should meet.

2. It monitors the number and security state of each VM according to policy as part of internal usage policy, alerting if a rogue VM is discovered. It takes both immediate automatic mitigation steps and alerts administrators. Mitigation steps can include moving the image to a sandbox area for provisioning and eliminating any networking possibilities as a quarantine measure. It controls multiple platforms both on-premise and in the cloud.

3. The monitoring system alerts the administrator of anonymous situations and actions taken.

4. The monitoring system mitigation steps, including automatic and administrator actions, establish a properly provisioned VM ready to be added to the network and enterprise.

As an impact, when procuring HBSS, the requirements need to include a VM discovery system and master VM monitoring system. With regard to VM security, written policy must be developed and maintained by a group responsible for overseeing corporate policy.

Mechanisms

- *Hardened Virtual Server Image* – Hardened virtual server images are installed by the VIM.

- *Hardware-Based VM Discovery System* – A hardware-based VM discovery system is installed as part of a platform's HBSS to communicate with the VM discovery system manager.

- *Host-Based Security System (HBSS)* – An HBSS is installed to include an automatic virtual machine discovery capability.

- *Hypervisor* – The hypervisor initiates establishment of VMs and does not inherently know if it is a hardened VM.

- *Virtual Infrastructure Manager (VIM)* – The VIM is used to create approved VM images and to install known VMs that are good.

Mobile BYOD Security

How can mobile device access to IT resources be secured?

Problem	Consumers often need to access enterprise information systems, whether they are on-premise or remote, using mobile devices including laptops, tablets, and smart phones, which pose special security requirements.
Solution	According to the BYOD security requirements, a security framework is established to monitor, control, and protect the mobile devices, their applications and data, and their network connections.
Application	An enterprise mobility management (EMM) system is implemented, covering the special security requirements of mobile devices.
Mechanisms	Enterprise Mobility Management (EMM) System

Problem

The cloud attribute of broad network access means that organizational capabilities are provided over the network and accessed through standard mechanisms that promote use by heterogeneous thin or thick client platforms such as laptops, tablets, mobile phones, personal digital assistants, and other mobile Internet devices.

Figure 8.20 illustrates the cloud attribute of broad network access. A service is available to many different kinds of devices, most often using TCP/IP communication and a Web browser-based delivery method that is similar across diverse computing platforms. The distribution of cloud services is normally provided by network and telecommunication carriers.

The platform operating systems are diverse, and each one can contain vulnerabilities. The apps can be pre-infected with malware instructed by hackers' command and control servers to steal information from the mobile device without alerting the users.

Organizations typically use mobile devices that are sometimes connected within an organization's security perimeter and sometimes exposed directly when traveling. Pervasive wireless communication poses a threat to security perimeters because there may not be a reliable way to form a boundary between external entities and internal entities. When uncontrolled paths to computing resources exist, the security perimeter is weakened or may not exist at all. These devices can create backdoors into systems by introducing an unknown network connection to a computer.

Figure 8.20

Broad network access providing support to diverse protocols.

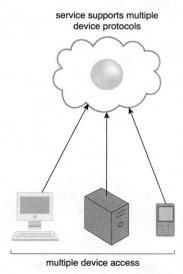

service supports multiple device protocols

multiple device access

In terms of legal risk, losing employee or client data can result in a company breach of industry compliance regulations, which could leave the company vulnerable to legal claims brought by the employee or client in question. In Figure 8.21, the need to secure a multitude of hardware platforms and operating systems, new networking paths, and new places for corporate data to reside is shown.

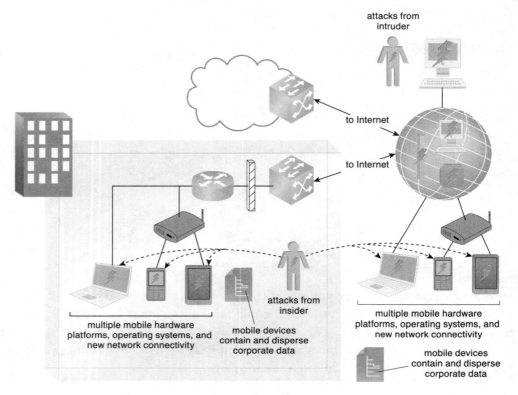

Figure 8.21
Security issues raised by mobile device usage.

Solution

BYOD requirements are developed in alignment with privacy and data security laws and industry compliance regulations. Device usage scenarios and use cases can be used to further develop BYOD security requirements. A flexible but enforceable policy is created to ensure that it effectively limits risk to the organization. The BYOD policy should complement other organization information security and governance policies.

According to the BYOD security requirements and policy developed, a security framework is established to monitor, control, and protect the mobile devices, their applications and data, and their network connections.

The following solutions address mobile device security issues, as shown in Figure 8.22:

A. Device (monitor)

- ownership type, either BYOD or corporate

- inventory of applications

- OS/version

- location including pre-defined geo-fencing

- compliance status indicating whether or not it is patched and contains only compliant applications

    Device (control)

- configure based on policy, push corporate security policy

- secure applications centrally using enterprise IdAM

- secure data access using enterprise IdAM

- audit to ensure policy is being enforced

    Device (protect)

- lost/stolen services – enable lock and wipe upon loss or theft

- protect data at rest and in motion

B. Network (monitor)

- monitor endpoints for compliance status

    Network (control)

- control corporate access with VPNs

    Network (protect)

- protect corporate network from mobile threats

C. Integrate with corporate SIEM and logging systems for visibility and monitor for compliance

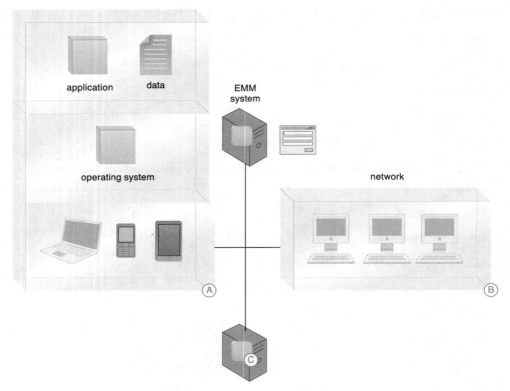

Figure 8.22
Monitoring, controlling, and protecting mobile devices.

Application

An enterprise mobility management (EMM) system is required to enforce policies and monitor usage and access. In a scenario where applications are installed directly on endpoints, IT has to determine and mandate the minimum specifications for OS and application support, performance, and other device-specific criteria. Corporate-owned personally enabled (COPE) devices can simplify the control issue.

The specific services made available on personally-owned devices and whether they will differ for specific work groups, user types, device types, and the network used needs to be determined. Network security capabilities must provide visibility into and protect against internal and external mobile threats, blocking of rogue devices, unauthorized users and non-compliant apps, and integration with SIEMs.

To protect the enterprise, network access control technology should be applied to authenticate people connecting to the network and check whether their devices have up-to-date antivirus software and security patches. Mobile devices should be put on a separate network segment. Industry standard security policies should be enforced, including whole-device encryption, PIN code, failed login attempt actions, and remotely wiping. A security baseline should be set and used to certify hardware/operating systems for enterprise use. Policy should contain control of mobile application deployment, patches and updates, and data ownership.

The monitoring related processing on personal devices can include the recording of geolocations and the tracking of Internet traffic. Companies must inform employees of the extent of the monitoring and ensure they are satisfied that the monitoring is justified by real benefits and does not unnecessarily infringe on privacy.

Mechanisms

- *Enterprise Mobility Management (EMM) System* – EMM provides the system for corporate enterprise management of BYOD and corporate supplied mobile devices.

Cloud Data Breach Protection

How can organizations provide protection against data breaches for cloud data?

Problem	Unprotected data is vulnerable to a wide variety of breaches by attackers that can have significant consequences on the cloud architecture security and/or the organization's business itself.
Solution	A system is established that provides encryption of sensitive data so that if it is lost, it is not readable by an attacker.
Application	Using validated encryption and governance that meets enterprise security assurance levels, data at rest is encrypted.
Mechanisms	Cryptographic Key Management System (CKMS), Threat Intelligence System

Problem

Industry data loss protection (DLP) compliance laws include the Health Insurance Portability and Accountability Act (HIPAA), the Sarbanes-Oxley Act (SOX), the Gramm-Leach-Bliley Act (GLBA), and others. With a multi-tenant cloud service, a flaw in one cloud consumer's application could allow an attacker access to their data and potentially every other tenant consumer's data as well. A common way in which data is ex-filtrated from enterprises is through the installation of malware and vulnerability exploits.

Figure 8.23 provides the following examples:

- Social engineering where the user is tricked into clicking a link to download and execute malware.

- Document hijacking, or "doc-jacking," where common documents containing exploits are delivered via network protocols.

- Malware delivered by something other than HTTP, such as email, a cloaked executable (.jpeg, .exe, .zip) or an infected USB drive, or malware delivered directly through a network intrusion.

- Once installed, malware can steal credentials or mount an attack from a trusted network to gain privileges and access to sensitive data.

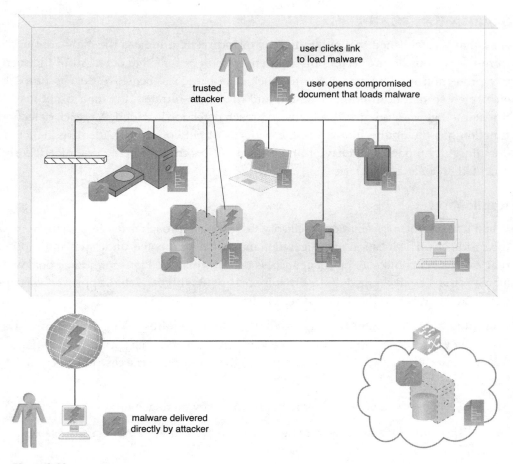

Figure 8.23
Various data breach attack vectors.

Evidence of malicious activity prior to data breaches is usually clearly documented in audit logs. If the organization knows about the activity, they can stop or mitigate the security threat. The longer it takes to discover a data breach, the more firmly rooted the attacker becomes, and more difficult and costly it becomes to discover and remove all of their malware. To quickly identify threats before they cause damage, realtime information and analysis of security events as they occur is required. The ability to rapidly spot and respond to actions that are out of the ordinary is required.

Solution

A system is established that either directly or indirectly mitigates the malware threats from the various attack vectors through encryption of sensitive data. All of the security protection mechanisms strive to block data breaches. Sensitive data is properly encrypted so that if all mitigations fail and data is ex-filtrated, the data is not lost. A threat intelligence system with a focus on breach detection is added. A breach detection function has the ability to analyze the patterns of network traffic, identify malicious domains, and model the behavior and impact of files that are being downloaded and executed on an attack surface.

Application

When prioritizing organizational security tasks, one approach is to view security from the inside out. The location of critical data must be documented under the assumption that an attacker could sooner or later access the information. Plans for how to deal with a breach must be developed. If data that is encrypted with validated, approved encryption is stolen, it is as if the data was never lost.

A cryptographic key management system (CKMS) is required, along with administrators, policy, and procedures, to manage key lifecycles and encryption of data. Figure 8.24 illustrates features of the data encryption that protects in the case of an actual data breach.

- A CKMS needs to be implemented to support key management.

- Policies and procedures need to be developed according to the security assurance level(s) required by the enterprise.

- Administrators need to be designated, trained, and given duties that together provide task administration. This separation of duties (SOD) protects against one or more people, depending on the assurance level, being able to attack the system alone.

- A split key cryptographic system supports SOD in that it takes more than one key to unlock and manage the CKMS, depending on the assurance level required. Keys are not stored with the data they protect.

- Data locations need to be inventoried and maintained to ensure rigorous protection of sensitive data.

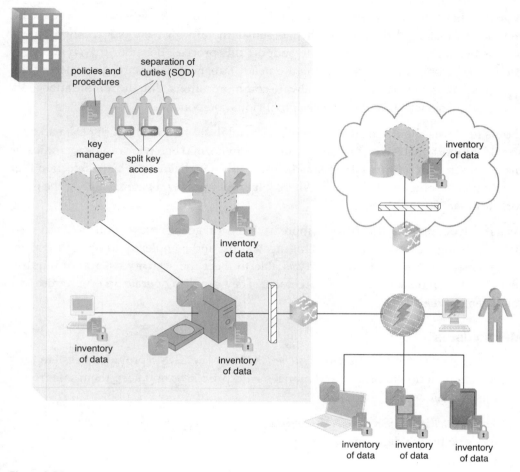

Figure 8.24

The use of enterprise encryption for sensitive data.

There are a number of considerations to be made, the first being in regards to the identification and classification of sensitive data since not all data requires DLP strategies.
It must be determined how sensitive data is currently being used and who requires
access to it, and identity and access management (IAM) must be employed to meet security requirements. In addition, DLP enforcement must be matched to the organizational
security policy to ensure compliance, not only for data at rest but for data in motion and
data endpoints as well.

A goal is the ability to identify zero-day malware on the network. Analysis needs to be conducted to establish proper placement of sensor monitoring technology. Development of sensitive data zone boundaries can support this process. Behavior-driven analytics need to be accomplished by analyzing the steady stream of data being generated by the organization's systems. Detecting malware communications with the remote attacker is as important as detecting the attacker's malicious components.

Inputs to SIEMs should include an intelligence analysis system and a Big Data adjunct should support analysis of data. A deviation from normal behavior can be an indicator that a breach is in progress. If an attacker encrypts a malicious payload, detection that encryption is being used in a place where it has not been used before can flag the issue for additional study.

As a result of applying this pattern, more backup storage is necessary due to encrypted data not being easily compressed. This creates cost and complexity to operating a key management system. If a third party is able to meet the security assurance requirements, they can outsource key management. They can also operate an on-premise key management regimen.

Mechanisms

- *Cryptographic Key Management System (CKMS)* – The CKMS provides a system for the organization to protect and manage enterprise keys and keep them safe from the attacker.

- *Threat Intelligence System* – A threat intelligence system is incorporated with a focus on breach detection.

Permanent Data Loss Protection

How can cloud consumers protect themselves from permanently losing their data?

Problem	Data can be permanently lost due to malicious attackers or from deletion by a cloud service provider, either through negligence or disaster. If encryption is being used on data and the encryption key is lost, the data is also lost.
Solution	A data retention policy is created and implemented as part of a security policy to mandate that backups of data and keys are created and maintained.
Application	Data is inventoried and assigned a sensitivity factor and a risk of loss factor, is encrypted and backed up in a location separate from the primary infrastructure, and the cloud consumer verifies that the cloud provider meets the data retention policy. A cryptographic key management system (CKMS) is implemented under the direct control of the data owner and is also backed up.
Mechanisms	Encryption, Cryptographic Key Management System (CKMS)

Problem

Data stored in the cloud can be lost due to malicious attackers, accidental deletion by the cloud service provider or user or administrator, or some type of disaster such as a fire or tornado. If unprepared, one of these events can result in the permanent loss of data. If a cloud consumer or cloud provider responsible for encrypting data loses the encryption keys, the corresponding encrypted data is also lost.

Data retention compliance requirements come from vertical industry governing laws such as the Payment Card Industry Data Security Standard (PCI DSS), the Health Insurance Portability and Accountability Act (HIPAA), Control Objectives for Information and Related Technology (COBIT), International Organization for Standardization (ISO) and International Electrotechnical Commission (ISO/IEC) 27002, the Sarbanes-Oxley Act (SOX), Security and Privacy Controls for Federal Information Systems and Organizations, the Gramm-Leach-Bliley Act (GLBA), and the Federal Information Security Management Act (FISMA), to name a few.

In Figure 8.25, the data loss vulnerabilities include the following:

A. Permanent deletion of data stored on-premise or in the cloud by a user, administrator, or attacker.

B. Permanent deletion of encryption keys stored on-premise or in the cloud by a user, administrator, or attacker.

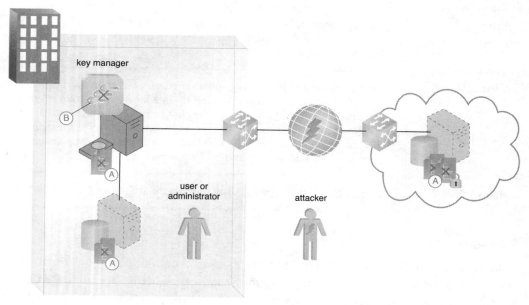

Figure 8.25

The loss of data occurs as a result of user/administrator mistakes or an attacker.

Solution

The organization's data custodians must develop and meet a retention policy by ensuring that the cloud provider has adequate processes to back up data in the cloud or anywhere it is located. The data includes any encryption keys used to encrypt the data. A data retention policy that includes requiring an inventory of data, its sensitivity, and a data loss risk assessment must be developed. Most compliance programs require a data retention policy and periodic audits to ensure the policy is being met.

Application

Data retention policy needs to be developed according to the most appropriate industry best practices, standards, and laws. Tools are available that provide templates to help identify types of data, such as personal identifiable information (PII). They provide a system to register the data in an inventory and identify risk of loss through malicious or criminal attack, system malfunction, or human error.

The backup of encryption keys is a critical and specialized piece of data retention policy. Normally, the separation of duties for cloud resource administrators that provide management of the cryptographic key management system (CKMS) is required.

Figure 8.26 illustrates the following:

A. Data retention policy, which normally meets a compliance requirement, requires an inventory of all sensitive data, the sensitivity level of the data, the risk of loss, and backup schedules and forms.

B. Backups of data and encryption keys are created according to policy. Backup copies are stored off-site and separate from operational data so that risks of loss are mitigated.

C. Periodic audits ensure compliance with policy.

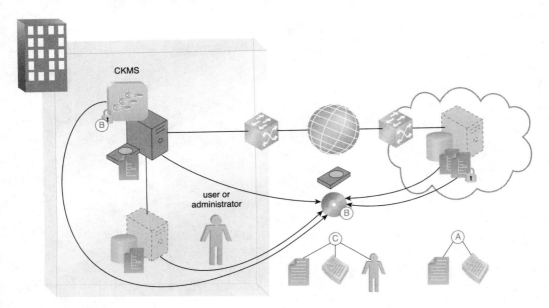

Figure 8.26
Permanent data loss risk mitigation in action.

Mechanisms

- *Encryption* – Encryption keys must be backed up to protect from encrypted data loss.

- *Cryptographic Key Management System (CKMS)* – The CKMS is used to house and manage encryption keys.

In-Transit Cloud Data Encryption

How can data be securely transmitted to, from, and within a cloud environment?

Problem	Data copied to and from a cloud environment transits networks and servers beyond the control of the organization and can be intercepted by malicious intermediaries.
Solution	A solution is implemented with capabilities that secure and protect data while it transfers between sender and receiver and also ensure that data will not be accepted by the receiver if the original data sent is modified.
Application	An encryption mechanism is implemented to encrypt data between sender and receiver for confidentiality, and a digital signature mechanism is implemented to provide integrity for the data.
Mechanisms	Cloud Storage Device, Cryptographic Key Management System (CKMS), Digital Signature, Encryption

Problem

Data between sender and receiver via the Internet requires security against malicious access in order to ensure data integrity and confidentiality. For example, an attacker can gain access and modify data before it enters the cloud environment, as shown in Figure 8.27. Data stored in a shared cloud environment can be susceptible to attack from other cloud consumers.

Solution

Data confidentiality and data integrity mechanisms are employed so that malicious intermediaries cannot observe the data or change it without detection. Cloud service providers are given the ability to read the data and check the integrity of the data.

Figure 8.27

An attacker intercepts data as it is being sent to Cloud Storage Device A.

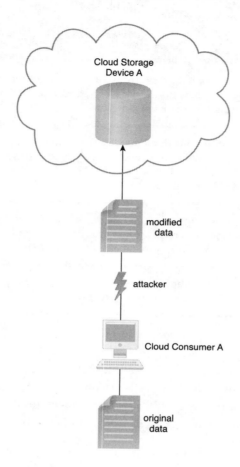

Application

An encryption mechanism is used to secure data as it travels between sender and receiver to provide confidentiality. The data is signed with a digital signature to provide for integrity checking. The cloud provider has the keys to decrypt the data and validates the digital signature of data received to ensure that it was not modified in transit, as shown in Figure 8.28.

If an attacker attempts to modify the data as it uploads into the cloud, the data will not be accepted by the receiver when they validate the digital signature, as illustrated in Figure 8.29.

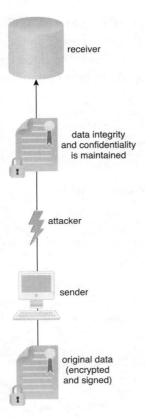

Figure 8.28

An attacker attempts to intercept data uploading into a cloud environment; however, the data is encrypted and signed before it is sent.

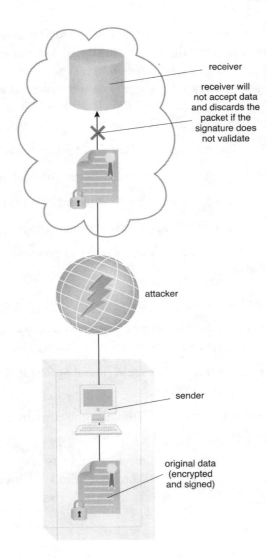

Figure 8.29

An attacker intercepts encrypted data before it is received by the cloud provider, and the receiver discards the packet as a result of maintaining data integrity and confidentiality.

When encrypting data between a cloud consumer and cloud environment, a client-side encryption method can be used with key management so that cloud consumers can own and manage the encryption key. When this pattern is applied inside the cloud environment to encrypt and secure data transferred inside the cloud, the encryption key management is handled by the cloud provider or cloud consumer depending on industry regulatory requirements using a cryptographic key management system (CKMS).

There are different levels of encryption used on data as follows:

- Data can be encrypted between the host and storage array.
- Data can be encrypted between the storage fabric and storage array.
- Data can be encrypted at the fabric layer.

All of the above options can be implemented simultaneously based on the required level of security.

Mechanisms

- *Cloud Storage Device* – Data stored on a cloud storage device can be encrypted and decrypted before entering or exiting the physical disks.
- *Cryptographic Key Management System (CKMS)* – A CKMS is used to manage encryption keys.
- *Digital Signature* – Digital signatures are used to sign data in transit and are validated by the cloud provider.
- *Encryption* – This mechanism is used to encrypt and decrypt data traveling into or out of physical disks stored in a cloud environment.

Chapter 9

Network Security, Identity & Access Management and Trust Assurance Patterns

Secure On-Premise Internet Access

Secure External Cloud Connection

Secure Connection for Scaled VMs

Cloud Denial-of-Service Protection

Cloud Traffic Hijacking Protection

Automatically Defined Perimeter

Cloud Authentication Gateway

Federated Cloud Authentication

Cloud Key Management

Trust Attestation Service

Collaborative Monitoring and Logging

Independent Cloud Auditing

Threat Intelligence Processing

This chapter acts as a continuation of Chapter 8 in that it continues to focus on cloud security architectures and solutions. This time, the areas covered are network security with an emphasis on external connectivity issues, the management of identities and access levels, and patterns that are applied to establish trust boundaries and characteristics.

Problem	The security profile for a network segment that has Internet access is equivalent to that of the Internet, which makes assets, internal or cloud, vulnerable to attacks over this segment.
Solution	A system is established whereby an Internet access segment consisting of network elements supports outbound interactions from the site to external entities via the Internet. All inbound interactions are handled via a controlled sharing (DMZ) segment. This DMZ segment contains mitigations to the current attacks and connection to cloud resources is established from a separate trusted network segment using cryptography.
Application	Using firewall and router security mechanisms, subnets with access controls lay the foundation for separating and protecting resources and at the same time provide required Internet access.
Mechanisms	Application Delivery Controller, Domain Name Service (DNS), Hardware Security Module (HSM), Intrusion Detection and Prevention System (IDPS), Security Information and Event Management (SIEM) System, Virtual Private Network (VPN)

Problem

The Internet connection is the first location where consumer and attacker need to be identified and separated as it is the primary point of entry for external attackers. Figure 9.1 provides an example where outbound interactions are initiated by consumers from within the enterprise that allow bi-directional data flow. This region contains the highest level of uncertainty because the untrusted network and trusted network are both present. Probes and brute force authentication attacks targeting infrastructure devices are common, and poorly designed networks will unintentionally allow enumeration of network accounts in credential stores.

Figure 9.1 shows the following threats to an enclave connected to the Internet:

A. Man-in-the-middle (MITM), session hijacking, cross-site scripting (XSS), malicious DNS attacks and distributed denial-of-service (DDoS) attacks are examples of the types of attacks that can be mounted. They are executed against any surface that is revealed to the Internet. One goal of these attacks is to install malware that further exploits enclave vulnerabilities.

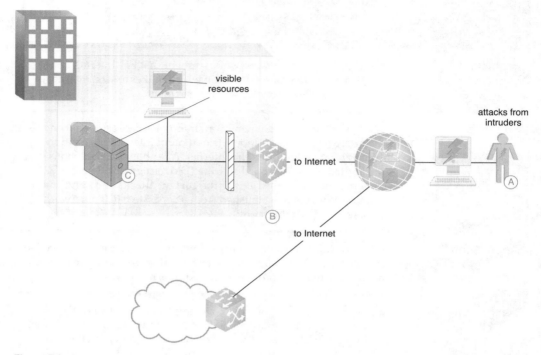

Figure 9.1
Examples of common Internet attacks.

B. Other attacks that can be encountered are malicious DNS responses that deceive internal components into interacting with malicious entities on the Internet or allowing botnet command and control server interactions with compromised internal hosts. DNS tunneling is often used to bypass access controls.

C. An example of malware is a botnet zombie that is installed on a visible resource and takes instructions from a remote attacker. Malware is installed on visible resources.

Solution

Secure network segmentation is introduced to protect internal networks from the Internet, starting with an external Internet-facing firewall. In Figure 9.2, firewalls and network address translation (NAT) provide protection from Internet intruders as follows:

A. Firewalled subnets provide segmentation to separate peered networks, participating in a DMZ architecture that protects all internal and external connections. The network segmentation architecture allows for mitigations to be put in place to combat the evolving taxonomy of Internet-based attacks.

B. For inbound access control, firewalls prevent attacks from the Internet. For outbound access control, the firewall allows authorized outbound interactions. For both inbound and outbound traffic, NAT provides information hiding capabilities.

C. To establish connection to cloud resources, VPNs are employed. This lays the groundwork to create cryptographically protected communication between cloud resources and on-premise protected resources.

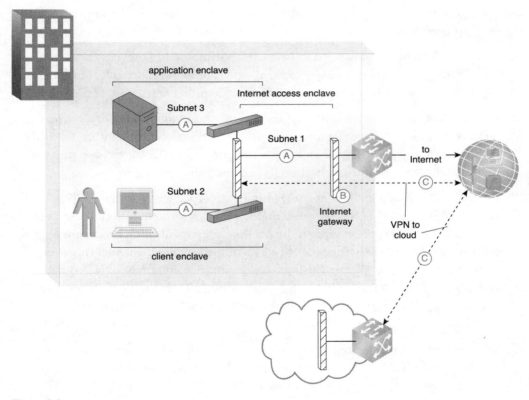

Figure 9.2
An example of subnet segmentation, firewalls, and NAT provider protection from Internet intruders.

Application

A security architecture is created using subnets that provide a foundation for multiple security services across the enclaves. Access cascades between enclaves through the firewalls so that any enclave can only connect to adjacent enclaves with the proper permissions. The architecture can be expanded to provide multiple enclaves for requirements such as infrastructure services, for example DNS and subsystems that are used by outward-facing Web services. Each function of the Web service can be isolated into a separate enclave. The enclave segmentation lays the groundwork to establish mitigations for various types of attacks. The concept of an application delivery controller (ADC) is used where a number of protection mechanisms are combined in a network device. Figure 9.3 illustrates mechanisms and their relationships in implementing the pattern.

A. Whitelists and blacklists are established and maintained to prevent users from interacting with known or suspected malicious entities and to protect internal assets from attacks. Black hole is used to provide protection against DDoS attacks.

B. A DMZ ADC acting as a security gateway performs a dual role in protecting against attacks and detecting anomalous information flow from within the DMZ. It provides application security and data loss protection (DLP), and can prevent data leakage and provide application level protection.

   Proxies and TLS accelerators are hosted in the Internet access enclave. They terminate encrypted TLS sessions so that the traffic can be monitored within the enclaves. Since encryption without inspection hides exfiltration occurring within enclaves, a TLS proxy that consists of a TLS offloading engine is incorporated. This engine can be accelerated using a hardware security module (HSM) with cryptographic acceleration that will accept inbound TLS traffic from consumers and decrypt it. This provides elimination of TLS processing on servers and support for application layer functions.

C. The firewalls are configured to perform stateful packet inspection of network traffic after the TLS proxy decrypts the communication. This allows inspection of unencrypted traffic as it traverses other enclaves.

D. The security architecture is expanded to provide other security services including network IDPS, application and database firewalling, in-line malware scanning, and load balancing. IDPS devices are necessary to safeguard the infrastructure as well as to examine the evolving taxonomy of Internet-based attacks.

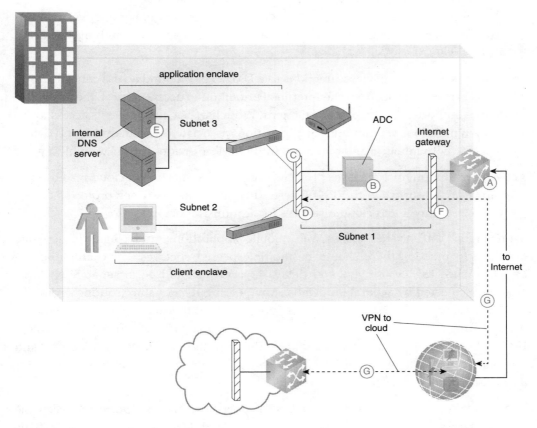

Figure 9.3

An example of the application of the Secure Internet Access pattern.

For pre-infection threat prevention, IDPS blocks exploitation of known application vulnerabilities. Anti-malware functions block exploitation of data-driven application vulnerabilities. The IDPS enforces protocols and data compliance. Post-infection threat prevention detects and blocks interactions with bot command and control servers. IDPS controls block leakage of sensitive data to destinations outside of the organization.

E. An internal DNS is configured to protect against DNS attacks. Clients and servers must point to trusted DNS servers within the enclave. The enclave DNS servers then connect to authoritative servers on the Internet. DNS servers within the network application enclave as well as all DNS clients within the other enclaves are not permitted direct Internet access for names resolution. For queries of external domains, clients and servers must perform lookups through the enclave DNS servers.

F. The Internet access enclave functions as a DMZ. For inbound access control, firewalls prevent attacks from the Internet. For outbound access control, the firewall allows authorized outbound interactions. Whitelist/blacklist prevents access to known malicious sites and use of applications associated with malware and data loss. For both inbound and outbound traffic, NAT provides information hiding.

G. With the on-premise enclaves protected, required connection to cloud resources can be accomplished with VPNs. These VPNs are routed between protected on-premise enclaves and cloud resources for administration.

Segmentation of enclaves places web, mobile applications, and clients in separate enclaves. In practice, there should be multiple peered enclaves. For example, infrastructure such as DNS servers and database servers should be in separate enclaves that are connected by separate firewalls. Any peering relationship (routing protocols, VPN, LDAP, etc.) must be mutually authenticated prior to establishing a trusted connection. This control helps defeat attack sources masquerading as trusted peers. Integrity checking must also be in place to defeat man-in-the-middle attacks. Identity and access management (IAM) must be implemented with separation of duties (SOD) for administrators.

The standalone Internet-facing firewall is intended to serve as a buffer between the Internet access enclave and the remaining enclaves within the peered segment. This approach prevents resource exhaustion attacks that target the Internet-facing firewall. External management and non-public information exposure are disabled on the outside interfaces. Access control lists (ACLs) are created with permit statements that match security policy and align with business requirements. This approach applies to both inbound and outbound traffic. ACLs must end with an explicit deny with logging enabled for dropped connections. An automatic routing black hole is implemented on the routers and firewall, and black hole routes are used to prevent traffic from crossing network segments. For example, a black hole route implemented on the border router is used to prevent a DDoS attack.

Logging of denied packets provides valuable insight including common attack vectors, taxonomies, and firewall administrator ACL change errors. This data is also valuable for effective data and event correlation across all network and security devices. Logging of the permitted traffic is a commonly accepted practice.

Data leakage prevention includes network-related information like internal IP addresses and routing tables. ICMP and other non-required vulnerable protocols are disabled to defeat reconnaissance efforts by attackers. All network devices must have a common authoritative time source via Network Time Protocol (NTP). This provides credibility for logging and data correlation.

An impact of using a suite of security mechanisms, besides the cost and complexity, is the critical need for automation. Security design should always first consider automation that includes incorporation of a security information and event management (SIEM) system to support incident alerting and auditing.

Mechanisms

- *Application Delivery Controller (ADC)* – The ADC concept is applied by combining security functions on some security devices.

- *Domain Name Service (DNS)* – DNS is secured against attacks by installing an internal DNS in a protected enclave.

- *Hardware Security Module (HSM)* — An HSM provides cryptograph acceleration for high cryptographic processing workload requirements.

- *Intrusion Detection and Prevention System (IDPS)* – IDPSs are installed as part of the ADC concept.

- *Security Information and Event Management (SIEM) System* – SIEM is used for alerting and auditing and to support coordination of the inputs from the various security mechanisms.

- *Virtual Private Network (VPN)* – The VPN is used to securely connect the on-premise resources to the cloud resources.

Problem	Solutions and service compositions can be required to execute partially in the cloud and partially on-premise due to scaling requirements, compliance regulations, or organizational policy, creating the need for secure connectivity.
Solution	A virtual private network (VPN) is used to establish an encrypted connection between the cloud service provider and the cloud consumer.
Application	A VPN tunnel is established between the cloud consumer gateway (CCG) and the cloud provider's virtual private gateway (VPG).
Mechanisms	Cloud Consumer Gateway (CCG), Virtual Private Cloud (VPC), Virtual Private Network (VPN), VPN Cloud Hub

Problem

Federal regulations, such as the Sarbanes-Oxley Act (SOX) and the Health Insurance Portability and Accountability Act (HIPAA) and laws and industry mandates such as the Payment Card Industry Data Security Standard (PCI DSS), often require organizations to maintain some processing and storage on-premise. Some on-premise IT capability may be maintained for continuity of operations and disaster recovery. The connection to two geographically dispersed locations combined with the complexities of the cloud poses connection security challenges. Figure 9.4 illustrates the security situation for a single cloud provider. The connection needs to protect against man-in-the-middle, snooping, and other attacks.

Solution

A cloud consumer gateway (CCG) is established on the cloud consumer side and connected to a virtual private cloud (VPC) using encryption. The encrypted connection is illustrated in Figure 9.5.

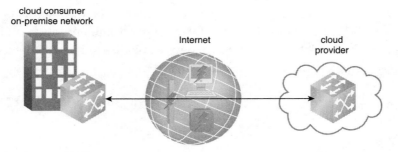

Figure 9.4
A consumer's on-premise network needs to connect to the cloud securely.

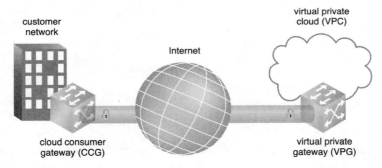

Figure 9.5
A secure connection is established between the cloud consumer network and virtual private cloud.

Application

The VPG is connected to the CCG via a virtual private network (VPN). The VPN extends the on-premise private network across the Internet or other public network, or wide area network (WAN). The VPN securely connects geographically separated offices of an organization, extending and creating one network. A customer edge (CE) device is located at the edge of the cloud consumer's network, providing access to the VPN. A provider edge (PE) device is a device or set of devices at the edge of the cloud provider network that connects to consumer networks through CE devices and maintains the VPN state.

VPNs ensure confidentiality and integrity of communication. They employ authentication mechanisms to ensure that the communication parties are who they claim to be, encryption to ensure confidentiality and integrity of data, and optionally, compression for efficient use of bandwidth.

The IPsec Security Protocol is a suite of protocols developed by the Internet Engineering Task Force (IETF) that provides standards for encryption, authentication, and compression at the network level. In Figure 9.6, a CE device is connected to a PE device, creating a VPN tunnel using the IPsec Protocol standard.

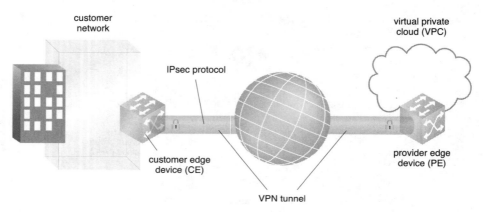

Figure 9.6
A customer network securely connected to a VPC.

In cloud computing, there are multiple configurations and network topologies that can be applied to this pattern. The pattern assumes a hardware device at each network, establishing the VPN. Software VPNs can be established within VMs or within any combination of VMs and physical devices. Another option for connection is the VPN hub-and-spoke with a VPN cloud hub. The cloud hub is a hub-and-spoke model that connects multiple branch offices and existing Internet connections with a VPC or multiple VPCs.

Figure 9.7 shows the VPN cloud hub architecture with connections to multiple VPCs. The dashed lines indicate the network being routed over their VPN connections between sites. One secure connection (A) is shown between Cloud Consumer Network 1 and VPC 1. A second connection (B) is shown between VPC 1 and VPC 2.

The major impact of establishing a VPN is networking and the security and management of encryption keys. The Cloud Key Management (444) pattern provides insight to these issues, as well as viable solutions. The network topology is complex, requiring concentrated focus from network designers and implementers and an understanding of routing protocols such as the Border Gateway Protocol (BGP), Open Shortest Path First (OSPF), and the Enhanced Interior Gateway Routing Protocol (EIGRP), which allows routes between sites connected by site-to-site VPN connections to be automatically learned. Security policy needs to be developed in regards to key management systems, and assurance level of the encryption needs to be determined based on the data sensitivity and risk of compromise. Once the VPNs are established, they must be monitored and must have automatic recovery provisioning when outages are encountered.

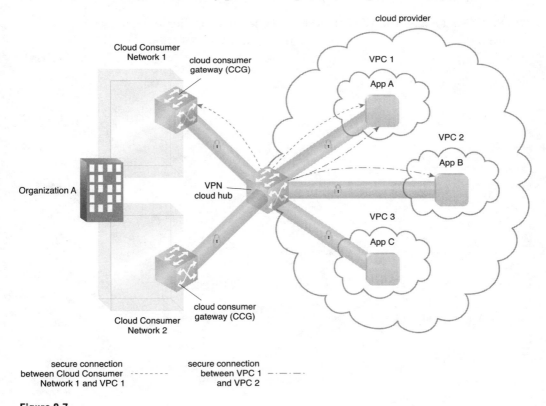

Figure 9.7
VPN connections are established via the use of a cloud hub.

Mechanisms

- *Cloud Consumer Gateway (CCG)* – The CCG is used by the cloud provider to terminate a cloud consumer's VPN.

- *Virtual Private Cloud (VPC)* – The VPC is used for normal processing while on-premise resources are used to house high value corporate data.

- *Virtual Private Network (VPN)* – The VPN is the selected method for encrypting the data in-transit.

- *VPN Cloud Hub* – The VPN cloud hub is used to consolidate the VPN connection from the on-premise network, as well as multiple connections to VPCs.

Secure Connection for Scaled VMs

How can connections be scaled to protect dynamically scaled VMs in a way that mitigates cloud provider lock-in?

Problem	When scaling cloud resources, differences between cloud consumer on-premise firewall, multiple cloud provider firewall, and network protection offerings can make it difficult to configure secure networking.
Solution	A system is established by controlling network traffic moving in and out of the VM using firewall agents or operating system firewalls. This creates a portable security solution that is location independent and scales as VMs are created.
Application	Using firewall agents or operating system-based firewalls, VMs can be pre-configured with a baseline of firewall policy, including VPN configuration, so that when VMs are created or live migrated in a cloud burst or other scaling activity, the associated firewall is also created or live migrated and pre-configured with firewall policy.
Mechanisms	Certificate, Cloud-based Security Groups, Digital Signature, Hardened Virtual Server Image, Live VM Migration, Virtual Firewall

Problem

Firewall rules are often managed in a hierarchical manner based on physical location, logical location of the assets on subnets, and functions of the server requiring network services. Within a particular firewall, rules are normally organized based on the logical architecture of the network. Policy grouping typically includes traffic entering the DMZ, traffic leaving the DMZ, and traffic entering or leaving the internal network, plus other network protection requirements. These policies can have hundreds of rules, including firewall virtual private network (VPN) configurations.

When VMs are created, isolation and security zones can be established through the use of firewalls, routers, switches, intrusion detection and prevention system (IDPS) devices, and other physical devices on the network in virtualization environments in order to meet security needs. As VMs are moved, the policies and required infrastructure need to move with them. However, the VMs are ephemeral in that hosts and IPs are constantly being created for the requested workload and removed when the resources are no longer needed.

Firewalls can become an issue during virtual machine replication, when either scaling in a homogeneous firewall environment or bursting into a heterogeneous firewall environment. Under these circumstances, firewall security must be handled quickly and automatically, as scaling or a burst is usually due to the immediate need for more processing resources.

Multiple firewall vendors' products can also become an issue. The consumer organization may be using one kind of firewall internally, but their cloud provider may not be supporting it. A second provider may be using another firewall solution. This can create the requirement to manage firewall policies across multiple vendor interfaces.

Figure 9.8 shows two consumer business processes being protected by a network or subnet-oriented firewall. There is a requirement to burst out to the cloud and at the same time maintain firewall protection. The issue lies in how to quickly configure the cloud firewall system to maintain the current level of protection.

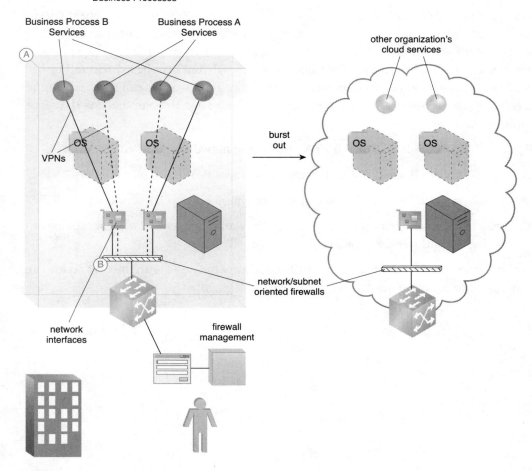

Figure 9.8

Organization A's cloud consumer needs to scale out from on-premise and may also need to scale from one cloud to another (A). Meanwhile, the firewall connectivity and security need to be managed in realtime (B).

Solution

A system is established that can use a single firewall policy, which is enforced regardless of execution location or firewall offering by a cloud provider. This can be done by using the firewall built into each operating system or by virtual firewall agents dedicated to each VM. By defining the rules within the virtual host-based firewall or firewall agents, protection is not dependent on location, and the rules can scale as VMs are created. Firewall rules can be set once, and no longer need to be updated if the server switches locations.

Figure 9.9 shows OS-level firewall VPNs providing network security as follows:

A. An OS or virtual agent firewall connects Business Process A's services via a VPN.

B. An OS or virtual agent firewall connects Business Process B's services via a VPN.

C. They are all managed by a policy-driven firewall management system capable of managing multiple OS type firewalls or firewall agents.

When services are burst into a cloud, the firewalls are included with the OS and are preconfigured to continue operations.

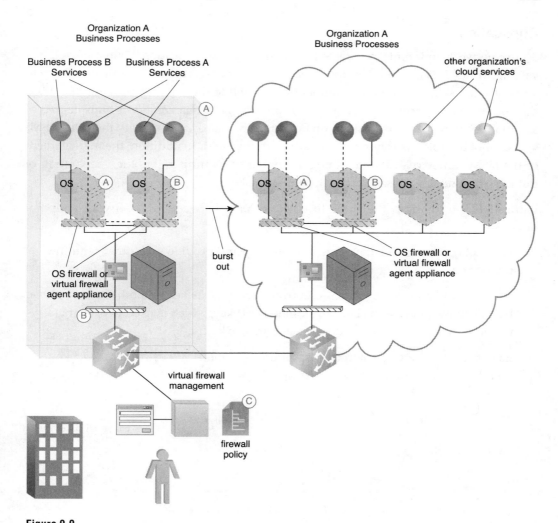

Figure 9.9

Organization A's services are burst out into a cloud, either by live migration or spin up from a hardened virtual server image. Virtual machine replication can be used to live migrate a VM from an on-premise configuration in a burst out to the cloud.

Application

Secure network endpoints are created using mutual authentication. With a virtual private network (VPN), each endpoint device, such as a firewall, must have a certificate to authenticate itself. Each endpoint authenticates itself to the other by proving that it has the corresponding private key using a cryptographic exchange. For a high degree of key management security, the key can be stored in a hardware security module (HSM) so it cannot be stolen without physical access to the HSM. In addition, the management of the HSM can be distributed among a number of administrators for a separation of duties so that no one person can compromise the keys.

Figure 9.10 summarizes the steps to create a VPN between two network endpoint devices:

1. Firewalls exchange certificates to authenticate and provide each other with their public key.

2. Each firewall creates a shared secret from their private key and other peers' public key. They each derive the Diffie-Hellman (DH) key, which is used to exchange material that will be used to derive a symmetric key.

3. Each firewall creates its own corresponding symmetrical key from the DH key and the material exchanges and sets up a VPN.

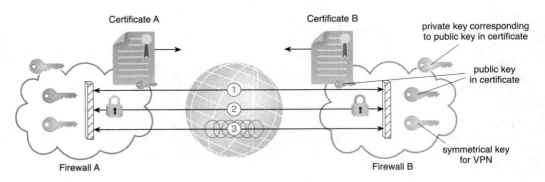

Figure 9.10
An example of the establishment of a VPN.

Organizations should create policies that move network associations required for virtual machines along with the virtual machines themselves. Virtualization-aware solutions that can manage network security policies and work with the hypervisor for added visibility and control need to be implemented. Hardened master VM template images used to create new servers must include the host firewall and firewall policy. Alternately, virtual firewall agents can be allocated to each VM and included in the image template. The template should use digital signatures to ensure integrity, assuming a proper signature validation is performed. As images are deployed on new servers, they inherit the parent image's latest security policies. Service security from a firewall standpoint becomes automatic when cloud bursting or scaling. As the IP address changes, other location-dependent factors such as network security automatically change configurations or are assisted by an administrator.

Implications for using OS-based firewalls include the potential of lowering costs since those firewalls are included in the OS pricing. This pattern is vendor independent, an impact of which is that a third party or combination of third party components is likely required to implement the pattern. If firewall agents are used, there will be license costs as well as the need for a management console.

For security reasons, it is important to monitor network traffic and alert to anomalies. The organization should not use virtual networking unless a coordinated virtual network monitoring system is in place. Otherwise it is not possible to monitor virtual networking since it does not traverse the network layer.

Mechanisms

- *Certificate* – Certificates are used for mutual authentication of VPN endpoints.

- *Cloud-based Security Groups* – Cloud-based security groups support resource scaling referencing firewall policy.

- *Digital Signature* – The digital signature is used to establish and verify the integrity of VM image templates.

- *Hardened Virtual Server Image* – Hardened virtual server images are established to include pre-configured virtual firewalls for scaling.

- *Live VM Migration* – Enables migration of virtual servers from one location in a burst out without service interruption.

- *Virtual Firewall* – A virtual firewall appliance (virtual software) is paired with each VM to establish a VPN that is easily relocated along with the associated services it connects and protects.

Cloud Denial-of-Service Protection

How can cloud services be protected against denial-of-service attacks?

Problem	Cloud denial-of-service (DoS) attacks are multifaceted and prevent consumers of cloud services from accessing their cloud resources.
Solution	A cloud DoS protection service is incorporated into the security architecture to shield the cloud provider from DoS attacks.
Application	A network DoS protection service is incorporated and updates are made to the domain name service (DNS) to route all cloud provider traffic through the protection service, which filters attack traffic and routes only legitimate traffic to the cloud provider. Alternately, the cloud provider can route traffic to a DoS protection service when experiencing an attack, or create their own DoS protection service.
Mechanisms	Domain Name Service (DNS), Traffic Filter, Traffic Monitor

Problem

There are three categories of DoS attacks: volume-based attacks, protocol attacks, and application layer attacks. A volume-based attack is when a DoS forces a cloud victim to use overwhelming amounts of network bandwidth. This causes unsupportable network usage, leaving the cloud services without network resources and causing non-responsiveness. These DoS attacks include distributed denial-of-service (DDoS) and distributed reflector denial-of-service (DRDoS). The attacks focus on multiple layers of the networking stack. Volume-based attacks include UDP floods, ICMP floods, and other spoofed-packet floods.

A DNS reflection attack is another type of volume-based attack whereby the attacker sends a request for a large DNS zone file with the source IP address spoofed as the IP address of the intended victim. The file is sent to a large number of open DNS resolvers who then respond to the request, sending the large DNS zone answer to the IP address of the intended victim. The attacker's requests themselves are only a fraction of the size of the responses, allowing the attacker to amplify their attack to many times the size of the bandwidth resources they control. The goal of the attack is to saturate the bandwidth of the attacked site, and the magnitude is measured in bits per second (Bps).

An example of a transport layer volume-based attack is an acknowledge (ACK) attack. A server initiating a TCP session first sends a synchronize (SYN) request to the receiving server. The receiving server responds with an ACK, after which data can be exchanged. In an ACK reflection attack, the attacker sends large amounts of SYN packets to servers with spoofed source IP addresses pointing to the intended victim. The servers then respond to the victim's IP with an ACK, creating the attack. Like DNS reflection attacks, ACK attacks disguise the source of the attack, making it appear to come from legitimate servers. The goal of the volume-based attack is to saturate the bandwidth of the attacked site, and the magnitude is measured in bits per second (Bps).

Protocol attacks include SYN floods, fragmented packet attacks, Ping of Death, Smurf DDoS, and others. This type of attack consumes actual server resources or those of intermediate communication equipment, such as firewalls and load balancers, and is measured in packets per second. As an example, in a Smurf attack, an attacker will spoof the source address of the Internet Control Message Protocol (ICMP) ping packet and send a broadcast to all computers on that network. ICMP is a connectionless protocol commonly used for diagnostic purposes that does not use any port number and works in the network layer. If networking devices do not filter this traffic, they are broadcast to all computers in the network. Because ping does not include a handshake, the destination has no means of verifying if the source IP is legitimate. The router receives the request and passes it on to all the devices that sit behind it. Each of these devices then responds back to the ping. The attacker is able to amplify the attack by a multiple equal to the number of devices behind the router.

Application layer attacks include attacks on application vulnerabilities. Comprised of seemingly legitimate and innocent requests, the goal of these attacks is to crash the application, such as a Web server. The magnitude is measured in requests per second. Exhausting a Web server's thread pool is one example of an application layer attack. Another is the low-rate denial-of-service (LDoS) attacks that can tie up a Web server.

Botnets are made up of computers with malicious software installed, turning them into zombies that have conceded control to a command and control server. The controller of a botnet is able to direct the activities of these compromised computers to attack a victim, either directly or indirectly through the attack examples listed above, as well as others.

In Figure 9.11, the attacker has distributed a number of zombies, which are remotely controlled malware that can be directed at a victim as part of a DDoS attack. The attacker is also aware of a set of services that can be spoofed into responding to the victim's

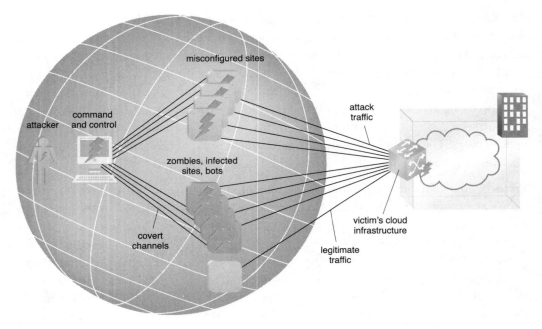

Figure 9.11

A series of advanced DDoS attacks, which blend multiple techniques.

imitated address. In this example, the attacker controls the botnet zombies that are compromised with malware, as well as other computers that inadvertently participate in attacks to launch DDoS attacks against the cloud provider's infrastructure. These zombies communicate on a covert channel to connect with the command-and-control server that the attacker controls.

Solution

A DoS protection service is engaged, diverting all traffic that would otherwise directly hit the victim's server infrastructure to the mitigation service network of datacenters, including attack traffic. Once traffic has shifted, the mitigation service absorbs the flood of attack traffic at the network edge, filters out the attack traffic, and prevents it from reaching the target's infrastructure, allowing only the legitimate traffic through to the cloud provider.

Application

One approach strategy is to reroute traffic through the DDoS service provider when an attack is detected. Another more expensive option is to have the traffic flow through the service provider for fully automated detection and mitigation. This mitigation strategy is highly effective but can introduce additional latency and complexity to Internet connection and routing. The cloud provider engages a DoS attack mitigation service and updates DNS to route all traffic through the mitigation service. The cloud provider can also install a management network to accomplish the same function. Using an on-demand cloud DoS defense service for a network saturation attack coupled with an on-premise cloud resource defense that is always on provides protection against the whole spectrum of attacks.

Figure 9.12 illustrates the use of a DoS mitigation service. The service has the resources to monitor traffic with a traffic monitor to absorb the DoS attack and filter out and forward legitimate traffic to the cloud provider using a traffic filter. An implication is that DoS mitigation systems need to be tested periodically. Failure to regularly test those systems can lead to inadvertent amplification of an attack if the mitigation systems fail.

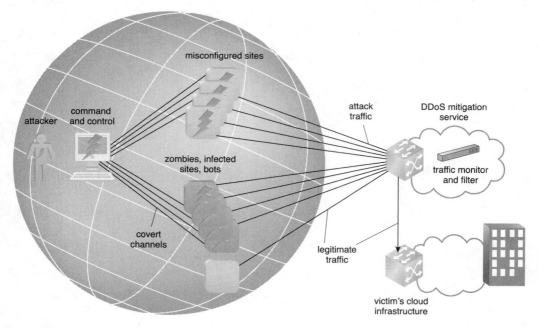

Figure 9.12
The DDoS mitigation service in action.

The solution is essentially a high capacity front end plus a mechanism that allows traffic with certain characteristics and origins to be ignored. An implication is that, in the hybrid scenario, the consumer's outer network needs equipment to notify the DoS service when an attack is experienced, to take over the network traffic for filtering and forwarding of the good traffic. In all cases, the cloud service has their traffic initially routed to the DoS service protection provider.

Mechanisms

- *Domain Name Service (DNS)* – The DNS must be updated to route the cloud provider's addresses through the DDoS mitigation service.

- *Traffic Filter* – The traffic filter is used to filter out malicious traffic.

- *Traffic Monitor* – The traffic monitor is used to detect DoS attack traffic.

Cloud Traffic Hijacking Protection

How can cloud communication be protected from traffic hijacking?

Problem	Attackers can often locate Internet service providers (ISPs) whose internal or ISP-to-ISP Border Gateway Protocol (BGP) session is susceptible to a man-in-the-middle attack. Once located, an attacker can potentially advertise any prefix they want, causing some or all traffic to be diverted from the real source toward the attacker.
Solution	A series of mechanisms is established to ensure mutually authenticated and encrypted communications data channels where possible, encryption and integrity protection of data in transit between the cloud consumer and cloud provider, as well as the monitoring and alerting of traffic anomalies.
Application	Cloud traffic hijacking attacks can be mitigated using either a third party and/or on-premise traffic monitoring system in conjunction with validated encryption and digital signatures, or authentication codes for the data in transit.
Mechanisms	Cryptographic Key Management System (CKMS), Digital Signature, Encryption, Traffic Monitor

Problem

The Border Gateway Protocol (BGP) can be used to launch traffic hijacking attacks by using fundamental flaws in the protocol itself. BGP, which calculates the quickest route for Internet traffic to travel in order for it to reach the destination IP address, can be subverted by undermining the trust relationship established by default between low-level Internet protocols.

IP hijacking, which can also be referred to as BGP prefix or route hijacking, is the seizing of groups of IP addresses by an attacker through the corruption of Internet routing tables. At the global level, individual IP addresses are grouped together into prefixes owned by an autonomous system. An example of autonomous systems is large Internet service providers.

The routing tables between autonomous systems are maintained using the BGP, which is the standard routing protocol used to exchange information about IP routing between autonomous systems. Attackers can infiltrate routers and take advantages of vulnerabilities in the BGP to route communications through their systems before routing it to the proper destination.

Communications traffic routes can be hijacked and routed to or through an attacker's compute resource, as shown in Figure 9.13. They may be able to modify or passively monitor the data, or spoof the entire cloud service's site.

1. A compromised router enables a hijack to occur. Internet routers are capable of being secured, but there are inevitably routers that are not secured or susceptible to new vulnerabilities. Attackers can access vulnerable routers and execute man-in-the-middle (MITM) and/or hijack attacks.

2. The victim's route after hijack. Normal routing of the network is disrupted and the packets are forwarded towards the attacker's part of the network and are at the mercy of the offending autonomous system.

3. Cloud data can be copied or modified on the hijacker's server as an MITM attack.

As a result of insecure communications protocols and routing equipment that can be compromised, there is a need to mitigate the constant risk.

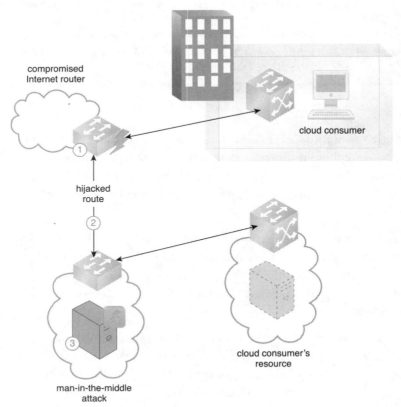

Figure 9.13

A communications traffic hijacking in progress.

Solution

Multiple precautions must be taken in order to protect from traffic hijacking, including traffic monitoring, data in-transit encryption, and integrity protection.

Application

Figure 9.14 depicts countermeasures that can be taken to prevent or mitigate traffic hijacking, as follows:

1. Where possible, encrypted communications channels are established either through VPNs or TLS sessions.

2. The data is signed and encrypted to protect confidentiality and integrity. As the data is being handled, it is assumed that there are malignant intermediaries on resources that are beyond the organization's direct control. If a hijack occurs, the data is not compromised.

3. Strong authentication of resources is used. PKIs with keys that are stored in hardware security modules (HSMs) are used for resources to authenticate to the cloud consumer. Properly evaluated and configured crypto-modules mitigate spoofing of resources. A cryptographic key management system (CKMS) is implemented to manage encryption keys.

4. Network paths are monitored for suspicious behavior. Possible network hijack alerts are received and processed in realtime.

Until all routers in use by the organization are secured, including Internet routers, traffic hijacking can occur. Using signed and encrypted data, the MITM cannot observe or modify the data without the modification being detected. Although traffic hijacking can still occur, the application of this pattern ensures that data is not compromised and that the cloud consumer is alerted to the hijack.

Key management is critical to encryption and integrity security. Key management and traffic monitoring can be managed from a third party service or within the organization. The important aspect of traffic monitoring is determining what normal traffic flow is and providing alerts for anomalous traffic.

Implications include the need for personnel to be assigned with the responsibility to monitor and respond to possible traffic hijack alerts.

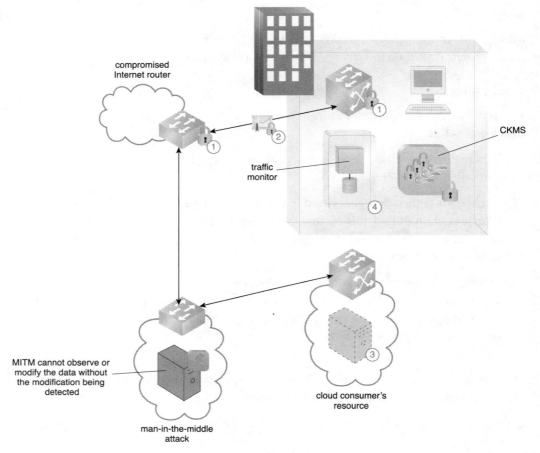

Figure 9.14

Various traffic hijacking mitigations are executed.

Mechanisms

- *Cryptographic Key Management System (CKMS)* – A CKMS manages the crypto-graphic keys used to encrypt the data prior to transmission and decrypt it at the destination.

- *Digital Signature* – A digital signature is used to ensure the integrity of the data in transit.

- *Encryption* – Encryption is used to ensure the confidentiality of the data in transit.

- *Traffic Monitor* – The traffic monitor is used by this pattern to detect traffic hijacking by noting normal traffic flow and alerting to anomalous traffic flow.

Problem

Generally, an organization's network architecture consists of an internal network that is protected from external networks, including the Internet, by a fixed defense of firewalls and routers. Cloud resource delivery and deployment models place boundaries in constant motion due to characteristics such as resource pooling and rapid elasticity. The advent of phishing attacks and addition of bring your own devices (BYODs) have the effect of placing untrusted access inside the perimeter. Many organizations have a requirement to connect on-premise resources with cloud resources. As an example, Figure 9.15 illustrates common attacks on vulnerabilities of resources on the extended network.

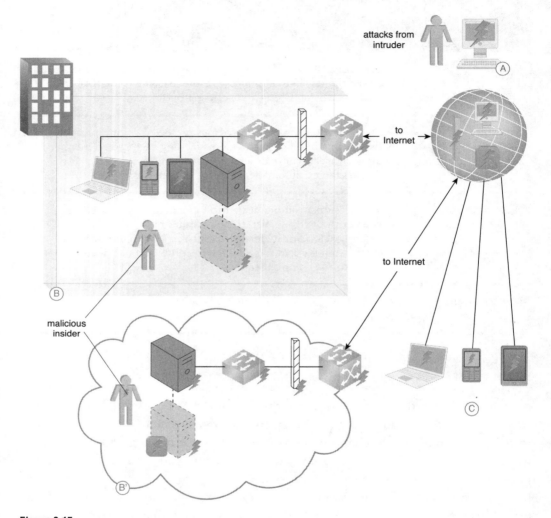

Figure 9.15

External attacks from intruders based worldwide (A). On-board attacks, from both on-premise and in the cloud (B). Vulnerabilities from mobile BYOD devices connected on-premise, in the cloud, or on the Internet (C).

Solution

A system is established that gives application owners the ability to create secure perimeters where and when they are required. Automatically defined perimeters (ADPs) are logical components that operate under the control of the cloud service or application owner. An ADP is based on a simple process of first identifying the device requesting access, then querying the identity system to determine what the cloud consumer is allowed to access, and then connecting the cloud consumer to the approved cloud applications with dynamically secured networking. ADPs provide access privileges to the protected infrastructure only after cloud consumer identification, authentication, and determination of access privileges. ADPs require endpoints to authenticate and be authorized before access is granted to protected resources. Connections are created between cloud consumers and cloud providers in realtime.

Application

The ADP controller regulates which services can communicate with each other. The controller may rely on authentication services, attribute services, geolocation services, policy services, and other security mechanisms to manage access.

The initiating services authenticate and communicate with the ADP controller to request a list of services to which they can connect. Protected services reject all communication from any resource except the ADP controller and any services that the ADP allows. The participating services accept connections only at the request of the ADP controller.

Figure 9.16 illustrates an ADP architecture containing ADP services and ADP controllers.

Figure 9.16

ADP cloud services can either be: access managed by requests to ADP controllers that rely on the organization's identity and access management (IAM) (A), cloud providers that initially only respond to the ADP controller and then only to cloud consumers that have been authorized by the ADP controller (B), cloud consumers requesting a single service, multiple services, or a service orchestration (C).

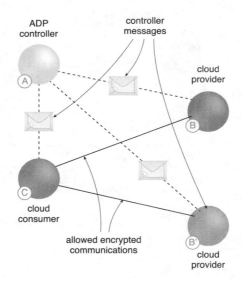

In Figure 9.17, the organization must provision participating services to respond to requests, as shown in the following steps:

1. The initial cloud consumer authenticates to the ADP controller.

2. The ADP controller determines a list of cloud service providers to which the initial consumer is authorized to communicate.

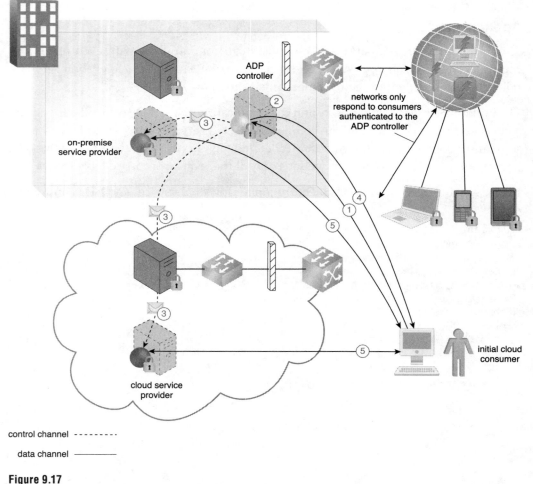

control channel - - - - - - - -

data channel —————

Figure 9.17

The participating cloud resources authenticate to the ADP and register with it when they are initially brought online.

3. The ADP controller securely instructs the requested cloud providers to accept communication from the initial cloud consumer as well as any required security policies such as the type of encrypted communications. It opens any network protections blocking the transaction.

4. The ADP controller securely gives the initial consumer the list of accepting providers as well as any security policies required for communications.

5. The initial consumer starts a secure connection to all authorized accepting providers.

The initial consumer starts a secure connection to all authorized accepting providers. For scaling and uptime requirements, the ADP infrastructure can be replicated and load balanced. The ADP brings together public key infrastructure (PKI), transport level security (TLS), Internet Protocol security (IPsec), security assertion markup language (SAML), and others. The ADP pattern is not intended to be applied to stand on its own. Other required protection, detection, and reaction-related patterns, such as Threat Intelligence Processing (465), should be applied as required, as well as concepts such as identity federation, attestation service, and geolocation to enable connectivity from any device to any infrastructure.

Connectivity in an ADP is based on a privilege model in which device identities are verified before access to application infrastructure is granted. Application infrastructure is effectively black, which is a US Department of Defense term that means the infrastructure cannot be detected.

Mechanisms

- *Automatially Defined Perimeter (ADP) Controller* – The ADP controller is used to manage secure connections between cloud consumers and cloud providers to maintain a secure perimeter.

- *Virtual Private Network (VPN)* – The VPN is used to create encrypted connections among the cloud consumers and cloud providers for an ADP session.

Cloud Authentication Gateway

How can cloud-based IT resources be made accessible to cloud service consumers with diverse protocol requirements?

Problem	Cloud consumers are compelled to support multiple authentication, communication and session protocols when cloud service providers deliver components, applications and service compositions with diverse protocol requirements.
Solution	An authentication service is implemented, allowing standard authentication, communication and session establishment from a cloud consumer to the authentication service. The authentication service then authenticates to the cloud resource on behalf of the cloud consumer using the diverse protocols required by the cloud provider.
Application	An authentication gateway service (AGS) is established as a reverse proxy front end between the cloud consumer and the cloud resource, which intercepts and terminates the consumer's encrypted network connection, authenticates the cloud consumer, authenticates itself and the consumer to the cloud provider, and then proxies all communication between the two. All three parties are authenticated in some combination of transport level or application level communication.
Mechanisms	Authentication Gateway Service (AGS), Certificate, Certificate Authority (CA), Certificate Revocation List (CRL), Certificate Trust Store, Public Key Infrastructure (PKI), Secure Token Service (STS), Virtual Private Network (VPN)

Problem

Applications, components and service compositions use multiple authentication mechanisms and protocols (Figure 9.18). This is especially true for legacy applications that have been moved into a cloud and can put multiple requirements on the cloud consumer for authentication, encrypted communication, and session establishment using tokens such as digital certificate, name/password, Kerberos, and Security Assertion Markup Language (SAML). Common communication protocols include HTTP, JSON-RPC, File Transfer Protocol (FTP), Simple Mail Transfer Protocol (SMTP), Secure Shell (SSH), and others.

Figure 9.18

A cloud service consumer must support authenticating to Cloud Service A with a certificate over the HTTPS protocol and setting up a Kerberos session (A) and authenticating to Cloud Service Provider B with a username/password over the JSON-RPC protocol and setting up a session with a session object (B).

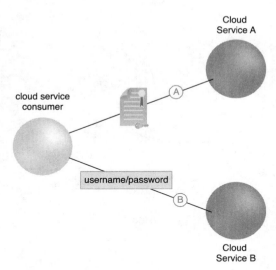

Solution

An AGS is established as a front end between the cloud consumer and the cloud service. The cloud consumer can be a person or a non-person entity (NPE), such as a component or Web service. The AGS intercepts and terminates the cloud consumer's connection, authenticates the cloud consumer using a set of common standard protocols and tokens, and then acts on behalf of the cloud consumer in communication with the cloud service. In this arrangement, all traffic between the cloud consumer and the cloud service passes through the AGS.

Figure 9.19 illustrates the concept of an AGS. The cloud consumer can either use a certificate or a username/password, depending on the desired cloud service authentication requirements.

1. The cloud consumer requests a cloud business service using one standard protocol, HTTPS, and two types of identity tokens, certificate or username/password. It uses a session ID to maintain an established session.

2. The AGS authenticates the cloud consumer.

3. The AGS then authenticates itself and the cloud consumer to the requested cloud service provider using the authentication and session protocols particular to the specific service.

4. The AGS sets up a standard session between itself and the cloud consumer.

Without the AGS, the cloud consumer needs to process every protocol and token required by the cloud provider services involved at the authentication and session layer.

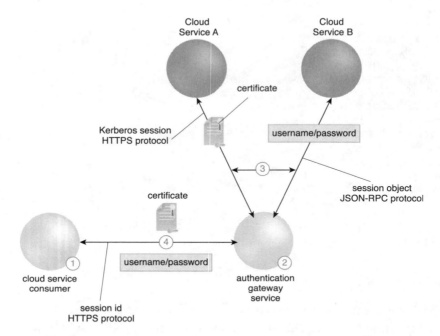

Figure 9.19

A consumer only needs to support a single set of standard protocols using the AGS.

Application

A cloud-based AGS performs authentication to cloud services as a reverse proxy between the cloud consumer and cloud providers. This allows a single standard authentication API for the cloud consumers and accommodates the various authentication schemes required by the cloud providers. Figure 9.20 shows how the introduction of an AGS simplifies authentication and session establishment for the cloud consumer while increasing security. For certificate-based authentication, the AGS manages downloading of the CRLs for all relying party (RP) provided services, conducts certificate validation, and manages sessions between the cloud providers and cloud consumers. For cloud consumers with username/password tokens, the AGS provides a single secure location for managing and authenticating usernames and passwords.

To ensure security, an AGS can be located within the security enclave of the cloud resources relying on the gateway as a reverse proxy. There are patterns whereby the AGS can reside within a cloud consumer's enclave. The service can support REST- and SOAP-based Web service architecture protocols between the AGS and the cloud consumer. It can also support other component-based protocols between the AGS and the cloud services. The pattern is extensible and can handle any required combination of protocols on either side of the AGS. It acts as a broker and protocol translator for cloud services. The AGS provides a central point from which to monitor consumer access to resources.

The AGS has the capability to establish a one-way (as with username/password) or client-authenticated (as with mutual certificate authentication) TLS session, cloud consumer to AGS proxy, and AGS to cloud provider. It can also rely on Internet Key Exchange (IKE)-based VPNs for network security. However, all three parties are authenticated in some combination of transport level or application level communication.

The AGS performs as an authentication service as well as a proxy and application gateway. In Figure 9.20, the normal flow is as follows:

1. The cloud consumer attempts to access Cloud Service A. It is routed to the AGS as a proxy after a domain name service (DNS) lookup. Cloud Business Service Provider A requires the Kerberos protocol.

2. The AGS authenticates to the cloud consumer using its certificate, and the cloud consumer presents its credential. As part of authenticating the claimed identity presented in the cloud consumer's credential, the AGS checks the credential's authenticity and validity. Username/password credentials are validated locally against a directory or an account store (not shown). Certificates are validated by checking whether or not the credential is issued from a trusted source, whether or not it has expired, whether or not the certificate policy allows the current use, and also checks the revocation status of the credential from the CRL. The AGS certificate trust store holds the trusted issuing CA root certificates.

3. Once the cloud consumer is authenticated, the AGS provides a token request to the secure token service (STS) according to the cloud service's requirements, and receives a token with the consumer's attributes. With the Kerberos protocol, the STS performs key distribution center functions.

4. The AGS presents the authentication token to the requested cloud service. If the cloud service provider determines proper authorization and access privileges, it provides a Kerberos token and resource to the AGS.

5. The AGS provides a separate standard session token to the cloud consumer along with the resource. The cloud consumer continues an open session over the HTTPS/TLS with the cloud service provider as long as the session token and Kerberos are valid.

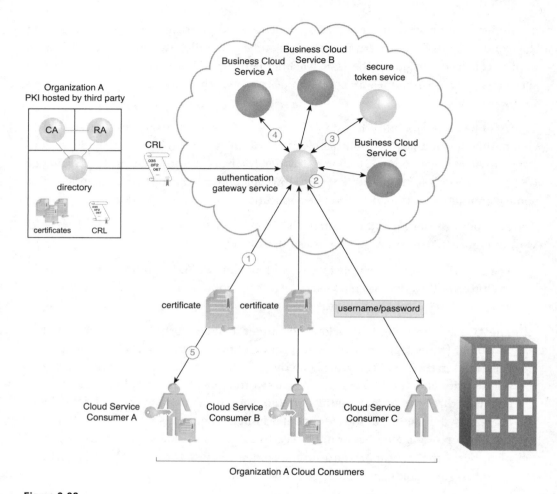

Figure 9.20

The AGS as a reverse proxy brokering among multiple authentication, communication and session protocols.

For other cloud providers with differing protocols, such as Business Service B and Business Service C in Figure 9.20, the concept of an authentication proxy using standard protocols with the cloud consumer and varied protocols with the cloud services is the same. Business Service B requires SAML tokens and Business Service C requires the JSON-RPC protocol. The AGS proxies the requests to the cloud consumers in a single standard way and mediates the varied protocols required by the cloud service providers.

An AGS may perform other functions, such as load balancing and logging. It provides a central location to log all authentication and resource accesses. It also provides a central place for CRL processing, alleviating multiple CRL downloads for every individual service.

An impact of using an AGS is that it becomes a single point of failure and a critical security infrastructure component that must be rigorously protected. AGSs need to be established in a high-availability load balanced configuration for continuity of operations (COOP) and be protected with firewall and routing access controls. All communication between cloud consumers and cloud provider services passes through the AGS, creating scaling and bandwidth issues. The AGS can ignore all traffic that is part of an authenticated session or monitor the session as an application gateway, which requires more processing power.

Mechanisms

- *Authentication Gateway Service (AGS)* – The AGS provides a reverse proxy to provide standard authentication to the cloud consumer and in turn authenticates to cloud services that have diverse protocols on behalf of the cloud consumer.

- *Certificate* – X.509 digital certificates are one form of standard cloud consumer identity claims used by the AGS.

- *Certificate Authority (CA)* – The CA issues the certificates used to fulfill the authentication requests for the application of this pattern.

- *Certificate Revocation List (CRL)* – The CRL is referenced to determine whether the certificates used in this pattern are revoked.

- *Certificate Trust Store* – The certificate trust store is referenced by the AGS to determine if the submitted certificate is issued from a trusted CA.

- *Public Key Infrastructure (PKI)* – A PKI establishes trust and issues certificates for an organization.

- *Secure Token Service (STS)* – The STS issues tokens to the AGS according to the standards and specifications required by the cloud services.

- *Virtual Private Network (VPN)* – The VPN is one method of creating a secure connection using X.509 certificates using the Internet Key Exchange (IKE) protocol.

Federated Cloud Authentication

How can X.509 certificates from a federation of cloud consumers be authenticated when an associated certificate revocation list fails?

Problem	If the certificate revocation list (CRL) corresponding to a cloud consumer's certificate is unavailable, either from communication or public key infrastructure (PKI) failure, cloud service providers are unable to authenticate submitted certificate credentials.
Solution	Federated authentication allows cloud services to authenticate cloud consumers incorporating a certificate status checking responder on the local area network (LAN), which supports authentication independently when the CRL for a given organization is unavailable due to failure.
Application	A local certificate validation service (CVS) is implemented to check the revocation status of submitted certificates from multiple organizations.
Mechanisms	Certificate, Certificate Authority (CA), Certificate Revocation List (CRL), Certificate Trust Store, Certificate Validation Service (CVS), Public Key Infrastructure (PKI)

Problem

A requirement of a federated enterprise is to share data among business partners across multiple organizations, meaning that the architecture must support authentication from individuals and services of diverse organizations. PKI certificates can be used throughout an enterprise to identify people as well as resources, including cloud services (REST and web services), transport layer security (TLS) and virtual private network (VPN) connection endpoints, as well as other components. These certificates must be validated when used for identification, authentication, and integrity checking. An interruption of the validation process by the denial of a current CRL for a given organization's certificates can ripple throughout a cloud provider's services that rely on certificates, resulting in an authentication denial-of-service.

The need to integrate composite cloud services across the enterprise and to share data among cloud consumers from diverse organizations securely and reliably derives from the requirement to provide authentication mechanisms adaptable to disconnected, intermittent, and limited (DIL) connectivity and varying performance and scaling requirements. When using X.509 certificates for cloud consumer identity claims, relying parties (RPs) normally download and check an issuing certificate authority (CA)'s CRL for the listing of the certificate. Figure 9.21 illustrates a certificate revocation process that compares a digital certificate's serial number with those on the issuing authority's CRL. The appearance of the serial number on the CRL indicates that the certificate has been revoked.

Certificate revocation processing occurs in the following steps, shown in Figure 9.21:

1. The CRL is downloaded from the PKI public repository and cached. When it expires, another current CRL is downloaded. If a current CRL is not available, certificate validation stops and RPs that require authentication normally stop authenticating.

2. A cloud consumer submits a certificate for access to a cloud resource. It is received by the authentication service.

3. The CRL is checked for a valid signature. It is checked to see if it is current. If not, the certificate cannot be validated, and processing normally stops at this point. If the CRL is valid, the certificate is checked to see if its serial is listed on it.

Figure 9.21

An authentication service checking the certificate revocation status.

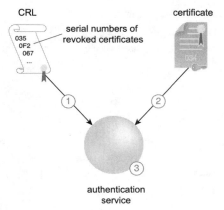

If a CRL is expired, the application normally rejects the authentication request from a cloud consumer, which can cause service disruption issues. Large and multiple CRLs can also cause source repository and network bandwidth performance issues, and consequently, continuity of operations (COOP) issues.

Solution

A local CVS is established, enabling the cloud consumer to authenticate to a resilient authentication service capable of validating certificates even using a stale CRL. An Online Certificate Status Protocol (OCSP) responder consumes CRLs and issues individual replies in response to revocation status requests about individual or groups of certificates. OCSP responders are capable of signing their own replies, and can continue to sign responses based on an expired CRL. This ensures continuity of operations if a failure in communications with the CRL repository or a failure of the PKI itself occurs. Figure 9.22 illustrates the process of a CVS using OCSP. When the cloud consumer needs services, in this case a component as a cloud service consumer:

1. It sends the required certificate to an authentication service to be authenticated.

2. The authentication service sends a request to the CVS that includes the issuer and serial number of the certificate.

3. The CVS compares the serial number with the associated issuer's CRL to determine if the certificate is revoked.

4. The CVS signs a response indicating if the certificate is good, revoked, or unknown.

Figure 9.22

The process of a CVS using OCSP.

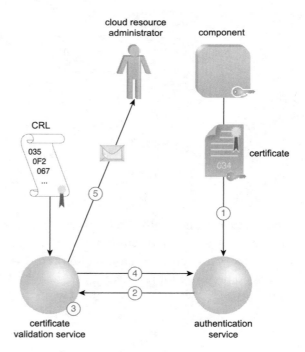

5. The CVS also checks to see that the CRL is valid. If the CRL is stale and the CVS cannot retrieve a current one, the CVS can be configured to send an alert to a cloud resource administrator notifying of a stale CRL. However, the CVS continues to sign revocation responses and the infrastructure continues to operate normally.

Application

A validation architecture is designed based on the validation security requirements of the cloud consumer. A CVS is implemented along with an authentication gateway service (AGS) to proxy authentication requests. A key component of the validation architecture is the establishment of trust. The security requirements establish the trust assurance level that the validation system needs to have.

CVSs are deployed to the local nodes to preserve operations during DIL conditions and to ensure performance reliability. They consume CRLs from the participating CAs when connectivity is available. When connectivity is not available, the local CVSs can respond based on stale CRLs and automatically notify administrators without disrupting the operation of any RPs. As a result, the cloud consumer is able to authenticate to a resilient authentication service that can validate certificates using a stale CRL.

In the case of multiple PKIs issuing millions of X.509 certificates, a local CVS allows large CRLs, sometimes on the order of hundreds of megabytes, to be managed by providing individual signed responses based on a downloaded CRL. Otherwise, the RP services must all download and manage the CRLs directly, increasing the required bandwidth of communications links and increasing the load on the directory servers holding the CRL.

Figure 9.23 shows two separate organizations, one that issues its own certificates to cloud consumers and one that uses a third party. Both organizations share a common authentication service that accepts certificates from either organization. Their certificates are issued from their respective PKIs. Each PKI contains a CA to issue the certificates, a registration authority (RA) to approve issuance of the certificates, a public directory containing the issued certificates, and the CRL.

Organization A's users are not able to authenticate to the federated authentication service because the CRL for their PKI is not available, and the one held by the cloud authentication service has expired. Organization B's users continue to successfully authenticate to the federated authentication service as there is no availability interruption to their associated CRL.

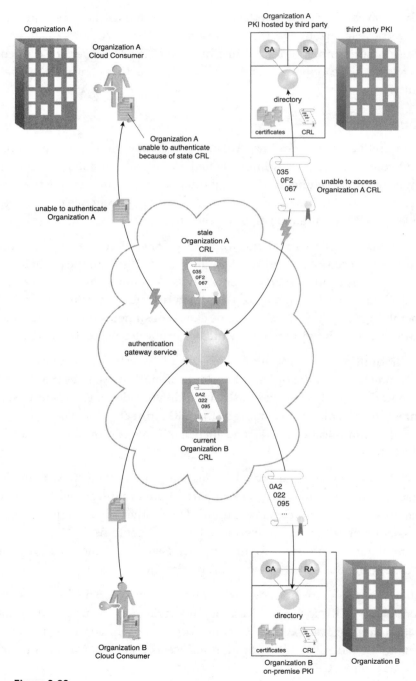

Figure 9.23

With the implementation of a CVS, the availability problems associated with an expired CRL are mitigated.

The following steps are shown in Figure 9.24:

1. The cloud consumer wants to gain access to a cloud resource and attempts to connect to it via the AGS. The AGS requests authentication of the cloud consumer. It initiates a client/2-way certificate authenticated TLS session, enabling the cloud consumer to access their certificate, which is protected by a PIN. The cloud consumer enters their PIN to authenticate themselves to the private key and provides credentials to the cloud provider. The cloud consumer also authenticates the AGS's certificate.

2. The AGS authenticates the cloud consumer's certificate received during TLS session establishment. To authenticate the claimed identity presented in the cloud consumer's credential, the AGS checks the authenticity and validity to determine whether the credential is issued from a trusted PKI, whether it is expired, and whether the certificate policy allows the current use. The AGS certificate trust store holds the trusted issuing CA root certificates.

3. The AGS sends a request for a revocation check to the CVS with the certificate serial number in question, as well as the issuer. However, the CRL corresponding to the CA that issued the certificate has expired and a fresh one is not available.

4. The CVS provides a revocation status (good, bad, or unknown) based on Organization A's expired CRL and signs the response. This shows that the CVS is providing a signed validation based on an expired CRL. The CVS notifies the cloud resource administrator that the CRL is expired.

5. Assuming successful authentication and privileges, the AGS provides the resource.

Combined with all local security services, such as directory services for user accounts, the CVS ensures indefinite operation of all systems in the enclave in the event that they are cut off from the corresponding CRL of the enterprise security services. A Server-based Certificate Validation Protocol (SCVP) server in place of an OCSP server offloads all of the above validation processing from the AGS to the server.

There are several implications to implementing local CVS responders. The infrastructure requirements increase the size, complexity, and overall management costs of the IT environment. The signing CVSs have certificates and signing keys that need to be managed. Their security assurance level should be the same as the PKI for which they are authenticating.

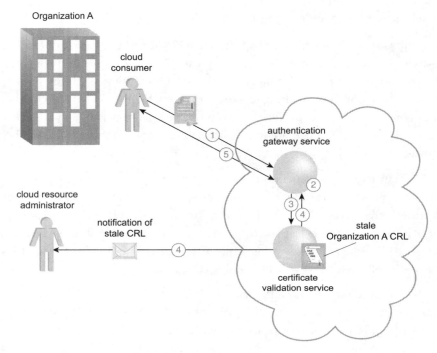

Figure 9.24
Resilient certificate validation in a cloud.

Local infrastructure issues include:

- *Selections of Mode of Validation* – There are two modes of CVS operation: pre-signed validations and validations that are signed as they are issued. Pre-signed validation has performance advantages in providing a local CVS, but does not have any COOP advantages. The pre-signed OCSP responses are signed based on the current CRL and expire when the CRL expires. OCSP validations that are signed when they are issued can continue to be signed based on a stale CRL. Procedures and profiles must be developed to guide the RP on which mode to select based on requirements and how to configure the validator. SCVP is also an option to consider.

- *Trust Model* – There are multiple trust models for trusting the CVS. They must be analyzed and selected according to the security requirements.

- *RP Connection to Service* – Procedures and profiles must be developed to enable local relying parties to connect to the local CVS.

- *DIL Procedures* – Procedures and profiles need to be developed in case of wide area communications failure and inability to access a valid CRL. In such cases, the local administrators must be notified, and mission critical systems must continue to operate normally with an awareness of the risk and procedures activated to locally revoke certificates if required.

- *Federation of Users* – CVSs have the ability to trust more than one PKI and therefore allow users from diverse organizations to share data by validating all their certificates. The trust of participating organizations' processes for vetting their individuals and services in order to issue credentials must also be addressed by determining security assurance levels of the PKIs involved. Procedures and profiles need to be in place to evaluate assurance policies of other PKIs for appropriateness for access to resources and configure CVSs to validate their certificates as required.

Mechanisms

- *Certificate* – X.509 digital certificates are the only form of cloud consumer identity claims used when applying this pattern.

- *Certificate Authority (CA)* – The CA issues the certificates and CRLs to be used to fulfill the authentication requests.

- *Certificate Revocation List (CRL)* – The CRL is referenced to determine whether the certificates are revoked.

- *Certificate Trust Store* – The certificate trust store holds issuing CA root certificates for multiple trusted organizations and is referenced by the AGS to determine if a submitted certificate is issued from a trusted CA.

- *Certificate Validation Service (CVS)* – The CVS is used by RPs to determine the validity of the submitted digital certificate and can continue to provide validation based on a stale CRL.

- *Public Key Infrastructure (PKI)* – The PKI issues certificates to each associated organization for use in authentication.

Problem	While encryption is foundational to cloud security, the management of encryption keys is one of the most difficult challenges in cloud computing. Failure to adequately manage encryption keys can lead to a range of administrative and security problems.
Solution	A cloud key management system is employed, available either as a physical or virtual network attached device.
Application	A cryptographic key management system (CKMS), optionally using a hardware security module (HSM) for key protection that consists of systems, personnel and policies is implemented to manage keys for encryption of all required data for both on-premise and cloud resources.
Mechanisms	Cryptographic Key Management System (CKMS), Hardware Security Module (HSM)

Problem

Encryption is used throughout the enterprise as the foundation for the security of data and platforms, including databases, identities, and network connections. The secure management of keys is critical as the compromise of keys can result in a compromise of the foundation of security systems.

Figure 9.25 shows the following common locations of keys that are used in the enterprise:

A. Asymmetric keys are used for identity, non-repudiation, and authentication. Asymmetric or symmetric keys can be used by an application to protect data.

B. TLS keys are asymmetric and are commonly used to securely exchange symmetric keys to protect data in motion.

C. VPN keys can be either symmetric or asymmetric, protecting data in motion. The VPN keys at the outer routers may be managed by the cloud provider or consumer.

D. Symmetric keys are used to provide VM security and data at rest.

E. VPN keys may be implemented on subnets and can also protect connections to the cloud.

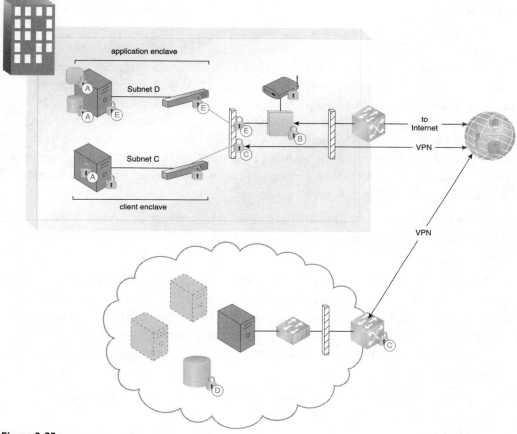

Figure 9.25
An example of organization keys, both on-premise and in the cloud.

This example shows the requirement of a cloud consumer to manage a number of keys both for their on-premise resources and for their cloud resources.

Solution

A key management system is employed to manage the enterprise keys. It consists of administrators, policies, procedures, components, and devices used to protect, manage, and distribute cryptographic keys. A key management system includes all devices or sub-systems that can access an unencrypted key or its metadata. Encrypted keys and their cryptographically protected (bound) metadata can be handled by components and transmitted through communications systems and stored in media that are not considered to be part of a key management system.

Application

A cryptographic key management system (CKMS) is employed, supporting split key, separation of duties (SOD), and multi-person administration, and available either as a physical or virtual network attached device. The CKMS must encrypt the encryption keys and, depending on the requisite assurance level, provide for SOD, which requires multiple administrators to accomplish a particular administration task. Under SOD, split key technology is incorporated so that each administrator holds part of the split key and it takes as many administrators as required by the assurance level to supply all the parts of a key to unlock the CKMS. Depending on the throughput requirements, the key manager or a collection of key managers can be housed in a VM, automated and located near the workload that is being secured.

The major functions of the CKMS are illustrated in Figure 9.26. In this illustration, using a CKMS allows keys and encryption policy to be controlled by the cloud consumer data owner.

A. The CKMS houses and protects the cloud consumer's keys in the key manager in encrypted form. For example, application keys are keys used by applications for their cryptographic operations and stored and protected within the HSM security boundary. Any operations requiring keys that are stored in the CKMS are performed by the CKMS on behalf of the end user, which prevents the end user from directly accessing the stored keys.

B. The lifecycle management (creation, renewal, management, destruction) of the keys is provided by CKMS administrators, who hold infrastructure keys that underpin the security of the CKMS. As an example, CKMS administrators hold control keys to unlock the CKMS for management purposes. Control keys are keys used to authorize the use of application keys in order to enforce security policies.

It normally takes more than one administrator to accomplish a CKMS function under the SOD principle. A split key system is used to support SOD so that multiple administrators are required in order to complete an administrative task, which is done by combining the keys that they separately control.

C. The keys corresponding to the encryption of various resources are stored in the CKMS and decrypted and activated by CKMS administrators with control keys. Public key infrastructure (PKI) issues asymmetric keys to identify consumers. Keys issued to non-person entities (NPEs), such as Web servers, are examples of keys managed by the CKMS. A log entry can be generated for each successful and unsuccessful use of key material in the CKMS, providing an audit trail for compliance and regulation purposes.

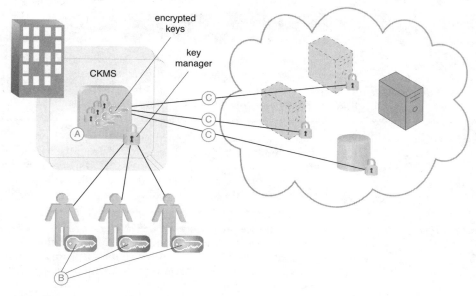

Figure 9.26
A sample CKMS architecture.

Depending on the required security assurance level, the CKMS can be housed in a hardware security module (HSM). An HSM is a dedicated cryptographic processor that is specifically hardened for the protection of the crypto key lifecycle. HSMs are trust anchors that protect the cryptographic infrastructure of organizations by support-ing securely managing, processing, and storing cryptographic keys inside a hardened, tamper-resistant device. Implementing a CKMS operated by the cloud consumer orga-nization is a trustworthy way to ensure the security of keys.

An impact is that there is a cost and complexity to operating a key management system. If a third party can meet the security assurance requirements for outsourcing key man-agement, it can be an alternative to operating an on-premise key management regimen. Most compliance regulations reference NIST FIPS 140 standards and requirements for using evaluated cryptographic modules for CKMSs.

Mechanisms

- *Cryptographic Key Management System* (CKMS) – The CKMS provides a system to protect and manage organization keys and keep them safe from the attacker.

- *Hardware Security Module (HSM)* – The HSM is used to store keys in hardware for a higher level of security assurance.

Trust Attestation Service

How can the security status of a cloud platform be communicated to cloud consumers?

Problem	Cloud platform security can be opaque to the cloud consumer that has compliance and regulatory security requirements. This can compromise the ability to verify the platform assurance level, which may be critical for some federal and regulated organizations.
Solution	An attestation service is implemented to maintain a trust policy for every attested host. It also evaluates reports from the hardware roots of trust from trusted platform modules (TPMs) on each node to determine whether each node has undergone a trusted boot and is in compliance with the security policy.
Application	An attestation service provides assurance that the protected environment is correctly invoked using the TPM, measuring the integrity by validating digital signatures on the software running in the protected environment. An attestation identity key credential exchanged during a secure boot is used to establish mutual trust between the TPM and the attestation service. The orchestration engine uses the attestation service to select the appropriate compute platform required by workloads.
Mechanisms	Attestation Service, Digital Signature, Orchestration Engine, Trusted Platform Module (TPM)

Problem

To meet the security compliance requirements, the cloud consumer most often needs to know whether or not a compute resource is running a compliant BIOS, OS, hypervisor and VM at boot time. In a cloud environment, the entity requesting this information could be a resource scheduler or orchestrator trying to schedule a service on a set of available nodes or compute services. Figure 9.27 illustrates the need to securely record and report the security status of a compute resource.

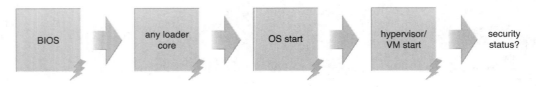

Figure 9.27
A general platform boot sequence.

Solution

The attestation service accurately determines the state of the security relevant BIOS configuration items on each platform. This allows the attestation service to report on and act on the items with which the organization is concerned. Figure 9.28 illustrates the sequence of events in the secure boot reporting to the attestation service. Secure transmission of BIOS integrity measurements ensures that the measurements are not modified, disclosed, or forged in-transit by malicious parties.

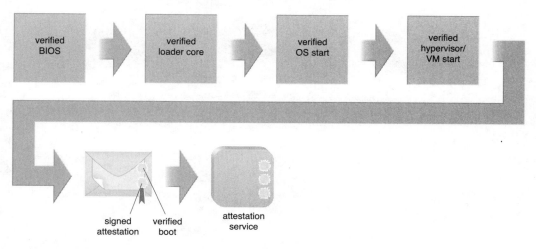

Figure 9.28
A trusted platform boot process.

Application

Measured boot can take measurements of different software components used in the OS boot process including the BIOS, OS loader, kernel, and drivers, and sign with a digital signature before securely storing the measurements in a trusted platform module (TPM). These measurements can be used by an attestation service to check the integrity of a given platform and to show that the platform has not been infected by malware. This attestation security service is a remote attestation service and can be provided by a trusted third party. It attests that the boot process of a particular machine is secure and that the anti-malware software on that machine is functioning properly. Figure 9.29 illustrates the use of an attestation service in the following steps:

1. A secure firmware boot prevents running an unknown OS loader by checking signatures called measured boot.

2. An early boot starts, first containing the OS, kernel, drivers, and other system files, and enforces security policy. It continues with a higher level of security booting of anti-malware, third party drivers, hypervisor, and VM operating system.

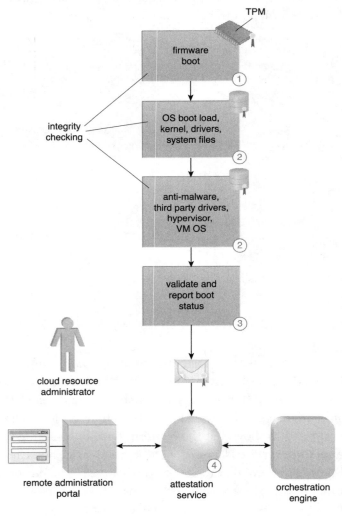

Figure 9.29
A secure boot with trust attestation.

3. Digitally signed TPM boot measurements are recorded during the boot and sent securely to an off-box attestation service for analysis using attestation identity keys.

4. An attestation service provides the security status to the orchestration engine and authorized cloud administrators through an administration portal.

Attestation makes the status information from various roots of trust visible and usable by other entities. In the TPM-based implementation, it provides a digital signature of platform configurations in the TPM, extended with specific measurements for various launch modules of the software with the attestation service validating the digital signature of status messages. This is done so that subsequent agents cannot alter or replace the data without detection, and so the source of the data is known.

The implications of this pattern include the need to focus protection on the attestation service and to securely connect and authenticate to the attestation service, as it is central to reporting the security status of cloud resources.

Mechanisms

- *Attestation Service* – The attestation service provides levels of compute node security assurance to cloud consumers.

- *Digital Signature* – A digital signature is used to provide integrity of code.

- *Orchestration Engine* – The orchestration engine refers to the attestation service to ensure provisioned resources with the required security assurance level.

- *Trusted Platform Module (TPM)* – The TPM provides a tamper-resistant hardware security module (HSM) to hold keys and provide cryptographic processes.

How can cloud monitoring and logging activities be coordinated between a cloud consumer and a cloud provider?

Problem	The cloud introduces a distributed compute platform that extends and distributes the organization's computing boundaries and diminishes governance control. This introduces uncertainty in regards to whether it is the cloud consumer or cloud provider who is responsible for specific security monitoring and auditing tasks.
Solution	The organization determines security monitoring and auditing requirements, divides them between internal on-premise and external cloud providers, and establishes a security monitoring system that integrates both.
Application	Because of the distributed nature of security monitoring and the resulting collection of audit information, a process for sharing of audit information across parties is implemented. A coordinated implementation of security information and event management (SIEM) systems is accomplished or the cloud provider may provide attestations instead of direct monitoring capabilities to meet security monitoring and auditing requirements.
Mechanisms	Security Information and Event Management (SIEM) System

Problem

The organization has a responsibility to monitor for attacks and unauthorized local and remote connections. They are required to monitor for evidence of unauthorized disclosure of organizational information, and must detect any violation of computer security policies, industry compliance requirements, or standard security practices. One of the potential downsides of moving workloads to the cloud environment is loss of direct control. The enterprise security control requirements shift from the organization's enterprise network alone to include the cloud. Administrators who previously had direct access to physical servers and console access to all logs and security monitoring output may now have limited accessibility.

However, according to best practices and many regulatory compliance requirements, organizations are accountable for the risk incurred by use of services provided by external providers and must address this risk by implementing compensating controls. Enterprises need to obtain sufficient assurance and security monitoring capabilities from external cloud providers to ensure that required security controls are in place. The issue is to work with the cloud provider to ensure that security monitoring tools meet compliance requirements, and that they are implemented to capture logs and machine data from operating systems, applications, and hardware devices.

The following requirements of cloud service types must be taken into account with security monitoring and logging:

- Private cloud – operated solely for one organization
- Community cloud – shared by several organizations
- Public cloud – available to any customer
- Hybrid cloud – two or more clouds (private, community, or public) that are connected

Depending on the service offering, for example IaaS, PaaS, or SaaS, only some of the necessary logs are directly available. Figure 9.30 illustrates the distributed nature of security monitoring in the cloud. The monitoring of identities accessing resources, security status of the resources, and security status of resource connectivity is vital to ensure secure transactions. Issues include the following facts:

A. Network traffic is spread out, including mobile devices accessing the network remotely.

B. Wireless network traffic extends the network.

C. The security status of resources that are distributed to the cloud, including their location, must be established, as well as on-premise resources.

D. Mobile devices, including tablets, phones, and laptops, must be monitored.

E. Man-in-the-middle attacks come from network devices on the Internet as well as agents placed inside data centers.

F. Malicious agents are constantly probing networks for vulnerabilities.

G. Malicious insiders have privileges within the enterprise but have malicious intent.

H. Authentication attempts originate from both internal and external consumers.

The various service model relationships between the cloud consumer and provider extend the organization's network boundary and greatly increase the organization's reliance on the cloud service provider's security practices.

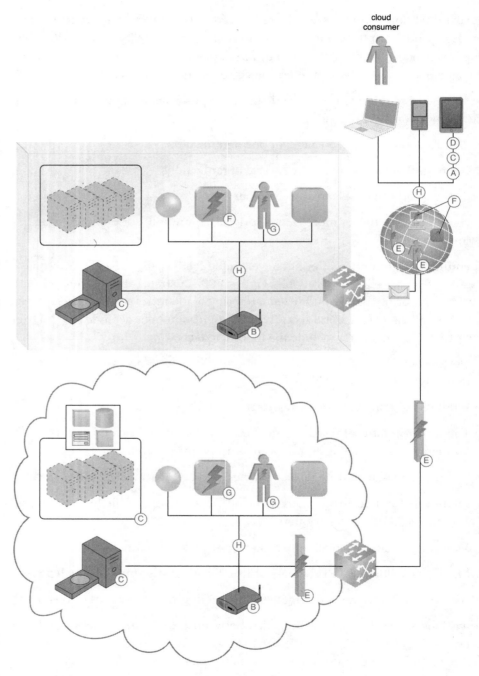

Figure 9.30

Organizational IT resources extend beyond the on-premise boundary.

Solution

Functional and regulatory security and privacy requirements are determined to meet logging and security monitoring purposes. The auditing and security monitoring capabilities must meet any rules, laws, and regulations that bind the organization. Risk management supports identifying the set of requirements and control measures that must be used by the cloud consumer to monitor the cloud provider's compliance with the services they offer. The information technology practices of the organization that pertain to the governance, policies, procedures, and standards used for logging and security monitoring of deployed or engaged services are extended to cloud computing environments.

Details about the system architecture of a cloud are analyzed and used to specify the protection required from the security and privacy controls, including mitigating risk by employing mechanisms and procedures for logging and for the continuous monitoring of the security state of the system. The mitigations that the organization normally uses to secure its data and infrastructure must extend to the cloud service provider. This requires the ability to accept the service provider's attestation that its policies and procedures provide the required levels of protection.

Application

With regards to many types of industry compliance requisites, there are distinct requirements that security monitoring take place within the information system. This is achieved through security identification and event management (SIEM) for collecting and analyzing security events. Since cloud providers deliver features such as on-demand provisioning and multi-tenancy, the security monitoring solution must take into account the dynamic aspect of cloud computing boundaries. To ensure the continued effectiveness of the controls, the organization needs to manage the security monitoring environment and ensure that contractual obligations, rules, applicable laws, regulations, and policies that bind the organization are being met.

Audit data from various systems needs to be normalized for follow-on processing. The SIEM mechanism augmented by Big Data techniques can analyze security event data in realtime for internal and external threat management, and can collect, store, analyze, and report on log data for incident response, forensics, and regulatory compliance.

Organizations must create, protect, and store the audit records required to establish the monitoring, analysis, and reporting of inappropriate information system activity and ensure that the actions of individuals and components can be traced. The need to protect sensitive audit logs and the integrity of audit data is mandatory for effective security monitoring and is required by many compliance standards. The enterprise must implement a reference monitor that is tamperproof, always invoked, and that ensures that the security monitoring system is functioning properly. The tamperproof property of the reference monitor prevents attackers from compromising the function of the mechanism. The always invoked property prevents adversaries from bypassing the mechanism and compromising the security policy.

The following high-level steps to setting up a security monitoring program are shown in Figures 9.31 and 9.32:

1. Security requirements are developed, starting with industry regulatory requirements and other security measures considered necessary by the organization.

2. Security monitoring requirements from a regulatory compliance standpoint and other organizational monitoring requirements are derived from the security requirements.

3. Candidate SLA clauses for negotiation with prospective cloud providers are developed as a tool for evaluating the selected provider.

4. The cloud service provider delivers self-assessments of the ability to meet security monitoring requirements, either directly or indirectly, through third-party audit attestation.

5. After selecting a cloud provider, a third-party organization's assessment is obtained that provides certifications of the candidate cloud service provider's ability to meet the required level of security assurance.

6. A cloud provider's security controls are implemented and integrated with the rest of the organization's resources' security controls, and their monitoring system is integrated with the organizational security monitoring system. Threat logic is developed that is suited to the shared environment and meets regulatory requirements for an effective alerting and reporting capability.

7. Continuous monitoring of the distributed enterprise commences, coordinating activities on-premise with the cloud provider. The cloud provider institutes continuous monitoring in accordance with the cloud consumer's requirements and the SLA.

8. Periodic audits of the combined enterprise are conducted as required by the industry, incorporating audit attestations from the cloud provider.

9. The third-party assessment organization conducts periodic assessments of the cloud provider as required.

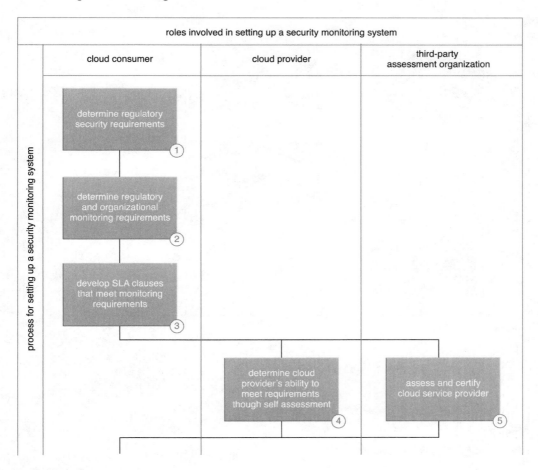

Figure 9.31
A sample process for selecting a cloud provider (Part I).

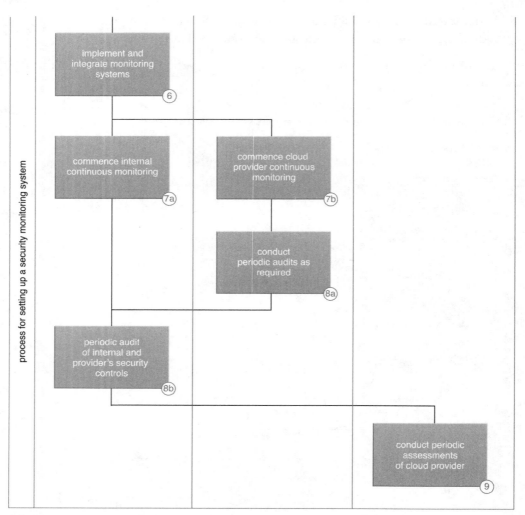

Figure 9.32
A sample process for selecting a cloud provider (Part II).

Organizations must accept the service provider's attestation that its policies and procedures afford the organization the required levels of protection through independent audit reports or audits they conduct themselves. Ideally, security monitoring includes external monitoring of cloud assets and internal monitoring of on-premise resources. Security monitoring needs to be implemented through solution patterns and mechanisms (for example intrusion detection and prevention systems (IDPS), vulnerability scanning, endpoint protection mechanisms, device and application authentication, audit record monitoring, and network monitoring) and the output from security monitoring should serve as input to the SIEM implementation. In turn, the SIEM implementation serves as the backbone to information security continuous monitoring and incident response programs.

SIEM is critical to an effective security monitoring program. Advanced SIEM correlates event, threat, and risk data to accurately detect attacks in progress, serves as an investigation platform, and produces compliance reports resulting from security event monitoring. System monitoring relates to the health, performance, and processing consumption of an IT system. Application performance management (APM) is an overarching system monitoring application. Having a robust APM solution in which the SIEM can receive detailed audit information from workload transactions creates an important, mature, and insightful situational awareness capability.

Mechanisms

- *Security Information and Event Management (SIEM) System* – The SIEM collects audit data, performs realtime analysis of events against threat logic, and provides security alerting of monitored events.

Independent Cloud Auditing

How can cloud-hosted IT resources be audited for compliance and SLA requirements when they are not owned or accessible by cloud consumers?

Problem	Assessments for security requirement objectives of confidentiality, integrity, and availability need to be performed by cloud consumers, providers, and third-party participants to ensure legal, security compliance, audit policy, and service level agreement (SLA) requirements are met. However, depending on the cloud service and delivery models, the organization does not own all the IT resources being consumed.
Solution	A specialized auditing approach is implemented in coordination with the cloud consumer, cloud provider, and a third-party cloud auditor.
Application	Auditing implementation, including configuration of security information and event management (SIEM) systems, can be determined based on regulatory compliance requirements and collaboration responsibilities between the cloud consumer, cloud provider, and a third party.
Mechanisms	Security Information and Event Management (SIEM) System

Problem

In order to meet industry compliance requirements, IT systems require implementation of strong auditing and compliance processes and procedures before a system can be approved for operation. The cloud consumer organization typically does not own or control all the underlying system resources that implement system capabilities when employing cloud resources.

Figure 9.33 provides an illustration of resource sharing between a typical cloud consumer and cloud provider. Policies, processes, and technical controls in support of regulations and auditing and legal requirements must be developed, requiring coordination between the cloud consumers and providers. All resources must be secured in a way that meets the required security levels and must be audited to prove compliance.

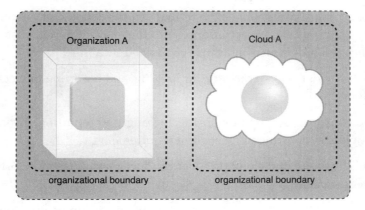

Figure 9.33
Cloud consumer organizations do not have full control of cloud-hosted IT resources.

Solution

A third-party cloud auditor conducts an independent assessment of cloud services, information system operations, performance, and security of a cloud implementation.

Figures 9.34 and 9.35 illustrate the general process of setting up auditing:

1. The cloud consumer determines regulatory applicability for the use of a given cloud service.

2. In coordination with the cloud provider, the cloud consumer determines division of compliance responsibilities between the cloud provider and cloud consumer.

3. The cloud provider's ability to produce evidence needed for compliance is determined.

4. The cloud consumer's role in providing evidence from their on-premise resources and in bridging the gap between cloud provider and required audit information is determined.

5. Security controls for cloud consumers and cloud providers are implemented.

6. A trusted third party conducts certification and accreditation (C&A) of the enterprise with close cooperation of the cloud consumer and cloud provider. It is beneficial to include the auditor so that they can comment on the viability of audit data collection plans. Certification is an evaluation of processes, systems, and other associated artifacts based on an industry norm or standard, usually conducted

by a third party. Accreditation is the formal determination that the certification program is administered in accordance with the relevant norms or standards of the certification program, usually also conducted by a third party.

7. The cloud provider sets up monitoring, logging, and reporting to meet audit requirements.

8. The cloud consumer sets up monitoring, logging, and reporting, incorporating the cloud provider's reporting to meet audit requirements.

9. The cloud consumer and cloud provider conduct continuous monitoring for compliance requirements.

10. The cloud auditor collects evidence from the cloud consumer and cloud provider that is used to conduct an audit.

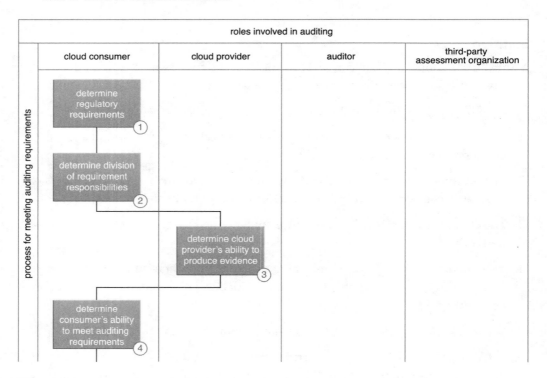

Figure 9.34

A sample cloud auditing process (Part I).

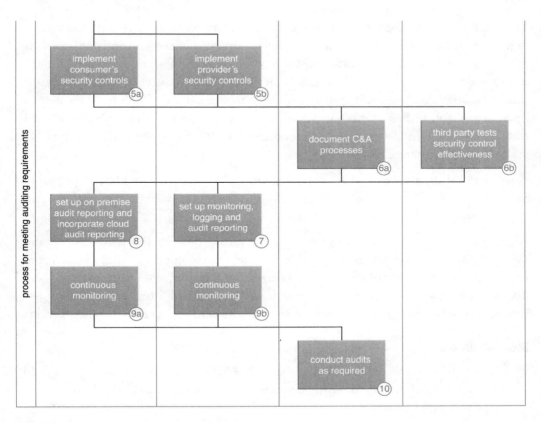

Figure 9.35

A sample cloud auditing process (Part II).

Application

Cloud service consumers and cloud service providers make their performance and security data available for auditors in accordance with relevant compliance frameworks such as the Payment Card Industry Data Security Standard (PCI DSS), the Health Insurance Portability and Accountability Act (HIPAA), Control Objectives for Information and Related Technology (COBIT), International Organization for Standardization (ISO) and International Electrotechnical Commission (ISO/IEC) 27002, the Sarbanes-Oxley Act (SOX), NIST Special Publication 800-53, Security and Privacy Controls for Federal Information Systems and Organizations, or another industry-oriented standard.

The cloud auditor makes an assessment of the security controls of the information system in order to determine the extent to which the controls are implemented correctly, operating as intended, and producing the desired outcome with respect to the security requirements for the system. The security auditing requires the verification of the compliance with regulation and security policy of the security controls for management, operational, and technical mechanisms implemented within the organizational information system boundary to protect the confidentiality, integrity, and availability of the system and its information.

A security information and event management (SIEM) system should be implemented to coordinate logging of event sources including operating systems, applications, databases, network and security components.

Among other implications, organizations must create, protect, and retain information system audit records to the extent needed to enable the monitoring, analysis, investigation, and reporting of unlawful, unauthorized, or inappropriate information system activity. They must also ensure that the actions of individual information system users can be uniquely traced to those users so they can be held accountable for their actions.

Mechanisms

- *Security Information and Event Management (SIEM) System* – A SIEM system is used to conduct continuous monitoring as required and coordinate the collection of information for auditing.

Threat Intelligence Processing

How can actionable threat indicators be generated to detect threats and prevent cloud vulnerability exploits?

Problem	Organizations are not normally able to take advantage of the large volume of available threat data that can provide indications of the kind of attacks to expect and where they can originate. This can result in missed opportunities to detect hidden security vulnerabilities and prevent them from being exploited.
Solution	Incorporating a threat intelligence system into the cloud security architecture allows organizations to forecast attacks, alert administrators and cloud consumers, and utilize the intelligence to prevent and defend against future attacks.
Application	A threat intelligence system is implemented to receive and process external intelligence feeds, as well as intelligence gained from analyzing attacks internally. It automatically queues security systems such as security information and event management systems (SIEMs), the network forensics monitor, endpoint threat detection and response systems (ETDRs), and intrusion detection and prevention systems (IDPSs), and alerts cloud administrators and consumers.
Mechanisms	Endpoint Threat Detection and Response (ETDR), Honeypot, Intrusion Detection and Prevention System (IDPS), Malware Hash, Network Forensics Monitor, Sandbox, Security Information and Event Management (SIEM) System, Threat Intelligence System

Problem

With its high volume of threat data and sophistication of threats, the threat landscape poses severe security challenges for an organization seeking to prevent exploits of their vulnerabilities. For example, there are domain names, applications, and countries of origin that should be blacklisted to reduce particular types of threats. Events such as specific application attacks, ports and services that are vulnerable, and the current malware being detected need to be collected and analyzed as part of security planning. The issue lies in finding a way to collect, analyze, and integrate threat intelligence knowledge operationally into cloud security systems for exploit prevention.

Figure 9.36 shows the following internal and external sources of information for threat intelligence:

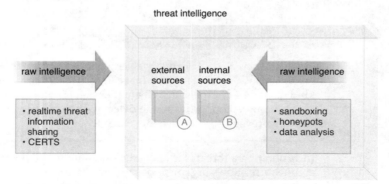

Figure 9.36
Common sources of information for threat intelligence.

A. External intelligence sources include:

- Raw intelligence from threat data such as malicious IP addresses, domain name system (DNS) names, URLs, malware hashes, etc.
- Threat information sharing from organizations, companies, and crowd sourcing.
- Computer Emergency Readiness Team (CERT) alerts.

B. Internal intelligence sources include:

- Raw intelligence from malicious activity detected inside the organizational boundaries.
- Information gathered from operating unknown executables in a sandbox.
- Observations of malicious activity in honeypots.
- Analysis of data observed that is internal to the organization.

As a result of this large volume of threat data, there is a need to analyze and create queuing for the organization's protection mechanisms. For example, if a participant of an information sharing organization experiences a zero-day attack and makes the characteristics of the attack available to the information sharing participants, they can take measures to protect from the attack.

Solution

Threat intelligence provides indications and warnings about threats that are likely to occur. Threat intelligence can provide attacker tactics, techniques, and procedures that organizations have experienced and mitigations that organizations have found that are effective against certain types of threats. Threat intelligence includes collecting and analyzing threat actors, exploits, malware, vulnerabilities, and compromise indicators. It is fed by collaborative realtime threat intelligence received from the community, as well as internal analysis. Exploit prevention derives from an understanding of threats and threat behavior.

Figure 9.37 shows collection, analysis, distribution, and use of analysis information. The data is automatically distributed to attack mitigation components in the enterprise, providing automatic update of security configurations. The automatic updates extend to cloud consumers' browser protection systems.

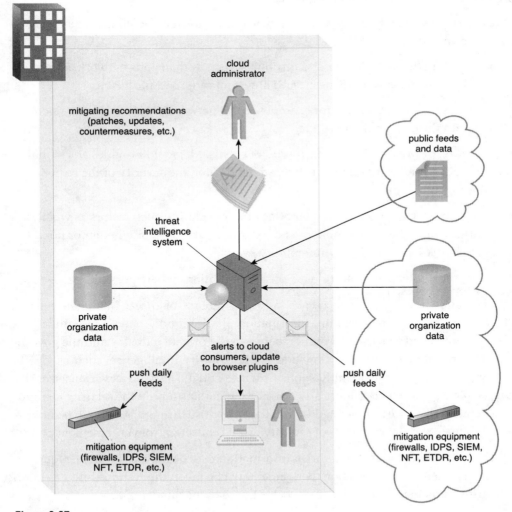

Figure 9.37

An example of a typical threat intelligence analysis architecture.

Application

A threat intelligence system is implemented, which alerts the organization to threat agents, their intended targets, attack campaigns, and known tactics, techniques, and procedures (TTPs). Using a threat intelligence system, the organization can institute threat prevention controls for actionable intelligence in the form of indicators and attack descriptions. Those indicators allow organizations to anticipate attacks before they unfold, and also to recognize their significance when detected in the network. An automatic update to protection mechanisms is configured for a realtime protection component of the threat intelligence system.

Actionable intelligence from threat intelligence can inform cloud consumers and providers, and includes:

- Observed malicious behavior and attributes, such as malicious network addresses, domain name resolution requests, URLs, system calls, and file hashes.

- Where attacks are observed, for example on the network, inside emails or documents, on the disk, in memory, etc.

- Criticality/priority of the event or series of events. Metadata provides additional information on the confidence level for the indicator, the severity of the corresponding attack, etc.

- How to protect against a particular attack by considering such factors as whether the attack should be blocked on the network or on the host, or whether or not a patch should be applied for vulnerability.

- Automatic updates to protection device configurations where possible.

Organizations should expect to receive a steady stream of threat intelligence without requiring manual intervention. Information Sharing and Analysis Organizations (ISAOs) share cybersecurity information between the private industry and the government. Threat intelligence sources include public security intelligence, such as CERTs and Computer Security Incident Response Teams (CSIRTs), as well as various security analysts, security product vendors and other organizations within the security community. Threat intelligence is generated within the enterprise through honeypots, sandboxing techniques, and data analysis of security events collected from enforcement points.

Implications include the fact that threat information may be highly sensitive, requiring special agreements and protection. Personnel must be given the responsibility to manage sharing agreements and coordination for usage of the queueing data.

Mechanisms

- *Endpoint Threat Detection and Response (ETDR)* – The threat intelligence system uses the data collected from the ETDR and queues the ETDR with emerging threat profiles.

- *Honeypot* – The honeypot captures and observes malicious behavior and provides the information to the threat intelligence system.

- *Intrusion Detection and Prevention System (IDPS)* – The threat intelligence system uses the data collected from the IDPS and queues the IDPS with emerging threat profiles.

- *Malware Hash* – Malware hashes are collected by the threat intelligence system and distributed to anti-malware systems for reference.

- *Network Forensics Monitor* – The network forensics monitor is used to search for threats as queued from the threat intelligence system.

- *Sandbox* – When the sandbox finds a malicious executable, it provides the attributes to the threat intelligence system.

- *Security Information and Event Management (SIEM) System* – The SIEM is used to search for breaches as queued by the threat intelligence system.

- *Threat Intelligence System* – The threat intelligence system is used to analyze threat intelligence and queue defense mechanisms.

Chapter 10

Common Compound Patterns

Private Cloud

Public Cloud

Software-as-a-Service (SaaS)

Platform-as-a-Service (PaaS)

Infrastructure-as-a-Service (IaaS)

Elastic Environment

Multitenant Environment

Resilient Environment

Cloud Bursting

Burst Out to Private Cloud

Burst Out to Public Cloud

Burst In

Secure Burst Out to Private
  Cloud/Public Cloud

Cloud Balancing

Cloud Authentication

Resource Workload Management

Isolated Trust Boundary

This chapter provides some of the more common and important combinations of the patterns documented in previous chapters. Each such combination is classified as a compound design pattern.

"Compound Pattern" vs. "Composite Pattern"

A "composite" is generally something that is comprised of inter-connected parts. For example, you could legitimately refer to a service composition as a composite of services because the individual parts need to be designed into an aggregate in order to act as a whole. A "compound," on the other hand, can simply be considered the result of combining a specific set of things together. A chemical compound consists of a combination of ingredients that result in something new when mixed together.

The patterns in this chapter are referred to as "compound patterns" because they document the effects of applying multiple patterns together. One of the most interesting parts of this exploration is that certain combinations of patterns result in design solutions that we are already familiar with.

Compound Pattern Members

The patterns that comprise a compound pattern have a relationship with the compound pattern itself. Whether these patterns have dependencies with or impacts on each other is immaterial. When studying them as members of a compound pattern, we are only interested in the results of their combined application.

Joint Application vs. Coexistent Application

When we discuss the notion of combining patterns into compounds, it is important to clarify how patterns can be combined. A compound pattern can represent a set of patterns that are applied together to a particular program or implementation in order to establish a specific set of design characteristics. This would be referred to as *joint application*.

The compound patterns with patterns that are jointly applied are:

- Cloud Bursting (492)

- Burst Out to Private Cloud (493)

- Burst Out to Public Cloud (496)

- Burst In (499)

- Secure Burst Out to Private Cloud/Public Cloud (501)

- Cloud Balancing (503)

Alternatively, the patterns that comprise a compound pattern can represent a set of related features provided by a particular program or environment. In this case, a *coexistent application* of patterns establishes a "solution environment" that may be realized by a combination of tools and technologies.

Compound patterns comprised of patterns that coexist to establish such an environment are:

- Private Cloud (474)

- Public Cloud (476)

- Software-as-a-Service (478)

- Platform-as-a-Service (480)

- Infrastructure-as-a-Service (482)

- Elastic Environment (484)

- Multitenant Environment (486)

- Resilient Environment (490)

- Cloud Authentication (505)

- Resource Workload Management (506)

The same "hierarchy style" notation is used to express compound patterns comprised of patterns that are jointly applied and those applied in a coexistent manner.

Private Cloud

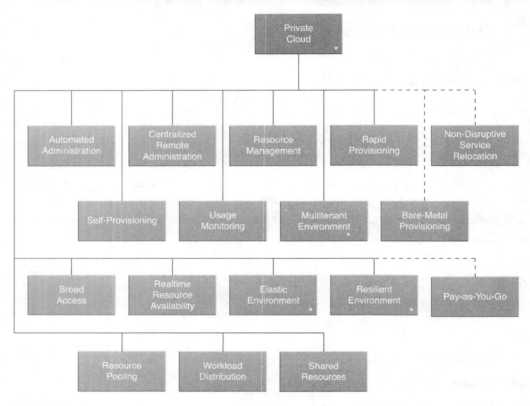

Figure 10.1
The Private Cloud compound pattern.

A private cloud is distinguished by its ownership by a single organization. From a technology architecture perspective, private clouds can be explored as single or multitenant environments. Multitenant variations of private clouds can exist (as per the Multitenant Environment (486) member pattern).

Some multitenant private clouds have a higher tendency of resembling Public Cloud (476). Note that despite its limited ownership, IT resources that are assembled to comprise a private cloud environment may belong to the organization acting as a cloud provider or they may be leased from an external service provider.

The Private Cloud compound pattern is comprised of the following core patterns:

- Automated Administration (310)
- Centralized Remote Administration (315)
- Resource Management (320)
- Self-Provisioning (324)
- Usage Monitoring (285)
- Broad Access (93)
- Realtime Resource Availability (292)
- Shared Resources (17)
- Workload Distribution (22)
- Resource Pooling (99)
- Rapid Provisioning (295)
- Elastic Environment (484)
- Resilient Environment (490)
- Multitenant Environment (486)

As indicated by the dashed lines in the preceding hierarchical diagram, the following extension patterns are part of the Private Cloud compound pattern:

- Bare-Metal Provisioning (305)
- Non-Disruptive Service Relocation (159)
- Pay-as-You-Go (288)

These optional patterns can be applied to enhance the functions and feature-sets of a private cloud environment. For example, they may represent extensions required by particular cloud consumers.

Public Cloud

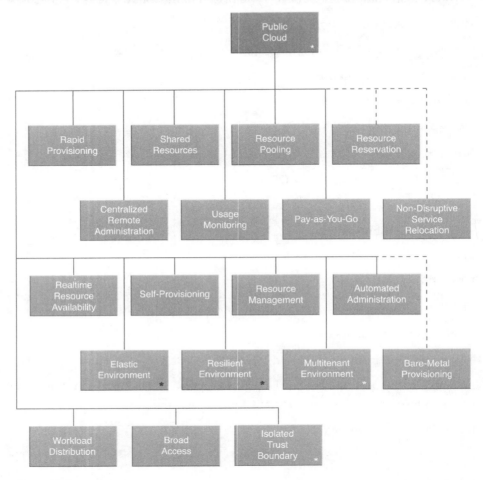

Figure 10.2

The Public Cloud compound pattern.

The Public Cloud compound pattern encompasses the patterns that comprised Private Cloud (474), and further expands upon the private cloud feature-set to provide multi-tenant functions in support of a broader range of diverse cloud consumers. Key aspects that distinguish the public cloud are its emphasis on resource sharing, billing, and the isolation of cloud consumer trust boundaries.

The administration of larger pools of IT resources that are unpredictably accessed and utilized by different cloud consumers can become a significantly more complex responsibility for public cloud providers.

The Public Cloud compound pattern is comprised of the following core patterns:

- Shared Resources (17)
- Resource Pooling (99)
- Rapid Provisioning (295)
- Workload Distribution (22)
- Centralized Remote Administration (315)
- Usage Monitoring (285)
- Pay-as-You-Go (288)
- Realtime Resource Availability (292)
- Self-Provisioning (324)
- Resource Management (320)
- Automated Administration (310)
- Broad Access (93)
- Elastic Environment (484)
- Resilient Environment (490)
- Multitenant Environment (486)
- Isolated Trust Boundary (508)

The Public Cloud compound pattern further contains the following extension patterns:

- Resource Reservation (106)
- Bare-Metal Provisioning (305)
- Non-Disruptive Service Relocation (159)

Software-as-a-Service (SaaS)

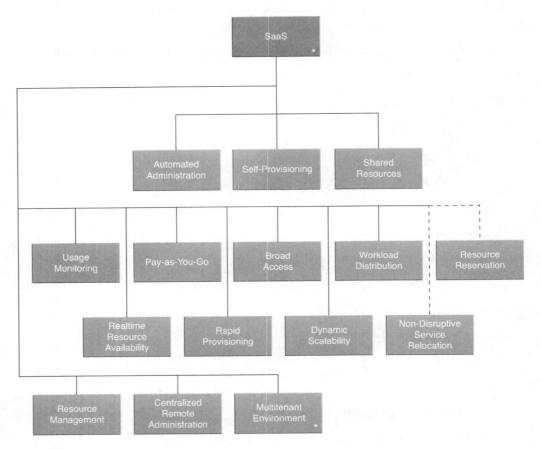

Figure 10.3

The SaaS compound pattern.

An SaaS implementation is the equivalent of a cloud-based service or application, owned by the cloud provider and made available to cloud consumers. Cloud consumers are not granted any significant control of the SaaS environment or its IT resources.

As with a PaaS environment, an SaaS implementation can be single-tenant but is more commonly multitenant. When part of multitenant environments, the application data, application profile, and/or database of each tenant is commonly hosted separately and isolated from each other. A single SaaS deployment is typically shared by multiple cloud service consumers, each of which is provided with its own runtime service instance.

The SaaS compound pattern is comprised of the following core patterns:

- Automated Administration (310)
- Self-Provisioning (324)
- Shared Resources (17)
- Usage Monitoring (285)
- Pay-as-You-Go (288)
- Broad Access (93)
- Dynamic Scalability (25)
- Realtime Resource Availability (292)
- Rapid Provisioning (295)
- Workload Distribution (22)
- Resource Management (320)
- Centralized Remote Administration (315)
- Multitenant Environment (486)

The SaaS compound pattern further contains the Non-Disruptive Service Relocation (159) and Resource Reservation (106) extension patterns.

Platform-as-a-Service (PaaS)

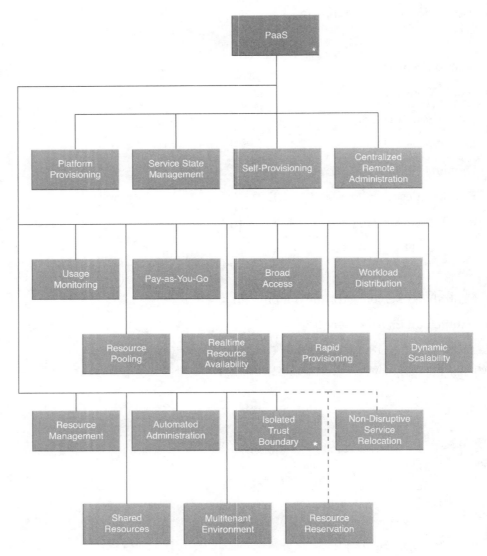

Figure 10.4
The PaaS compound pattern.

As with an IaaS environment, a PaaS environment is comprised of a collection of IT resources made available to a cloud consumer. The PaaS environment is distinguished by being more controlled, pre-defined, and primarily limiting cloud consumer usage and administration to tasks pertaining to the development and deployment of cloud services and cloud-based solutions.

A PaaS environment, by its nature, is most commonly used as part of a multitenant environment. However, single-tenant implementations are also allowable. Similarly, a PaaS can be implemented as part of a private cloud, but it is more commonly made available via a public cloud.

The PaaS compound pattern is comprised of the following core patterns:

- Platform Provisioning (301)
- Service State Management (61)
- Self-Provisioning (324)
- Centralized Remote Administration (315)
- Shared Resources (17)
- Usage Monitoring (285)
- Pay-as-You-Go (288)
- Broad Access (93)
- Workload Distribution (22)
- Resource Pooling (99)
- Realtime Resource Availability (292)
- Rapid Provisioning (295)
- Dynamic Scalability (25)
- Resource Management (320)
- Automated Administration (310)
- Multitenant Environment (486)
- Isolated Trust Boundary (508)

The PaaS compound pattern further contains the Resource Reservation (106) and Non-Disruptive Service Relocation (159) extension patterns.

Infrastructure-as-a-Service (IaaS)

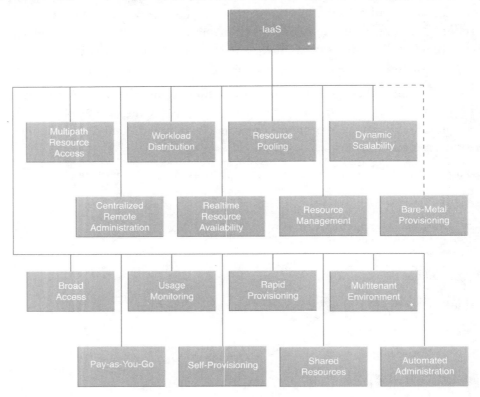

Figure 10.5
The IaaS compound pattern.

The IaaS compound pattern builds upon the architectural layers established by Private Cloud (474) and Public Cloud (476) to provide a concrete environment that offers raw IT resources (virtual and, optionally, physical) for open and independent usage and management by cloud consumers.

The member patterns of the IaaS compound pattern represent feature-sets, as provided to individual cloud consumers. Note that cloud consumers of commercial IaaS products are often able to choose the feature-set they will actually lease.

The IaaS compound pattern is comprised of the following core patterns:

- Multipath Resource Access (127)
- Workload Distribution (22)

- Dynamic Scalability (25)
- Broad Access (93)
- Rapid Provisioning (295)
- Centralized Remote Administration (315)
- Realtime Resource Availability (292)
- Resource Management (320)
- Automated Administration (310)
- Shared Resources (17)
- Resource Pooling (99)
- Pay-as-You-Go (288)
- Self-Provisioning (324)
- Usage Monitoring (285)
- Multitenant Environment (486)

The IaaS compound pattern further contains the Bare-Metal Provisioning (305) extension pattern.

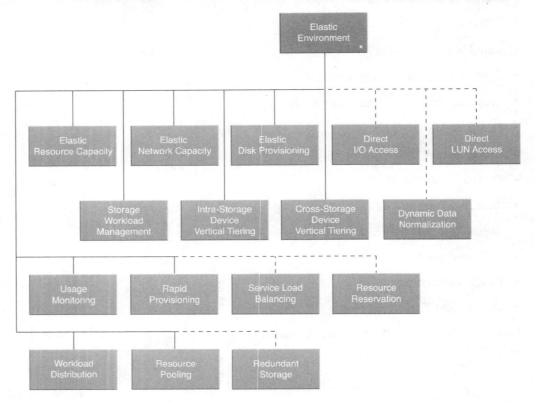

Figure 10.6
The Elastic Environment compound pattern.

The Elastic Environment compound pattern represents a collection of patterns that coexist in an environment to provide the dynamic feature-set required to realize the elasticity characteristic of a cloud.

This compound pattern is a member pattern of the following compound patterns:

- Private Cloud (474)
- Public Cloud (476)

The Elastic Environment compound pattern is comprised of the following core patterns:

- Elastic Resource Capacity (37)
- Elastic Network Capacity (42)
- Elastic Disk Provisioning (45)
- Storage Workload Management (64)
- Intra-Storage Device Vertical Tiering (81)
- Cross-Storage Device Vertical Tiering (74)
- Workload Distribution (22)
- Usage Monitoring (285)
- Rapid Provisioning (295)
- Resource Pooling (99)

The Elastic Environment compound pattern further contains the following extension patterns:

- Direct I/O Access (169)
- Direct LUN Access (173)
- Dynamic Data Normalization (71)
- Resource Reservation (106)
- Redundant Storage (119)
- Service Load Balancing (32)

Multitenant Environment

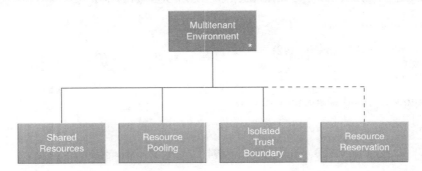

Figure 10.7
The Multitenant Environment compound pattern.

The Multitenant Environment compound pattern represents a collection of patterns that co-exist in a physical environment to provide the feature-set required to realize the multitenancy characteristic of a cloud.

This compound pattern is a member pattern of the following compound patterns:

- Private Cloud (474)

- Public Cloud (476)

- PaaS (480)

- SaaS (478)

The Multitenant Environment compound pattern is comprised of the following core patterns:

- Shared Resources (17)

- Resource Pooling (99)

- Isolated Trust Boundary (508)

...and the following extension pattern:

- Resource Reservation (106)

Compound patterns that include Multitenant Environment as a member pattern usually share some or all of its four member patterns. This redundancy is intentional, as the Multitenant Environment compound pattern combines its member patterns to form a distinct (compound) feature-set that can act independently from when the features of its member patterns are applied separately.

Multitenancy is sometimes mistaken for virtualization because the concept of multiple tenants is similar to the concept of virtualized instances. The differences lie in what is multiplied within a physical server acting as a host:

- *Virtualization:* Multiple virtual copies of the server environment can be hosted by a single physical server. Each copy can be provided to a different user, can be configured independently, and can contain its own operating system and applications.

- *Multitenancy:* A physical or virtual server hosting an application is designed to allow usage by multiple different users. Each user feels as though they have exclusive usage of the application.

Because the Multitenant Environment compound pattern includes the Resource Pooling (99) and Shared Resources (17) patterns, it inherits their respective and cumulative risks:

- overlapped trust boundary

- resource constraints

These concerns are mitigated by the application of the following patterns:

- Isolated Trust Boundary (508)

- Resource Reservation (106)

The following steps are shown in Figures 10.8 and 10.9:

1. The cloud provider selects and groups the underlying shared resources based on requirements dictated by its cloud consumers. The cloud provider then creates a resource group.

2. A parent-level resource pool is created from the resource group and a smaller resource pool is created for each cloud consumer. Each set of resources is allocated from the parent resource pool.

3. Cloud services designated for sharing to cloud consumers can be shared.

4. Any cloud consumer-specific or dedicated cloud services and IT resources are allocated.

5. Each cloud consumer is given a dedicated administration portal and service catalog access.

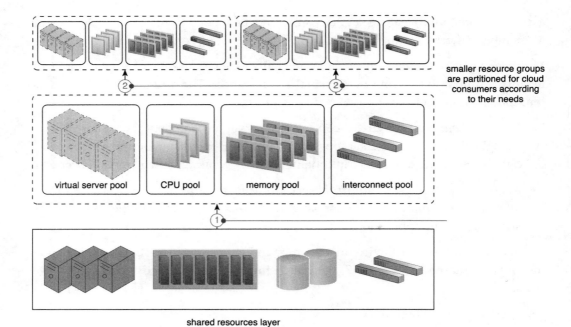

Figure 10.8

The common architectural layers of a cloud-based multitenant environment (Part I).

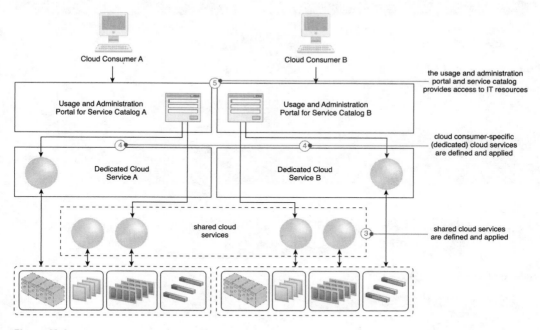

Figure 10.9

The common architectural layers of a cloud-based multitenant environment (Part II).

Resilient Environment

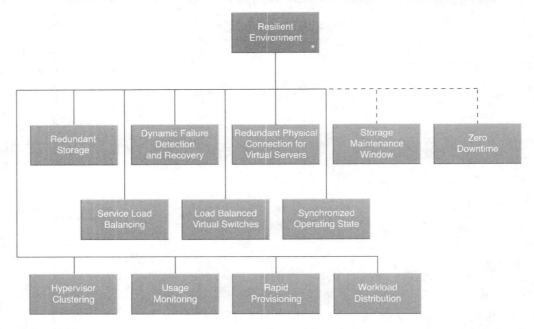

Figure 10.10
The Resilient Environment compound pattern.

The Resilient Environment compound pattern represents a collection of patterns that coexist in a physical environment to provide the failover feature-set required to realize the resiliency characteristic of a cloud.

This compound pattern is a member pattern of the following compound patterns:

- Private Cloud (474)
- Public Cloud (476)

The Resilient Environment compound pattern is comprised of the following core patterns:

- Redundant Storage (119)
- Dynamic Failure Detection and Recovery (123)
- Redundant Physical Connection for Virtual Servers (132)

- Service Load Balancing (32)

- Load Balanced Virtual Switches (57)

- Synchronized Operating State (138)

- Hypervisor Clustering (112)

- Usage Monitoring (285)

- Rapid Provisioning (295)

- Workload Distribution (22)

The Resilient Environment compound pattern further contains the following extension patterns:

- Storage Maintenance Window (147)

- Zero Downtime (143)

Cloud Bursting

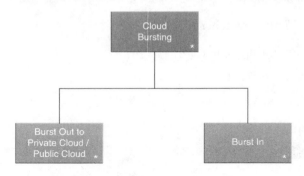

Figure 10.11
The Cloud Bursting compound pattern.

Cloud Bursting is a specialized cloud architecture that allows IT resources to scale from on-premise environments to clouds, based on pre-defined usage thresholds. When documented as a design pattern, Cloud Bursting is defined as a compound pattern that is comprised of two primary compound patterns:

- Burst Out to Private Cloud (493) or Burst Out to Public Cloud (496)

- Burst In (499)

Each of these two patterns can be applied as part of a cloud bursting architecture, or independently as part of other forms of cloud architecture.

"Bursting out" enables one environment to dynamically scale (burst) IT resources to another environment. The bursting out cloud architectures explored in this section are specific to bursting out from an on-premise environment to a cloud environment. There are two variations of this compound pattern that depend on whether bursting out occurs to a private cloud or public cloud:

- Burst Out to Private Cloud (493)

- Burst Out to Public Cloud (496)

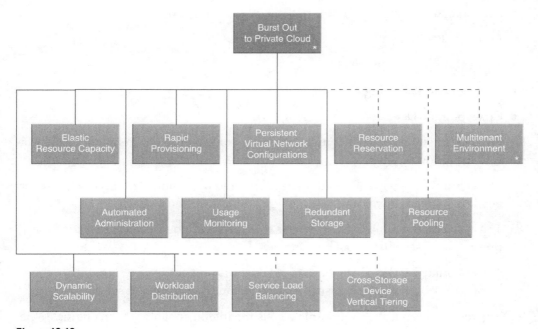

Figure 10.12
The Burst Out to Private Cloud compound pattern.

Burst Out to Private Cloud is a compound pattern comprised of the following patterns:

- Elastic Resource Capacity (37)
- Rapid Provisioning (295)
- Persistent Virtual Network Configuration (227)
- Automated Administration (310)
- Usage Monitoring (285)
- Redundant Storage (119)
- Dynamic Scalability (25)
- Workload Distribution (22)

This pattern further contains the following optional patterns:

- Resource Reservation (106)
- Resource Pooling (99)
- Multitenant Environment (486)
- Service Load Balancing (32)
- Cross-Storage Device Vertical Tiering (74)

Figure 10.13 illustrates a typical burst out from an on-premise environment to a private cloud in the following steps:

1. The cloud consumer requests that are monitored by an automated scaling listener begin to increase in volume.

2. The automated scaling listener detects that received requests have exceeded the pre-defined usage threshold.

3. The automated scaling listener initiates the burst out scaling by signaling to the resource replication mechanism for more instances of the cloud service.

4. The resource replication mechanism calls the intelligent automation engine in the private cloud to automate the generation of more instances.

5. The system established by the application of Rapid Provisioning (295) executes the creation of more requested instances of the cloud service.

6. A load balancer can be optionally incorporated to automatically forward subsequent cloud consumer messages to cloud service instances while bursting remains active.

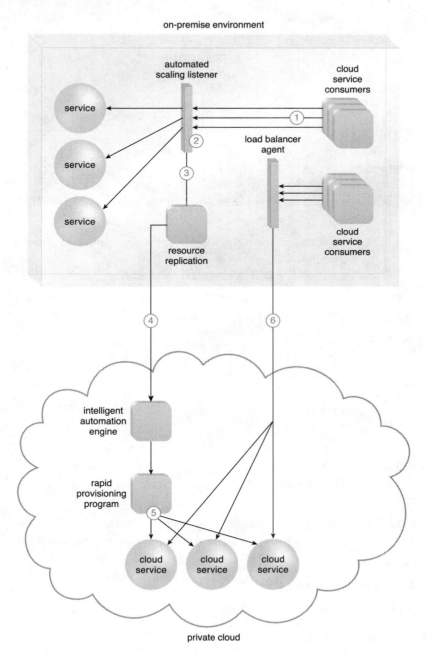

Figure 10.13

An example of a typical burst out from an on-premise environment to a private cloud.

Burst Out to Public Cloud

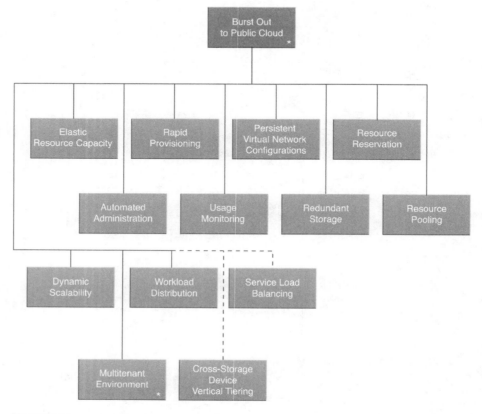

Figure 10.14

The Burst Out to Public Cloud compound pattern.

Burst Out to Public Cloud is a compound pattern comprised of the same patterns as Burst Out to Private Cloud (493), except that the following patterns are no longer optional:

- Multitenant Environment (486)
- Resource Pooling (99)
- Resource Reservation (106)

Architecturally, bursting to a public cloud is similar to bursting to a private cloud with the exception of the multitenancy characteristics that the public cloud must accommodate to ensure that occurrences of bursting out do not impact other cloud consumers or IT resources.

Figure 10.15 illustrates the steps to executing a burst out from an on-premise environment to a public cloud. The step descriptions are almost identical to performing a burst out to a private cloud, as listed under Burst Out to Private Cloud (493). The primary difference is that the multitenant architecture encompasses a resource pool.

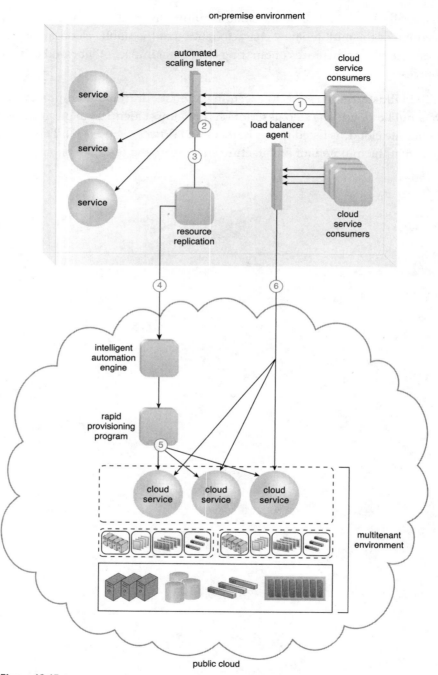

Figure 10.15

An example of a typical burst out from an on-premise environment to a public cloud.

Burst In

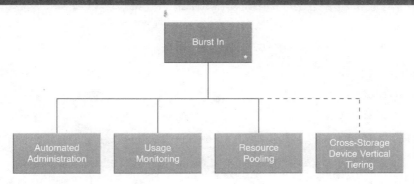

Figure 10.16
The Burst In compound pattern.

"Burst In" is the counterpart to the aforementioned "Burst Out" compound patterns, in that it is a compound pattern that establishes a system that retracts IT resources from an environment that has reached a low level of utilization. A cloud can burst in to an on-premise environment or to another cloud.

The Burst In compound pattern is comprised of the following core patterns:

- Automated Administration (310)
- Usage Monitoring (285)
- Resource Pooling (99)

It also includes the following extension pattern:

- Cross-Storage Device Vertical Tiering (74)

While the patterns are the same when bursting in from a private or public cloud, the resultant scenarios can differ. Figure 10.17 shows a private cloud architecture wherein the Burst In pattern is applied, as follows:

1. Reduced cloud service consumer requests are received.

2. The automated scaling listener determines that the reduction in usage warrants a burst in via the scaling in of cloud services.

3. The automated scaling listener signals the intelligent automation engine to delete the cloud service instances that were previously replicated and provisioned as a result of the burst out.

4. The intelligent automation engine runs a script that interacts with the rapid provisioning program to delete the cloud service instances.

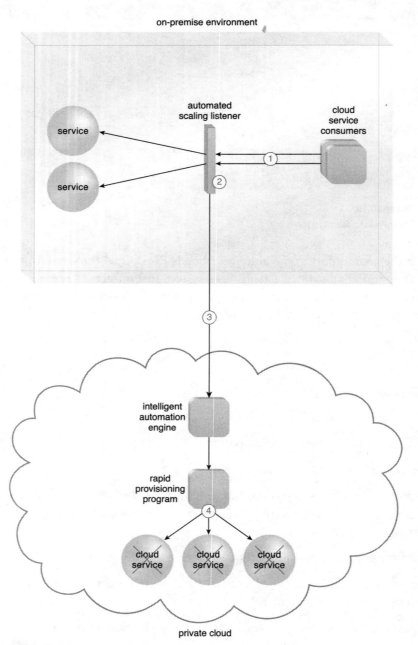

Figure 10.17

Bursting in from a public cloud is based on a comparable cloud architecture, resulting in an interaction scenario similar to the one just described. The primary difference is in Step 4. When bursting in from a public cloud, IT resources are typically released and moved back to the resource pool after the cloud service instances are deleted.

Secure Burst Out to Private Cloud/ Public Cloud

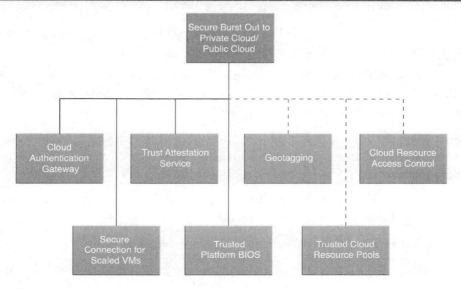

Figure 10.18

The Secure Burst Out to Private Cloud/Public Cloud compound pattern.

Secure Burst Out to Private Cloud/Public Cloud is a compound pattern that provides additional features for the purpose of securing the cloud architecture resulting from the application of Burst Out to Private Cloud (493) or Burst Out to Public Cloud (496). Cloud bursting requires confirmation of the security level of cloud resources and access privileges, security level of the associated communications channels, and secure authentication of cloud consumers and providers.

When Burst Out to Private Cloud (493), Burst Out to Public Cloud (496), and Burst In (499) are combined, a cloud architecture supporting bi-directional bursting is established.

In order to securely burst out to public or private clouds:

- The cloud platforms need to be confirmed to be at the security assurance level required by the workload and the cloud consumer needs access privileges.

- The network connecting the cloud consumer and prospective cloud platforms needs to be secure to the required assurance level.

- The endpoints involved need to authenticate each other to the required security assurance level.

The Secure Burst Out to Private Cloud/Public Cloud compound pattern is composed of the following required patterns:

- *Cloud Authentication Gateway* (430) – Enables initiating and receiving endpoints for communications to mutually authenticate.

- *Trust Attestation Service* (448) – Confirms the security assurance level of compute platforms and compute pools and makes the information available to properly authenticated consumers.

- *Secure Connection for Scaled VMs* (409) – Ensure that an encrypted and authenticated communications channel is established for scaling of virtual machine compute platforms.

- *Trusted Platform BIOS* (337) – Has been established to a specified security assurance level through a trusted boot process.

The following member patterns are considered optional extensions:

- *Geotagging* (341) – Enables workload orchestration services to confirm the proper location of compute resources.

- *Trusted Cloud Resource Pools* (354) – Have aggregated trusted compute platforms of the same security assurance levels if the workload requires them.

- *Cloud Resource Access Control* (364) – Uses attributes of the cloud consumer to determine if they have the privileges to access the resource.

It is assumed that the original on-premise resources and workload have been properly secured. If anything changes at any time during the burst out or burst in process, confirming the security of any new platform and required authorizations, connections, and authentication of endpoints must always be accomplished.

Cloud Balancing

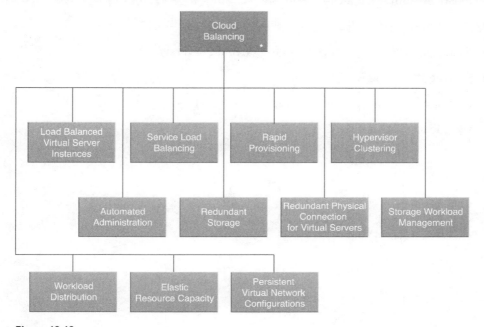

Figure 10.19
The Cloud Balancing compound pattern.

The Cloud Balancing pattern establishes a specialized cloud architecture in which IT resources can be load-balanced across multiple clouds. The benefits of a cloud-balanced architecture lie in the improved performance and efficiency of balanced IT resources. Cloud balancing can also be implemented to improve IT resource availability, whereby failed instances of IT resources are balanced by having cloud consumer requests automatically forwarded to redundant instances on another cloud.

The Cloud Balancing compound pattern is comprised of the following core patterns:

- Load Balanced Virtual Server Instances (51)
- Service Load Balancing (32)
- Rapid Provisioning (295)
- Hypervisor Clustering (112)
- Automated Administration (310)

- Elastic Resource Capacity (37)

- Redundant Storage (119)

- Redundant Physical Connection for Virtual Servers (132)

- Storage Workload Management (64)

- Persistent Virtual Network Configuration (227)

- Workload Distribution (22)

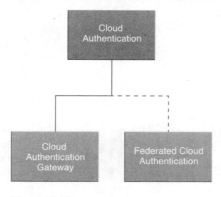

Figure 10.20
The Cloud Authentication compound pattern.

The application of this pattern results in a security management system with feature-sets that correspond to the application of the following required pattern:

- *Cloud Authentication Gateway* – With respect to authentication and access management, Cloud Authentication Gateway (430) provides for the authentication of cloud consumers as a necessary security step before presenting the consumer to the requested cloud resources' access control mechanisms. The access control mechanisms can be assured that a cloud consumer is who they claim to be, to the required level of security assurance, as they render an access control decision.

The following pattern is considered an optional extension:

- *Federated Cloud Authentication* – When business partners are sharing information, Federated Cloud Authentication (436) provides for authentication of a federation of credentials in support of the authentication portion of the compound pattern.

Resource Workload Management

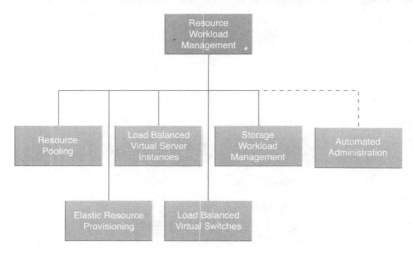

Figure 10.21

The Resource Workload Management compound pattern.

This compound pattern represents an environment that ensures that workloads are distributed in a manner that minimizes over-utilization and under-utilization while maximizing resource usage and efficiency.

This compound pattern is comprised of the following patterns:

- *Load Balanced Virtual Server Instances* – This pattern is responsible for distributing virtual servers across the hypervisors, based on the required computing capacity of each virtual server. This ensures that none of the hypervisors are over-utilized or under-utilized.

- *Storage Workload Management* – This pattern considers the amount of I/O throughout and data processing required by each cloud consumer, service, application, and virtual server being hosted in storage, in order to balance the workloads between cloud storage devices for even distribution.

- *Load Balanced Virtual Switches* – This pattern is applied to prevent congestion and bottlenecking on the virtual switch's physical uplinks.

The following pattern is considered an optional extension:

- *Automated Administration* – When Automated Administration (310) is applied with the use of the automated scaling listener mechanism, the automated administration system can initiate the workload to add another physical uplink whenever the load is increasing and there are no standby physical uplinks.

> **NOTE**
>
> In addition to the characteristics and features established by the application of the aforementioned patterns, a resource workload management environment will often further require storage performance and capacity assurance features to ensure that the storage workload management system will not cause any SLA breaches or performance impacts, and will further ensure that there is sufficient free space at the destination cloud storage device before a service, application, or virtual server is moved there.

Isolated Trust Boundary

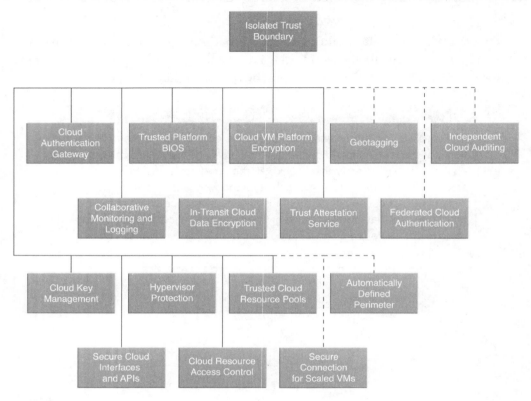

Figure 10.22

The Isolated Trust Boundary compound pattern.

The Isolated Trust Boundary is foundational to the multitenancy characteristic of the cloud. This pattern is primarily comprised of security and virtualization patterns that combine to prevent overlapping trust boundaries in a multitenant implementation.

The attribute of being trusted means being verified to a level of assurance and confidence that the information originator, information recipient, processing, and networking meet security requirements. The security assurance level is the measure of confidence that the security functions, features, practices, policies, procedures, mechanisms, and architecture of organizational information systems accurately mediate and enforce established security policies. Specific assurance-related security controls embodied in these patterns can be implemented by organizations based on the security requirements of their information systems. The member patterns must be applied to the security assurance level required by the organization.

Executing trusted workloads in a multitenant environment requires confirmation of the security level of cloud-based IT resources and access privileges, confirmation of the security level of the associated communications channels, and secure authentication of cloud consumers and providers.

The aforementioned requirements are typically achieved as follows:

- All cloud consumer and provider endpoints for a workload execution must be authenticated to the required level of assurance.

- Compute platforms involved in workload execution must be secured to the required level of assurance.

- Networks connecting endpoints involved in workload execution must be secured to the required level of assurance.

- Monitoring, logging, and alerting provide alerts to transaction anomalies and create audit trails to establish trustworthiness and accountability for a transaction.

The Isolated Trust Boundary compound pattern is comprised of the following patterns:

- *Cloud Authentication Gateway* (430) – This pattern enables initiating and receiving endpoints to mutually authenticate communication.

- *Cloud Resource Access Control* (364) – This pattern uses attributes of the cloud consumer to determine if they have the privileges to access the resource.

- *Cloud VM Platform Encryption* (350) – This pattern ensures that VM backups, snapshots, and live migration create files of the organization's VMs and are kept secure from data leakage.

- *Cloud Key Management* (444) – Encryption is foundational to security, and key management is critical to managing an organization's encryption keys.

- *Collaborative Monitoring and Logging* (452) – This pattern allows cloud consumers and providers to establish the required information to ensure the organization is meeting its industrial compliance requirements.

- *Hypervisor Protection* (344) – This pattern ensures the hypervisor, whose security is essential for the VMs it manages, is kept secure.

- *In-Transit Cloud Data Encryption* (391) – This pattern ensures that data traveling between the organization and cloud and between cloud services is protected at the network level.

- *Trust Attestation Service* (448) – This pattern confirms the security assurance level of compute platforms and compute pools for execution of a trusted workload.

- *Trusted Cloud Resource Pools* (354) – This pattern aggregates trusted compute platforms of the same security assurance levels as required by the workload.

- *Trusted Platform BIOS* (337) – This pattern establishes the specified platform security assurance level through a trusted boot process.

- *Secure Cloud Interfaces and APIs* (360) – This pattern ensures that cloud services require authentication to the proper level of assurance.

The following patterns are considered optional extensions:

- *Automatically Defined Perimeter* (425) – This pattern establishes protected communications between cloud consumers and providers.

- *Geotagging* (341) – This pattern enables workload orchestration services to confirm the proper location of compute resources.

- *Federated Cloud Authentication* (436) – This pattern allows a federation of organizations to interoperate by trusting and authenticating each other's credentials.

- *Independent Cloud Auditing* (460) – This pattern provides attestation to industry regulatory authorities that the organization is meeting their security and privacy responsibilities.

- *Secure Connection for Scaled VMs* (409) – Whether or not scaling is involved, the pattern ensures that an encrypted and authenticated communications channel is established between virtual machine compute platforms.

Appendix A

Cloud Computing Mechanisms Glossary

Technology mechanisms represent well-defined IT artifacts that are established within an IT industry and commonly distinct to a certain computing model or platform. The technology-centric nature of cloud computing requires the establishment of a formal level of mechanisms to be able to explore how a given pattern can be applied differently via alternative combinations of mechanism implementations. This not only standardizes proven practices and solutions in a design pattern format, it further adds standardization to pattern application options. It is for this reason that the following mechanisms have been defined and are formally associated with design pattern profiles.

Additional content from select Cloud Certified Professional (CCP) course modules has been assembled into an expanded version of Appendix A that has been made available by Arcitura Education via the InformIT Web site. This content examines each mechanism in closer detail and provides supplementary diagrams. To download this version, register the book at www.informit.com/title/9780133858563. (To register your book, click the Register Your Product link on this page. You are prompted to sign in or create an account. When asked for the ISBN, enter 9780133858563. This is the print book ISBN and must be entered even if you have a digital copy of the book. The expanded version of the appendix can then be accessed by clicking the Access Bonus Content link in the Registered Products section of your account page.) The content from the expanded version of Appendix A is also available at www.cloudpatterns.org.

Application Delivery Controller (ADC)

The application delivery controller (ADC) is used to combine security functions, such as application layer security, distributed denial-of-service (DDoS) protection, advanced routing strategies, and server health monitoring combined with basic application acceleration and server load balancing, in one device. It is typically placed in a data center between the firewall and one or more application servers in the DMZ.

Attestation Service

An attestation service is responsible for assessing the integrity of cloud compute nodes through techniques introduced by the trusted computing technology and trusted platform modules (TPMs). Remote attestation services are critical for implementing secure compute platforms in the cloud. They check whether a platform is launched with known-good firmware and software components, communicating the security trust level or trustworthiness of a platform to users and supporting visibility and auditability.

Attribute Authority

The attribute authority, also known as an attribute store, is a directory or database in which systems can create, read, update, and delete (CRUD) consumer attributes. It is a trusted source of consumer attributes to support making attribute-based access control (ABAC) decisions. The attribute authority is considered an identity provider (IdP) that provides user attributes to an attribute consumer. Attributes are encoded into signed tokens, such as Security Assertion Markup Language (SAML) tokens, for consumers to submit to providers to support determination of access privileges.

Attribute-Based Access Control (ABAC) System

Attribute-based access control (ABAC) is a logical access control model used by relying parties that controls access to objects. Attributes may be considered characteristics of anything that may be defined and to which a value may be assigned. In its most basic form, ABAC relies on the evaluation of the attributes of the consumer and the resource and a formal relationship or access control rule defining the allowable operations for consumer/resource attribute and environment condition combinations.

Audit Monitor

The audit monitor mechanism is used to collect audit tracking data for networks and IT resources in support of, or dictated by, regulatory and contractual obligations.

Authentication Gateway Service (AGS)

The authentication gateway service (AGS) provides proxy/brokered authentication for applications unable to natively support PKI authentication. Brokered authentication allows for a more secure and standard authentication method utilizing hardware-based credentials. The service can also provide username/password authentication. Once a consumer's credential is verified via a directory or PKI service, the AGS can be configured to query other data sources, such as identity attribute services, and pass this data on to the application. Once passed to the application, attributes can be utilized in support of capabilities such as attribute-based access control (ABAC).

Automated Scaling Listener

The automated scaling listener mechanism is a service agent that monitors and tracks communications between cloud service consumers and cloud services for dynamic scaling purposes. Automated scaling listeners are deployed within the cloud, typically near the firewall, from where they automatically track workload status information.

Automatically Defined Perimeter (ADP) Controller

The automatically defined perimeter (ADP) controller uses secure channels to control ADP participating hosts. ADP hosts can either initiate connections or accept connections managed by interactions with the ADP controller. This architecture separates the control plane from the data plane, enabling greater security and scalability. All end-points attempting to access a given infrastructure must be authenticated and authorized prior to entrance. The ADP relies on authentication and access control mechanisms. It mitigates many network-based attacks such as scanning, distributed denial-of-service (DDoS), injection attacks, OS and application vulnerability exploits, man-in-the-middle (MITM), cross-site scripting (XSS), cross-site request forgery (CSRF), pass-the-hash (PTH) and other attacks.

Billing Management System

The billing management system mechanism is dedicated to the collection and processing of usage data as it pertains to cloud provider accounting and cloud consumer billing. Specifically, the billing management system relies on pay-per-use monitors to gather runtime usage data that is stored in a repository that the system components then draw from for billing reporting and invoicing purposes.

Certificate

A certificate is a data file that binds the identity of an entity to a public key, and contains the user's identification and a signature from an issuing authority. It is also referred to as a digital certificate, X.509 certificate, or a public key certificate. Certificates are issued from a public key infrastructure (PKI), which provides a registration authority to determine the identity of the certificate holder or subject to a required level of assurance, and a certification authority to issue the certificate. The PKI also contains a repository of the issued certificate and the certificate revocation list (CRL).

Certificate Authority (CA)

The certificate authority is the public key infrastructure (PKI) entity that digitally signs certificates and certificate revocation lists (CRLs). The CA generates some certificate information but is primarily responsible for collecting information from authorized sources and entering that information into a certificate before signing. The CA digitally signs and issues a subscriber's certificate when authorized by the appropriate trusted person, called a registration authority.

Certificate Revocation List (CRL)

The certificate revocation list (CRL) is a signed list that is published and maintained by each certification authority (CA) that lists all of its revoked certificates still within their validity dates. When a CA revokes a certificate, the CA administrator (CAA) prepares a new CRL and posts it to the directory server. The CRL has additional fields, including the reason for revocation and date and time for the next update. When a consumer requests access to a resource, the resource can allow or deny access based on the CRL entry for the issuer of the certificate of that particular consumer.

Certificate Trust Store

The certificate trust store provides a mechanism for trusting self-signed root certificates from internal and other organizations. It is essentially a container for certificate trust lists. Provisioning certificate stores with only the certificate issuers trusted by the organization is critical. The stores must also be locked down so that they cannot be updated without a secure process. Relying parties must consult their certificate trust store to determine if a particular submitted certificate is trusted.

Certificate Validation Service (CVS)

A certificate validation service (CVS) provides certificate validation using revocation checking with the Online Certificate Status Protocol (OCSP) or the Server-based Certificate Validation Protocol (SCVP) for all aspects of validation checking. Complete certificate validation requires that the certificate is issued from a trusted source, which requires building a validated chain of intermediate certificates up to a trusted root, which involves checking all of the digital signatures. The certificate must be within its validity period, within its appropriate usage, and not revoked.

Cloud Consumer Gateway (CCG)

The cloud consumer gateway (CCG) is a secure network router anchored on the cloud consumer side of a cloud provider connection. The CCG is a hardware or software-based appliance located on the customer premises that serves as a bridge between local networks and remote cloud-based networks. Optimally, gateway encryption is managed by the cloud consumer and is required by many industry compliance regulations.

Cloud Storage Data Placement Auditor

The cloud storage data placement auditor mechanism is used to govern and control where datasets can be stored. This mechanism can be used to enforce policies on where each dataset can or cannot be stored and perform frequent checks and audits of each dataset's storage location to ensure the appropriate cloud storage device is used according to the requirements established in the service contract.

Cloud Storage Device

The cloud storage device mechanism represents storage devices that are designed specifically for cloud-based provisioning. Instances of these devices can be virtualized, similar to how physical servers can spawn virtual server images. They are commonly able to provide fixed-increment capacity allocation in support of the pay-per-use mechanism. Cloud storage devices can be exposed for remote access via cloud storage devices.

Cloud Storage Device Performance Monitor

The cloud storage device performance monitor mechanism is used to ensure pre-defined levels of performance are met using a policy-driven model of storage allocation. The cloud storage device performance monitor mechanism can perform further functions, such as automatically checking the current location of datasets against the pre-defined required performance metrics in order to ensure datasets always reside in a cloud storage device that matches its requirements. It can send an alert if data resides in a cloud storage device that does not meet the cloud consumer's requirements.

Cloud Storage Management Portal

The cloud storage management portal mechanism allows cloud consumers and cloud service consumers access to interact with and control data stored in a cloud environment. This mechanism can be implemented to store data in the cloud in different formats, including structured or unstructured datasets. It can also be implemented to store data in different types of cloud storage devices and to allow cloud consumers to access data regardless of its type and underlying cloud storage device type.

Cloud Usage Monitor

The cloud usage monitor mechanism is a lightweight and autonomous software program responsible for collecting and processing IT resource usage data.

Cloud Workload Scheduler

The cloud workload scheduler automates, monitors, and controls the workflow throughout the cloud infrastructure. This automation usually manages hundreds of thousands of workloads per day from a single point of control. A workload is a process or set of processes that can be componentized, individually operated upon, and produce a product, with the abstraction being above the network, hardware, and operating system layers but requiring security at each layer.

Cloud-based Security Groups

The process of resource segmentation creates cloud-based security group mechanisms that are determined through security policies. Networks are segmented into logical cloud-based security groups that form logical network perimeters. Each cloud-based IT resource is assigned to at least one logical cloud-based security group, which is assigned specific rules that govern the communication between security groups.

Cryptographic Key Management System (CKMS)

The cryptographic key management system (CKMS) consists of policies, procedures, components, and devices that are used to protect, manage, and distribute cryptographic keys and certain specific information, called metadata. A CKMS includes all devices or sub-systems that can access an unencrypted key or its metadata. Encrypted keys and their cryptographically protected metadata can be handled by computers and transmitted through communications systems and stored in media that are not considered to be part of a CKMS.

Digital Signature

The digital signature mechanism is a means of providing data authenticity and integrity through authentication and non-repudiation. A message is assigned a digital signature prior to transmission, which is then rendered invalid if the message experiences any subsequent unauthorized modifications. A digital signature provides the evidence that the message received is the same as the one created by its rightful sender.

Domain Name Service (DNS)

The domain name service (DNS) is an Internet service that translates domain names into IP addresses. Since domain names are alphabetic, the corresponding IP addresses are determined by a DNS lookup. The DNS is a network of servers that maps Internet domain names to their numeric IP addresses. Information from all the domain name servers across the Internet are gathered together and housed at the central DNS registry that is then distributed on the Internet.

Encryption

The encryption mechanism is a digital coding system dedicated to preserving the confidentiality of data. It is used for encoding plaintext data into a protected and unreadable format.

Endpoint Threat Detection and Response (ETDR)

Endpoint security refers to the protection of an organization's network when accessed via remote devices such as laptops or other wireless and mobile devices. Endpoint threat detection and response (ETDR) focuses on the endpoint as opposed to the network, threats as opposed to only malware, and officially declares incidents and the collection of tools' primary usage for both detection and incident response.

Enterprise Mobility Management (EMM) System

EMM is a comprehensive approach to securing mobile devices such as smartphones and tablets. EMM typically involves some combination of mobile device management (MDM), mobile application management (MAM), and mobile information management (MIM).

Failover System

The failover system mechanism is used to increase the reliability and availability of IT resources by using established clustering technology to provide redundant implementations. A failover system is configured to automatically switch over to a redundant or standby IT resource instance whenever the currently active IT resource becomes unavailable.

Geotag

A geotag is a data receptacle in a trusted platform module (TPM) that holds geolocation attributes and provides the mechanism for geolocation capability. Geolocation tagging is initiated by a cloud administrator when the server is first provisioned in the data center. This allows a cloud consumer to specify the location(s) where a workload should be placed, and to verify whether virtual servers and workloads are running in the correct geographic location. The geographic location determination capability supports many industry regulatory compliance requirements.

Hardened Virtual Server Image

The hardened virtual server image is a template for virtual service instance creation that has been subjected to a hardening process. This generally results in a virtual server template that is significantly more secure than the original standard image. Hardened virtual server images help counter the denial of service, insufficient authorization, and overlapping trust boundaries threats.

Hardware-Based VM Discovery System

The hardware-based VM discovery system operates in the physical hardware and provides the capability to locate hypervisors in memory, analyze nested virtualization setups showing the relationships among the same machines, and also provides a transparent mechanism to recognize and support the address space of the virtual machines.

Hardware Security Module (HSM)

The hardware security module (HSM) is a dedicated hardware cryptographic processor that is designed for the protection of the encryption key lifecycle. HSMs provide the capability to securely manage, process, and store encryption keys inside a hardened tamper-resistant device that is also resistant to bus probing. HSMs normally have features that provide tamper evidence, such as logging and alerting, and tamper resistance, such as deleting keys upon tamper detection. HSMs are mission critical as they manage the cryptography that is foundational for security, and are typically clustered for high availability.

Honeypot

Honeypots are decoy systems implemented to gather information on an attacker. They are hosts that have no authorized users other than the honeypot administrators because they serve no business function. Honeypots collect data on threats and activity directed at them is considered suspicious. Honeypots can be set up inside, outside, in the DMZ of a firewall design, or in all three locations. They are most often deployed inside of a firewall for control purposes. Honeypots are variants of standard intrusion detection and prevention systems (IDPSs) but with a greater focus on information gathering and deception.

Host-Based Security System (HBSS)

The host-based security system (HBSS) is automated and standardized security software used to provide host-oriented security on servers, desktops, and laptops rather than at the boundary, such as on routers and switches, to protect against both internal and external threats. HBSS is a suite of security applications that protect at the host server level. It contains security systems such as the host intrusion prevention system (HIPS) and firewall and virus scan. It protects multiple weak points simultaneously, especially at the client. HBSS provides detailed report capabilities, realtime asset status, central configuration management, and defense-in-depth protection of the latest cyber threats.

Hypervisor

The hypervisor mechanism is a fundamental part of virtualization infrastructure that is primarily used to generate virtual server instances of a physical server. A hypervisor is generally limited to one physical server and can therefore only create virtual images of that server. Similarly, a hypervisor can only assign the virtual servers it generates to resource pools that reside on the same underlying physical server.

Identity and Access Management (IAM)

The identity and access management (IAM) mechanism encompasses the components and policies necessary to control and track user identities and access privileges for IT resources, environments, and systems. IAM mechanisms exist as systems comprised of four main components that are authentication, authorization, user management, and credential management.

Intrusion Detection and Prevention System (IDPS)

Intrusion detection and prevention systems (IDPS) automate the process of monitoring the events occurring in a computer system or network, and attempt to identify possible incidents, log information about them, stop them, and report them to security administrators. They are typically used to record information related to observed events, notify security administrators of important observed events, and automatically generate reports, with remediation actions performed manually after human review of the report. Many IDPSs can also be configured to respond to a detected threat using a variety of techniques, including changing security configurations or blocking the attack.

Live VM Migration

Live VM migration can be used to migrate virtual servers from one location to another without service interruption if both the source and destination locations are using a compatible hypervisor brand and version. Live migration moves running virtual machines from one physical server to another without impacting virtual machine availability. This is done by pre-copying the memory of the migrating virtual machine to the destination server. An administrator or orchestrator that initiates the live migration must determine which computer to use as the destination for the live migration, considering the security requirements. The guest operating system of the migrating virtual machine is not aware that the migration is happening, so no special configuration for the guest operating system is needed. Networking must be managed.

Load Balancer

The load balancer mechanism is a runtime agent with logic fundamentally based on the premise of employing horizontal scaling to balance a workload across two or more IT resources to increase performance and capacity beyond what a single IT resource can provide. Beyond simple division of labor algorithms, load balancers can perform a range of specialized runtime workload distribution functions that include asymmetric distribution, workload prioritization, and content-aware distribution.

Logical Network Perimeter

A logical network perimeter establishes a virtual network boundary that can encompass and isolate a group of related cloud-based IT resources that may be physically distributed. It is defined as the isolation of a network environment from the rest of a communications network.

LUN Masking

The LUN masking mechanism is used to configure required security policies to present the storage LUNs to only those systems and cloud storage devices that require access via the interfaces and configuration options provided by physical storage vendors.

Malware Hash

Malware hashes are used by virus protection systems to identify viruses. They consist of calculated numerical values of code unique to the virus. Malware authors have learned to customize viruses for each infected machine, challenging anti-virus systems.

Multi-Device Broker

The multi-device broker mechanism is used to facilitate runtime data transformation so as to make a cloud service accessible to a wider range of cloud service consumer programs and devices.

Network Forensics Monitor

The network forensics monitor captures, records, and analyzes network events in order to discover the source of security attacks or other problem incidents. Computer forensics involve the preservation, identification, extraction, documentation, and interpretation of computer media for evidentiary and/or root cause analysis. Network forensics monitors aid in acquiring and analyzing evidence.

Orchestration Engine

Orchestration is the automated coordination and management of computer resources and services. Orchestration provides for deployment and execution of interdependent workflows completely on external resources. A cloud orchestration engine manages complex cross-domain workflows, involving systems, enterprises and firewalls, and processes including handling exceptions.

Pay-Per-Use Monitor

The pay-per-use monitor mechanism measures cloud-based IT resource usage in accordance with predefined pricing parameters and generates usage logs for fee calculations and billing purposes. The data collected by the pay-per-use monitor is processed by a billing management system.

Physical Uplink

A physical uplink is used by virtual servers to communicate with the virtual and physical servers that are hosted outside of their virtual switch. This path must be guaranteed to be redundant and reliable at all times.

Platform Trust Policy

The platform trust policy is a security assurance policy for a platform, such as its secure launch control policy restricting applications to only execute on platforms that meet a specified trust assurance level. Compliance and auditing mechanisms must demonstrate that critical, personal, or sensitive data has only been processed on platforms that meet trust requirements.

Public Key Infrastructure (PKI)

The public key infrastructure (PKI) mechanism exists as a system of protocols, data formats, rules, and practices that enable large-scale systems to securely use public key cryptography. This system is used to associate public keys with their corresponding key owners while enabling the verification of key validity. A PKI enables the use of encryption and digital signature services across a wide variety of security services and applications.

RAID-level Idenfitier

The RAID-level identifier mechanism is used to provide RAID-level information on cloud storage devices. If cloud storage device vendors provide APIs or SDKs, this mechanism can be implemented automatically for integration into the management portal mechanism. If no API or SDK is provided, the cloud storage administrator should manually populate the information using available features or options.

Ready-Made Environment

The ready-made environment mechanism is a defining component of the PaaS cloud delivery model that represents a pre-defined, cloud-based platform comprised of a set of already installed IT resources, ready to be used and customized by a cloud consumer. These environments are utilized by cloud consumers to remotely develop and deploy their own services and applications within a cloud. Typical ready-made environments include pre-installed IT resources, such as databases, middleware, development tools, and governance tools.

Remote Administration System

The remote administration system mechanism provides tools and user interfaces for external cloud resource administrators to configure and administer cloud-based IT resources. A remote administration system can establish a portal for access to administration and management features of various underlying systems.

Resource Cluster

The resource cluster mechanism is used to group multiple IT resource instances so that they can be operated as a single IT resource. This increases the combined computing capacity, load balancing, and availability of the clustered IT resources.

Resource Management System

The resource management system mechanism helps coordinate IT resources in response to management actions performed by both cloud consumers and cloud providers.

Resource Replication

Resource replication is defined as the creation of multiple instances of the same IT resource, and is typically performed when an IT resource's availability and performance need to be enhanced. Virtualization technology is used to implement the resource replication mechanism to replicate cloud-based IT resources.

Sandbox

Sandbox is a testing environment that isolates untested or unknown code. Sandboxing protects operational systems and their data from unknown code that may have arrived on the network from unknown external sources. It can provide threat intelligence by analyzing code behavior, and can be used in conjunction with rogue executables captured in a honeypot.

Secure Token Service (STS)

A secure token service (STS) issues security tokens as a result of consumer requests for single sign-on (SSO) tokens. The STS authenticates the consumer and issues a security token that contains consumer claims and is protected from manipulation by a digital signature. Example tokens issued include Kerberos and SAML.

Security Information and Event Management (SIEM) System

SIEM combines security information management (SIM) and security event management (SEM) functions into one security management system. SIEM collects relevant data about an enterprise's security posture in multiple locations and analyzes all the data from a single point of view, providing the capability to spot trends and patterns that may be the result of malicious activity.

Single Sign-On (SSO)

The single sign-on (SSO) mechanism enables one cloud service consumer to be authenticated by a security broker, which establishes a security context that is persisted while the cloud service consumer accesses other cloud services or cloud-based IT resources. Otherwise, the cloud service consumer would need to re-authenticate itself with every subsequent request.

SLA Management System

The SLA management system mechanism represents a range of commercially available cloud management products that provide features pertaining to the administration, collection, storage, reporting, and runtime notification of SLA data.

SLA Monitor

The SLA monitor mechanism is used to specifically observe the runtime performance of cloud services to ensure that they are fulfilling the contractual QoS requirements that are published in SLAs. The data collected by the SLA monitor is processed by an SLA management system to be aggregated into SLA reporting metrics. This system can proactively repair or failover cloud services when exception conditions occur, such as when the SLA monitor reports a cloud service as "down."

State Management Database

A state management database is a storage device that is used to temporarily persist state data for software programs. As an alternative to caching state data in memory, software programs can offload state data to the database in order to reduce the amount of runtime memory they consume. As a result, the software programs and the surrounding infrastructure are more scalable.

Storage Path Masking

The storage path masking mechanism is used to discover the available paths to a cloud storage device or physical storage device in a similar way to the multipathing mechanism. This mechanism can be used to establish concurrent communication over multiple pathways, and to hide some or all paths to a cloud or physical storage device from systems or applications.

Sub-LUN Migration

A logical unit number (LUN) is a unique identifier used to designate individual or collections of hard disk devices for address by a protocol associated with a SCSI, iSCSI, fibre channel (FC), or similar interface. A sub-LUN is a higher granularity designation of a LUN. Sub-LUN migration automates the process of moving data to optimum storage devices by, for example, detecting data that has a high access rate and temporarily moving it to faster storage. When requests for the data drop off, it is moved back to the disk location where the original copy is stored.

Threat Intelligence System

A threat intelligence system provides evidence-based threat knowledge, including context, mechanisms, indicators, implications, and actionable advice for use in countering threats. Threat intelligence can provide information about an emerging threat to an asset that can be used to inform decisions as to how the subject will respond to that threat. Common forms of threat intelligence data include security threats, threat actors, exploits, malware, vulnerabilities, and compromise indicators.

Traffic Filter

Traffic filtering is a method used to provide network security by filtering network traffic based on many types of criteria. Traffic filters are used as distributed denial-of-service (DDoS) protection devices that provide ingress filtering, rate limiting, reverse address lookup, and network traffic monitoring. Inbound filters are employed by routers to limit traffic towards a network to authorized traffic only, and to specify rules and policies that govern a specific port, service, server, or network. Inbound filters are implemented in network hardening and security planning to manage the traffic flow and allow only secure and trusted networks, hosts, or autonomous systems to access the protected network.

Traffic Monitor

Network traffic monitoring is the process of reviewing, analyzing, and managing network traffic for any abnormality or process that can affect network performance, availability, and/or security. The traffic monitor allows categorization of a network's bandwidth usage. It provides network administrators with realtime data as well as long-term usage trends for all network devices.

Trusted Platform Module (TPM)

A trusted platform module (TPM) is a tamper-resistant integrated circuit built into some computer motherboards that can perform cryptographic operations, such as key generation, and protect small amounts of sensitive information, such as passwords and cryptographic keys. The TPM securely stores artifacts used to authenticate the platform, including passwords, certificates and encryption keys. The TPM is used to store platform measurements that help ensure that the platform remains trustworthy. Authentication and attestation are necessary steps to attain trust to a policy-specified level of assurance.

Virtual Appliance

A virtual appliance typically comes in the open virtualization format (OVF) and is either a pre-installed and configured virtual server image or a pre-installed virtual server that can be imported and used immediately.

Virtual CPU (vCPU)

Virtual CPU (vCPU) is the amount of processing power that a hypervisor provides to a virtual server. Four to eight vCPUs can usually be allocated to each physical core to accommodate varying workloads.

Virtual Disk (vDisk)

A virtual disk (vDisk) is a specialized variation of the cloud storage device mechanism that exists as a single file or a set of files split into smaller parts that represent the virtual server's hard disk. A virtual disk is the consolidation of hard drives that are allocated to a virtual server before or after its creation.

Virtual Firewall

The virtual firewall is software running in a virtual server that controls and filters communication to, from, and between virtual servers. It is a network firewall service or appliance running within a VM that provides the protection and monitoring functions of a physical network firewall.

Virtual Infrastructure Manager (VIM)

The virtual infrastructure manager (VIM) coordinates the server hardware so that virtual server instances can be created from the most expedient underlying physical server. The VIM is a commercial product that can be used to manage a range of virtual IT resources across multiple physical servers.

Virtual Network

The virtual network is a combination of virtual switches and their uplinks to a physical network that isolates a network environment. The virtual network requires a minimum of one physical uplink and one virtual switch, although it can have more virtual switches.

Virtual Private Cloud (VPC)

The virtual private cloud (VPC) is the segmentation of a public cloud service provider's multitenant environment to support private cloud computing. The VPC provides secure data transfer between an organization's on-premise and public cloud provider, ensuring isolated boundaries from every other customer's data both in transit and inside the cloud provider's network.

Virtual Private Network (VPN)

The virtual private network (VPN) is a network that uses a public telecommunication infrastructure, such as the Internet, to provide consumers with secure connections to their organization's network. The VPN ensures privacy through security procedures and tunneling protocols, including the Layer Two Tunneling Protocol (L2TP). Data is encrypted at the sending end for transmission and decrypted at the receiving end.

Virtual RAM (vRAM)

Virtual RAM (vRAM) is the amount of RAM that a hypervisor allocates to a virtual server. When a virtual server is created with a certain amount of RAM, a hypervisor must allocate the same amount of vRAM to that virtual server.

Virtual Server

The virtual server, also known as virtual machine (VM), is a form of virtualization software that emulates a physical server and is used by cloud providers to share the same physical server with multiple cloud consumers by providing cloud consumers with individual virtual server instances.

Virtual Server Snapshot

Snapshotting a virtual server is a method of creating a full restore point for the virtual server, including the virtual server's applications, hardware settings, and operating system.

Virtual Server State Manager

The virtual server state manager enables the virtual server to be paused and saved in any state. This can be performed in the middle of any action, such as copying files or installing the operating system. Virtual server state managers are supported by all hypervisors.

Virtual Switch

A virtual switch is a logical network switch that operates at the hypervisor level. Network interface cards (NICs) are emulated into a single virtual switch.

Virtualization Agent

The virtualization agent mechanism is an agent that is installed inside the virtual server and typically provides load-enhanced drivers for the virtual servers to add various types of common functionality, synchronization of the date and time of the virtual server to the host, and securing of communication between the virtual server and hypervisor.

Virtualization Monitor

The virtualization monitor is a specialized variation of the usage monitor mechanism that provides monitoring functionality specific to virtualization-related usage. A variety of virtualization monitors can be used to perform different forms of monitoring. Virtualization monitors are typically implemented as service agents.

VPN Cloud Hub

The VPN cloud hub provides secure communication between distributed data centers using a hub-and-spoke model with VPC architecture. It enables connection to organizational data centers, whether on-premise or in the cloud, in order to function as part of a single, private network. These networks can use IPsec or TLS in hardware or software.

Appendix B

Alphabetical Design Patterns
Reference

Provided here for quick reference purposes is an alphabetical list of design patterns in this book with corresponding page numbers.

Automated Administration (310)

Automatically Defined Perimeter (425)

Bare-Metal Provisioning (305)

Broad Access (93)

Burst In (499)

Burst Out to Private Cloud (493)

Burst Out to Public Cloud (496)

Centralized Remote Administration (315)

Cloud Authentication (505)

Cloud Authentication Gateway (430)

Cloud Balancing (503)

Cloud Bursting (492)

Cloud Data Breach Protection (382)

Cloud Denial-of-Service Protection (416)

Cloud Key Management (444)

Cloud Resource Access Control (364)

Cloud Storage Data at Rest Encryption (181)

Cloud Storage Data Lifecycle Management (184)

Cloud Storage Data Management (187)

Cloud Storage Data Placement Compliance Check (190)

Cloud Storage Device Masking (194)

Cloud Storage Device Path Masking (198)

Cloud Storage Device Performance Enforcement (201)

Cloud Traffic Hijacking Protection (421)

Cloud VM Platform Encryption (350)

Collaborative Monitoring and Logging (452)

Cross-Hypervisor Workload Mobility (247)

Cross-Storage Device Vertical Tiering (74)

Detecting and Mitigating User-Installed VMs (369)

Direct I/O Access (169)

Direct LUN Access (173)

Dynamic Data Normalization (71)

Dynamic Failure Detection and Recovery (123)

Dynamic Scalability (25)

Elastic Disk Provisioning (45)

Elastic Environment (484)

Elastic Network Capacity (42)

Elastic Resource Capacity (37)

External Virtual Server Accessibility (244)

Federated Cloud Authentication (436)

Geotagging (341)

Hypervisor Clustering (112)

Hypervisor Protection (344)

Independent Cloud Auditing (460)

Infrastructure-as-a-Service (IaaS) (482)

In-Transit Cloud Data Encryption (391)

Intra-Storage Device Vertical Data Tiering (81)

IP Storage Isolation (218)

Isolated Trust Boundary (508)

Load Balanced Virtual Server Instances (51)

Load Balanced Virtual Switches (57)

Memory Over-Committing (86)

Mobile BYOD Security (376)

Multipath Resource Access (127)

Multitenant Environment (486)

NIC Teaming (90)

Non-Disruptive Service Relocation (159)

Pay-as-You-Go (288)

Permanent Data Loss Protection (387)

Persistent Virtual Network Configuration (227)

Platform Provisioning (301)

Platform-as-a-Service (PaaS) (480)

Power Consumption Reduction (330)

Private Cloud (474)

Public Cloud (476)

RAID-Based Data Placement (214)

Rapid Provisioning (295)

Realtime Resource Availability (292)

Redundant Physical Connection for Virtual Servers (132)

Redundant Storage (119)

Resilient Environment (490)

Resource Management (320)

Resource Pooling (99)

Resource Reservation (106)

Resource Workload Management (506)

Secure Burst Out to Private Cloud/Public Cloud (501)

Secure Cloud Interfaces and APIs (360)

Secure Connection for Scaled VMs (409)

Secure External Cloud Connection (404)

Secure On-Premise Internet Access (397)

Self-Provisioning (324)

Service Load Balancing (32)

Service State Management (61)

Shared Resources (17)

Single Root I/O Virtualization (178)

Software-as-a-Service (SaaS) (478)

Stateless Hypervisor (278)

Storage Maintenance Window (147)

Storage Workload Management (64)

Sub-LUN Tiering (210)

Synchronized Operating State (138)

Threat Intelligence Processing (465)

Trust Attestation Service (448)

Trusted Cloud Resource Pools (354)

Trusted Platform BIOS (337)

Usage Monitoring (285)

Virtual Disk Splitting (204)

Virtual Server Auto Crash Recovery (155)

Virtual Server Connectivity Isolation (231)

Virtual Server Folder Migration (223)

Virtual Server NAT Connectivity (240)

Virtual Server-to-Host Affinity (252)

Virtual Server-to-Host Anti-Affinity (258)

Virtual Server-to-Host Connectivity (265)

Virtual Server-to-Virtual Server Affinity (267)

Virtual Server-to-Virtual Server Anti-Affinity (272)

Virtual Switch Isolation (235)

Workload Distribution (22)

Zero Downtime (143)

About the Authors

Thomas Erl

Thomas Erl is a top-selling IT author, founder of Arcitura Education Inc., and series editor of the *Prentice Hall Service Technology Series from Thomas Erl*. With more than 200,000 copies in print worldwide, his books have become international bestsellers and have been formally endorsed by senior members of major IT organizations, such as IBM, Microsoft, Oracle, Intel, Accenture, IEEE, HL7, MITRE, SAP, CISCO, HP, and many others. As CEO of Arcitura Education Inc., Thomas has led the development of curricula for the internationally recognized Big Data Science Certified Professional (BDSCP), Cloud Certified Professional (CCP), and SOA Certified Professional (SOACP) accreditation programs, which have established a series of formal, vendor-neutral industry certifications obtained by thousands of IT professionals around the world. Thomas has toured more than 20 countries as a speaker and instructor. More than 100 articles and interviews by Thomas have been published in numerous publications, including *The Wall Street Journal* and *CIO Magazine*.

Robert Cope

Robert Cope has more than 25 years of experience in mission-critical systems development, spanning all aspects of the software system engineering lifecycle from architectural development, experimentation and prototyping, requirements development, design, implementation, and operations to acquisition program management for large systems. With more than 10 years in research, development, and implementation of security architecture, Public Key Infrastructure (PKI) security technology, and security services for large organizations, he has vast experience in information assurance, identity management deployment, operations, and maintenance of large-scale high assurance identity management enclaves.

Robert is the CEO of Homeland Security Consultants, a Federal Risk and Authorization Management Program (FedRAMP)–approved Third Party Assessment Organization (3PAO) for certifying cloud services. He led the development of the virtualization and cloud computing architecture for a large organization and was the chief architect responsible for the development of an enterprise authentication service, leading a team to integrate the organization's identity and access management service architecture using Model Based System Engineering (MBSE) and the System Modeling Language (SysML).

Robert is a Certified Trainer for Arcitura's Cloud School and SOA School. He has been a contributing member of the National Institute of Standards and Technology (NIST) Cloud-adapted Risk Management Framework (CRMF) and a contributing member of the Organization for the Advancement of Structured Information Standards (OASIS) IdCloud Technical Committee. He is also a member of the International Council on Systems Engineering (INCOSE).

Amin Naserpour

A certified IT professional with more than 14 years of experience in solution architecture and design, engineering, and consultation, Amin Naserpour specializes in designing medium to enterprise-level complex solutions for partially to fully virtualized front-end infrastructures. His portfolio includes clients such as VMware, Microsoft, and Citrix, and his work consists of integrating front-ends with back-end infrastructure-layer solutions. Amin designed a unified, vendor-independent cloud computing framework that he presented at the 5th International SOA, Cloud + Service Technology Symposium in 2012. Certified in cloud computing, virtualization, and storage, Amin currently holds Technical Consultant and Cloud Operations Lead positions for Hewlett-Packard, Australia.

Index

A

ABAC. *See* attribute based access control (ABAC)

access control, 513

ADC. *See* application delivery controller (ADC)

ADP. *See* automatically defined perimeter (ADP) controller

AGS. *See* authentication gateway service (AGS)

application delivery controller (ADC), 403
    defined, 512

application layer attacks, 417

attestation service, 190, 192, 358, 451
    defined, 512

attribute authority, 368
    defined, 513

attribute based access control (ABAC), 368
    defined, 513

attribute store. *See* attribute authority

audit monitor, 21, 24, 69, 79, 103, 110, 126, 144, 287, 294, 318
    defined, 513

authentication gateway service (AGS), 363, 366-368, 435
    defined, 513

Automated Administration design pattern, 38, 284, 302, 475, 477, 479, 481, 483, 493, 499
    profile, 310-314

automated scaling listener, 22, 28, 31, 40, 43, 55, 69, 79, 85, 213, 287, 314
    defined, 514

automatically defined perimeter (ADP) controller, 429
    defined, 514

Automatically Defined Perimeter design pattern, 510
    profile, 425-429

B

bandwidth, 43

Bare-Metal Provisioning design pattern, 475, 477, 483
    profile, 305-309

bare metal virtualization, 344

basic input/output system (BIOS), 337

BGP (Border Gateway Protocol), 421

billing management system, 291, 318
    defined, 514

BIOS (basic input/output system), 337

BIOS/firmware rootkits, 337

bootkits, 338

Border Gateway Protocol (BGP), 421

botnets, 417

Broad Access design pattern, 16, 318, 475, 477, 479, 481, 483
    profile, 93-95

Burst In compound pattern, 473, 492
   profile, 499-500
Burst Out to Private Cloud compound
   pattern, 473, 496-497, 501
   profile, 493-495
Burst Out to Public Cloud compound
   pattern, 473, 492, 501
   profile, 496-498

C

CA. *See* certificate authority (CA)
capacity watchdog system, 52-55
capitalization in design pattern
   notation, 13
CCG. *See* cloud consumer gateway (CCG)
CCP (Cloud Certified Professional), 6
Centralized Remote Administration
   design pattern, 284, 293, 321, 475, 477,
   479, 481, 483
   profile, 315-319
certificate, 358, 435, 443
   defined, 514
certificate authority (CA), 435, 443
   defined, 515
certificate revocation list (CRL), 435, 443
   defined, 515
certificate trust store, 430, 435-436, 443
   defined, 515
certificate validation service (CVS), 443
   defined, 515
CKMS. *See* cryptographic key
   management system (CKMS)
Cloud Authentication compound
   pattern, 473
   profile, 505
Cloud Authentication Gateway design
   pattern, 502, 505, 509
   profile, 430-435
Cloud Balancing compound pattern, 473
   profile, 503-504
cloud-based security groups, 354, 358, 364,
   368, 409, 415
   defined, 517

Cloud Bursting compound pattern, 473
   profile, 492
*Cloud Computing: Concepts, Technology &
   Architecture* (Erl), 2-5, 14
cloud consumer gateway (CCG), 408
   defined, 516
Cloud Data Breach Protection design
   pattern, profile, 382-385
Cloud Denial-of-Service Protection design
   pattern, profile, 416-420
Cloud Key Management design pattern,
   406, 509
   profile, 444-447
Cloud Resource Access Control design
   pattern, 502, 509
   profile, 364-368
cloud service types, 453
cloud storage data aging management, 186
Cloud Storage Data at Rest Encryption
   design pattern, profile, 181-183
Cloud Storage Data Lifecycle Management
   design pattern, profile, 184-186
Cloud Storage Data Management design
   pattern, profile, 187-189
cloud storage data placement auditor, 192
   defined, 516
Cloud Storage Data Placement Compliance
   Check design pattern, profile, 190-193
cloud storage device, 21, 24, 31, 49, 55, 63,
   69, 73, 79, 85, 103, 110, 117, 122, 131, 142,
   145, 154, 164, 171, 176, 183, 186, 189, 192,
   197, 209, 213, 217, 226, 250, 282, 299, 308,
   314, 394
   defined, 516
Cloud Storage Device Masking design
   pattern, profile, 194-197
Cloud Storage Device Path Masking
   design pattern, profile, 198
Cloud Storage Device Performance
   Enforcement design pattern, profile,
   201-203
cloud storage device performance monitor,
   201-203
   defined, 516

cloud storage device pools, 101
cloud storage management portal, 189,
    217, 220
    defined, 517
**Cloud Traffic Hijacking Protection design
    pattern, profile, 421-424**
cloud usage monitor, 21, 24, 31, 36, 40, 43,
    48-49, 55, 60, 63, 69, 80, 85, 104, 111, 126,
    145, 164, 171, 176, 287, 291, 294, 314, 318
    defined, 517
**Cloud VM Platform Encryption design
    pattern, 509**
    profile, 350-353
cloud workload scheduler, 357-358
    defined, 517
coexistent application
    of compound patterns, 473
    defined, 13
**Collaborative Monitoring and Logging
    design pattern, 509**
    profile, 452-459
community clouds, 453
compound patterns
    Burst In, 473, 492
        profile, 499-500
    Burst Out to Private Cloud, 473, 492,
        496-497, 501
        profile, 493-495
    Burst Out to Public Cloud, 473, 492, 501
        profile, 496-498
    Cloud Authentication, 473
        profile, 505
    Cloud Balancing, 473
        profile, 503-504
    Cloud Bursting, 473
        profile, 492
    coexistent application of, 473
    composite patterns versus, 472
    defined, 12-13
    design patterns as members, 472
    Elastic Environment, 473-477
        profile, 484-485

Infrastructure-as-a-Service, 20, 473
    profile, 482-483
Isolated Trust Boundary, 477, 481,
    486-487
    profile, 508-510
joint application of, 472
Multitenant Environment, 473-483,
    494-496
    profile, 486-489
Platform-as-a-Service, 473, 486
    profile, 480-481
Private Cloud, 473, 476, 482-486, 490
    profile, 474-475
Public Cloud, 20, 473-474, 482-486, 490
    profile, 476-477
Resilient Environment, 473-477
    profile, 490-491
Resource Workload Management, 473
    profile, 506
Secure Burst Out to Private
    Cloud/Public Cloud, 473
    profile, 501-502
Software-as-a-Service, 20, 473, 486
    profile, 478-479
CPU pools, 101
CRL. *See* certificate revocation list (CRL)
**Cross-Hypervisor Workload Mobility
    design pattern, profile, 247-251**
**Cross-Storage Device Vertical Tiering
    design pattern, 485, 494, 499**
    profile, 74-80
cryptographic key management system
    (CKMS), 183, 197, 353, 386, 390, 394,
    424, 447
    defined, 517
**custom reporter (Usage Monitoring design
    pattern), 287**
**custom scripts (Rapid Provisioning design
    pattern), 296**
CVS. *See* certificate validation service
    (CVS)

D

data normalization, 71-73
data source loader, 290
data transport mechanism, 186
denial-of-service (DoS) attacks, 416-420
deployment agent, 306
deployment component, 306
deployment data store, 296
design patterns. *See also* compound patterns
    benefits of, 10
    defined, 2
    as members of compound patterns, 472
    list of, 536
    notation for
        capitalization, 13
        page number references, 13
    profile format, 11-12
    Web site, 6, 14
Design Patterns: Elements of Reusable Object-Oriented Software (Gamma, et al), 3
Detecting and Mitigating User-Installed VMs design pattern, profile, 369-374
digital certificates. *See* certificate
digital signature, 340, 349, 359, 394, 415, 451
    defined, 518
DIL procedures, 443
Direct I/O Access design pattern, 43, 164, 178-179, 485
    profile, 169-172
Direct LUN Access design pattern, 485
    profile, 173-177
discovery agent, 306
distributed denial-of-service (DDoS) attacks, 416
distributed reflector denial-of-service (DRDoS) attacks, 416
DNS reflection attacks, 416
domain name service (DNS), 403, 420
    defined, 518

driver rootkits, 338
Dynamic Data Normalization design pattern, 16, 485
    profile, 71-73
Dynamic Failure Detection and Recovery design pattern, 98, 490
    profile, 123-126
dynamic horizontal scaling, 28-31
dynamic relocation, 29
Dynamic Scalability design pattern, 38, 99-100, 479, 481, 483, 493
    profile, 25-31
dynamic storage provisioning, 46
dynamic vertical scaling, 29

E

Elastic Disk Provisioning design pattern, 485
    profile, 45-50
Elastic Environment compound pattern, 473, 475, 477
    profile, 484-485
Elastic Network Capacity design pattern, 485
    profile, 42-44
Elastic Resource Capacity design pattern, 485, 493, 504
    profile, 37-41
EMM system. *See* enterprise mobility management (EMM) system
encryption, 181-183, 197, 390, 394, 424
    defined, 518
endpoint threat detection and response (ETDR) system, 469
    defined, 518
enterprise mobility management (EMM) system, 381
    defined, 519
External Virtual Server Accessibility design pattern, 242
    profile, 244-246

F

failover system, 122, 126, 136, 142, 145, 154
    defined, 519
Federated Cloud Authentication design
    pattern, 505, 510
    profile, 436-443
federation of users, 443
firewalls (Secure Connection for Scaled
    VMs design pattern), 409-415
fixed-disk storage allocation, 45

G

gateway. *See* cloud consumer gateway
    (CCG)
Geotagging design pattern, 502, 510
    profile, 341-343
geotags, 192, 343, 359
    defined, 519

H

hardened virtual server images, defined,
    519
hardware-based VM discovery system, 374
    defined, 520
hardware security module (HSM), 340, 447
    defined, 520
honeypots, 469
    defined, 520
host-based security system (HBSS), 375
    defined, 521
hosted virtualization, 345
HSM. *See* hardware security module
    (HSM)
hybrid clouds, 453
hypervisor
    defined, 521
    purpose of, 222
Hypervisor Clustering design pattern, 98,
    269, 491, 503
    profile, 112-118
Hypervisor Protection design pattern, 509
    profile, 344-349

I

IaaS. *See* Infrastructure-as-a-Service
    compound pattern; Infrastructure-as-a-
    Service environments
icons in pattern profiles, 11
identity and access management (IAM)
    system, 189, 363, 366-368
    defined, 521
IDPS. *See* intrusion detection and
    prevention system (IDPS)
Independent Cloud Auditing design
    pattern, 510
    profile, 460-464
Infrastructure-as-a-Service compound
    pattern, 20, 473
    profile, 482-483
Infrastructure-as-a-Service environments,
    flexibility in, 222
intelligent automation engine, 43, 311-314
intelligent watchdog monitor, 125-126
interconnect pools, 101
In-Transit Cloud Data Encryption design
    pattern, 510
    profile, 391-394
Intra-Storage Device Vertical Data Tiering
    design pattern, 485
    profile, 81-85
intrusion detection and prevention system
    (IDPS), 403, 469
    defined, 522
IP Storage Isolation design pattern, profile,
    218-220
Isolated Trust Boundary compound
    pattern, 477, 481, 486-487
    profile, 508-510
IT resources
    dynamic scaling, 27
    horizontal scaling, 22
    sharing, risks and challenges, 20

J-K

joint application
  of compound patterns, 472
  defined, 13

kernel rootkits, 338
Key Management design pattern. *See*
  Cloud Key Management design pattern

L

live VM migration, 40, 56, 145, 165, 251, 257,
  264, 271, 277, 334, 415
  defined, 522
Load Balanced Virtual Server Instances
  design pattern, 254, 261, 269, 276, 331,
  503, 506
    limitations of, 253
    profile, 51-56
Load Balanced Virtual Switches design
  pattern, 237, 245, 491, 506
    profile, 57-60
load balancer, 22-24, 33-36, 56, 60, 70, 287
  defined, 522
logical network perimeter, 21, 24, 43, 56, 60,
  70, 104, 111, 118, 131, 136, 145, 171, 229,
  308, 318,
    defined, 523
LUN masking, 197, 220
  defined, 523

M

malware hashes, 469
  defined, 523
management loader, 306
management portal. *See* cloud storage
  management portal
measured boot, 339
mechanisms in pattern profiles, 12
Memory Over-Committing design
  pattern, 16
    profile, 86-89
Mobile BYOD Security design pattern,
  profile, 376-381

multi-device broker, 94, 318
  defined, 523
Multipath Resource Access design
  pattern, 482
    profile, 127-131
multitenancy, virtualization versus, 487
Multitenant Environment compound
  pattern, 473-475, 477, 479, 481, 483, 494,
  496
    profile, 486-489

N

nested resource pools, 102
network bandwidth, 43
network forensics monitor (NFM)
  defined, 524
NIC Teaming design pattern, 16
  profile, 90-92
Non-Disruptive Service Relocation design
  pattern, 180, 260, 475, 477, 479, 481
    profile, 159-165
normalization (Dynamic Data
  Normalization design pattern), 71-73
notification service for this book series, 7

O

Open Virtualization Format (OVF),
  converting virtual servers to, 248
operating system baseline (Rapid
  Provisioning design pattern), 296
orchestration engine, 451
  defined, 524
O/S boot load bootkits, 338
OVF (Open Virtualization Format),
  converting virtual servers to, 248

P-Q

PaaS. *See* Platform-as-a-Service compound
  pattern; Platform-as-a-Service
  environments
page number references in design pattern
  notation, 13

parent resource pools, 101
pattern languages, defined, 11
Pattern-Oriented Software Architecture (Buschmann, et al), 3
pattern profile format, 11-12
patterns, defined, 10. *See also* compound patterns; design patterns
Patterns of Enterprise Application Architecture (Fowler), 3
Pay-as-You-Go design pattern, 284-285, 475, 477, 479, 481, 483
    profile, 288-291
pay-per-use monitor, 31, 41, 43, 50, 63, 80, 85, 104, 165, 171, 176, 287, 291, 318
    defined, 524
Permanent Data Loss Protection design pattern, profile, 387-390
Persistent Virtual Network Configuration design pattern, 144, 164, 234, 493, 504
    profile, 227-230
physical RAM pools, 101
physical server pools, 100
physical uplink, 60, 92, 136, 145, 229, 234, 238, 243, 246, 251
    defined, 524
PKI. *See* public key infrastructure (PKI)
Platform-as-a-Service compound pattern, 473, 486
    profile, 480-481
Platform-as-a-Service environments, networking interfaces, 222
Platform Provisioning design pattern, 284, 481
    profile, 301-304
platform trust policy, 343, 359
    defined, 524
PNIC hardware devices, functionality, 179
pools. *See* Resource Pooling design pattern
Power Consumption Reduction design pattern, profile, 330-334
Prentice Hall Service Technology Series from Thomas Erl, 2-6

pre-signed validations, 442
Private Cloud compound pattern, 473, 476, 482, 484, 486, 490
    profile, 474-475
private clouds, 453
problems in pattern profiles, 11
protocol attacks, 417
Public Cloud compound pattern, 20, 473-474, 482, 484, 486, 490
    profile, 476-477
public clouds, 453
public key certificates. *See* certificate
public key infrastructure (PKI), 435, 443
    defined, 525

R

RAID-Based Data Placement design pattern, profile, 214-217
RAID-level identifier, 217, 220
    defined, 525
Rapid Provisioning design pattern, 284, 302, 475, 477, 479, 481, 483, 485, 491, 493-494, 503
    profile, 295-300
ready-made environment, 304
    defined, 525
Realtime Resource Availability design pattern, 284, 319, 475, 477, 479, 481, 483
    profile, 292-294
Redundant Physical Connection for Virtual Servers design pattern, 245, 490, 504
    profile, 132-137
Redundant Storage design pattern, 98, 485, 490, 493, 504
    profile, 119-122
remote administration system, 104, 111, 319
    defined, 525
requirements in pattern profiles, 11
Resilient Environment compound pattern, 473, 475, 477
    profile, 490-491

resilient watchdog system, 123-125

resource borrowing, 106

resource cluster, 24, 36, 56, 118, 145

> defined, 526

resource constraints, 106

Resource Management design pattern, 475, 477, 479, 481, 483

> profile, 320

resource management system, 104, 111, 304, 308, 319

> defined, 526

Resource Pooling design pattern, 20, 28, 38, 98, 106-107, 475, 477, 481, 483, 485-487, 494, 496, 499

> profile, 99-105

resource replication, 21, 24, 31, 36, 41, 44, 50, 56, 60, 63, 104, 111, 118, 122, 131, 136, 142, 145, 154, 165, 171, 177, 193, 229, 300, 304, 309, 314

> defined, 526

Resource Reservation design pattern, 20, 88, 98, 100, 477, 479, 481, 485-487, 494, 496

> profile, 106-111

Resource Workload Management compound pattern, 473

> profile, 506

rootkits, types of, 337

S

SaaS. *See* Software-as-a-Service compound pattern; Software-as-a-Service environments

sandbox, 469

> defined, 526

Secure Burst Out to Private Cloud/Public Cloud compound pattern, 473

> profile, 501-502

Secure Cloud Interfaces and APIs design pattern, 510

> profile, 360-363

Secure Connection for Scaled VMs design pattern, 502, 510

> profile, 409-415

Secure External Cloud Connection design pattern, profile, 404-408

secure firmware boot, 339

Secure On-Premise Internet Access design pattern, profile, 397-403

secure token service (STS), 368, 435

> defined, 526

security information and event management (SIEM) system, 403, 459, 464, 469

> defined, 526

Self-Provisioning design pattern, 297, 302, 318, 475, 477, 479, 481, 483

> profile, 324-329

sequence logger, 296

sequence manager, 296

server groups, 35

server images, 296

server templates, 296

Service Load Balancing design pattern, 485, 491, 494, 503

> profile, 32-36

Service State Management design pattern, 481

> profile, 61-63

Shared Resources design pattern, 16, 99-100, 106, 475, 477, 479, 481, 483, 486-487

> profile, 17-21

sibling resource pools, 101

SIEM. *See* security information and event management (SIEM) system

Single Root I/O Virtualization design pattern, profile, 178-180

single sign-on (SSO), defined, 527

SLA management system, 126, 165, 294, 309

> defined, 527

SLA monitor, 126, 165, 287, 294, 319

> defined, 527

SOA Design Patterns (Erl), 3

Software-as-a-Service compound pattern, 20, 473, 486

> profile, 478-479

Software-as-a-Service environments, networking interfaces, 222
solutions in pattern profiles, 12
SSO (single sign-on), defined, 527
statefulness, 61-63
Stateless Hypervisor design pattern, profile, 278-282
state management database, 63, 142
   defined, 527
Storage Maintenance Window design pattern, 491
   profile, 147-154
storage path masking, 220
   defined, 528
storage pools, 101
Storage Workload Management design pattern, 485, 504, 506
   profile, 64-70
STS. *See* secure token service (STS)
sub-LUN migration, 213
   defined, 528
Sub-LUN Tiering design pattern, profile, 210-213
symbols, legend, 5
Synchronized Operating State design pattern, 491
   profile, 138-142

T

thin provisioning, 46-48
Threat Intelligence Processing design pattern, profile, 465-469
threat intelligence system, 386, 469
   defined, 528
TPM (trusted platform module), 193, 339-340, 343, 349, 359, 451, 529
traffic filter, 420
   defined, 528
traffic monitor, 420, 424
   defined, 529
trust attestation service. *See* attestation service

Trust Attestation Service design pattern, 502, 510
   profile, 448-451
trusted boot, 339
Trusted Cloud Resource Pools design pattern, 502, 510
   profile, 354-359
Trusted Platform BIOS design pattern, 502, 510
   profile, 337-340
trusted platform module (TPM), 193, 339-340, 343, 349, 359, 451, 529
trust models for CVS, 442

U

usage database, 286
Usage Monitoring design pattern, 284, 289, 475, 477, 479, 481, 483, 485, 491, 493, 499
   profile, 285-287
usage monitoring station, 286
usage reporter, 287

V

vCPU. *See* virtual CPU (vCPU)
vDisk. *See* virtual disk (vDisk)
VIM. *See* virtual infrastructure manager (VIM)
virtual appliance
   Cross-Hypervisor Workload Mobility design pattern, 251
   defined, 529
virtual CPU (vCPU)
   Cross-Hypervisor Workload Mobility design pattern, 21, 41, 56, 104, 111, 145, 251
   defined, 529
Virtual Disk Splitting design pattern, profile, 209
virtual disk (vDisk), 145, 209, 251
   defined, 530
virtual firewall, 234, 415
   defined, 530

virtual infrastructure manager (VIM), 21, 41, 56, 60, 89, 92, 104, 111, 118, 136, 146, 165, 172, 177, 209, 226, 230, 234, 238, 246, 251, 257, 264, 271, 277, 282, 334, 375
  defined, 530
virtual machines (VMs). *See* virtual server
virtual network, 146, 243, 251, 239
  defined, 530
virtual private cloud (VPC), 408
  defined, 531
virtual private network (VPN), 403, 408, 429, 435
  defined, 531
virtual private network (VPN) cloud hub. *See* VPN cloud hub
virtual RAM (vRAM), 21, 41, 56, 89, 104, 111, 146
  defined, 531
virtual server, 21, 24, 31, 41, 44, 51-56, 60, 63, 105, 111, 118, 131-137, 142, 146, 165, 172, 177, 230, 248, 300, 304, 314, 353, 369-374, 522
  defined, 531
Virtual Server Auto Crash Recovery design pattern, profile, 155-158
Virtual Server Connectivity Isolation design pattern, profile, 231-234
Virtual Server Folder Migration design pattern, profile, 223-226
Virtual Server NAT Connectivity design pattern, profile, 240-243
virtual server pools, 100
virtual server snapshot, 251
  defined, 532
virtual server state manager, 251
  defined, 532
Virtual Server-to-Host Affinity design pattern, profile, 252-257
Virtual Server-to-Host Anti-Affinity design pattern, profile, 258-264
Virtual Server-to-Host Connectivity design pattern, profile, 265-266

Virtual Server-to-Virtual Server Affinity design pattern, 234
  profile, 267-271
Virtual Server-to-Virtual Server Anti-Affinity design pattern, profile, 272-277
Virtual Switch Isolation design pattern, profile, 235-239
virtual switches, 56-60, 92, 118, 137, 146, 165, 230, 234, 239, 243, 246, 251, 266
  defined, 532
virtualization, 19, 487
  types of, 344
virtualization agent, 89, 146, 158
  defined, 532
virtualization monitor, 56, 89, 118, 146, 209, 334
  defined, 533
VMs (virtual machines). *See* virtual server
volume-based attacks, 416-417
VPC. *See* virtual private cloud (VPC)
VPN. *See* virtual private network (VPN)
VPN cloud hub, 408
  defined, 533
vRAM. *See* virtual RAM (vRAM)

W

Web sites
  www.cloudpatterns.org, 6, 14
  www.cloudschool.com, 6
  www.servicetechbooks.com, 2, 6-7
  www.servicetechmag.com, 6
  www.servicetechspecs.com, 6
  www.whatiscloud.com, 6, 14
Workload Distribution design pattern, 475, 477, 479, 481-482, 485, 491, 493, 504
  profile, 22-24
workloads, defined, 517

X-Y-Z

X.509 certificates. *See* certificate

Zero Downtime design pattern, 98, 491
  profile, 143-146

ABOUT THE SERIES

The Prentice Hall Service Technology Series from Thomas Erl aims to provide the IT industry with a consistent level of unbiased, practical, and comprehensive guidance and instruction in the areas of service technology application and innovation. Each title in this book series is authored in relation to other titles so as to establish a library of complementary knowledge. Although the series covers a broad spectrum of service technology-related topics, each title is authored in compliance with common language, vocabulary, and illustration conventions so as to enable readers to continually explore cross-topic research and education.

servicetechbooks.com/community

ABOUT THE SERIES EDITOR

Thomas Erl is a best-selling IT author, the series editor of the Prentice Hall ServiceTechnology Series from Thomas Erl, and the editor of the Service Technology Magazine. As CEO of Arcitura Education Inc., Thomas has led the development of curricula for the internationally recognized Big Data Science Certified Professional (BDSCP), Cloud Certified Professional (CCP), and SOA Certified Professional (SOACP) accreditation programs, which have established a seriesof formal, vendor-neutral industry certifications. Thomas has toured over 20 countries as a speaker and instructor. Over 100 articles and interviews by Thomas have been published in numerous publications, including the Wall Street Journal and CIO Magazine.

SOA Governance: Governing Shared Services On-Premise & in the Cloud
by Stephen Bennett, Thomas Erl, Clive Gee, Robert Laird, Anne Thomas Manes, Robert Schneider, Leo Shuster, Andre Tost, Chris Venable

ISBN: 0138156751
Hardcover, 675 pages

SOA with REST: Principles, Patterns & Constraints for Building Enterprise Solutions with REST
by Raj Balasu -bramanian, Benjamin Carlyle, Thomas Erl, Cesare Pautasso

ISBN: 0137012519
Hardcover, 577 pages

Cloud Computing: Concepts, Technology & Architecture
by Thomas Erl, Zaigham Mahmood, Ricardo Puttini

ISBN: 9780133387520
Hardcover, 528 pages

SOA with Java: Realizing Service -Orientation with Java Technologies
by Thomas Erl, Satadru Roy, Philip Thomas, Andre Tost

ISBN: 9780133859034
Hardcover, 592 pages

Next Generation SOA: A Concise Introduction to Service Technology & Service-Orientation
by Thomas Erl, Clive Gee, Jürgen Kress, Berthold Maier, Hajo Normann, Pethuru Raj, Leo Shuster, Bernd Trops, Clemens Utschig-Utschig, Philip Wik, Torsten Winterberg

ISBN: 9780133859041
Paperback, 208 pages

Cloud Computing Design Patterns
by Thomas Erl, Robert Cope, Amin Naserpour

ISBN: 9780133858563
Hardcover, 528 pages

Service-Oriented Architecture: A Field Guide to Integrating XML and Web Services
by Thomas Erl

ISBN: 0131428985
Paperback, 534 pages

Service-Oriented Architecture: Concepts, Technology & Design
by Thomas Erl

ISBN: 0131858580
Hardcover, 760 pages

SOA Principles of Service Design
by Thomas Erl

ISBN: 0132344823
Hardcover, Full-Color, 573 pages

Web Service Contract Design & Versioning for SOA
by Thomas Erl, Anish Karmarkar, Priscilla Walmsley, Hugo Haas, Umit Yalcinalp, Canyang Kevin Liu, David Orchard, Andre Tost, James Pasley

ISBN: 013613517X
Hardcover, 826 pages

SOA Design Patterns
by Thomas Erl

ISBN: 0136135161
Hardcover, Full-Color, 865 pages

SOA with .NET & Windows Azure: Realizing Service-Orientation with the Microsoft Platform
by David Chou, John deVadoss, Thomas Erl, Nitin Gandhi, Hanu Kommalapati, Brian Loesgen, Christoph Schittko, Herbjorn Wilhelmsen, Mickey Williams

ISBN: 0131582313
Hardcover, 893 pages

Arcitura™
Big Data Science School

Vendor-Neutral Big Data Training & Certification
15 Course Modules • 15 Exams • 6 Certifications

The Big Data Science Certified Professional (BDSCP) program from the Arcitura Big Data Science School is dedicated to excellence in the fields of Big Data science, analysis, analytics, business intelligence, technology architecture, design and development, as well as governance. A collection of courses establishes a set of vendor-neutral industry certifications with different areas of specialization. Founded by best-selling author, Thomas Erl, this curriculum enables IT professionals to develop real-world Big Data science proficiency. Because of the vendor-neutral focus of the course materials, the skills acquired by attaining certifications are applicable to any vendor or open-source platform.

For more information, visit: **www.bigdatascienceschool.com**

Certified Big Data Science Professional
Certified Big Data Scientist
Certified Big Data Consultant

Certified Big Data Engineer
Certified Big Data Architect
Certified Big Data Governance Specialist

Arcitura™
the IT education company